fP

YANKS

The Epic Story of the American Army

in World War I

JOHN S. D. EISENHOWER

with Joanne Thompson Eisenhower

THE FREE PRESS

New York   London   Toronto   Sydney   Singapore

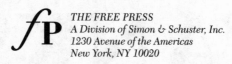

THE FREE PRESS
A Division of Simon & Schuster, Inc.
1230 Avenue of the Americas
New York, NY 10020

The Free Press and colophon
are trademarks of Simon & Schuster, Inc.
Designed by Edith Fowler
Manufactured in the United States of America

10   9   8   7   6   5   4   3   2   1

Library of Congress Cataloging-in-Publication data

Eisenhower, John S. D.
   Yanks : the epic story of the American Army in
World War I / John S. D. Eisenhower.
      p. cm.
   Includes bibliographical references and index.
   1. United States. Army—History—World War,
1914–1918.   2. World War, 1914–1918—
Campaigns—Western Front.   3. United States.
Army. American Expeditionary Forces—History.
I. Title.
D570 .E37 2001
940.4'1273—dc21   2001023124
ISBN 0-684-86304-9

TO

Dorothy W. "Dodie" Yentz

CONTENTS

BOOK THREE
THE AEF FIGHTS INDEPENDENTLY:
ST. MIHIEL AND THE MEUSE-ARGONNE

MAPS

AUTHOR'S NOTE

"THE HISTORY of the Victorian Age," writes Lytton Strachey in his Preface to *Eminent Victorians,* "will never be written: we know too much about it." That paradoxical and somewhat arresting statement serves as Strachey's excuse for selecting four lives to depict an entire age of British history, but it applies to any subject on which mountains of material have been written.

The First World War, often referred to as the Great War, certainly falls into that category. Too much is known about that vast conflict to permit one book to cover the entire war in anything but a textbook fashion. The "explorer of the past," to continue with Strachey, "will row out over that great ocean of material, and lower down into it . . . a little bucket, which will bring up to the light of day some characteristic specimen."

With that idea in mind, I have not attempted to write a comprehensive story of the Great War. Instead I have focused on the American Expeditionary Force (AEF), commanded by General John J. Pershing. In describing the inception of the AEF in early 1917 and its subsequent development and employment until the war's end in late 1918, I have not attempted to give a rounded picture of the whole war, which includes the actions of many nations on many fronts. Nevertheless, the story of the AEF and how it fit into the general scheme of the war is worth a study in itself.

The saga of the AEF is not, on the whole, a cheery one. The overseas experiences of the American troops—"doughboys"—bore little relationship to the rousing patriotic songs such as George M. Cohan's "Over There," or to the parades and banners. It entailed arduous duties, performed in the wet, the cold, sometimes the heat, with death always lurking, mostly in the front line infantry battalions but elsewhere as well. There was heroism, but there was also cowardice. At first there was ignorance of the job to be done—"innocence" might be a better word. Yet the end result was inspiring. A great many people pulled together to attain a great accomplishment.

In a way, the story of the AEF in the Great War is part of my background, perhaps something I needed to put on paper in order to work it out of my system. I was born in an Army family slightly less than four years after the last gun was fired in the Meuse-Argonne; my first vivid memories are those of trudging over the battlefields with my father, Major Dwight D. Eisenhower, and my mother. During 1928 and 1929 my father was a member of General Pershing's American Battle Monuments Commission, with offices in Paris. One of his tasks was to draft the official *Guide to the American Battlefields in France*. The end result was a remarkable book; it remains today the best available guide for the student of the war to follow. The final edition was not published until 1938, and I have no idea what proportion of my father's original words survived. I also have no idea of how the study of the terrain in northern France helped him in later campaigns across the same territory fifteen years later. But I know that accompanying him on his many tours around the territory made a lasting impression on me. At age six, I was even privileged to shake the hand of the Great Man himself, John J. Pershing!

It is not surprising that, as a youngster, I viewed the Great War in a romantic fashion. Heroic charges, reduction of fearsome enemy machine gun nests, the roar of artillery, the exploits of the air aces—those were my boyhood fantasies, based on true stories but far from the grim truth.

Others have viewed the AEF and its role in the Great War much differently. Some have thought it unnecessary; others have succumbed to excessive disillusionment over the disparity between the patriotic mouthings of our propagandists and the grisly facts of the Argonne or of Château Thierry. The latter views, when carried to the extreme, are no more right nor wrong than my childhood concepts. They are just viewed from different angles, both extreme.

The purpose of this book, therefore, is to strike a balance, to examine how the AEF came about, to describe the gargantuan efforts needed to create it, supply it, train it, and fight it, and in so doing to show how the modern American Army was born. Since many of my sources are personal memoirs written by survivors, I have not dwelt at length on the immense tragedies felt by so many families. Nevertheless, it is my hope that this single, modest volume will provide some perspective on one of the truly pivotal events in American history.

JOHN S. D. EISENHOWER

BOOK ONE

CREATING THE AEF

PROLOGUE

AT GERMAN ARMY HEADQUARTERS in northern Silesia, Kaiser Wilhelm II of Germany called a council of his top military advisers. Representing the Army were the venerable Field Marshal Paul von Hindenburg and his mercurial but brilliant chief of staff, Erich Ludendorff. Admiral Henning von Holtzendorff, chief of the naval staff, and Admiral Karl von Müller, chief of the naval cabinet, represented the Navy. Chancellor Theobald Bethmann Hollweg represented the German Reichstag.

The date was January 9, 1917, a critical point in the war between the Central Powers (Germany, Austria-Hungary, Turkey, and Bulgaria) and the Western Allies (Britain, France, Russia, Italy, and Romania). The German campaign to destroy Romania as a fighting force had just finished successfully, but the situation on the all-important Western Front, where the Kaiser's soldiers faced the British and French, was stalemated. And time was not on Germany's side.

The question—Could unrestricted submarine warfare in the Atlantic Ocean be reinstituted?—was foremost in everyone's mind. The European Allies had suffered a bad harvest in 1916, and Britain was more than ever dependent for her very survival on the sea lanes by which she received food and supplies from the United States. Even under the current restrictions on submarine activity, Allied shipping losses were already severe; if the tempo were stepped up, Holtzendorff insisted, Britain would be knocked out of the war within six months.

Kaiser Wilhelm and Chancellor Bethmann Hollweg were dubious about Holtzendorff's claims. The Kaiser fluctuated in his policies from day to day, but Bethmann consistently opposed this drastic measure on the basis that it would certainly bring the United States into the war on the side of the Allies. Furthermore, Bethmann was drawing up a peace plan for Europe, which had been requested by American President Woodrow Wilson. It was in Germany's interest, he believed, to explore that avenue first.

Bethmann, however, was fighting a losing battle. Both Hindenburg and Ludendorff adamantly supported the submarine policy and were unafraid of bringing America into the war. Even if America entered, Hindenburg believed, German submarines would prevent America from sending any troops to Europe. Ludendorff was more blunt, declaring that he did not "care two hoots about America." Holtzendorff then reiterated his position, on his "word of honor," that "not one American will land on the continent."

Bethmann Hollweg gave way. "Your Majesty," he said, "I cannot counsel you to oppose the vote of your military advisers."

The die was cast. Kaiser Wilhelm directed that unrestricted submarine warfare would begin as of February 1, 1917.[1]

BY THE BEGINNING OF 1917, the Great War in Europe had been raging for two and a half years, most of that time in a condition of bloody stalemate on the Western Front. The German war machine had invaded Belgium and France in August of 1914, and at one point had driven all the way to the Marne River, only a few miles east of Paris. There it had been halted, however, and driven back to the line of the Aisne. On that critical front the two sides—France and Britain on the one hand, Germany on the other—stood eyeball-to-eyeball in a long line of trenches extending all the way from Switzerland to Nieuport, on the North Sea.[2] In East Prussia and Poland, the German forces had been battling those of Czarist Russia, with more decisive results.

Throughout this period the United States had remained officially neutral. Its people were generally sympathetic to the Western Allies, but Americans in general had no desire to participate in the hideous bloodletting that was gripping the continent of Europe. President Woodrow Wilson, meanwhile, was making use of his position as the head of the great neutral power in an attempt to mediate peace between the two sides, a "peace without victory." He did not see his moral authority as a mediator compromised by the fact that American bankers were supplying the Allies with financial backing, nor that segments of American industry were selling them war material.

The Allies, especially Britain, wished that Wilson would cease pursuing an elusive peace and would bring the United States into war on their side. Recognizing, however, that the overriding sentiment of the American public favored official neutrality, the Allies settled for whatever help the Americans would give them under current conditions. The Germans, of course, were well aware that America was aiding the Allies, but they tolerated that limited aid as vastly preferable to an outright declaration of war. In the meantime, the Kaiser's government had been encouraging Wilson to continue his peacemaker role.

President Wilson would have been happy to do just that, but circumstances were pushing America in another direction. Newspapers spread sensational reports of German brutality, perpetrated especially against Belgian and French civilians, and American resentment toward Germany had progressively grown because of the German use of the submarine against Allied and neutral shipping. When a U-boat sank the British liner *Lusitania* in 1915, 128 American passengers were lost. That event planted the seeds of an active anti-German feeling in America.

America had been on the brink of declaring war in late March 1916, when a German submarine sank the French passenger ship *Sussex*, with several American lives lost. Wilson's protest and threat to break diplomatic relations had intimidated Germany for the moment, and the Kaiser's government suspended its policy of unrestricted submarine warfare. Wilson's terms, however, were well-nigh impossible for the Germans to comply with for any length of time. They called for submarines to give early warning to intended victims. If a merchant ship submitted, the ship would be searched. Failing that, the submarine commander was responsible for rescuing the crews and passengers. These restrictions robbed the submarine of the element of surprise, its greatest asset. Following those terms, in fact, had rendered the German submarine campaign only partially effective. Nevertheless the German government had been living with them for nearly a year.

GERMANY POSSESSED a significant asset in its efforts to keep America from joining the Allies, her ambassador to the United States, Count Johann von Bernsdorff. A skinny, dapper little man, Bernsdorff was a superb envoy, whose formidable diplomatic talents had been taxed to the fullest in encouraging Wilson to continue his peacemaking efforts while at the same time keeping his own government convinced that it was in Germany's best interest to conciliate Wilson. A congenial bon vivant, popular in the right circles, he was accorded liberal entrée to the high and mighty. He enjoyed the atmosphere of Washington and was friendly with President Wilson's friend and confidant, Colonel Edward M. House. Much of Bernsdorff's influence with the President, in fact, resulted from his friendship with House.

Bernsdorff's little world of capital intrigue predictably came to an abrupt end on February 1, 1917, when he received the fateful message from Berlin announcing the resumption of unrestricted submarine warfare. The Americans, he knew, would never stand for that. The world's most industrialized nation, with all its resources of matériel and manpower, would now almost certainly join the Allies.

Bernsdorff did what little he could to ease the blow. He sent a long and laborious letter to his friend House, attempting to portray the Kaiser's actions as consistent with Wilson's efforts to promote a "peace without victory" in Europe. The new policy of unrestricted submarine warfare, he claimed, would terminate the war very quickly, during which time the Kaiser's government would "do everything possible" to safeguard American interests. In the meantime he "begged" Wilson to continue working to bring about peace.

House was in New York when he received Bernsdorff's personal letter. Recognizing that a crisis of epic proportions loomed, he dropped everything else and took the midnight train for Washington. The next morning he was closeted with President Wilson and Secretary of State Robert Lansing at the White House. The three men compared the text of the official German letter with Bernsdorff's personal note to House and found them similar. In only one respect were the two messages different. The official letter contained an insulting addition, the terms under which the Germans would allow one American ship a week to pass through the submarine blockade. The American steamers would have to follow a lane designated by the Germans, displaying distinguishing marks (red and white stripes) on the hulls, and flying a red and white checkered flag. Furthermore, the American government must promise that the ships so favored carried no contraband.[3]

By sheer coincidence, a third German message arrived in Washington that day. This one listed the terms that Germany would accept as the price of a negotiated peace. Arrogant and restrictive, the Kaiser's government demanded a restoration of Germany's losses since 1914 but a retention of its gains. The terms included "restitution of the part of Upper Alsace occupied by the French," establishment of a new frontier that would protect Germany and Poland from Russia, freedom of the seas, and special guarantees to protect Germany from French invasion along the strategic military avenue through Belgium. Further, the note demanded that Germany's colonies, seized by the Allies during the war, be reinstated, that German businesses be compensated for their losses, and that mutual compensation be given for the freeing of occupied territories—almost all of which Germany had taken from France.[4] The British and French would be treated as the losers in the war, at least on points if not by a knockout.

Faced with these three messages, and conscious of the angry reaction they were bound to stir up in the American public, the conferees quickly concluded that a break in diplomatic relations was inevitable. The question of timing remained, however. Would it be better to give Bernsdorff his passports immediately, based on these letters, or would it be better to await some overt act, some solid proof that the German government meant what it said? After some discussion, Wilson decided to break diplomatic relations at once.

On Saturday morning, February 3, 1917, President Wilson addressed a joint session of the United States Congress. He presented the current crisis between the United States and Germany as serious but not yet irreparable. Breaking diplomatic relations with Germany did not, he insisted, mean that war was inevitable. Still clinging to the hope that the Great War might still be settled without American armed intervention, Wilson clung to an optimistic note:

> I refuse to believe that it is the intention of the German authorities to do in fact what they have warned us they will feel at liberty to do. . . . Only actual overt acts on their part can make me believe it even now. . . . We wish to serve no selfish ends. We seek to stand true alike in thought and action to the immemorial principles of our people. . . . These are the bases of peace, not war. God grant we may not be challenged to defend them by acts of wilful injustice on the part of the Government of Germany![5]

THOUGH NOT YET RESIGNED to war, the President consented to allow some very limited measures in order to cope with the renewed submarine threat. The most obvious of these was to permit the arming of American merchant vessels. Even this he supported only reluctantly: American merchant ships might be armed, he said, but the government would furnish neither the guns nor the gunners. Wilson clung to the hope that Germany might modify her position regarding the unlimited use of U-boats even after a submarine sank the American merchant vessel *Housatonic* without warning on February 6. But by the time that the American vessel *Lyman M. Law* was sunk on the 16th of February, some of Wilson's cabinet members were becoming vehement in favor of the government's arming merchant vessels.[6]

ACROSS THE CONTINENT, about 150 miles over the border between the United States and Mexico, a strange impasse kept American eyes turned southward. The treatment of that running sore would clear the path for America's entry into the Great War.

In March 1916, nearly a year before the current crisis with Germany had broken out, the Mexican bandit Francisco (Pancho) Villa had raided the American town of Columbus, New Mexico, and seventeen Americans had been killed. An enraged public had forced President Wilson to send the American Punitive Expedition into Mexico to pursue Villa. Mexican President Venustiano Carranza had reluctantly permitted this incursion at first, but after nearly a year of Yankee presence in Chihuahua, his patience had worn thin. Villa remained at large; of the three skirmishes the Americans had fought during that time, two had pitted the Americans against Mexican government troops, not Villistas. Carranza, no friend of the United States, began issuing threats, causing the Americans to give up the chase and concentrate at Casas Grandes, in the Mexican state of Chihuahua. There the Yankees drilled for months, waiting. Now, on February 5, 1917, Wilson ordered them back across the border into the United States. Their leader, a fifty-seven-year-old brigadier general named John J. Pershing, would soon have more daunting foes to face.

Despite that conciliatory move, President Wilson was not allowed to put the Mexican problem out of his mind. The Kaiser's government, aware of Carranza's sympathy for their cause and his dislike of Americans,[7] sought to exploit his leanings for its own ends. For some months German agents had been making significant inroads into the Mexican Army and civil government, and so successful were they that overconfidence set in, causing them to overplay their hand. The German foreign secretary, Arthur Zimmermann, sent a message to Ambassador von Bernsdorff in Washington on January 16, 1917, to be forwarded to the German ambassador in Mexico City, Count von Eckhart. In it Germany made Mexico a proposal of an alliance, including a promise to

> . . . make war together, make peace together. Generous financial support and *understanding on our part that Mexico is to reconquer the lost territory in Kansas, New Mexico, and Arizona.*[8]

Those were the territories (inaccurately described) that Mexico had lost to the United States in the war of 1846–1848. American awareness of the Zimmermann Telegram, as it came to be known, would obviously create a tremendous surge of resentment in the public.

Unfortunately for the Germans, British Naval Intelligence had long since broken the code they had been using to protect the secrecy of such messages. The Zimmermann Telegram was soon being deciphered by British cryptographers in the celebrated Room 40. The experts finished their work by February 19, and five days later the British government turned the Zimmermann Telegram over to Walter H. Page, the American ambassador in London.[9] When Page transmitted it to Washington the next day, Wilson's ambivalence sustained another sharp blow. In his indignation [10] he resolved to notify Congress the next day.

Wilson's disclosure of the Zimmermann Telegram caused a violent reaction among the American public. As soon as the President stepped down from his appearance before Congress, that body unhesitatingly voted him authority to "employ any instrumentalities or methods that may be necessary and adequate to protect our ships and our people in their legitimate pursuits on the seas."[11] Still, the President proceeded cautiously. In his presentation he did not mention Zimmermann by name. He continued to insist that the "overt act" had not yet been committed.

From that point on, however, the United States moved inexorably toward war. On March 18, three American ships were sunk by German submarines, and the next day the Russian Czar, Nicholas II, was deposed by rebellious Menshevik forces in St. Petersburg. Idealists who longed to view the European struggle as one between democratic powers and tyrants were now placated. The Western democracies were no longer allied with a ruler generally regarded as equally despotic as the Kaiser himself; America could enter the war on the Allied side with a clear conscience.

On Tuesday, March 20, 1917, Woodrow Wilson met again with his cabinet and found it unanimous in favor of war. The sentiment was doubly significant because its membership included men who were by disposition pacifists, Secretary of War Newton D. Baker and Secretary of the Navy Josephus Daniels among them. Daniels, who seemed to feel the import even more than the others, was reportedly in tears.[12] Even then Wilson did not commit himself. On the next day, however, he issued a call for Congress to meet on April 2, two full weeks before the date he had previously set.

At the joint session on Monday evening, April 2, 1917, President Woodrow Wilson asked the Congress to declare war on Imperial Germany. It was a difficult, even searing moment for him. "It is a fearful thing," he said, "to lead this great peaceful people into war, into the most terrible and disastrous of all wars, civilization itself seeming to be in the balance. But," he went on,

the right is more precious than peace, and we shall fight for the things which we have always carried nearest our hearts—for democracy, for the right of those who submit to authority to have a voice in their own Governments, for the rights and liberties of small nations, for a universal dominion of right by such a concert of free peoples as shall bring peace and safety to all nations and make the world itself free.[13]

The members of Congress rose to a standing ovation when the President finished speaking. Even Wilson's critics agreed that he was reflecting their own views. On April 4 the Senate adopted the resolution for war by a vote of 82–6. Two days later the House of Representatives followed with a vote of 373–50. On April 6, 1917, Wilson signed the resolution.[14]

The United States was at war with Imperial Germany and the Austro-Hungarian Empire.

CHAPTER ONE

A VISIT FROM PAPA JOFFRE

JOSEPH JACQUES C. JOFFRE, Marshal of France, was an amiable and optimistic man, known affectionately in France and the United States as "Papa." Until late 1916 he had been the head of the French Army. Though he no longer held that position by the time the United States was approaching war against Germany, Americans were only vaguely aware of his demotion.

Long a leader in the coterie of French officers who believed they could defeat Germany by sheer audacity, Joffre had been in command of the French Army when the Great War began in early August 1914. At that point, his personality had a profound effect on the course of history. In the first few weeks it seemed that the Germans would repeat their triumph of 1870, in which the French Army was routed, with Emperor Napoleon III actually taken prisoner. But Joffre's balance and continual optimism held the French Army together, and the exhausted Germans were driven back to a line along the Aisne River. Joffre was hailed as the "Hero of the Marne," his name a household word in America as well as Europe.

But that was 1914, and since then fate had not been kind. Once the armies on the Western Front had settled into their prolonged, ghastly stalemate, the luster attached to Joffre's name gradually wore off. He was widely blamed for French unpreparedness when the Germans attacked Verdun in 1916, and the pressure for his removal became strong. He resigned as chief of the French Army in December of 1916, succeeded by General Robert Nivelle.[1] The exalted title, Marshal of France, was then conferred on Joffre; the honor carried a hollow ring. He was perhaps surprised, therefore, when French Premier Alexandre Ribot called him into his office on April 1, 1917.

The Premier had an important challenge for Joffre. The United States, he said, was expected to declare war against Germany within the next few days, and if that should come to pass, Ribot would send René Viviani, a former French Premier and currently Lord Chancellor, on an important mission to Washington. Would Joffre be willing to make the trip as a member of the party? Ribot wished to exploit the fact that the victory of the Marne was still remembered in the United States, and Joffre was still a hero, ideal to represent the French Army to the American people.[2]

Joffre had reservations about accepting. General Nivelle's great spring offensive on the Aisne was about to take place, and excitement was in the air; he hated to be absent from France at that time. On reflection, however, he did not take long in accepting. The entry of the United States in the war was a tremendously important event, and the government of France needed to know more about America's capabilities and plans. It might also be possible to guide the new ally in its first efforts. Joffre notified Premier Ribot that he was available and began making preparations even before the mission was confirmed.

As Ribot had anticipated, the United States Congress declared war on Germany on April 6, 1917, and by the middle of the month the Viviani mission was organized and ready to go.[3] The French Premier did not issue detailed, binding instructions to the members. He simply directed Joffre to establish "a general outline of the policy which will govern the co-operation of the American forces with the Allied Armies."[4] How Joffre went about it was up to him.

Up to that time, Joffre had devoted little or no thought to the American military situation, so when he began to study the numbers he was struck by the small size of the American Army. Regulars and National Guardsmen together totaled only 200,000 men,[5] so that force would have to be multiplied many times to be of any value in Europe, where the Allies had nearly four million men on the Western Front and the Germans about 2.5 million.[6]

The easy part of the task, Joffre believed, would be to recruit and train the enlisted soldiers; the difficult problem would be to create an officer corps. Developing leaders competent to hold their own in battle against the highly professional German Army could not be accomplished instantaneously.

To make American troops immediately effective, therefore, Joffre's first inclination was to urge the Americans to furnish the French and British "with men instead of armies." If troops were sent to France organized only into companies and battalions, they could be incorporated quickly into French regiments for training and service at the front. There would therefore be "no occasion for training general officers and staff for the larger units, only captains and majors being needed."[7]

Joffre quickly discarded that idea, however, because he knew the Americans would never accept it. No great nation, especially the Americans, would "allow its citizens to be incorporated like poor relations in the ranks of some other army and fight under a foreign flag."[8] He therefore determined that he would start from that premise as he entered discussions in America.

THE VIVIANI PARTY left Paris by train on the morning of April 15, 1917, and that evening sailed aboard the French cruiser *Lorraine II* from the Brittany port of Brest. Two American journalists were aboard,[9] and Joffre, ever conscious of how useful the press could be in presenting the French position, successfully set about to win them over. But the nine-day voyage was no holiday; one of the newsmen remarked on how busy Joffre kept his small staff. "The Marshal," the reporter wrote, "is prepared, if President Wilson should ask, to indicate what, in his judgment, America might do."[10]

One development cast a pall over the passengers of the *Lorraine II*. A few days out of port the ship's radio picked up crushing news: General Robert Nivelle's touted offensive on the Aisne River had floundered with an appalling loss of life.[11] Joffre owed nothing to the man who had undercut and succeeded him, but the Hero of the Marne was too big to take any comfort in Nivelle's failure. Joffre grieved both for France and for Nivelle. But not for long. Temporary defeat always inspired Joffre to greater efforts, and this disaster only convinced him, as he later wrote, "that a gigantic effort would have to be demanded of the Americans; what must be done, and without a moment's delay, was to mobilize in the service of the Allied cause all of America's resources."[12]

On the evening of April 24, the *Lorraine II* entered Hampton Roads, Virginia, where she was greeted by the North Atlantic Squadron of the American Navy. The fleet commander, Admiral Henry T. Mayo, boarded the vessel, along with the popular French ambassador, Jules Jusserand, and the assistant secretary of the navy, Franklin D. Roosevelt. In a lavish message of welcome, Admiral Mayo declared that being sent to meet this distinguished party was the "greatest honor of his career."[13] The brief ceremonies completed, the Viviani party transferred to the President's yacht, the *Mayflower,* for the trip up the Chesapeake Bay and the Potomac River. They arrived in Washington on the following morning, the party standing at respectful attention as the vessel passed under the cliffs of Mount Vernon.

Down to meet the *Mayflower* when she docked at Washington's Navy Yard was Secretary of State Robert Lansing, along with a British delegation, headed by Foreign Secretary Arthur Balfour. It was a festive occasion. The shops of Washington were closed for the day, and the whole population of the city, Joffre later wrote, was out to meet the guests.

THE TWO MISSIONS in Washington—French and British—both performed dual functions. To the public, their activities appeared to be mostly ceremonial. In that capacity they often acted together, though in a sort of undeclared competition. In public they vied for the headlines and behind doors they acted as salesmen for their own national viewpoints regarding America's future role in the war. It created an odd situation.

In public, Joffre was the main attraction in the French party; the venerated war hero far overshadowed a mere former Premier. In the British party it was the head, Foreign Minister Balfour, who carried the appeal. A previous Prime Minister, Balfour was a suave and charming aristocrat, but an aristocrat who wore his position lightly, possessed of an acute sensitivity to the democratic predispositions of the American public. His greatest single coup in warming American hearts came about by a caper. He secretly eluded his security guards and sneaked away to enjoy a lunch with a personal friend of long standing, an American not currently associated with government.

The most memorable public event was a ceremony in which the French and British delegations placed wreaths at the tomb of George Washington at Mount Vernon. The French came as the nation that had rendered the Americans vital aid in attaining American independence from Britain. But George Washington had been born an Englishman. So Balfour paid homage to

the immortal memory of George Washington . . . who would have rejoiced to see the country of which he was by birth a citizen and the country his genius called into existence fighting side by side to save mankind from military despotism.[14]

Even Balfour's eloquence, however, could not overcome the trump cards the French held in the friendly competition of public relations. Americans had not forgotten that the French were once our indispensable allies in our war of independence against the British. Thus Joffre could say in a press conference, "France and America will see with pride and joy the day when their sons are *once more fighting shoulder to shoulder in defense of liberty.*"[15] That was a sentiment not even the most articulate Englishman could completely counter.

Joffre stayed in Washington for ten days, during which time he addressed both houses of Congress individually. On the afternoon of May 4, he began a week's tour of the principal cities of the Eastern United States, and the American people poured out their affection. He was an appealing character; his clear blue eyes, young-looking face, and direct manner more than compensated for his sixty-five years and well-rounded torso. His fame was still magic to Americans, and his appearances gave the American people a chance to honor the brave people of France, as personified in him. In St. Louis he endeared himself to the Americans by entering a barber shop and unobtrusively awaiting his turn for a haircut. He paid his respects to Abraham Lincoln in Springfield and to Ulysses S. Grant in New York. He placed wreaths at statues of Joan of Arc and Lafayette, and visited West Point, the American Valhalla of military professionalism. Everywhere he was received with such tumultuous welcomes as to astonish him. It was a fitting tribute to a fine old soldier.

CEREMONIES, no matter how important, were only window dressing; the real significance of the French and British missions lay in the series of hardheaded discussions held with senior American officials in Washington. For Joffre the most important meeting was the one held on April 27, with Army Chief of Staff Hugh Scott and his deputy, Major General Tasker Bliss. They met at the Army War College.

Joffre started out on the line he had concluded while still back in Paris. The Americans, he said, could obviously not take part of the battlefront immediately. Yet, if they waited until they had mobilized, trained, and supplied a powerful army, they might arrive in France too late to save the degenerating military situation. It would be better, he said, to act now with such elements as are ready.

To accomplish that end, Joffre recommended that the Americans form a single unit, even if only a division, to be sent to France immediately to symbolize American participation. Such a division would first go into training in the French rear areas for a period of from four to six weeks. It could then be sent to a relatively quiet sector of the front before being committed to a more active part of the line. The arrival of that unit would be the first visible step on the road to later cooperation.

Joffre did not presume to dictate how the Americans could establish the large force that would eventually turn the balance of power in Europe, but he reiterated his conviction that the biggest problem would lie in the training of new officers and noncommissioned officers. Privates in the ranks, he insisted, were far easier to train, and the French would be very willing to help.

Little of what the Marshal said was new to Hugh Scott and Tasker

Bliss. Scott's questions to Joffre, therefore, centered around logistical problems. Could a port of debarkation in France be allocated to the Americans? What about rolling stock? And above all, what did the Marshal visualize regarding the command relationships between the Americans and their allies?

To many questions Joffre had at least partial answers. The French had already considered the question of a port of debarkation and recommended that the Americans be given use of La Pallice, near La Rochelle, on the Bay of Biscay. That seaport had both landing quays and an adequate water supply. Storage space was short, but that could be built. Its facilities, he estimated, were adequate to support more than the one American division he was requesting immediately, but he had doubts about its ability to support the 400,000 to 500,000 men visualized by the planners. That matter could be addressed later.

Joffre had anticipated that the Americans would be sensitive about the question of command relationships, so he came prepared to treat the subject diplomatically. Though the first American troops in France would obviously have to serve under French Army commanders, he was quick to assure his hosts that the Americans should soon have an army of their own. It was bad, he emphasized, to divide an army. The Americans agreed.

Before the meeting broke up, Joffre made a special request for special service troops and equipment—railroads, automobiles, and trucks in particular, which the French needed badly. Scott saw no difficulty in meeting that need.

WHILE JOFFRE was conferring with the Americans, so was British Major General George T. M. Bridges, a member of the Balfour mission. On April 30, three days after Joffre met with Scott and Bliss, Bridges penned a letter to Major General Joseph E. Kuhn, president of the War College, which was charged with planning for the General Staff.[16] Whereas Joffre had supported a separate American army from the beginning, Bridges concentrated on appealing for American draftees to fill up depleted British units. Like the French, the British Army was striving to maintain its strength by yearly reinforcements from the new "class" of recruits, the young men just reaching draft age. That source of manpower, however, could not keep the ranks of the British Army filled; nearly all its units were far below strength. The answer Bridges offered to solve that grim situation was to draw directly from the American manpower pool.

Specifically, Bridges urged that 500,000 newly inducted American recruits be sent to England at once for training and integration into British units.[17] Unconvincingly, he promised that the individual Americans could later be removed and placed in an American army—when such was formed. The great advantage of this plan, he said, would be that almost immediately America would be actively participating in the struggle. In the process, they would be suffering casualties, "without which it is difficult to realize the war."[18] The Americans were not yet prepared for the frankness of Bridges's words nor for his aloof manner. He therefore received a cool reception.

Bridges came close to overstepping his bounds in the tenuous ethics of alliances. Despite the premise that "we are all in the same boat," he fell prey to making sniffing references to Britain's Gallic ally. He emphasized the question of language, claiming that the French had "few English-speaking officers." Americans "will soon get tired of being instructed through interpreters." In a possible attempt at humor, and assuming that Americans were still just misplaced Anglo-Saxons, he said, "If [you Americans serve] with the French, you would probably want your own food supply also."[19]

The principle of placing American recruits into British or French units came to be known to the Americans as "amalgamation." Quick to detect its unsuitability for the American objectives was General Bliss. Rejecting the scheme because it would cause "greatly disproportionate loss of life" without gaining its object, Bliss foresaw an important political and psychological danger to American interests. "When the war is over," he wrote to Secretary of War Baker, "it may be a literal fact that the American flag may not have appeared anywhere on the line because our organizations will simply be parts of battalions and regiments of the Entente armies."[20]

On some points, however, Bridges and Joffre agreed: the Americans needed training in modern warfare and both offered the services of their own nation's instructors. More immediately, both pleaded for an immediate show of American force. "The sight of the Stars and Stripes," Bridges wrote, "will make a great impression on both sides."[21]

WITH IT ALL, Joffre was the man the Americans listened to. When he departed Washington for his trip around the country, he left a paper setting forth his views. When he returned on May 10, he learned to his delight that the War Department had drawn up a memorandum based almost entirely on his recommendations. It called for the organization of a single division, composed largely of Regular Army men, to be sent to France as early as June 1, 1917. Nobody expected the 1st Division to be fully trained in modern warfare. That would take place in France. But all agreed that a recognizable American force should be sent to France immediately.[22]

Joffre's work was done. He returned to France to render his report, having capped a military career with a diplomatic triumph. He had made a great contribution to eventual Allied victory. He had helped the Americans to begin thinking in concrete terms about their specific role in the coming campaigns. He had also uncovered some of the basic problems that would continue to plague American war planning: the very real, often selfish differences between French and British needs, and the unique political needs of America as a proud participant in this now truly worldwide conflict.

Marshal Joseph "Papa" Joffre had planted the seeds that would grow to be the two million man American Expeditionary Force.

CHAPTER TWO

A NATION AT WAR

THE UNITED STATES was at war with Germany and fully committed to sending a major expeditionary force to France. Implementing this commitment would call for unprecedented efforts and sacrifices. President Wilson was fully aware of the magnitude of the task. "It is not an army that we must shape and train for war," he said in a draft proclamation, "it is a nation." The effort would involve not only the military, but the industrial and the moral forces of the country as well.[1]

When war was declared, active public support was wide but not universal. Few citizens contested the action in itself; resentment of German arrogance and ruthlessness had seen to that. But pockets of resistance still survived; for example, Senator James K. Vardaman, a Mississippi Democrat, had attempted to prevent the passage of the war declaration practically up to the last minute.[2] Vardaman was a known Southern isolationist, and he did not represent a very large segment of the population, but enough people held similar viewpoints as to constitute a cause for concern. No American territory had been attacked to enrage the public, as would be the case with the Japanese raid on Pearl Harbor a quarter century later. In 1917 the general attitude of mere acceptance had to be transformed to one of zeal.

To mobilize public support, the President called on an intense man named George Creel, who had been an avid and visible supporter of Wilson's reelection campaign of 1916. Creel did not appear to be a man Wilson would prefer to associate with. True, both were native Virginians, but Wilson's family had spent the Civil War in relative safety and comfort in Augusta, Georgia, whereas Creel's people had been so impoverished that they pulled up stakes and migrated to Missouri just to eke out an existence. Creel, unlike Wilson, had been raised in a hard luck, street-smart

world; his background of privation had made him an aggressive chal-
lenger of established society.

Creel was a man of action. He had pursued a varied career as a
newspaper reporter, politician, professional boxer, and even police commissioner, always driven by a fiery intensity. As a newspaper man he had
proudly lived up to the label of "muckraker." In recent years he had been
engaged in attacking the Pendergast political machine in Kansas City; another target of his pen was the prevalence of cruel and abusive child
labor.[3] Creel had come to view the academic, lofty Wilson as a fellow re-
former. It was on that basis that Creel had published his supportive campaign tract, *Wilson and the Issues*.[4] Wilson was grateful, and when the
time came to create the Committee on Public Information on April 13,
1917, he turned to this firebrand crusader as its chairman.

Creel lived up to all of Wilson's expectations. He set up an office on
Jackson Square, across Pennsylvania Avenue from the White House, and
there he began recruiting a group of journalists dedicated to spreading
the word of the war's righteousness across the land.[5] The committee's Division of News distributed more than six thousand press releases in the
course of the war, and Creel later claimed that more than twenty thousand newspaper columns were derived from material issued in Committee on Public Information handouts. He enlisted the help of prominent
motion picture personalities—Mary Pickford, Douglas Fairbanks, and
Charles Chaplin among them. An appearance by those three luminaries
to sell Liberty Bonds on Wall Street brought a crowd of thirty thousand
people.[6] He organized a stable of cheerleaders that called themselves the
Four Minute Men, who traveled the country giving short pep talks at
rallies and in theaters. Creel even called on the great explorer Roald
Amundsen to spread the word.

Creel enjoyed his role, reveling in its sometimes heady aspects. One
day a Frenchwoman, whom he described as "very lovely," came into the
office and introduced herself as the Marquise de Courtivron. Her father
was Prince Polignac, who had fought for the South during the Civil War.
On his deathbed the Prince had requested that his sword be returned to
the state of Virginia. "Very timidly," Creel later recalled, "she asked if it
could be arranged without too much trouble. The Marquise was sent not
only to Richmond but to every other capital below the Mason and Dixon
line, and the whole South cheered her."[7]

The exuberant spirit that Creel engendered was infectious. Con-
temporary songwriters did their part to stir up patriotic fervor. "Over
There" became George M. Cohan's greatest musical hit, followed closely
by Irving Berlin's wistful "Oh, How I Hate to Get Up in the Morning."

Sentimental songs included "Roses of Picardy." Upbeat, morale-raising songs included "Pack Up Your Troubles" in both England and America. "K-K-K Katy" brought smiles. The Great War came to be thought of as a "singing war."

As might be expected, Creel offended some people, especially sober-minded citizens. Charges of censorship were leveled against him in some quarters. A zealot in promoting his product, Creel refused to tolerate any criticism toward the cause; since he dispensed the news, he had much power to control what the public learned. Nevertheless, Creel played a major role in changing the minds of people who for three years had observed strict neutrality in the war. In a remarkably short time his efforts completely reversed their reluctance.[8]

GEORGE CREEL'S ROLE in marshaling public support, while well-nigh indispensable, would have been meaningless if the enthusiastic men and women he was inspiring could not be organized into a cohesive war effort. Since President Wilson showed little personal interest in military matters, that task fell to an unusual degree on the shoulders of Secretary of War Newton Baker, who became, in the words of his biographer,

> the bridge between the people and the Army which was to translate the people's strength into armed power; the bridge between the President and the people; between the Congress and the Army, with its colossal demands for appropriations; between the parents and the son in the ranks; between the shoemaker and the soldier who wore out shoes on the march; between the soldier's stomach and the kitchen.[9]

Baker was an ideal man for the job. He had been in his position about a year when the United States entered the war, and before coming to Washington he had been a successful lawyer, a solicitor of the city of Cleveland, and later an extremely effective mayor of the same city. He was devoted to Woodrow Wilson and had been Wilson's avid supporter in the presidential election in 1912. The pacifism he shared with the President was mitigated by his advocacy of military preparedness. Above all, Baker had earned a reputation for an ability to work with others.

He did not look the part of the man of Mars. Only forty-six years old, small of stature, and unpretentious, his prominent eyeglasses gave him the appearance of a schoolmaster. But by the time war came, this quiet little man had proved to be quite capable of directing armies and headstrong commanders.

His relations with Chief of Staff Hugh Scott were cordial. He re-

spected the old Indian fighter and early in the partnership had allowed
Scott to play the role of a tutor. But Scott and the other generals who
served under Baker had learned early that when the Secretary said no,
that was exactly what he meant.

He also worked well with Secretary of the Navy Josephus Daniels.
Daniels went so far, in fact, as to describe the two of them as "yoke fellows," a relationship that Daniels somewhat hyperbolically called "the
perfect working together of the Army and the Navy, which made them invincible in the World War."[10]

BAKER'S EXECUTIVE ABILITY would be taxed in the months ahead, because the War Department had neither an adequate General Staff nor an
effective chief of staff to head it. The men assigned to the General Staff
were competent officers, thanks to the Army's excellent school system,
but they were far too few. The traditional American fear of undue military influence in government had caused the Congress to limit the General Staff Corps to a paltry fifty-five officers, of whom only twenty-nine
could be stationed in Washington.[11]

General Scott was a fine old officer, but he was only months away
from the mandatory retirement age of sixty-four. Moreover, he hated
office work.[12] His shortcomings were partially offset by his deputy chief
of staff, Tasker Bliss, who was a meticulous man, at home behind a desk.
Bliss was a scholar, who had studied European military systems first-
hand, and who earned Baker's admiration for his "habit of deliberate
and consecutive thinking, his mind a comprehensive card index."[13] Some
said that Bliss spent too much time on trivia and lacked the ruthlessness
necessary in a strong chief. But for the moment Baker had nobody to replace these two old soldiers with, so his own role took on added importance.

The War Department itself was an antiquated structure, with parts
acting almost independently of the head. Throughout American history,
the Army's various bureaus—Adjutant General, Corps of Engineers,
Quartermaster, and Ordnance—had operated as fiefdoms, and the relatively new General Staff, organized only in 1903, could not control them.
The only chief of staff who could tame them temporarily was General
Leonard Wood, who served from 1910 to 1914, and his success would
have been impossible without the wholehearted backing of then Secretary of War Henry L. Stimson.[14] The rest of the chiefs stayed in office for
only short terms, that prestigious position being awarded as a sort of gold
watch to senior officers nearing the mandatory retirement age. The
heads of the bureaus, on the other hand, held their offices for years,

maintaining strong, independent congressional ties, arguing for appropriations on their own.

In a way, however, it was well that the bureaus were so strong. With a totally unprepared nation being faced with a gigantic mobilization, they were the part of the structure that knew their business. Having operated during peacetime, the Corps of Engineers knew how to construct camps; the Adjutant General knew how to keep personnel records and make assignments; the Ordnance Department could develop weapons like the superb Springfield M-1903 rifle. The nation was therefore able to mobilize. Even so, it came at a cost. Independent agencies bid against each other, as well as against the Navy. It was inevitable that much wastage of government money was going to occur.

MUCH HAD HAPPENED during Baker's first year as Secretary of War. Soon after his arrival in early 1916, the public began to appreciate the need for an expanded, modernized army, and on May 20 Congress passed the National Defense Act of 1916, which provided for the authorized strength of the Regular Army to be raised to a level of 175,000 men, a goal to be reached at the end of five years. The act was motivated, however, by concern over relations with Mexico, not potential war with Germany. Among other shortcomings, it provided for a very limited expansion, to only 286,000 men, even in time of war. Of greater significance for the future was the emphasis it placed on the Army's reserve component, the National Guard, for which it authorized a ceiling of 400,000 men.

When war came nearly a year later, both Wilson and the Congress realized that the National Defense Act of 1916 could never provide even the 500,000 men the United States originally expected to send to Europe. A new bill was necessary, and the terms of that bill would determine the very nature of the army that was to be built.

The vast size of the proposed new army dictated that, as in previous American wars, it would consist largely of citizen-soldiers, men brought in from civil life and trained under the supervision of the Regulars.[15] During the year that the previous act had been in effect, the total number of men in uniform came to 130,000 Regulars and about 70,000 National Guardsmen. Assuming that a total of a million men were needed, from what sources would the additional 800,000 men come? Would the nation have to implement a draft or could it raise that large number of troops solely from volunteers? Would the newly organized divisions be called Regular, National Guard, or something else?

Professionals, understandably, advocated expanding the Regular Army by fleshing out its ranks into a so-called Continental Army, exclusively under federal control.[16] That idea was quickly discarded because of opposition from the politically powerful National Guard, which would never stand for it, but in case of emergency even the National Guard could not be expanded quickly enough to make up the shortage in manpower. So Baker and his associates settled for a compromise: expand the Regular Army by creating twenty Regular divisions and eighteen National Guard divisions. Whatever additional divisions were needed would be organized in a separate category called the National Army.[17] The Regulars and the Guardsmen would generally come from the first volunteers that flocked to the colors, but the question remained as to how to raise the members of the National Army.

One man felt no ambivalence on the subject. From the start, Chief of Staff Hugh Scott would consider no solution whatever except for a national draft. He shared his views forcibly with Baker, who agreed. Baker then presented that recommendation to President Wilson, carefully presenting all sides of the debate. Some people, he advised, would object to a draft on constitutional grounds. Others remembered the bitter experiences the Union had undergone during the American Civil War, only fifty years earlier.[18] After some discussion, Wilson and Baker made a courageous decision in favor of a draft, and the bulk of the American people supported it.[19]

Baker and Wilson early came to one important conclusion. It was essential, they realized, that the American citizenry should be made to feel that the draft was theirs, not something imposed by an autocratic military. To accomplish that end, they directed that the inductees would be selected by draft boards made up of local citizens, appointed by the various governors throughout the country. To popularize the process, the bill cast the board members themselves in the position of draftees. Citizens so serving were not to be paid, and any attempt to avoid such onerous duty would be labeled a misdemeanor.[20]

As might be expected, some resistance met the draft bill in Congress. Its progress was further hampered by the followers of Theodore Roosevelt, who introduced what became known as the Roosevelt Amendment, which held approval of Wilson's draft proposal hostage to a provision authorizing the former President to organize a division of volunteers.

Theodore Roosevelt, despite his zeal for preparedness, was actually more of a hindrance than a help in America's effort to mobilize for war, because his personal desire to participate in any fighting caused considerable embarrassment. His early offer to organize a division, rendered the day after Bernsdorff's fateful message, was rejected coldly but politely.[21] Roosevelt then swallowed his pride and called personally on the man who had defeated him at the polls and whom he had been attacking as "timid" in recent months. The meeting was friendly,[22] but nothing came of it. Wilson supported Baker's decision to reject Roosevelt's offer to raise a division, much to the relief of the General Staff.

The Selective Service Act was passed on May 19, 1917, mobilizing the manpower of the nation. It provided for the first registration of citizens between twenty-one and thirty-one to be held on June 5. In the course of the war, two more registrations would finally increase the range of ages from eighteen to forty-five inclusive. An impressive 24 million men were eventually registered, of which 2.8 million were actually inducted into service at one time or another. The draftees would soon be as fully accepted in the military as the Regulars, Guardsmen, and volunteers—and their desertion rate would be the lowest of those in any category.[23]

ON THE MORNING OF JULY 20, 1917, Secretary of War Baker stood blindfolded in his office, the cameras of the press whirring. He was to draw the first number in the lottery to determine who should be the first men called to active duty. Baker was to be followed by Senator George E. Chamberlain, of Oregon, chairman of the Senate Committee on Military Affairs. Many dignitaries participated. The last drawings were made by Acting Chief of Staff Tasker Bliss and General Enoch Crowder, whose office had written the draft act and who, now designated as Provost Marshal General, would actually conduct the draft.[24]

Baker reached into a glass jar that contained 10,500 registration numbers written on slips of paper. He took hold of one and read it out: Number 258. Any man holding that number would immediately report to the draft board.

America's full manpower was now committed to the cause. The first men had been selected to create the National Army of the American Expeditionary Force.

CHAPTER THREE

THE SELECTION
OF GENERAL PERSHING

ON THE LAST DAY of Marshal Joffre's visit to Washington, Secretary of War Baker introduced him to Major General John J. Pershing, the recent commander of the Punitive Expedition in Mexico. Baker and Wilson, having agreed to send a small force to France immediately, had selected Pershing to head it. As the Secretary sketched a rundown of Pershing's distinguished career, Joffre caught the names New Mexico, Dakota, Cuba, and the Mexican frontier. Commenting that Pershing was a "fine-looking soldier," the elderly Frenchman predicted that Pershing would soon be commanding millions of men. "Please tell him," Joffre said, "that he can always count on me for anything in my power."[1]

In making this introduction, Baker did not convey the amount of soul-searching that had gone into the selection. It was one of the most important decisions that Baker and President Wilson would ever make, as the officer selected would have to be capable of carrying tremendous responsibility on his own. Secretary Baker could not look over the shoulder of the man sent to command in Europe.

Pershing had not always been Baker's first choice. In early 1917 the most prestigious field officer in the United States Army was Major General Frederick Funston, commanding the Southern Department at San Antonio, Texas. Funston was an aggressive officer, who had entered the Army in 1898 through the National Guard of Kansas. He had distinguished himself in the Philippine Insurrection, earning the Congressional Medal of Honor at the Battle of Calumpit. After that he personally led a daring and spectacular raid, actually capturing the rebel leader, Emilio Aguinaldo. Seventeen years a general officer, Funston was expected to lead any force the United States would put into the field.

It was not to be. The command picture changed drastically during the evening of February 19, 1917. The circumstances were later vividly recalled by General Douglas MacArthur.

MacArthur, a major at the time, was assigned that evening as the all-night duty officer for the Army General Staff in the old State, War, Navy Building[2] across Executive Avenue from the White House. He had performed this chore many times before, and the duties were routine. On this particular evening the Adjutant General duty officer was Lieutenant Colonel Peyton C. March. March was fifteen years senior to MacArthur, but he was a personal family friend of long standing, so that evening promised to be a pleasant visit. Neither MacArthur nor March expected any excitement before the staffs returned to the offices the next day.

At about 10:00 P.M., the quiet was shattered. A messenger delivered a dispatch from San Antonio. MacArthur watched March's face as he read it; MacArthur quickly sensed something important. General Funston, the message disclosed, had died of a massive heart attack that evening while dining out at a local hotel. Word had to be delivered to Secretary Baker without delay.

Delivering the message, however, would not be a pleasant or easy task. Secretary Baker, MacArthur knew, was hosting a dinner party in honor of the President himself, and the strictest orders had been issued that the party was not to be disturbed. Nevertheless, MacArthur left the Army command post and headed for Baker's downtown residence.

As he expected, MacArthur was stopped at the door, and no amount of pleading could get him past the guards. However, as he fruitlessly argued, he discovered that he could get a glimpse into the dining room from the entrance hall. Eventually he succeeded in making himself noticed among the lighthearted guests—by the President himself.

Wilson was familiar with MacArthur, and, caught up in the gaiety of the evening, called out, "Come in Major, and tell all of us the news. There are no secrets here." The other guests applauded.

MacArthur steeled himself and stepped forward. "Sir, I regret to report that General Funston has just died." The men around the table caught their breaths and soon thereafter scattered in a stampede.

Wilson and Baker, though somewhat shaken, took the news in stride. As MacArthur waited for instructions, they beckoned for him to follow as they went into an adjacent room. First the President dictated a message of sympathy to Mrs. Funston. Then turning to Baker, he asked, "What now, Newton, who will take the Army over?"

Baker, perhaps stalling for time, turned to MacArthur. "Whom do you think the Army would choose, Major?"

"I cannot, of course, speak for the Army, but for myself the choice would unquestionably be General Pershing."

Wilson looked at the young officer for a long moment. Then he said quietly, "It would be a good choice."[3]

WILSON'S REACTION was widely shared, and almost certainly would have been reached without MacArthur's contribution. Even though Funston had been Pershing's superior, Pershing might have been selected in any case, for Baker and Scott had come to realize that Pershing possessed certain qualities that Funston lacked. The most obvious of these was an ability to deal with people who held opposing views. Pershing was no diplomat, but compared to the impetuous Funston, he was a model of self-restraint. With Funston out of contention, the choice would be even easier.

Pershing had long been a marked man in the Army. After graduating from West Point in the Class of 1886, he had been assigned to frontier duty in the campaigns against the Sioux that culminated in the Battle of Wounded Knee in 1890. He performed outstanding services in the Spanish-American War, and in an engagement near the famous San Juan Hill he came to the notice of Lieutenant Colonel Theodore Roosevelt. In 1901 the new President Roosevelt made some arbitrary promotions that included elevating Captain Pershing to the rank of brigadier general, jumping three grades and passing over hundreds of Regular officers. Later, when Pershing married the comely and vivacious daughter of United States Senator Francis E. Warren, of Wyoming, Roosevelt himself attended the ceremony at the Washington Cathedral. During the recent troubles on the Mexican border, it was Pershing who was sent into Mexico in pursuit of Villa, though his superior, Frederick Funston, had coveted that field command.

Pershing was more admired than liked. By nature he was an austere, aloof man, and his rigid insistence on military punctilio earned him enemies. When he was assigned as a tactical officer at West Point, his obsession with stern discipline made him extremely unpopular with the cadets. Seizing on his previous assignment to the 10th Cavalry, a regiment of Negro soldiers, the cadets saddled him with a sobriquet that was toned down to "Black Jack." Euphonious, the nickname stuck with Pershing throughout his career, long after its origin was forgotten.

Pershing's reserve was deepened by the burden of a personal tragedy. Three years earlier his vivacious young wife and two small daughters had perished in a tragic fire at the Presidio of San Francisco. Only his son, Warren, away on a holiday, was left. To some extent Pershing unjustifiably blamed himself for the tragedy. Assigned to command the 8th Cavalry Brigade at El Paso, Texas, he had left his wife and children in comfortable and supposedly safe quarters at the most desirable post in the West to spare them the hardships of the Texas frontier. Throughout the rest of his life, which lasted another thirty-four years, Pershing never remarried.

The personal tragedy did not, however, cause Pershing to give up his life or his career. Instead, he threw himself into his military duties with even greater single-mindedness, proving his abilities by his aggressive conduct in Mexico; if he could be faulted in any way, it was only for overzealous execution of President Wilson's vague orders regarding the objectives of the Punitive Expedition.

Other candidates were considered as prospective commanders of the AEF. Two of them were former Army chiefs of staff. Foremost among Pershing's competitors was Major General Leonard Wood, the Army chief of staff between 1910 and 1914. In that position, Wood had been highly effective, arguably the only effective Army chief since the office was created in 1903. Part of Wood's success at that time was due to his relative youth—he was only fifty years old. Inspired by his friend Theodore Roosevelt, he called himself a "preparedness man"—others called him a "military evangelist." Convinced that it required only six months to train a soldier, even an officer,[4] he established several volunteer officer training camps, the most noted of which was at Plattsburgh, New York. So popular was this program that the trainees paid their own expenses, even though graduation did not offer regular commissions.

When his term as chief of staff expired, Wood continued on active duty as the commander of the Eastern Department, with headquarters at Governors Island, New York City. There he continued to promote the concept of officer training programs, and in 1915 he formally established the Plattsburgh Movement.[5]

But despite his stellar performance as chief of staff, Wood had shortcomings, one of which was a genius for stirring up controversy. He advocated military preparedness so blatantly that the Wilson administration—always determined to avoid saber-rattling—had become alarmed. His longtime personal friendship with former President Roosevelt was a doubtful asset, especially when he seemed to espouse Roosevelt's sharp attacks on what Roosevelt considered Wilson's cowardice in trying to keep America out of the war. In contrast to Pershing, who disdained political activity, Wood had been openly eyeing the presidency for years. While he was in command of the Army's Eastern Department he used the proximity of his headquarters to New York City to court the friendship of men on Wall Street, presumably with a view to using them as a political power base. When he provided a rostrum from which Roosevelt attacked the Wilson administration on the preparedness issue, Secretary Baker transferred him to command the Southeastern Department, with headquarters in Charleston, South Carolina. When asked why he had taken such action, Baker answered icily:

> I think General Wood has been very indiscreet, and I think the appearance of political activity which he had allowed to grow up about many of his actions has been unfortunate for his reputation as a soldier.[6]

But Pershing, also, had opponents, some of whom were spreading rumors that he, like Wood, had been disloyal to Wilson, especially with regard to the President's policies toward Mexico. Some of these rumors reached Baker, who brought them up with Hugh Scott. Scott quickly rejected any such allegations and lost no time in warning Pershing to be "extremely careful about such matters."[7] This came as a shock to Pershing, who was more than eager to participate in the coming campaigns, and who dearly wanted the goodwill of his superiors. The reports, he wrote in a letter addressed to Scott but ultimately designed for Baker, were "entirely without foundation." The President had been confronted with "very serious conditions" and his acts had been prompted by only the "highest of motives." Pershing's own attitude toward Wilson was "one of entire friendliness" and the President could count on him "to the last extremity, both as to word and deed, for loyalty and fidelity, in any task that may be given me to perform."[8] And immediately after Wilson's appearance before Congress asking for a declaration of war, Pershing sent the President an emotional (and doubtless sincere) letter of congratulations on Wilson's "soul-stirring, patriotic address." He sent another in the same vein to Baker.[9]

Baker weighed the merits of the two men, Pershing and Wood. He then submitted his recommendation to President Wilson.

PERSHING KNEW THAT HE was the leading contender, but the decision was slow in coming. He was therefore puzzled when he received a message from his father-in-law, Senator Warren, asking about his proficiency in the French language. Stretching the truth considerably, Pershing replied that his French was very good. His answer was unimportant. Warren's true message was to tell Pershing that he was at least a strong contender for the assignment in France.

Certainty came quickly. On May 2, 1917, Pershing received a message from General Scott:

For your eyes only. Under plans under consideration is one which will require among other troops, four infantry regiments and one artillery regiment from your department for service in France. If plans are carried out, you will be in command of the entire force. Wire me at once designation of the regiments selected by you and their present stations.[10]

Pershing set about making his selections. From the units that he had taken into Mexico, he chose four infantry regiments, the 16th, 18th, 26th, and 28th. To support them he selected the 6th Field Artillery Regiment. He then departed, as ordered, for Washington.

ON MAY 10, 1917, occurred the first meeting between the two men who would work hand in glove for the rest of the First World War, the two most important officials involved directly with the United States role in the conflict. Major General John Pershing, newly arrived in the nation's capital, strode into the State, War, Navy Building to report to the Secretary of War. Their first talk covered only general topics. Pershing was surprised to find Baker younger and smaller than he had expected, especially when hunched behind his desk. But when Baker spoke, Pershing felt the force of his personality. After a brief discussion of Pershing's recent expedition into Mexico, Baker referred to Pershing's new appointment, assuring the general that his selection had been based solely on his record. Pershing expressed his appreciation and said he hoped that Baker would have no occasion to regret the choice. Pershing left the office "with a distinctly favorable impression of the man upon whom, as head of the War Department, would rest the burden of preparing for a great war."[11]

AT THE TIME of this visit, Pershing understood that he was going to France only as a division commander. He would be completely comfortable in that capacity; after all, the Punitive Expedition that he had recently commanded in Chihuahua had reached a strength of some fifteen thousand men at one point. A day or so later, however, Baker called him in again with the sobering news that the President had changed his role. Pershing would now go to France as the Commander-in-Chief of any American forces that would eventually be sent, not merely as a division commander. Pershing was directed to select his staff and depart for Europe as soon as possible, and not to wait for the 1st Division to accompany him.

Pershing was rocked by this new assignment. It was, of course, a promotion and an expression of approval, but it would entail a far more complicated set of challenges. He shook off his concern quickly, however, and began to think about whom he should take. He would, of course, have the pick of any of the officers of the Army, because his responsibilities would now include the development of an entire theater of war, including a supply system as an integral part of his organization. Since he would be dealing on an equal basis with allies, he needed a staff of more than just warriors.

As Pershing went down the list of officers he was familiar with in his career, he hit upon the name of Major James G. Harbord, whom he had known in the cavalry and the Philippine Constabulary. Harbord was not a West Point graduate; he had, in fact, enlisted as a soldier in January of 1889. But from the start, Harbord's record had been exemplary. Pershing had faith in the records and in the Army's unofficial rating system by word of mouth among officers, and Harbord was the man he chose as his future chief of staff.[12]

In all, Pershing selected thirty-one men as staff members at the outset, and he began making final preparations for his contingent to leave for France. It was difficult, however, for him to set an exact date for departure, because the Atlantic Ocean was infested with German submarines, and the *Baltic,* on which he and his staff were to sail, had been instructed to wait until the naval authorities deemed the risk to be acceptable.

He did not waste his time. While waiting around Washington, Pershing visited with various old friends and corresponded with others. One bit of correspondence was difficult to handle. On May 20, 1917, he received a letter from former President ("Colonel") Theodore Roosevelt,[13] who was playing all angles to get involved in the war. The ostensible purpose of the Colonel's letter was to request that Roosevelt's two sons, Theodore Jr. and Archibald, be allowed to enlist as privates in Pershing's command, even though they were both officers in the Reserve Corps, stationed at Plattsburgh. Granting such a request would fly in the face of President Wilson's order that only Regulars were to go abroad in the first contingent. Appended as a postscript, however, was the real reason for Roosevelt's letter:

> If I were physically fit, instead of old and heavy and stiff, I should ask myself to go under you in any capacity down to and including a sergeant; but at my age, and condition, I suppose that I could not do work you would consider worth while in the fighting line (my only line) in a lower grade than brigade commander.[14]

This was not a welcome request. Fortunately, Pershing had no need to respond because he possessed no authority in the matter. He referred the letter to Secretary Baker, who, to Pershing's intense relief, rejected the former chief executive's request.

Another encounter would prove to be more productive. When lunching at the Metropolitan Club in Washington, Pershing was joined by an old friend from his days at Lincoln, Nebraska, Charles G. Dawes, who had applied for a commission in the Engineer Corps. Noting Dawes's complete lack of practical experience in the field, Pershing was amused by his friend's pretensions to be an engineer. He did, however, have a great respect for Dawes's ability as a businessman, so on return to the War Department, he spoke to Baker in Dawes's behalf.[15] He would never regret that action.

On May 24, 1917, Pershing accompanied Baker to the White House for a short conference with President Wilson. It was their first meeting, and it consisted almost solely of formalities and pleasantries; to Pershing's mild disappointment the President said nothing about the role his Army should play in cooperation with the Allied Armies, but both expressed mutual confidence, the President promising his "full support."[16]

Finally, Pershing was informed that the *Baltic* would sail on the 28th of May. During the waiting period, Pershing and his chief of staff, James Harbord, had been assigned an office across the hall from that of General Bliss, who was acting chief of staff in the absence of Scott. There, in an attempt to formalize the particulars of their mission, the two composed their own draft letter of instructions. They then took their draft across to General Bliss, who, in the name of the Secretary of War, signed it. Later in the same day, however, Pershing received another formal letter of instructions, this one from Secretary Baker himself:

1. The President designates you to command all the land forces of the United States operating in Continental Europe and in the United Kingdom of Great Britain and Ireland, including any part of the Marine Corps which may be detached for service there with the Army.

. . . .

3. You are invested with the authority and duties devolved by the laws, regulations, orders and customs of the United States upon the commander of an army in the field in time of war. . . .

4. You will establish, after consultation with the French War Office, all necessary bases, lines of communications, depots, etc., and make all the incidental arrangements essential to active participation at the front.

5. In military operations against the Imperial German Government, you are directed to cooperate with the forces of the other countries employed against that enemy; but in so doing the underlying idea must be kept in view that the forces of the United States are a separate and dis-

tinct component of the combined forces, the identity of which must be preserved. This fundamental rule is subject to such minor exceptions in particular circumstances as your judgment may approve. The decision as to when your command, or any of its parts, is ready for action is confided to you.

That order resembled, but not quite duplicated, the instructions that Bliss had signed. Pershing was little concerned because both sets of orders gave him practically unlimited powers. In only one respect did they differ. Baker's order did not specify which nation, Britain or France, Pershing should work more closely with. Bliss's directed him to "plan and conduct active operations in conjunction and in cooperation with the French armies operating in France against Germany and her allies." Pershing was still not worried. As he read the orders, he concluded that "the general character of our mission" meant cooperation with any of the Allied Armies in France.[17]

ON MAY 27, 1917, Pershing's special train departed from Washington, bound for New York,[18] and the next morning he and his staff checked in at Governors Island, their point of departure. Later that day the Pershing party were to go by a government tugboat, the *Thomas Patten,* out to meet the *Baltic.* The circumstances were not auspicious, for the day was dark, rainy, and windy. In an effort to prevent the public from learning what was going on, Pershing and his party were bundled up in scruffy civilian clothes, "collars turned up in the absence of umbrellas or raincoats." Elizabeth Coles Marshall, wife of Captain George C. Marshall, watched them out her window and regarded them as an unimposing group. "They were such a dreadful-looking lot of men," she later told her husband, "I cannot believe they will be able to do any good in France."[19]

CHAPTER FOUR

THE YANKS ARRIVE

As THE *BALTIC* plowed her way out of New York Harbor and into the Atlantic Ocean, the passengers aboard were apprehensive. Despite the supposed secrecy of the sailing, someone had failed to get the word. Numerous crates had been sitting in plain view on the wharf, blazoned with large letters identifying the various chiefs of supply departments. The newspaper reporters, under no restriction, could readily surmise what was going on. From their stories, enemy agents could alert German U-boats to seek the *Baltic* out. None of the passengers, even Pershing himself, realized that the cooperative press would voluntarily keep details about the party's departure secret—which turned out to be the case.[1] For the immediate moment, however, the greatest cause for anxiety was the fog. Nervous passengers gradually became accustomed to the fog-horns, which blew every three minutes, but they were relieved when, after two days, the pea soup lifted and the ship burst into the sunlight.

Despite the concern that would endure through the entire voyage, Pershing and his staff put the ten days of the Atlantic crossing to good use, and much work was done. The schedule in Washington had been hectic; it would be the same in France. But on the high seas there was little to infringe on Pershing's time. Pershing and Harbord worked closely, considering at the outset how to organize the headquarters they were about to establish in France. As a basis for future planning, Pershing set a tentative figure of a million men as the ultimate strength of the American Expeditionary Force. He and Harbord also gave much thought as to the sector on the Western Front where it would be most advantageous to situate the American Army.[2]

The rest of the staff were kept busy also. Based on Pershing's assumption of a million man AEF, boards of experts met to make plans for

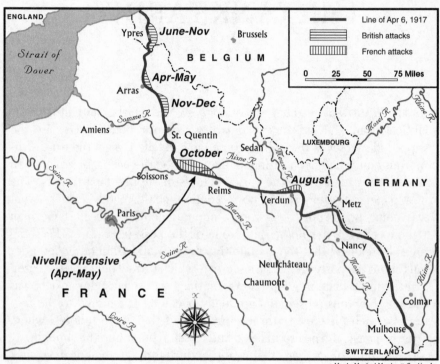

1. The Western Front in 1917.

Map by Maryland Mapping & Graphics, Inc.

The Western Front changed very little during the year of 1917, after the Americans joined in the war. At the left end of the line the British attacked in Flanders. In the middle, the much anticipated Nivelle offensive of April failed miserably. The offensive at Verdun was a limited affair, designed to restore French morale after the Nivelle failure.

surveying facilities for ports, railways, and lines of communications without delay on arrival in France.[3] Other boards studied machine gun requirements, artillery requirements, and other equipment they would need. Pershing also decreed that his fledgling Air Service, part of the Signal Corps in the United States, would be independent.

ON JUNE 5, 1917, eight days after leaving New York, the *Baltic* began to zigzag, which meant that the ship was entering the "danger zone" of the North Atlantic, infested with German U-boats. As planned, two American destroyers, a half mile off each side of the ship, escorted her in. After proceeding up the Mersey River, the *Baltic* docked at Liverpool at 9:30 A.M. on the 8th of June.

Pershing's arrival was a joyous event, one that would be duplicated in countless ceremonies across England, and later in France. He and his staff were seen as harbingers of an American intervention so desperately needed in those dark days. Pershing himself was welcomed warmly as the human embodiment of Allied hopes. In Liverpool, Pershing and his staff were greeted by a party consisting of the Lord Mayor and his wife, together with local representatives of the British Army and Royal Navy. An honor guard was on hand, and a band played the two national anthems. Pershing considered the occasion to be of great symbolic significance, though the ceremony was unremarkable. It was, in his words, "the first time in history that an American Army contingent was ever officially received in England."[4] Pershing's comments to the welcoming party were informal and played to the feelings of the crowd.

> Speaking for myself personally, the officers of my staff, and the members of my command, we are very glad indeed to be the standard bearers of our country in this great war for civilization. To land on British soil and to receive the welcome accorded us seems very significant and is deeply appreciated. We expect in course of time to be playing our part, and we hope it will be a very large part, on the Western Front.[5]

From the moment he debarked from the *Baltic* to the moment Pershing left British soil, his time was filled with ceremonies, some useful, others less so. In London, he was greeted at Euston Station by Lord Derby, the British Secretary of State for War, Field Marshal Sir John French, and the American ambassador, Walter H. Page. As the newly arrived Americans drove through the streets, Pershing noticed that nobody paid any heed to the American uniforms; the "Yanks" had already become a commonplace sight in London.

The following day, Pershing paid a formal call on King George V at Buckingham Palace. The King, Pershing thought, was remarkably acute, though unimpressive physically. At the end of the call, the King asked Pershing to do everything possible to promote cooperation between the "English speaking peoples." Still fixated by the prevailing British notion that Americans were only slightly removed Englishmen, he said, "The Anglo-Saxon race must save civilization." Dramatically, the King declared that America's entry into the war caused his "life dream to be realized."[6]

Later that morning Pershing visited with the American ambassador, Walter Page. Page had attained great popularity in Britain when, back in the days of American neutrality, he had made loud public pronouncements deploring America's slowness in entering the World War on the side of the Allies. "Now," Page said to Pershing, "I am able to hold up my head and look people squarely in the eye." Pershing noted that this lack of loyalty to Commander-in-Chief Woodrow Wilson sat badly with many Americans, but he believed that Page's high standing in Britain would continue to make him useful in his present position.[7]

Pershing then called on Admiral William S. Sims, that distinguished old sailor, now retired, who was directing the movements of United States naval vessels, especially destroyers, from his office in the American embassy. Sims was dissatisfied with the efforts of the Navy Department in Washington to supply the much needed destroyers that Britain had requested. Until more of those vessels arrived, Sims could promise nothing by way of protection for American troopships crossing the Atlantic. Pershing could understand Sims's point, but the conversation did nothing to lighten his view of prospects for a quick buildup of his army.

The busy schedule Pershing was subjected to was just what his position demanded at the moment. Without an army to command, he was still cast largely in the role of an ambassador. But through it all, he remained a soldier first and foremost. He particularly valued his visit with General Sir William Robertson, chief of the Imperial General Staff. On June 12 he witnessed a tactical demonstration arranged by Field Marshal Sir Arthur Paget, Commander of the Home Forces. Pershing was struck by the brevity of the training period given to British recruits: nine weeks. That short period, the British explained, was sufficient for trench warfare. British recruits were not expected to conduct open warfare. Pershing was puzzled by this complete preoccupation with trench warfare as opposed to maneuver.

As Pershing went through his succession of official visits, the British continued to press on him their need for American help. From Lord

Derby, the Secretary of State for War, and from Prime Minister David Lloyd George, Pershing received the same messages:

1. American forces should be brought overseas quickly, in American bottoms;
2. the Americans should be associated with the British, as fellow Anglo-Saxons, rather than with the French; and
3. the most effective way for the Americans to be employed in British units would be as individual replacements or in small units, to fill out experienced British tactical formations.

Pershing agreed with the first idea; he had doubts about the second; and he violently disagreed with the third. However, he did not make an issue of these matters while he was a guest on British soil. He would hear variations of those viewpoints time and again in the months to come.

All in all, Pershing made a favorable impression on the British populace. One writer outdid himself, conjecturing that Pershing's appearance ensured a speedy end to the war in Europe as the result of America's entry. Another, A. G. Gardiner, said Pershing's arrival had

> the aspect of the dawning of a new epoch in the war, even in British eyes, while in France, whose endurance in the face of her tremendous sacrifices is the admiration of the world, the advent of the commander of the American expeditionary force will bring high encouragement and hope, such as can only be measured by the depth of her sorrows in these last three years.

Gardiner lauded Pershing himself, asserting that "Englishmen who have met the American commander unite in paying high tribute to his qualities."

With those tributes to see him off, Pershing and his staff left the United Kingdom for the French port of Boulogne on the morning of June 13. Pershing had learned much in Britain that would be of use to him later. He had also shown the British the face of the coming Yank: courteous but resolute.

THE ENGLISH CHANNEL was uncommonly smooth that June morning as Pershing's contingent of the American Expeditionary Force landed at Boulogne. In France, as in Britain, Pershing was met by the most prominent of public men and welcomed with even greater fervor the moment he set foot on French soil. The party at Boulogne included two men who would stay with Pershing's headquarters throughout the war. One of these was Colonel Jacques Adelbert de Chambrun, who had left his seat in the Chamber of Deputies to don the uniform of a colonel, and the other was Brigadier General Peltier, the one-armed veteran who became a liaison officer between Pershing's headquarters and the French. The British were represented by Lieutenant General Fowke, adjutant general of Field Marshal Sir Douglas Haig's British Expeditionary Force. Meeting Pershing in Paris late in the afternoon were all the important officials of the French War Department: Paul Painlevé, the Minister of War; Marshal Joffre; René Viviani; Major General Ferdinand Foch (chief of staff);[8] and United States Ambassador William G. Sharp. No time had been set aside for speeches, much to Pershing's relief.

What happened then stunned the American general; it also demonstrated to the world how eager the French were to have the Americans join them in fighting the Germans. As reported in the *New York Times* the next day, Pershing took all parts of Paris "by storm, from the President of the Republic, commanders of the army and Ministers of the Government down through the ranks and grades to the humblest little midinettes, who lined his route to throw flowers and kisses. No other man since the war began received such a magnificent, wholehearted welcome." Nor could any man, the enthusiastic reporter added, "have risen to meet it in a more splendid and dignified manner."[9] When Pershing addressed the deputies in the Chamber, the applause lasted several minutes.

Pershing was in his element when engaged in this sort of activity. His natural bearing and dignity were just what the French craved. "Since the days of Murat, the *beau sabreur*," one reporter observed, "French crowds have always adored military leaders who looked the part." A highlight of the ceremonies in Paris took place on June 14 with Pershing's visit to the tomb of the Emperor Napoleon I. Pershing was conducted down to the inner crypt, handed the key, and asked to unlock the heavy wrought iron gate, an honor normally reserved to heads of state. Pershing stood solemnly before the tomb, head uncovered, and paid his respects to "one of the world's great commanders."[10] The French rejoiced. Even Pershing's reverent manner in inspecting the Emperor's sword was mentioned. Let policies wait for another day.

Pershing never actually spoke the words "Lafayette, we are here," as ascribed to him. They were uttered by Colonel Charles E. Stanton, speaking for him at Lafayette's tomb outside Paris on the 4th of July. Nevertheless, those words represented Pershing's sentiments and the aura that surrounded him in mid-June of 1917.

A more sobering line, and more relevant, was spoken by Ambassador Sharp at dinner the day the Pershing party arrived in Paris. Expressing the same feelings as Ambassador Page, he said, more appropriately,

> You cannot realize the satisfaction I feel that we are in the war and that you are here to prepare for our participation. It is a great day for America and for France. The civilian now gives way to the soldier. I hope you have not arrived too late.[11]

ACROSS THE ATLANTIC, at Governors Island, Captain George Marshall, age thirty-six, was anxious for fear that he, for one, would be "too late." He had felt keen disappointment as he had escorted Pershing's contingent from headquarters down to the dock for the boat ride out to the *Baltic*. Marshall was ambitious, and he knew that the paths to military advancement lay overseas. He envied that scraggly-looking group of officers departing the United States in the rain.

Marshall realized, of course, that he had little cause for complaint. He had not been a member of Pershing's Punitive Expedition into Mexico the year before, and young officers such as George Patton had earned their priority in the sands of Chihuahua. And for the moment Marshall had plenty on his hands. As senior aide to the ailing Major General J. Franklin Bell, he had found himself inundated with work ever since Bell had settled down at Governors Island in late April. The rather small officer training camp at Plattsburgh Barracks, New York, had to be transformed into a major facility that could train young officers for the tasks ahead. And Marshall found himself coping with innumerable requests the general was receiving from young men eager to be assigned to the training school. The backlog had already reached some four hundred to five hundred. Employing four stenographers at one time, and sometimes talking to two people on the phone at once, Marshall underwent what he later described as "the most strenuous, hectic, and laborious" weeks of his life.[12]

Organizing the camps involved a myriad of details. There were major matters such as selecting locations and finding personnel to run them; and seemingly mundane administrative problems such as securing an adequate supply of mattresses, blankets, and even pillows for the training camps.

Marshall's break came a few days after Pershing's departure, when he accompanied General Bell to Washington to straighten out the matter of command arrangements for the ports of embarkation. On that trip he learned that Major General William J. Sibert, an old friend of Pershing's, was organizing a contingent of troops soon to depart for France. Marshall went to Bell asking if the general would release him to go with that contingent. General Bell gave his blessing. Sibert's group would be called the 1st Division, and Marshall was assigned as the division G-3, or operations officer. For an officer of Marshall's age and rank, no greater plum could be asked for.

Marshall was allowed only a day and a half to prepare for an overseas assignment and to pack his wife up for departure to her home in Lexington, Virginia. By the afternoon of June 10 he reported to General Sibert at the Hoboken docks. His ship, the *Tenadores*, had once been part of the North German Lloyd Line before the United States government had confiscated her. Marshall was uncomfortable to see that all the dock workers loading the ships were still Germans, left over from the days when the ship had been one of theirs. "The average stevedore," he later wrote, "looked as though he were a member of the crew of some German submarine."[13] The same night that Marshall arrived at the dock, the infantry of the 1st Division began loading. The process went on the whole night in a dismal drizzle. It was not a cheerful setting.[14]

At 4:00 A.M. on June 14, the same day that General Pershing and his staff were touring Paris, the *Tenadores* slipped out of New York Harbor, carrying a battalion of the 28th Infantry. Off her port bow was the *DeKalb*, carrying the 5th Marine Regiment.[15] Three other transports made up the division, and they were escorted by two cruisers, one of them a converted vessel, three destroyers, and a fuel ship. The 1st Division was off for France, destined to play a major role in Pershing's AEF.

ABOUT TWO WEEKS LATER, on the morning of June 26, Marshall looked over the railing of the *Tenadores* at the French port of St. Nazaire. He was struck by the absence of men on the dock and in the town; most of the women were in mourning. The whole scene carried the eerie atmosphere of a funeral. There had been little time for anyone to prepare a welcome. General Pershing, in fact, had learned of the division's schedule only four days before it landed.[16]

Marshall was concerned about the impression the newly arrived Americans were making on their French hosts. After joining the division, he had learned the reason for its hasty departure, Marshal Joffre's urgent request that a unit, even makeshift, be sent to France to "show the flag." But the troops actually showing the flag would be in unimpressive condition, for they were not yet highly disciplined.

One incident at St. Nazaire especially troubled Marshall. About three days after the first troops had disembarked, a French peasant girl reported an attempted rape. The accused soldier denied any such intentions, and in his defense claimed that she had enticed him. No matter: the court sentenced him to thirty years of confinement and General Sibert approved the finding. Marshall assumed that the stiff punishment would probably be commuted when the man reached the United States, but the quick act of discipline made a great impression on the French—and also on the men of the 1st Division. But Marshall had another, more subtle concern: would the French underestimate American troops because of their appearance and the impression of imperfect discipline? Marshall feared that French officials would conclude that the Americans were "kindly, timorous oafs."[17] He wondered how the battalion of the 16th Infantry would look when it was sent to Paris for the historic parade along the Champs-Elysées, scheduled for July 4. Their lack of parade ground training would be obvious, and their often ill-fitting uniforms were hardly smart. To the French, who put a premium on military precision, that could be misleading.

Marshall had a point; indeed, General Pershing felt the same way. All too aware that the crack regiments he had trained in Mexico had been filled up with a large number of untrained recruits, he had at first refused to send any troops to the celebration. Under pressure, Pershing finally relented, and the 2d Battalion, 16th Infantry, was designated to represent the whole division. The men of the battalion were loaded into French boxcars for the trip to Paris.

If the appearance of the Americans, still wearing their broad-brimmed campaign hats, was not up to European standards, that detail was lost in the frenzy of enthusiasm of the crowds for the symbolism of American presence. The *New York Times* rhapsodized,

HUGE CROWDS GATHERED

FOR REVIEW CHEER FRANTICALLY

FOR THE AMERICANS

Paris turned out a crowd that no American city ever surpassed for size, enthusiasm, and profusion of the Stars and Stripes.

At Pershing's residence on the Rue de Varenne the crowds had gathered long before the scheduled starting time for the ceremonies to begin. At 8:00 A.M. "the resplendent Republican Guards executed a field reveille under Pershing's windows, and all routes toward the Invalides were thronged even before Pershing's men turned out." In the Tomb of Napoleon, President Raymond Poincaré presented American flags and banners; the "enthusiasm of the vast crowd reached its highest pitch when General Pershing, escorted by President Poincaré, Marshal Joffre, and other high French dignitaries passed along reviewing the lines of the Americans drawn up in square formations. . . . Vive les Américains! Vive Pershing! Vive les Etats Unis."[18]

It had been quite a show. When it was over, the 2d Battalion, 16th Infantry, reboarded the forty-and-eight trains * to Gondrecourt-le-Château, in eastern France, where they would begin many months of training.

IN PARIS, Major General Pershing had largely completed the last of his ceremonial duties by Saturday, June 16. With his staff set up at 31 rue Constantine, in downtown Paris, he left Paris in the morning, headed for Compiègne, about sixty miles north of the city. There he was to visit Major General Henri Pétain, General-in-Chief of the French Armies, who had relieved General Nivelle after the disastrous failure at Chemin des Dames on the Aisne River the previous April.

As Pershing and Harbord waited in the car outside Pétain's headquarters, Colonel "Bertie" de Chambrun prepared them. Referring to the other French generals, he said, "They are all great men, but they are great men of the past. Wait until you see Pétain."[19] Once they were introduced, Harbord, at least, was quickly convinced that the French had at last found the right man. Physically, Pétain did not resemble the American preconception of a Frenchman. Harbord described him as "an erect, soldierly-looking man, bald, but originally with blond hair, wears a heavy mustache, walks briskly." Harbord misjudged Pétain's age by four years, estimating his age at about fifty-seven, whereas he was actually sixty-one.[20] He ascribed Pétain's Nordic coloring to the fact that the British had occupied the general's home town of Calais for hundreds of years, and that many of the local inhabitants had Anglo-Saxon ancestry.

Pétain's proven success matched his military bearing. After the defeat of the Nivelle offensive, numerous French regiments had resorted to passive resistance, willing to defend but refusing to attack. In addition a small but active mutiny had been attempted and put down, and some of the ringleaders had been executed. The bulk of the soldiers went unpunished, because their complaints were easy to understand. With a population of forty million people, France had lost two million men in this war, and many had not been granted leave to visit their families in three years.

Pétain had taken this situation to heart and had begun a policy of home leave. He had made his personality felt by visiting every French di-

---

* Forty-and-eights were so named because each car could carry forty men and eight horses.

vision personally. He dealt with their fears by assuring them that no more needless attacks would be ordered. He also devised a system of defense in depth in the static front lines. The results had been salutary.[21] Pétain, in Harbord's estimation, was "easily the strong man in authority over here now. He knows what France can do; probably what Germany can do; what the temper of his own people is; what their need of coal will be in the next cold winter; what their need of certain foodstuffs will be; the importance to them of steel, etc."[22]

Pershing's impression of his future colleague was consistent with that of Harbord. He made a point of Pétain's kindly expression, keen sense of humor, and his tendency not to talk much. Their conversation hinged almost entirely on military affairs and America's part in the war, which both men agreed could not amount to much until the spring of 1918. Above all he had hopes for their future relationship:

> My impression of Pétain was favorable and it remained unchanged throughout the war. Our friendship, which I highly treasure, had its beginning at this meeting. Complete cooperation is difficult even under the most favorable conditions and is rarely attained between men or peoples of different nationalities, but it seemed probable that Pétain's breadth of vision, his common sense and his sound judgment would make for understanding, and this proved to be the case.[23]

Pétain had other obligations that afternoon, but before lunch was over he offered Pershing the opportunity to take a look at the front. Major General Franchet d'Espérey, commanding a group of armies, conducted the Americans to an observation post about two miles from the front, where they could see the town of St. Quentin, then behind the German lines. For the first time Pershing and Harbord heard the continuous low rumble of artillery and the occasional staccato of a machine gun.

TO THAT STORM, America would soon have to add its own thunder, and between ceremonies Pershing and Harbord had been giving their problems and goals careful thought and had narrowed their prospective decisions down to five main items:

1. What shall be the ultimate total of our forces in Europe?
2. What shall be the organization of the troops with which we fight?
3. How shall they be supplied? What portion of supply can be obtained in Europe?

4. How shall shipments of supplies and troops be worked out with reference to each other?

5. For what period must we prepare as the probable duration of the war? [24]

Few of these questions could be dealt with out of hand. Pershing had now set a strength of a million men for the AEF, twice the size being assumed by the War Department at the moment. That upgrading vastly complicated the questions of organization and supply, and Pershing had little to go on in basing his supply requirements. The American Military Mission had given him a start in the matter of supply by arranging for the AEF's use of St. Nazaire, on the south coast of Brittany. Further than that he could not go, at least for the moment.

Organizing his staff was another matter. Amazingly, Pershing had no official guidance. A new version of the Field Service Regulations had been published in 1914, and though that document mentioned a chief of staff for a force in the field, it said nothing about the staff members beneath the chief. The current organization of the War Department in Washington was of no help either. It was broken down into three sections: combat, supply, and intelligence. That, Pershing and Harbord concluded, would never do as a pattern they could follow.

Pershing and Harbord were well aware of the War Department's history of chaos and were determined to prevent a duplication of that situation in France. In Pershing's headquarters the representatives of the Washington bureaus were called the Special Staff—Quartermaster, Engineers, Ordnance, Medical Corps, and later Transportation Corps. These staff sections could not function as independent entities, all reporting to the commander. Even if such a scheme were wise, Pershing himself did not have the unlimited time and energy necessary to supervise them all, even assisted by a chief of staff. An organization of "assistant chiefs of staff" to coordinate the special functions was the result. Pershing and Harbord were inventing the General Staff in the modern sense during their early days in Paris. As Harbord described it,

> We created five divisions, each under an Assistant Chief of Staff. For the time the designations were Administrative Policy, Intelligence, Operations, Co-ordination, and Training sections. The General felt that probably in normal times Training and Operations would be handled together, but for the emergency which now confronted him he decided that Training merited an Assistant Chief of Staff who could give his entire time to it. [25]

It was a prophetic decision. That organization dreamed up by Pershing and Harbord early in 1917 has existed, with some modification, to the present day. The assistant chiefs of staff were numbered by section, G-1, G-2, and so on.[26]

ONE OF PERSHING'S most urgent tasks was to establish an American area of operations, a sector in which the Americans would operate when they were eventually ready for combat. Such a matter had to be settled with the French. Not only were the Americans in France as guests, but President Wilson had determined, in general terms, that the United States should cooperate with Britain on the seas and with the French on the land. Besides, Pershing was going to be using French ports, French railroads, and French territory to house and train his million man army. In short, Pershing would have to look principally to Pétain for approval of his plans.

Pershing's choices for an American sector were limited. The northern sector along the English Channel and North Sea coast were of course restricted to the British. From centuries back, the British had invaded Continental Europe through Calais and Normandy. When the Duke of Wellington fought against Napoleon at Waterloo in 1815, he always kept a line of retreat open from Brussels back to the English Channel. Britain was later instrumental in establishing Belgium as an independent nation to act as a buffer between the Channel and any threat from the east. France's northwest coast was undisputedly British-dominated.

The French, too, had their priorities: French troops must always be the primary guards of the gates of Paris. Any sector in the Champagne region would have to be defended by French forces.

Pershing had his eye on another area, however, the sector around Verdun, running between the Argonne Forest and the Vosges Mountains. It was an area of great importance to Germany, for behind the lines in Lorraine lay the important coal fields of the Saar and the Longwy-Briey iron ore region. Besides that, the vital railway line that connected Metz with the German armies of the west ran across the front there. An Allied invasion into that territory would not only threaten these important features but would open into a natural avenue for the invasion of Germany itself through the Moselle Valley. As a practical consideration, the northeastern portion of France offered the best of the possible training and billeting areas for American troops. To support such a buildup in eastern France logistically, Pershing tentatively thought of a supply line running northward including Tours, Orléans, Montargis, Nevers, and Châteauroux. He had mentioned this sector to General Pétain almost on his arrival, and he had received at least Pétain's tentative approval.[27]

Pershing also needed to arrange procedures for coordination with

Pétain. To that end, the French Minister of War, Paul Painlevé, suggested that a group of French officers, all familiar with the French system, be placed at Pershing's "disposal." When Pershing had needs, he was to turn to the Liaison Group and pass his requests through them. To head the group, Painlevé offered the services of a man of stature, Marshal Joffre himself. Pershing, however, balked at the idea. It would be "pleasing to think of being associated with Marshal Joffre," he said, but he feared creating another channel to penetrate in order to reach those in authority. Besides, the proposal carried an overtone of "tutelage," which he resented. He therefore explained to the French War Minister that he preferred to make use of the French officers actually assigned to his staff. The officers of Pershing's supply departments could confer directly with their corresponding numbers in the French bureaus. That was the procedure he followed.[28]

WITH THE LOCATION of an American sector at least tentatively agreed, Pershing could begin establishing a line of communications to supply it. His staff studied the available French ports, always remembering Pershing's determination to keep American activities as independent as possible. That objective ruled out any offers, no matter how generously rendered, for the Americans to share British ports and lines of communications; in Pershing's eyes, sharing logistical arrangements could well lead to unwanted dependency. Moreover, the French and British forces numbered about five million men at that time,[29] and their lines of communications were already taxed. The Americans must have a line of supply of their own.

Pershing therefore decided to request the use of three main seaports on the French west coast, from north to south St. Nazaire, on the Loire; La Pallice, near Rochefort; and Paulliac, the seaport of Bordeaux on the Garonne River.[30] These ports were not being extensively used by the British and French, and they were far enough south that German submarines engaged in blockading Britain could not at the same time interfere with American shipping into these ports.[31]

These ports also provided reasonable connections with acceptable railroad lines. Two main, double-track lines were available, one leading from St. Nazaire and and the other from Bordeaux. The northern of these, from St. Nazaire, ran through the major French city of Tours, and the two lines converged at Bourges. Another line ran farther north from Tours to Chaumont. East of Chaumont and Dijon the railroad lines branched out to Neufchâteau on the north, Epinal in the center, and Belfort in the south, all points along the line of contact with the enemy.

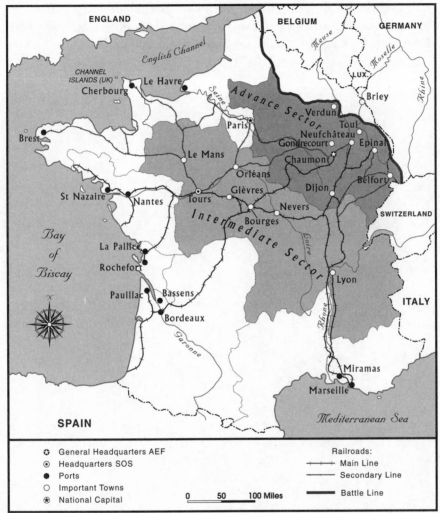

ENGLAND

BELGIUM

GERMANY

English Channel

Meuse

Moselle

Rhine

CHANNEL
ISLANDS (UK)

Le Havre

Cherbourg

Advance Sector

Verdun

Briey

Paris

Toul

Seine

Neufchâteau

Gondrecourt

Epinal

Brest

Le Mans

Chaumont

Orléans

Dijon

Belfort

St Nazaire

Gièvres

Nantes

Tours

Nevers

SWITZERLAND

Intermediate Sector

Bourges

Loire

*Bay
of
Biscay*

La Pallice

Rochefort

Lyon

Pauillac

Bassens

ITALY

Bordeaux

Rhône

Garonne

Miramas

Marseille

SPAIN

Mediterranean Sea

		Railroads:
☼	General Headquarters AEF	
⊙	Headquarters SOS	+−+−+ Main Line
●	Ports	—— Secondary Line
○	Important Towns	
✹	National Capital	▬▬▬ Battle Line

0   50   100 Miles

2. The American Line of Communications.

Map by Maryland Mapping & Graphics, Inc.

The American Line of Communications, maintained by the Services of Supply (SOS), was one of the great Yankee achievements of the war. The main railroad lines used by the SOS originated at St. Nazaire and south along the Bay of Biscay. Running south of Paris, they avoided interfering with French defense of their capital. They also left the Channel ports in the hands of the British. General Pershing justified this great expenditure of effort, insisting that if the United States were to become the dominant Allied military force in 1919, it would need to control its own supply system.

This logistical scheme would dictate the location of the various American headquarters. The logical place for a future headquarters of the Line of Communications, Pershing decided, was Tours, on the main railroad line. He also considered Chaumont, just behind Neufchâteau, as his own future headquarters. For Pershing and his small staff, the move from Paris into the field could not come soon enough.

CHAPTER FIVE

ORGANIZING THE AEF

TOWARD THE END OF JULY, 1917, General Pershing found a break in his hectic schedule and felt he could now accept the long-standing invitation of Field Marshal Sir Douglas Haig to visit the British Expeditionary Force. On Friday, July 20, Pershing left Paris accompanied by Harbord and his aide, Lieutenant George S. Patton. The ninety-mile car trip took them through a pleasant, hilly countryside. Crops were nearing harvest time, and the sight of the beautiful shade trees of Beauvais and Montreuil temporarily took Pershing's mind off his immediate concerns.

For a while after Pershing's party left Paris, the troops along the road were French. When British troops began appearing along the road, the visitors knew they had entered the British zone. At Montreuil, where the British main headquarters was located, the Americans were greeted by Lieutenant General Fowke, Haig's adjutant-general. Fowke had served with Pershing in Manchuria in 1901, when both were military observers with the Japanese Army.

While he was conferring with General Fowke, a matter came up that showed the Americans how grim and serious this war was to the British. Several British soldiers had been tried by a small, informal court that morning and had been found guilty of misbehavior before the enemy—desertion, running away in action, absence without leave when under orders for action. The culprits had been sentenced to death and were executed before sundown. The British showed no mercy when dealing with such conduct. Harbord remarked that the death sentence in the United States Army required the approval of the President.[1]

Late that afternoon, Pershing's party left Montreuil and drove the few miles to St. Omer, about twenty miles south of Dunkirk, where Field Marshal Haig kept his personal command post in an old château.[2] The

British commander greeted the Americans cordially, ignoring the dull roar in the background, part of the great artillery preparation supporting the British in the Second Battle of Ypres, only twenty miles to the east.

Haig and Pershing presented an interesting contrast. Pershing, always ramrod stiff during formal occasions, looks Prussian in their joint photograph. Haig, on the other hand, looks completely at ease, very much in charge of things. Both men, in common with most generals of the day, sported mustaches, but Pershing's was severe, while Haig's was lush and trimmed. Haig's appearance was impeccable. With his outwardly relaxed but determined bearing, he resembled the lord of a manor, substituting an immaculate uniform for pipe and tweeds. But no matter. Haig liked the formal, dignified Pershing, something he had not expected in an American.

When serious talks began, it was soon evident that Pershing was going to learn more from Haig than Haig was going to learn from Pershing. Pershing had no ready answer to the only question Haig was interested in: how quickly the American forces could be built up. He could offer little regarding the strength and degree of training he could attain. On the other hand, Pershing got a good picture of the British situation, especially when the two were joined by General Sir William Robertson, Chief of the Imperial General Staff. The two British generals were frank, admitting that they had lost some 175,000 officers and men in their recent offensive at Arras. To Pershing that shocking figure was the predictable result of a strategy based on attrition.[3] Whether Pershing knew it or not, the most ardent critic of both Haig and Robertson was the British Prime Minister, David Lloyd George.

Pershing also learned a great deal about the British experience with rail transportation. The BEF had tried at first to run their railroads with army engineers, and later with specially selected officers. Neither had worked, however, and they had finally turned the problem over to a civilian railroad expert, Sir Eric Geddes. Geddes had recently been replaced by an officer named Nash, and the name change gave rise to a bit of British humor. The railroad marshaling yard had previously been called "Geddesburg"; the name had now been changed to "Nashville."[4]

ON HIS RETURN TO PARIS, Pershing found waiting for him an invitation to breakfast from British Prime Minister Lloyd George. Lloyd George, a radical Welshman, held the military high command in no awe, but he made a practice of trying to know all generals, both British and foreign. On the morning of their meeting, he was principally concerned with the political situation in Russia, which Lloyd George feared was now finished as a factor in the war. That grim circumstance emphasized the importance of the arriving Americans. But when Lloyd George mentioned American participation in Allied political discussions, Pershing said nothing. He would discuss the military implications but would not discuss political matters, as they were outside a soldier's purview.

THE U.S. 1ST DIVISION did not stay long in St. Nazaire, and the men were soon loaded up in French forty-and-eight boxcars to be transported to their training area in eastern France. Each train consisted of fifty cars, principally flats and boxes, with usually two small passenger cars on the end.[5] This rail transport was hardly luxurious, and the Americans cursed the fact that forty-man cars did not conform to their battalion organization. But riding, even in boxcars, was preferable to marching, and soon the division was unloading at Gondrecourt-le-Château, the small town in Lorraine situated about twenty miles northwest of Neufchâteau and some sixty miles south of Verdun. Gondrecourt provided ample ground in the general area where the employment of the Americans was contemplated. There they settled down for serious training.

Other divisions would follow the 1st. The 2d, unlike the Big Red One, as the 1st was known, was being constituted in France from units that had come overseas independently. In addition to those two Regular divisions would follow two National Guard units, the 26th "Yankee" Division and the 42d "Rainbow" Division. These divisions were made up of units that had seen service on the Mexican border in 1916, composed of men with some experience, essentially comparable to the two Regular divisions.

By this time in the war, mid-1917, the growing capabilities of aerial reconnaissance were beginning to affect the deployment of troops even far to the rear of the front line. Encampments as far back as Gondrecourt could be detected by enemy aircraft and then bombed. For that reason the newly arriving Americans were not being housed in separate camps; rather, despite the long-held American tradition against quartering troops with civilians, the men of the new divisions were being billeted as guests of the French population. It was a manageable arrangement out in the country, where almost every farmhouse had a large barn adjacent as part of the property, capable of housing a substantial number of troops. The troops quickly came up with a humorous name for those barns: they called them "forty-and-eights" in imitation of the military transport cars—but in this case, forty men in the second floor of the barn and eight horses below.

The officers, on the other hand, were allowed to find their own billets, quite often with the French family that owned the barn the men slept in. George Marshall, for one, found a room in a small house with an agreeable courtyard and garden outside the window. Its owner was a Madame Jouette, whom he described as "a rather homely, vigorous French woman of forty-five years." Besides Madame Jouette and her husband, the household consisted of a young refugee woman and her eight-year-old daughter. The Jouettes' son had been captured at Verdun the year before, and was presently a German prisoner of war. Marshall was to spend six months in that little house, his small room containing only a cot, a washstand, and two chairs. He later described that period as the "Winter of Valley Forge" and attributed his ability to keep a stiff upper lip to the good nature of Madame Jouette.[6]

Training for the 1st Division was not an easy matter. The French instructors, told to push the Americans hard for quick service in the line, overestimated the division's state of readiness. The designation Regular was misleading. The troops that Pershing had trained in Mexico were highly professional, but each of his old regiments had carried a strength of only seven hundred men, of whom half had since been removed for assignment elsewhere; new recruits then filled them to their current strength of two thousand. Almost all the old noncommissioned officers had been promoted to the officer ranks, and those now serving as NCOs had come from the ranks of the newly inducted privates. As a result, it was necessary to instill discipline before technical training could be of much use. And the stakes were high. The 1st Division, vaunted as the "pick of the American Army," could not be allowed to perform badly in its first test of battle.

The French instructors had much to learn about American psychology. They soon discovered that their new wards were virtually unfettered by tradition, new at war, yet very adaptable. The French instructors, who by this time had become set in their ways of conducting the war, found the Americans puzzling. Writing about the Americans, a French memorandum said,

> American units arriving in France have only had, up to the present time, very incomplete instructions . . . gymnastic exercises, close order drill, rifle fire in small warfare, having but little relation to actual warfare. . . . The officers are usually strong, athletic, intelligent, and very ambitious to learn. Lacking a solid military foundation, personal temperament dominates. . . . In relations with all officers, it should be borne in mind that they have an extremely well-developed sense of amour-propre, based on their pride in belonging to one of the greatest nations in the world. Consequently, an attitude of superiority over them should be assiduously avoided, a fact which in no way prevents absolute subordination required by the service.[7]

A copy of that memo fell into American hands. One commentator wrote,

The offensive spirit of the French and British Armies has largely disappeared as a result of their severe losses. Close association with beaten forces lowers the morale of the best troops. . . . In many respects, the tactics and technique of our Allies are not suited to American characteristics or the American mission in this war. . . . Berlin can not be taken by the French or the British Armies or by both of them. It can only be taken by a thoroughly trained, entirely homogenous American Army. An American Army can not be made by Frenchmen or by Englishmen.

To that anonymous note, Pershing appended one of his own: "This is entirely my own view."[8]

Despite the difficulties involved, the division worked hard, and the soldiers did their jobs. Marshall noted that they "worked overtime and all the time, sang French songs and were virtually Frenchmen during training periods, at the same time being criticized as American rookies."[9] No wonder that men of the 1st Division looked back on those months of training at Gondrecourt as among the most difficult of the war.

Fortunately the difficulties of language and psychology were eased by the high quality of the men of the 47th French *Chasseurs Alpins* (known as "Blue Devils"), also headquartered at Gondrecourt. One of the duties of these veteran Frenchmen was to assist in the training of the Americans, and they made a great impression. Marshall described them as "picked fellows of an unusually vigorous type; they wore a dark blue tunic and an Alpine hat of the same shade . . . with a magnificent fighting record." Their general, a "little, wiry man with one eye, which shot sparks every time he talked," was however part of the problem. He never did get used to the fact that the Americans at that time needed basic as well as advanced training.[10]

As the operations officer of the 1st Division, George Marshall was in a position of considerable prestige. He was quickly promoted from his original rank of captain to major. Still, he was underranked. Longtime Army usage in the American Army, however, called for authority to be vested in one's position rather than his rank insignia, and the officers and men that Marshall dealt with accepted his position without question. The Army could not have functioned in any other manner.[11]

Before he could begin serious training, Marshall was saddled with the unusual task of selecting training areas for the three other divisions who would follow the 1st in that eastern part of France. First he had to find a cantonment near Neufchâteau for the 26th (Yankee) Division, an assignment that forced him to travel more than a hundred miles a day. Once the 26th was settled, Marshall placed the newly constituted 2d Division at Bourmont, about halfway between Neufchâteau and Chaumont. He later did the same for the 42d (Rainbow) Division. Those four divisions—the 1st, 2d, 26th, and 42d—were the only American divisions that would spend the entire winter of 1917–1918 in France.

ON AUGUST 19, 1917, Marshall and several other high-ranking officers of the 1st Division staff were accorded a rare privilege, that of witnessing a French division in the attack. The operation consisted of a limited attack northward on both sides of the Meuse River north of Verdun. It had been inspired by a need to reinstill confidence and aggressiveness in the French infantry, gravely weakened by the failure of General Nivelle's offensive in April. It was to be executed by the French Moroccan Division, an elite unit that considered itself to be the "great assault division" of the French Army.

To ensure that the attack would succeed, the concentration of heavy and light artillery on German positions on the Morte Homme, in the vicinity of Chattaincort on the west side of the Meuse, was described to Marshall as "the greatest artillery concentration up to that time in history"—twenty-two artillerymen to every twenty French infantrymen! Never mind that such a concentration would be impossible over a wider front; this attack had to go.[12]

The scheme of maneuver was complicated, including an attack by one battalion along a ridge running parallel to the front but out ahead of it. Nevertheless, the French knew what they were doing, and the assault, limited though it was, accomplished its mission of simply advancing a few thousand yards.

AS THE 1ST DIVISION was getting settled, Pershing and Harbord were doing the same, looking for a suitable location for a major headquarters in the French countryside. Both had had enough of the hustle and bustle of Paris, and they longed for a place where they and the staff could concentrate on their work. On August 3 the two generals lunched at the Hôtel de France, in Chaumont, and were impressed with what the town had to offer. Chaumont at that time had a population of twenty thousand people, and it was young by European standards, having been founded in A.D. 950. It did, however, boast a great deal of history, and Harbord ruminated on the days when Chaumont had been the meeting place for the Dukes of Burgundy, Champagne, and Lorraine. What attracted Pershing's attention, however, was Chaumont's practicability in a modern war. It was served by a major railroad line, located handily on the planned artery between St. Nazaire and Verdun. Above all it provided a large public building in the center of town, perfect to house a headquarters. Private homes abounded, enough to billet all the officers of the headquarters, and the engineers could construct barracks for the enlisted men.[13]

In Pershing's mind the matter was settled. Though there was work still to be done in Paris, he moved his headquarters to Chaumont by early September. From that date on, the name Chaumont would be synonymous with Headquarters, American Expeditionary Force.

Getting settled in Chaumont was a huge task, and a matter of utmost importance was that of establishing communications, without which even the most capable group of staff officers would be unable to function. This need brought on a major adjustment for Pershing and his group of old-line regular officers, the inclusion of women in this all-male society. From the outset, it was obvious that competent, if not professional telephone operators were sorely needed. A typical situation went like this:

> "Hello, this is Colonel Wilson, and I want to speak to Major Johnson in Tours."
> *"Pardon, je ne comprends pas. Répétez, s'il vous plaît."*
> "I said Major Johnson in Tours and hurry up."
> *"Monsieur, quel est le nom, s'il vous plaît?"*
> "Look, dammit. Don't you understand? I want . . ."[14]

That type of dialogue could not be tolerated for long if a headquarters were to control units many miles away from it. A top priority was therefore set on improving the overused French telephone system and training the people who would use it. The Army Signal Corps began installing miles of new permanent pole lines and leasing other lines from the French. The need was great: in the United States at that time there were fourteen telephones for every hundred persons; in France there were only one and a half per hundred. Before the war was over the figures would be impressive: 12,000 miles of line leased from the French and 22,000 miles of new wire laid.[15]

Soon after the headquarters of the AEF moved to Chaumont, Pershing put in a request to the War Department for a hundred American telephone operators fluent in French. These women would not be assigned to combat units, but "will do as much to help win the war as the men in khaki."[16] By the time that American fighting units were assigned to active sectors of the front, the system was working smoothly. "No civil telephone service that ever came under my observation," Pershing later wrote, "excelled the perfection of ours after it was established."[17]

There was more to the buildup of the AEF than amassing infantry, artillery, tanks, and planes.

IN LATE SUMMER 1917, the SS *Manchuria* was sailing from Iceland to Liverpool. Aboard her was the United States 9th Infantry Regiment, destined to become part of the 2d Division. Twenty-year-old Lieutenant Ladislav Janda was a member of M Company of that regiment. Lud Janda, as everyone called him, was in many ways typical of the young men who had volunteered for service just after the war had broken out some five months earlier. Born in Cedar Rapids, Iowa, of Bohemian parents, he had been an engineering student at Iowa State College, Ames, before signing up. A product of an officer training camp, he had joined this nominally Regular unit and with it had left Chicago by train in August, about a month earlier.

In other ways, however, Lud Janda was far from ordinary. He was a keen student and observer, a fine athlete, and mature far beyond his years. His letters home to his family, to whom he was very close, were written with more than a soldier's stiff upper lip; they were ebullient. Janda at least pretended to enjoy everything that happened, even when his own life was in danger.

The *Manchuria* had left New York alone, early in the month of September, and at Halifax, Nova Scotia, it had rested two days waiting for its convoy to be assembled. When the eight ships of the convoy pulled out on September 12, Janda was disappointed to note that, due to the inclusion of a couple of tramp steamers, the speed of the convoy would be held down to only nine knots. Each ship, including the *Manchuria*, carried guns. One, carrying a grand total of eight, had been designated as a "cruiser."

When the convoy was two days out of port, it was joined by eight British destroyers for protection against the concentration of German submarines that clustered around the British Isles. These British destroyers, Janda noted with a touch of envy, could go four times as fast as the convoy. They were "little devils," only about 225 feet long, but they cut circles around the other ships, able to turn in a distance equal to their own length. Watching them, Janda's mind went back to a motion picture that showed fierce Indians riding around a circle of frightened settlers in their covered wagons. He was glad, in this case, that the "Indians" were friendly, not hostile.

Before leaving New York, Janda had recorded three wishes for the trip. The first was to hit a storm; the second was to get in a fight; and the third was that they land safely despite both. All three wishes were to be granted.

Unfortunately for Janda's youthful spirits, he missed the fight. Early one morning, before he and his comrades had arisen, the destroyers escorting the *Manchuria* detected a submarine and attacked it with depth charges. Hearing the noise, Janda rushed out on deck, only to miss the show. He never knew for sure whether the charges dropped by the destroyers had sunk or even damaged the U-boat, but seeing no debris and hearing nothing further, he concluded ruefully that they had not.

On the last night of the trip, nature granted Janda's second wish, for a storm. They had been experiencing rough weather all the way across, but "this was a real one":

> We could now see it coming, in the distance about 6:30 and Holy Moses, when it hit us! Roy Olson (Duluth) and I spent the greater part of the evening on deck. You can't imagine what a real wind at sea is. It blew with such force that a person was shoved and mauled around on the starboard side like chaff, even when holding on to the rail with both hands. Now we were on the upper deck, and the old ship would dip her nose into the water and up would come the water clear up on top. The wind was so strong that when you attempted to look at it, it would try to tear off your eyelids. It was not groaning or moaning through the rigging but was shrieking. Just as though a person were blowing on a whistle as hard as he could about ten feet from your ear. The waves breaking and flopping on deck sounded like cannonading. That was how I came to go out on deck first. I thought I heard and was going to see a sub fight.

The next morning the waters were quieter. By seven o'clock the *Manchuria* was rounding the northern part of Ireland, which "certainly looked pretty,"[18] and finally docked safely at Liverpool on September 22, 1917.

NOT EVERY SHIP was as lucky as the *Manchuria*, but by the time of her sailing, the U-boat menace had begun to diminish. Considerable credit for solving the U-boat problem belongs to Admiral William Sims.

Just after America entered the war, and Sims was assigned as United States naval representative in Europe, he met with Britain's First Sea Lord, Admiral Sir John Jellicoe, and what Jellicoe revealed gave him a shock. Up to that time Britain had refrained from sharing highly secret information about shipping losses with the neutral Americans, but now Jellicoe gave Sims the true figures. To them he added a simple, powerful warning: "It is impossible for us to go on with the war if losses like this continue." Both men agreed that at the moment Germany was winning the war. Worse than that, there was nothing they could come up with for the moment to reverse the situation.[19]

The answer was found, not from any single measure but from a combination of them. The two admirals convinced their respective governments that shipbuilding must be raised in priority. Pressure was exerted on neutral nations to contribute ships to the Atlantic crossings. Japan, at war with Germany in the Far East, contributed fourteen destroyers. Both the British and American navies began programs for laying minefields in waters near German U-boat installations. Spotter aircraft and radio intercept activities were speeded up. The United States Navy came up with an additional nineteen destroyers.

Of all the measures, the most effective was the establishment of the new convoy system, a joint British-American venture. Up to the time of Germany's declaration of unrestricted submarine warfare, the Royal Navy had attempted to maintain the sea lanes to Britain by patrolling a corridor leading all the way across the Atlantic, hoping to keep a strip of water clear of U-boats. The system had failed. Allied shipping was going to the bottom at an unacceptable rate—844 ships since the first of February—and during that time it was estimated that not more than ten of the ninety submarines available to Germany had been sunk. Germany was constructing U-boats so rapidly that their fleet was even gaining strength.[20]

There were objections to the convoy system, to be sure. For one thing, it was slow: a convoy could go no faster than its slowest ship. Further, the arrival of a convoy temporarily overloaded the capacity of the ports, because all the ships, which had previously arrived one at a time, now descended on a port all at once. Finally came the question of the rights of the shipowners. Traditionally, ship captains were an undisciplined lot, accustomed to keeping their own schedules rather than waiting for a convoy to leave port.

The decision to go to the convoy system was made easier by the stark fact that the other system had failed. To raise the average speed of the convoys, the Allies sorted them into fast, medium-speed, and slow groups. For the periodic overload of port facilities, a scheme was worked out whereby the convoy would split up so that individual ships could proceed to various ports once the danger zone had been crossed. As to the rights of the ship captains, the question was simple. The convoy system would afford protection and the corridor system had not. If they wanted that protection, they would have to cooperate. They did.

All together these measures produced results. The peak in losses had come in April 1917, with 852,000 gross tons sunk. In May the losses had dropped to 500,500 tons, and by November of 1917 it had dropped further, to 200,000 gross tons. That was still too much, but for the moment, potential losses did not deter the Americans from sending men overseas as soon as they were trained and shipping was available.

WITH MEN LIKE JANDA on their way, and with Pershing preparing to receive the troops that would follow the original divisions, Secretary of War Newton Baker, back in Washington, was heading the effort to create, equip, and train them. He needed a strong chief of staff, and he had come to the reluctant conclusion that General Hugh Scott lacked the needed energy. So Baker attached Scott to a group headed by former Secretary of War Elihu Root that was going to Russia to confer with Russia's revolutionary leader, Alexander Kerensky. In Scott's absence, Baker placed his deputy, Tasker Bliss, in his stead as acting chief. After Scott's retirement, Bliss would be chief of staff in his own right. Though Bliss himself was due to retire in a period of a few months, he was capable of carrying on while Baker cast around for the man he wanted to succeed him.

Baker needed all the help he could get. The draft registration of June 5, 1917, had signed up all men from the ages of twenty-one to thirty-one. Subsequent registrations would sign up nearly 11 million men. Of the total 24 million registered, about 2.8 million would eventually be called into service.[21] The results would be salutary in the long run, but the process would be slow. Most of the recruits brought into service would be assigned to National Army divisions, and the first of those would take a year in getting overseas.

To receive and train the new recruits, Baker and Bliss set up a series of camps and cantonments, mostly concentrated in the eastern portion of the United States. Their construction was authorized in May 1917 at about the same time as the draft bill was passed, and by July the last site was procured. Before the war was over, a total of thirty-two camps and cantonments would be established, about half assigned to the National Guard, all of these located south of the Virginia–North Carolina border. The other half, designated for the National Army, were mostly located north of that line.[22] The Regular divisions were spread out among those thirty-two establishments.

In the beginning, the National Guard divisions were generally better prepared than were most of those that carried Regular Army numbers. The Guard units, which numbered from 24 to 42,[23] were already in being when war was declared, at least on paper, whereas no Regular Army divisions were organized. Of the two Guard units going immediately to France, the 42d (Rainbow) received the bulk of the publicity, and its nickname became more universally recognized than its number.[24] The Rainbow Division became a sought-after assignment for many regular officers. Colonel Douglas MacArthur, who enjoyed considerable influence, was named at the outset as its chief of staff.

All divisions—Regular, National Guard, and National Army—were organized similarly. Each comprised a thousand officers and 27,000 men. The infantry was organized in two brigades, with two regiments assigned to each (hence the term "square" division). It would also include an artillery brigade and a battalion of engineers. This made an American division approximately twice the size of either an Allied or a German division. Theoretically, the large size would give the division extra staying power; and in an Army where officer talent was spread thin, it was supposed to make better use of that resource.

All of these divisions, except for the 1st and the 2d, received at least some training in the United States before being shipped overseas. The average training time, including that given to the later National Army divisions, was six months.[25] In this training period the Americans were aided by instructors from the French and British Armies. Though the numbers were small—286 French instructors and slightly fewer British—their influence was great. For it was they who taught the teachers, von Steuben style. The French instructors emphasized the sophisticated aspects of war—artillery, liaison, minor tactics, and fortifications—while the British emphasized individual subjects—gas, physical training and the bayonet, machine gun, sniping, and mortar. Though most of the training was conducted by American officers, the contributions of these French and British were invaluable.[26]

To SUPPLY THE COMBAT TROOPS, Pershing needed an organization that could deliver food, clothing, and ammunition immediately to the front, while at the same time storing enough supplies to insure continued combat operations in case the pipeline should be cut somewhere along the line. The organization capable of performing these functions would be a major command, headed by a general officer. The problems he faced would be so complex that they would be without precedent in American military history.

Harbord and the staff began studying the problems from the beginning and soon came up with four basic questions to be answered:

1. What reserve must be accumulated against possible interruption of the flow of supply?

2. How and where should the supplies be stored?
3. What should be the means for unloading at the ports, and reloading for shipment to the front or to storage?
4. What organization was needed?[27]

In the absence of previous experience, Harbord and his staff determined, rather arbitrarily, that the Americans should strive to maintain a level of ninety days of supply (a goal that was never reached). Starting at the more modest objective of forty-five days of supply, the Americans had to decide where the greatest threat would occur to an uninterrupted flow: in transit by rail from the ports to the railhead, or from danger of being overrun by a successful German drive? The result was a compromise: the Line of Communications was to be divided into three parts: (a) a Base Section, (b) an Intermediate Section, and (c) an Advance Section, with ten days' storage each in the Base Section and the Advance Section. The bulk of the supply level (twenty-five days) was to be stored in the Intermediate Section. Before the end of the war, eight Base Sections would be organized, starting with St. Nazaire and Bordeaux, but extending also to London, Le Havre, and even Italy.[28]

To direct this gargantuan effort, Pershing selected an officer who had commanded a regiment under him on the Mexican border in 1914, Major General Richard M. Blatchford. Blatchford was a year older than Pershing and had little experience in this kind of work, but he was a good soldier and when Pershing asked, he accepted the challenge.[29] To the extent possible, Pershing attempted to cloak Blatchford with complete authority. He could not, however, delegate powers to a subordinate that he did not possess himself. The railroads on which the lines of supply depended were intrinsically part of the infrastructure of France, and the French would not relinquish complete control of even a section of their rail net. Not even the British, who had been in position for nearly three years and were holding a definite section of the line, had been able to attain total control of the rail lines from the channel ports to the BEF. And much of the means of making the railroad run—rolling stock, trackage, repair shops, and people—would have to be French.

Pershing did, however, have a bargaining chip for negotiations: he could offer American-built locomotives that would fit the French gauges. The French asked for huge numbers of these but settled for three hundred. In exchange, the French eventually granted practical, if not titular, control of the railroad lines the Americans would use. They always, within the limits of their ways, gave a high degree of cooperation.[30]

Railroading was one of two areas where Pershing was forced to water down Blatchford's authority. Drawing on the British experience, he obtained the services of a civilian railroad expert, William W. Atterbury, general manager and operating vice president of the Pennsylvania Railroad, and a man who had assisted in supplying Pershing's troops during the Punitive Expedition in Mexico. The other area was that of local procurement of supplies from French sources, placed under the authority of Pershing's old friend, Charlie Dawes, with whom he had visited at the Metropolitan Club before leaving for France.

Dawes, a fifty-two-year-old banker from Ohio, proved to be ideal for the position of Civilian Procurement Officer.[31] Unlike Atterbury, who insisted on maintaining his civilian status, he was brought into service in uniform. He served loyally, never showing any feeling that his prominence in civilian life merited higher rank, and before the war was over he would attain the rank of brigadier general.[32]

IN LATE 1917, Brigadier General Benjamin D. Foulois, of the Air Service, reported to General Pershing at Chaumont. The two men knew each other well from the days when Foulois had commanded Pershing's First Aero Squadron in Mexico a year and a half earlier. Pershing knew Foulois to be a practical man as well as a first-class pilot, and he had made use of the airman's talents as his supply officer in Mexico for a time.

Pershing wanted Foulois with him, and before leaving Washington he had asked that Foulois be released from his duties with the Signal Corps to join the staff of the AEF. The War Department had refused on the basis that Foulois was irreplaceable for the moment but could be released in six months. The Chief Signal Officer made good on his promise, and Foulois was now available to replace Brigadier General William L. Kenly, a nonpilot, as Chief of the Air Service, AEF.

Kenly had no objection to being replaced by Foulois, but the change caused considerable anguish to Colonel William B. (Billy) Mitchell, a flamboyant airman who carried the title of Chief of the Air Service in the Zone of Advance—that is, in the combat zone.[33] Mitchell had been comfortable serving under the titular authority of Kenly, but Foulois was anathema to him. The two men had been rivals for some years, and there was nothing friendly about the rivalry.

In many ways Foulois and Mitchell had much in common. Both had entered the Army to fight in the Spanish-American War in 1898. Both were mavericks, with a disdain for the traditional Army way of doing things. Both had secured their pilot wings unconventionally; Foulois by teaching himself to fly (with the help of the Wright brothers) and Mitchell much later by taking flight training from a civilian instructor at his own expense. And both were farseeing airmen, men who had written articles on the vast possibilities, as yet unrealized, of air power.

There the resemblances ended. Foulois, by far the more experienced aviator, was an executive, who saw aviation not just as a glamorous combat activity but as a large enterprise that had to be supported by staff work, procurement, and construction. Mitchell, though he had attained experience as a staff officer, lacked interest in management. Though Foulois and Mitchell were about the same age, Mitchell had at one time been a full colonel, deputy to the Chief Signal Corps Officer, while Foulois was still a major. Then their relative positions were reversed. When Congress passed an appropriations bill allocating a whopping $640 million to the Air Service, the resulting expansion necessitated conferring direct commissions on men from civilian life. Faced with a flood of new officers of varying grades, the War Department wisely conferred blanket promotions on Regulars to prevent the professionals from being smothered. Foulois was promoted straight from the grade of major to that of brigadier general.[34]

The two men's personal dealings also stood in strong contrast. Foulois, while something of a strutting, pipe-smoking prima donna himself, habitually went out of his way to smooth over personal matters; Mitchell was often indiscreet and critical. The targets of his barbs included the traditional Army hierarchy—and anyone who disagreed with him. Foulois himself headed the list.

For the moment, however, Foulois had other worries. The hundred staff officers he had brought with him—"carpetbaggers," in Mitchell's words[35]—were principally nonpilots, in keeping with Foulois's belief that competent American aviators were too much in demand to be wasted in desk duty. He set out to purchase supplies from the French, supplies that would never make it into the holds of transatlantic shipping; he arranged for storage space at Le Bourget and Orly airfields; and he established a vast assembly plant at Romorantin, a hundred miles south of Paris. In that one installation alone, he had 10,500 people employed by the end of the war; had hostilities gone into 1919, he had plans for over 47,500 workers.[36]

All this was fraught with problems; it would be months before American pilots would play a significant role in aerial combat over the front, but the foundations had been laid.

ALTHOUGH BARELY NOTICED in an Army or in a nation gearing up for the largest war it had ever fought, a significant event occurred on September 5, 1917: the first American casualties of the war. The victims were members of the 11th Engineers, a railroad unit, which had gone to work in the British zone as early as August 1917. On that morning, in the vicinity of Gouzeaucourt, near Cambrai, a German artillery shell exploded near the men as they worked, and two of them were wounded.[37] Since they were not part of an American division, however, their dubious honor has remained largely unnoticed.

CHAPTER SIX

THE SUPREME
WAR COUNCIL

WHILE THE AMERICANS were preparing to join in the fight on the Western Front, events elsewhere were causing alarm among the Allied governments and underscoring the urgency of the Yanks' forthcoming role. Russia was in turmoil, and the question remained whether her badly battered armies would remain in the fight. If not, several hundred thousand of the Kaiser's soldiers, including some of his best, would be freed for use on the Western Front.

The situation was not without hope. Alexander Fyodorovich Kerensky, the thirty-six-year-old leader of the Menshevik arm of the Communist Party, did not believe that the removal of the Czar necessarily called for an end to Russia's war effort. Unlike the more radical socialists, Kerensky had supported the war from its very beginning. He still believed, in fact, that he could conduct the war effectively while at the same time democratizing the Russian Army to conform to his moderately liberal beliefs. To cope with soldier dissatisfaction at the old Czarist abuses, Kerensky established a commissar system in the Army and set up boards to hear the complaints of his soldiers; at the same time he planned an ambitious new offensive in East Prussia. These efforts met with approval in the West. The abdication of the Czar, whom nobody missed, appeared to be a favorable development, especially in the eyes of the idealistic Woodrow Wilson, who was now relieved of being allied with an autocrat.

Kerensky's good intentions, however, were beset by bad luck. First, his much touted June offensive in East Prussia failed miserably, and many blamed him for that disaster. Morale in the Russian Army fell to a new low, and in a desperate effort to cope with this alarming condition,

Kerensky went to the front in person, hoping that his fiery rhetoric, which had been so successful in political circles, could inspire the troops to new efforts. It was a lost cause. When Kerensky personally replaced the popular General Lavr G. Kornilov as Commander-in-Chief, he lost the support of many of his followers. The Bolsheviks, under Lenin, made a bid to seize power in October of that year, and Kerensky was unable to marshal the forces to resist them. He went into hiding, later to make his escape to the West.

Once in power, the Bolsheviks began taking steps to bring the Russian war effort to a close. On October 26, immediately after the coup that put them in power, the Soviet Congress sent a telegram to all foreign governments calling for "an immediate armistice based on the nations' rights to self-determination."[1] Though that first move was rejected, all fighting on the Eastern Front ceased. By December 2, 1917, a truce was signed pending a final peace treaty. Russian soldiers, in the meantime, deserted by the thousands. "They voted for peace with their feet," Lenin was fond of saying.[2] It would be months before a final, harsh peace treaty was signed between Russia and Germany at Brest-Litovsk, Poland.[3]

By late October 1917, Germany could move good combat divisions from the Eastern to the Western Front, leaving only enough to keep an eye on the unstable Bolshevik government. The Western Allies would feel the brunt.

THE WORSENING CONDITION of the Russian Army during 1917 was indirectly responsible for another crisis on the Allied side, the Austro-German defeat of the Italians at Caporetto, Italy, and their retreat to the line of the Piave River north of Venice.

The front between the Italians and the Austrians, like the Western Front in France, had long been stalemated. There the two sides, with forces about equal in strength, had fought a series of indecisive battles. These actions were aimed only toward gaining more defensible terrain; neither side harbored any hope of knocking the other out of the war. The Italian front was about equal in length to that in France and Flanders but was manned by only about a third as many troops on either side. A good portion of the line, the northern, lay in mountainous country unsuited for large-scale operations. In that region the Austrians occupied considerable Italian territory; their advances had reached down as far south as the northern tip of Lake Garda. But behind that front lay the Alps. Neither side was going to mount large-scale operations in such terrain.

The Italian interest lay to the east, where the front ran approximately along the Austrian-Italian border. There they had a specific goal,

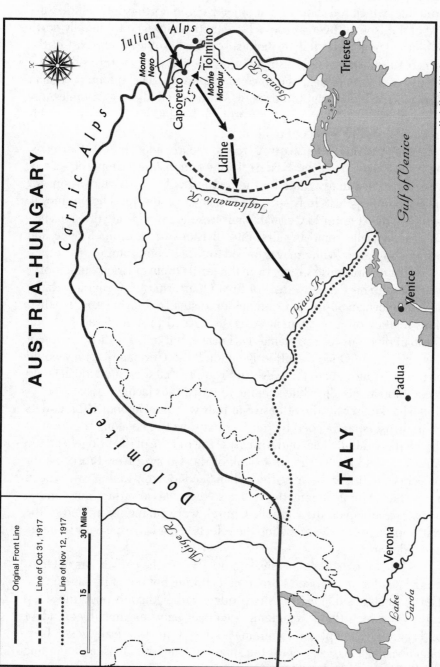

3. The Battle of Caporetto, October–November 1917.

The Battle of Caporetto, fought between the Austro-Germans and the Italians, did not bear directly on the Americans. However, the resounding Italian defeat led directly to the significant step of establishing a Supreme War Council, which in turn later led to the appointment of a military Commander-in-Chief, Ferdinand Foch.

the acquisition of the port of Trieste, at that time Austrian territory. The front line, which fell short of that objective, ran north–south a little ways east of the Isonzo River, a crooked stream that zigzagged generally north to south. Though the Italians held substantial ground to the east of the Isonzo, the Austrians held a single bridgehead on the western side in the vicinity of Tolmino, near the town of Caporetto. The autocratic Italian General-in-Chief, Luigi Cadorna, was concerned about a possible Austrian offensive, but he expected it to be a local affair. The extent of his enemy's plans did not occur to him.

The Austrian offensive was really spearheaded by the Germans. With the threat from the Eastern Front diminishing, Emperor Karl of Austria had begun to agitate for the removal of his Austrian divisions for employment against Italy—a fairly reasonable desire. Their removal, however, ran counter to German plans to keep second-rate divisions facing Russia while removing first-rate divisions to confront France and Britain. So Kaiser Wilhelm was forced to seek a compromise.

That compromise sprang from the fertile brain of Erich Ludendorff, who, despite his deceptive title of First Quartermaster General, was the de facto German Supreme Commander. Instead of moving Austrian divisions to Italy on a permanent basis, he agreed to send seven first-rate German divisions for the planned offensive, but only for the duration of this one action. Once the offensive ended, the German divisions would be removed and sent to the Western Front. In that way Ludendorff could accommodate his ally while keeping the Austrians facing Russia.

The date set for the offensive in Italy was late October 1917, and its main thrust, spearheaded by the Germans, would be along the front of the weakened Italian Second Army, making full use of the bridgehead the Austrians held across the west bank of the Isonzo River. Prospects for success were bright, because the Italian Second Army was known to be in a bad state. Morale among the Italian soldiers was low; the Communists, Socialists, and even the Catholic Church were calling for an end to the war, and the troops were feeling the effects. That was especially so in the Second Army.

The German-Austrian attack jumped off in the early hours of October 24. Cadorna had been warned of its timing but not of its nature. The Germans attacked along the sharp ridges rather than through the steep valleys between them, maintaining contact between units by an adept and aggressive telephone communication system. As a result, seven German divisions, massed against the single Italian 19th Division defending the Tolmino bridgehead, were unexpectedly successful. Led by mountain troops, among them the Wurtemberg Battalion, all coached in mountain warfare by the Austrians,[4] they broke through along a fifteen-mile breach, moving about a third of the way to German General Otto von Below's first objective, Monte Matajur. The Wurtemberg Battalion alone captured seventeen artillery pieces and 150 prisoners.[5] Though the rest of the Italian Second Army remained relatively intact (as well as the Third Army to the south), General Cadorna realized that a breakthrough of this magnitude could result in the enemy's cutting the Second Army off from the rear. Accordingly, during the first night after the attack, Cadorna ordered his army to fall back to a second line of defense, the key point of which was Monte Matajur, the German objective.

Once the lines had broken, the Italian retreat did not stop. The next day Cadorna met with General Luigi Capello, the popular but ailing commander of the Second Army, and together they decided to withdraw to the Tagliamento River, about sixty miles to the rear of the original front on the Isonzo. By October 31, six days after the offensive began, the Italian army had taken position there. The next day, November 1, Below, ignoring his strained logistical situation, assaulted the Tagliamento River line; it, too, crumbled in what was a headlong retreat. The Italians fell all the way back to the Piave.

To forestall the impending collapse of Italy, the French hastily ordered the dispatch of six divisions to Italy, and the British five, though the first of these did not arrive until November 6.[6]

The crisis soon passed. Once dug in behind the Piave River, the Italian troops found new strength. No longer were they engaged in an attempt to take Trieste; they were now defending their homeland. In addition, bad weather set in, and Ludendorff wanted his German divisions back. The front stabilized on the Piave. Meanwhile, Cadorno was relieved of command, replaced by the younger Armando Diaz, and Vittorio Orlando took over as Prime Minister of Italy.

In the Caporetto campaign, the Italians had lost 10,000 men killed, 30,000 wounded, and nearly 300,000 captured.[7] But the Italian will to fight had actually been stiffened; no longer was there a possibility of a separate, negotiated peace between the Italians and the Austro-Germans.[8]

THE CAPORETTO EPISODE was the culminating example of a crying need among the Allied armies: an improvement in the coordination between national armies and better overall direction of the war. Aside from the competition between the British and French for the future use of American troops, there was considerable disagreement over the proper use of available manpower in the Eastern Mediterranean and the Balkans, one

result of which was the virtual stranding of a large British-French expedition at Salonika. With the collapse of Russia as an ally and the freeing of
large numbers of German units for the Western Front, it was becoming
obvious that if the French and British did not improve the coordination
of their war efforts, disaster might strike before the great industrial and
manpower potential of the United States could be brought into play
against the common enemy.

Spurred on by this obvious need, the three Allied leaders—David
Lloyd George, Paul Painlevé, and Vittorio Orlando—agreed to meet at
Rapallo on the Italian Riviera on November 7. It was urgent that they
discuss the problem of coordination among the Allies. Sir William Robertson, chief of the Imperial General Staff, and Ferdinand Foch, chief of
the French Army Staff, would also attend.

On the way to the Rapallo Conference, Prime Minister Lloyd
George stopped in Paris and while there invited General Pershing to
breakfast. Still intent on becoming better acquainted with the American
general, he asked Pershing's opinion on creating a Supreme War Council.

Pershing was doubtful. He agreed that the lack of Allied coordination in the past had enabled the Germans to deal with the two allies
separately, but he recalled the gloomy results that had stemmed from
so-called councils of war throughout history. Could not a single military
supreme commander, charged with coordinating actions on the Western
Front, be appointed?

Lloyd George agreed with Pershing's point in theory, but he considered the chance of a supreme commander unlikely. After all, as Pershing
later recorded, "the French would object to any but a Frenchman, and
the British might not like that."[9]

At that breakfast meeting, Lloyd George invited Pershing to accompany him to the Rapallo Conference. The general respectfully declined,
doubting the propriety of his going without instructions from his own
government. He knew that both Haig and Pétain held serious doubts
about such a war council, and he had no wish to be caught in the middle
of such a disagreement. Further, he suspected that the British Prime
Minister was really seeking "some means of controlling the British
Army."[10] Lloyd George's distaste for what he considered Haig's profligacy
in expending British lives was no secret.

Accompanied by General William Robertson, Lloyd George arrived
at Rapallo the next day to meet with the French and Italian leaders. In a
remarkably short time the three Prime Ministers announced the establishment of a Supreme War Council. At the political level its membership
would consist of President Woodrow Wilson, Prime Minister Lloyd

George, Premier Painlevé, and Prime Minister Orlando. Its military members were to be Robertson, Bliss, and Foch, the three respective chiefs of staff. The political members were to meet periodically at Versailles, but the military representatives would watch the situations of the forces "day by day." As it turned out, Wilson would decline to participate personally, much as he approved of the concept of the council. Instead he would send Colonel Edward House to represent him, a mission that House doubtless relished.

In practice, the council, sitting at Versailles—a big concession on the part of the British—would do most of its work in the military, not the political, sphere. And even the military representatives could not be present on a full-time basis. Tasker Bliss, for example, retained his position as the U.S. Army chief of staff for a while, a member of Baker's personal "War Council," which the secretary established in mid-December.[11]

AT MIDNIGHT on the day of the Rapallo Conference, General Tasker Bliss was alone in his room at Claridges Hotel, London. The Army chief of staff was a member of a party headed by Colonel House, sent to confer with the British high command on the future conduct of the war. As was his custom, Bliss sat down to pen his daily letter to his wife, Nellie. First of all, he described the events of the voyage—the storms, the cruisers, the destroyers, and the airplanes. But then he turned to the serious war situation. Bliss, a sensitive man, saw pathos in it:

> The news tonight from Russia is very grave. That, on top of the disaster in Italy, is making everyone here very anxious. Mr. Lloyd George and the Chief of Staff, Gen. Robertson, went to Rome while we were at sea and have not returned. That may prolong our stay here. And it is possible that we may have to go to Rome. It is pitiful to see the undercurrent of feeling that the hopes of Europe have in the United States, pitiful, because it will be so long before we can really do anything, although the very crisis seems to be at hand.[12]

Bliss had some time on his hands. Since Robertson, Lloyd George, and other members of the British high command were away at Rapallo, he decided to visit France to confer with Pershing. It would be wise, he thought, for the two old friends to exchange all available information before Bliss had to participate in decisions important to Pershing and his command.[13]

Bliss was ideally suited for this kind of role. Though his admirer, Newton Baker, conceded that he "probably could not have drilled a squad," he was also a linguist and a scholar who could fit in with diplomats. He possessed tact, diplomacy, and breadth of outlook that Pershing lacked. Bliss would have been just as unqualified for Pershing's job of making war. Each man was properly cast in his own role.[14]

HOUSE AND BLISS arrived in Paris from London on November 22, and Pershing, embroiled in reorganizing his headquarters at Chaumont, reluctantly drove to join them. On arrival he and Harbord witnessed the beginnings of a tug-of-war. House, as President Wilson's alter ego, was being courted by both the French and British, and he was obviously enjoying it. The issue the two Allies were competing over was basic and very important: which country, France or Britain, would carry the chief responsibility for training the newly arriving Americans, and thus presumably would reap the greater benefits from their presence when they were ready to fight?

House, however, had no intention of committing himself, intending to defer the issue for another time. Such an attitude was totally foreign to a man like James Harbord, untutored in diplomatic strategies, and he rankled over the gist of House's plans, which he shared with the staff:

> No speeches, for some might blunder on the subject of Russia; and some of the little fellows might ask disagreeable questions. It will be our business to be pleasant and sympathetic to the small nations. Listen to what they say. Do not promise them anything. Do not tell them anything about tonnage. Be pleasant. It is our day to smile. Just circulate around among the little fellows and listen to their stories. Be kind and agreeable.

"If that isn't giving a stone when they ask for bread," Harbord concluded, "then I dunno."[15]

THE FIRST MEETING of the council took place on November 29, 1917, at the Crillon Hotel in Paris, where the American party was staying. As it approached, General Pershing was uncomfortable, concerned for fear that this new arrangement might mean a threat to his own position. Did the establishment of a higher authority reflect a feeling of dissatisfaction on Wilson's part with his own performance? Did the presence of Bliss at Versailles mean that he was to be supervised as closely as Douglas Haig was by David Lloyd George and Henri Pétain by Georges Clemenceau? The meeting—or rather the meetings leading up to the plenary session— would give some idea of what the future held.

Pershing had little to fear, at least for the moment. The first plenary meeting, conducted under Clemenceau's chairmanship, accomplished little other than establishing goodwill among the participants, all pleased that they had managed to set the Supreme War Council up at all.[16] But at the end of the meeting Pershing asked Robertson, Foch, and Bliss, the chiefs of staff of the three major armies, to meet with him informally.

This small group did business where the large unwieldy plenary session could not. The time had come, they all agreed, to set forth a definite program for the deployment of American troops for the coming spring. Deliberately presenting the rosiest picture possible, Pershing said he expected to have 650,000 American troops in France by the next July, which he would have organized into twenty-four divisions, in four corps. This ambitious program, which his audience listened to enthusiastically, not only pleased the Allies; it put the onus on them to come up with the shipping tonnage to make this objective possible. Clemenceau later embraced the concept. Pershing had accomplished more in this short time than all the generals and statesmen gathered in the unwieldy plenary meeting.[17]

BOOK TWO

APPRENTICESHIP: THE OPENING BATTLES

CHAPTER SEVEN

BAPTISM OF FIRE

GEORGES CLEMENCEAU'S nickname, the "Tiger," was well deserved, for the fiery seventy-eight-year-old Frenchman had led a long life of continual controversy. For forty-one years as a journalist and Radical Republican politician, he was in one fight after another. He was an odd mixture, a patriotic Frenchman but an enemy of the monarchy, the Church, and often the military. His career had been a series of ups and downs. In the late 1890s he was ousted as mayor of Montmartre on suspicion of bribery in connection with the abortive French effort to build a Panama Canal. Out of office in 1898, his reputation was restored when his newspaper, *L'Aurore,* published Emile Zola's open letter, "J'Accuse," helping to marshal public opinion in the dramatic Dreyfus case. He was Premier of France between 1906 and 1909 but was voted out of office for excessive zeal in quelling strikes that were threatening the foundations of the country. By November of 1917, however, France needed a strong leader, and Clemenceau was called on by President Poincaré to be Premier once more.

Clemenceau was well acquainted with the Americans, at least the Americans of his youth. In his twenties, he had found it prudent to leave France and live for a while in the United States because of his role as a leader of the radical opposition to the reign of Emperor Napoleon III. While residing in America he taught school in New England for a while and in 1864 he accompanied General Ulysses S. Grant's Army as a journalist at the siege of Petersburg. If he developed a friendship for the Americans during his years of asylum, however, it had little bearing on his attitude toward them in 1917. He viewed the arriving Yanks only in terms of their usefulness to France. The newcomers had to get into the fighting as soon as possible.

In early September 1917, two months before taking up the premier-
ship of France,* Clemenceau decided to visit Pershing's headquarters at
Chaumont. He arrived unannounced on a Sunday morning and, finding
the American general absent, continued on to visit the American 1st Division at nearby Gondrecourt. One of the infantry battalions of the division was having a field day, strenuous recreation consisting of races and
athletic competitions, and Clemenceau spent the day watching the various activities. When he left he declared himself pleased, especially to witness the drill of the machine gun crews. His real pleasure, however, came
in witnessing a boxing match. As Clemenceau took a ringside seat, two
fighters went after each other with such fury that he found himself splat-
tered with their blood. He left satisfied that the Americans may be in
need of training, but they would fight.[1]

The next day, Clemenceau again visited the 1st Division, this time
bringing General Noël Marie Edward de Castelnau, the French commander of the area in which sector Gondrecourt was located. General
William Sibert, commanding the 1st Division, received the two men in
his office.

Clemenceau had now formulated a plan designed to get the 1st Division trained sufficiently to go into the active line. As part of their combat indoctrination, he proposed to assign American troops, a battalion at
a time, into a quiet sector. To instruct them in proper procedures, each
battalion would be "brigaded"[2] with French troops. He had a specific
sector in mind, a portion of the line north of Lunéville, just to the east of
Nancy. He wanted to begin this process by mid-September. It was a question, he told General Sibert, of winning or losing the war.

Overt Yank participation was a paramount symbolic consideration.
French strength and morale were at an all-time low, and the appearance
of the Americans, whether in perfect condition or not, was necessary to
give them hope. Many months, he pointed out, had passed since America
had entered the war, and no American troops had yet been seen in the
line. The Americans must make some sacrifice to show they were in
earnest.

Sibert did his best to present the other side. The world was watching the 1st Division, he said, with the mistaken idea that it represented
the best of the veteran American Regular Army. In truth it was full of
new recruits, and it must be trained to its fullest before being sent into

---

* France had four Premiers during 1917: In March, Aristide Briand was replaced by
Alexandre Ribot; in September, Ribot was replaced by Paul Painlevé; on November 15
Clemenceau replaced Painlevé.

battle. Clemenceau was not there to listen, however, and he and Castle-
nau soon departed.[3] The division was not, as it turned out, ordered into
the line as early as Clemenceau had wanted, but from the time of his visit,
the men of the 1st knew that they would soon be committed as front line
troops.

GENERAL SIBERT'S arguments reflected Pershing's views. Unfortunately
for Sibert, however, his chief was holding him personally accountable for
the many deficiencies in the training of his troops. On September 6,
shortly after Clemenceau's visit, Pershing ordered a review to be held in
honor of French President Poincaré. The invitation had been issued on
the spur of the moment, and word reached 1st Division headquarters
only the afternoon before it was to take place. Captain George Marshall,
acting chief of staff, had to select the site in the waning hours of daylight,
and some of the participating troops, scattered for miles around the area,
were forced to march all night in order to reach their assembly positions
in time. President Poincaré professed to be delighted at seeing these
strong young men perform, but anyone could see that the performance
had been extremely ragged. When Marshall had selected the field the
night before, he had failed to notice that it was soggy from recent rains
and torn up by previous use. Pershing put great store in military smart-
ness, and he made no secret of his chagrin.

About a month after that unfortunate incident, Pershing came to the
1st Division training area to observe a demonstration of a battalion attack
on a fortified position. The demonstration went well, but when Pershing
asked Sibert for a critique, the latter's response was halting, indicating
that he was unfamiliar with the scenario. Pershing's hard feelings toward
Sibert now erupted, and he berated the division commander in front of
his staff and rose from his seat, heading for the door of the headquarters.
George Marshall, who had made the arrangements, jeopardized his own
future by protesting, even confronting the commanding general, with a
series of arguments justifying the difficulties the division was working
under. Pershing accepted this insubordination with a shrug, but it was becoming apparent that General Sibert's days as commander of the Big Red
One were numbered.[4]

By the second week of October 1917 the troops of the 1st Division
were finally put into action. An order arrived at division headquarters
that all the staff had been expecting: one battalion from each of the division's four infantry regiments would leave Gondrecourt and go into the
line. Those battalions would serve under the tutelage of the French 18th
Division, which was holding a six-mile sector on a pleasant plain about

ten miles east of Nancy, the general area that Clemenceau had mentioned earlier.[5]

The French command made sure that the American troops were to participate strictly under French control. General Sibert and his staff were instructed to remain at Gondrecourt, away from the action. Only one officer from the division headquarters could visit the scene, and he was admonished to give no orders whatsoever. Each American battalion would be placed under the command of a different French regiment. One artillery battalion from the 1st Division could fire in support, but its role was only to supplement the fires of the French artillery.[6] Each infantry battalion would stay in the line for ten days before being replaced by another battalion of the same regiment.

General Paul Emile Bordeaux, the commander of the French 18th Division, was a congenial man, but he suffered from an excessive concern to keep control firmly in his own hands, or at least in the hands of his own officers. Bordeaux might be excused for being chary regarding the competence of these new Americans, but he carried his caution too far by forbidding them to send patrols out ahead of their barbed wire protection. That restriction meant that the enemy would have the freedom of No Man's Land at night while the Americans would have to wait and fret in their trenches.[7] The first test of American combat troops would be conducted at a marked disadvantage.

The first ten days of occupation, by the 1st Battalion of each regiment, went smoothly. Inevitably, since this was the first combat the Americans had participated in, certain milestones were passed: at 6:05 A.M., October 23, 1917, the first shot from an American-manned gun was fired from Battery C, 6th Field Artillery. On the same day the first American infantrymen were wounded and treated in an American field hospital at Einville. Two days later the first American officer was wounded, and on October 27 a battalion from the 18th Infantry captured the first prisoner taken by American troops.[8] All this was routine activity in a quiet sector.

The calm was shattered on the night of November 2–3, as each 1st Battalion was in the process of being relieved by the 2d Battalion. The early part of the relief went well, encountering only the normal confusion that accompanies such activities, but at about 3:00 A.M. the doughboys were hit with a "blinding flash and a crash and a roar that seemed to upset and to blot out the very earth itself."[9] It was a major incoming artillery barrage, laid down to protect a German raid being conducted into American lines.

After the initial blast of the front line, the barrage concentrated on a single platoon of the 16th Infantry, making it impossible for that platoon

to withdraw and equally impossible for the battalion commander to reinforce it. A German patrol crept forward with Bangalore torpedoes, long,
snakelike devices filled with high explosive to clear out barbed wire, and
blew gaps in the protective wire. They rushed the isolated platoon with
grenades, pistols, trench knives, and bayonets. Within a few minutes the
firing ceased and the Germans made off with eleven American prisoners,
one of them a sergeant. Behind lay the bodies of Corporal James B.
Gresham, Private Thomas F. Enright, and Private Merle D. Hay. One of
the men had had his throat cut. They were the first Americans killed in
combat in an American unit in the First World War.[10] Marshall attributed
the enemy's ability to reach American lines with impunity to Bordeaux's
order forbidding them to patrol.[11]

The next day the three Americans were buried at the small town of
Bathelémont, just behind the lines where they had fallen. General Bordeaux himself conducted the service with some solemn remarks:

> The death of this humble Corporal and these Privates appeals to us with un-
> wonted grandeur. We will, therefore, ask that the mortal remains of these
> young men be left with us forever. We will inscribe on their tombs, "here lie
> the first soldiers of the United States to fall on the fields of France for jus-
> tice and liberty." The passerby will stop and uncover his head. The travelers
> of France, of the Allied countries, of America, and the men of heart, who
> will come to visit our battlefields of Lorraine, will go out of their way to
> come here to bring to these graves the tribute of their respect and gratitude.
> Corporal Gresham, Private Enright, and Private Hay, in the name of
> France I thank you. God receive your souls.[12]

The incident brought a bizarre sequel. After all the inquiries regarding the action had been completed, a message from Major Theodore
Roosevelt, Jr., commanding the 2d Battalion, 26th Infantry, arrived at 1st
Division headquarters requesting the privilege of making a retaliatory
raid. Approval was not easy in coming. General Bordeaux, whose division
had experienced many such attacks, saw the German incident as a routine affair, not worth the risk of a retaliation.

Young Roosevelt, however, was full of fervor, and he took full advantage of the warm feelings the French high command held for his
famous father. Through backdoor machinations, he finally secured Bordeaux's approval, and also the approval of General Sibert back in
Gondrecourt. Once his operation had been authorized, Major Roosevelt's enthusiasm, George Marshall later recorded, "knew no bounds,
and he embraced the French Lieutenant [who was to accompany him]
and proclaimed his complete satisfaction with the Army, the war, and the
world in general."

General Sibert approved the action but put his foot down on one point. Two brothers, Lieutenant Archibald B. (Archie) Roosevelt and his brother Theodore, both sons of the former President, were planning to participate in one raid that actually should have been led by a sergeant. Archie Roosevelt was in immediate command of the detachment, so Theodore was not allowed to go along, much to his disappointment.

Roosevelt and the French lieutenant rehearsed the action several times, and they developed a mutual liking and respect in the process. When the appointed night arrived, the two young officers led their small detachment out through No Man's Land, marking their route with a white tape. They experienced no difficulty in finding their objective, an old building. Immediately they laid siege to it, expecting to find it occupied by a German patrol.

No Germans were there, and that unforeseen circumstance caused the rapport between Roosevelt and the Frenchman to come to an end. They could not agree on what to do next and even began to argue over what exactly was their location. To solve the impasse, Roosevelt ordered the French lieutenant to return to the friendly lines. But Roosevelt still made no contact with the enemy and decided to return himself. On the way back his patrol exchanged some sharp rifle fire. Not with the Germans, however; with the Frenchman himself, who had become lost. Fortunately nobody was hurt and the incident went unreported in the press.[13]

As THE YEAR 1917 faded into 1918, the four original American divisions spent a cold and miserable winter on the Western Front in France. Winter clothing, requisitioned as early as July, failed to arrive in sufficient quantities. The weather was the coldest it had been in years. For the divisions in France, the winter of 1917 was their Valley Forge. As a result of the experience, the 1st, 2d, 26th, and 42d developed a feeling of being the "old reliables," the divisions destined to be used in the most difficult situations.

It would have been superhuman, however, if some degree of pessimism had failed to creep into the ranks. Part of the pessimism came from the French instructors, who were worn out and cynical, but part of it came from some frightening facts. Everyone knew that the Germans were moving divisions from the Eastern to the Western Front, that the Allied offensives of 1917 had been disappointing, and that no American divisions had arrived in France since the original four. Pershing's headquarters were within easy driving range of all four divisions, and any rumors of negative attitudes stood a good chance of reaching him. And reach him they did. The main culprits, in the reports that Pershing saw, were the commanders of the 1st and 26th Divisions, William Sibert and Clarence Edwards respectively.

Pershing had been harboring doubts about both men for some time. Sibert he considered too genial, not sufficiently forceful. Edwards, whose 26th Division felt a certain superiority over the Regular Army because of the elite nature of their peacetime organization, shared their commander's tendency to exaggerate the hardships his men were undergoing. Edwards, older than Pershing, had a sharp tongue, and his wit was always leveled at higher headquarters. Pershing's animosity toward Edwards was kept in check because Edwards did nothing overtly wrong.

On December 13, 1917, Pershing sent a stern message directed to Sibert and Edwards, as well as to one brigade commander from both the 1st and 26th. Without mincing words, he gave blunt warning that no officer's command was safe if he failed to produce results. He cited reports of "deep pessimism, including the apprehension of undue hardships to be undergone." He mentioned specifically the numbers of the enemy and a general impression that "the war is already well along toward defeat of our arms." He regretted that such impressions had been derived mainly from general officers, whose attitude should be exactly opposite. His final paragraph was threatening:

> The officer who cannot read hope in the conditions that confront us; who is not inspired and uplifted by the knowledge that under the leadership of our chief executive, the heart of our nation is in this war; who shrinks from hardship; who does not exert his own personal influence to encourage his men; who fails in the lofty attitude which should characterize the General that expects to succeed, should yield his position to others with more of our national courage.

He concluded that any officer who knowingly held negative attitudes should "in honor" apply for relief, and when "the visible effects of it on the command of such an officer reach me in the future, it will constitute grounds for his removal without application."[14]

That rebuke brought strong reactions from its targets. William Sibert demanded a court of inquiry. Clarence Edwards gave some lame excuses for his conduct. The two brigadiers, who later went on to prove themselves outstanding leaders in battle, were irate.[15] Of the four, however, only Sibert failed to survive the storm. Pershing's paternalistic attitude toward the 1st Division could not allow him to keep Sibert in command. On December 14, 1917, Robert Lee Bullard replaced him as commanding general of the Big Red One. Sibert went on to perform outstanding duties in the engineering field more suited to his temperament and training.[16]

IF PESSIMISM infected the 1st and 26th Divisions, it seems to have been overcome easily by Major General Charles Menoher, of the 42d (Rainbow) Division. Menoher was a fine soldier. Furthermore—and fortunately—he seemed to take no offense at being overshadowed in the public eye by his chief of staff, Colonel Douglas MacArthur.

MacArthur, who would later lay claim to recommending Pershing to President Wilson in March of that same year, was a marked man, both in his own eyes and in those of his associates. Tall and handsome—the son of one of the Army's heroes, General Arthur MacArthur—he saw himself as a man of destiny. Once an engineer, he had seen that the paths of glory lay in the combat units, and he had been influential in promoting the original idea of a Rainbow Division. He did not, however, expect to reap laurels behind the desk as the chief of staff of a division. Like the old soldiers of the nineteenth century, he was willing to take risks, grave risks, to achieve his ambitions.

But MacArthur had no intention of taking those risks without being noticed in the process. Claiming that flamboyance was part of leadership, he designed his own uniform. First he refused to wear the prescribed British-style steel helmet and in its place habitually wore a standard officer's garrison cap, with visor. He removed the grommet (stiffener) from the cap, and the effect was rakish, though it made him look somewhat like a German officer to the unsuspecting. In place of the standard officer's blouse he wore his old West Point sweater, with a large "A" on it, denoting that he had been a varsity baseball player while at the Academy. As a weapon he carried only a riding crop, and to top it all he sported a long muffler, knitted for him by his mother. He made a point of making friendships among his contemporaries and among his troops. A natural charmer, Colonel Douglas MacArthur was a popular officer among the men of the Rainbow Division.

Among Pershing's staff at Chaumont he was not so popular. Part of the mutual animosity may have been, as MacArthur claimed, the result of staff jealousy of the combat troops. But much of it stemmed from the high-handed way in which, soon after the 42d arrived in France, MacArthur had defied the will of the staff. As the troops of the Rainbow were making camp near Nancy, orders came from Pershing's headquarters reassigning thirty-three of the officers of the Rainbow to other divisions. After MacArthur had appealed unsuccessfully for a cancellation, he sent anguished messages to political friends in Washington pushing his case. Even that questionable action failed to make a difference, and MacArthur finally appealed to James Harbord, Pershing's chief of staff, and induced him to intervene. Harbord did so, and Pershing decided that some division other than the 42d would be the source of the needed officer replacements. The incident did nothing to endear MacArthur to the rank and file of the AEF staff whose will he had thwarted.[17]

Still, MacArthur's personal courage was legendary. Even while he was the division chief of staff, he determined to participate personally in some front line action. His opportunity came on the night of February 26, 1918, when the Rainbow was in the line near Lunéville, under the command of General Georges de Bazelaire. Learning that the French were planning a night raid on German lines, MacArthur secured the French commander's reluctant permission to go along. He did not, however, inform General Menoher. Attaining one permission was difficult enough, and MacArthur, secure in Menoher's approval, knew that he would be congratulated—if he returned alive.

When the night came, MacArthur joined the French party, dressed in his usual unorthodox attire, down to his shiny cavalry boots, bowing to prudence only to the extent of blackening his face and accepting the loan of a pair of wire cutters and trench knives. As MacArthur and one other American made their way out with the French, they were spotted by General Menoher—who said nothing.

The raid began with a toss of a grenade by one of the French *poilus,* and a German machine gun answered instantly. Enemy artillery laid down a barrage behind the raiders, temporarily cutting them off. But they pushed forward, and by the morning they returned to friendly lines with several German prisoners, one of them a colonel. MacArthur, prodding the colonel with his riding crop, was lacking the seat of his riding breeches. But the French were overjoyed to see the party return. MacArthur was given a French Croix de Guerre for the action, as well as a drink of cognac. Not to be outdone, General Menoher awarded him a Silver Star.[18] This was only the first of MacArthur's many feats of daring on the Western Front.

NOT ALL THE FIRST combat actions of American troops were as successful as that of Douglas MacArthur. The German raid on the position at Seicheprey in April 1918 stood in somber contrast.

Seicheprey was a small town in the Ansauville sector, about twenty-five kilometers northwest of Toul. The territory was part of the triangle known as the St. Mihiel Salient, a bulge into French lines left over from the campaign of 1914. Since then the French had made a couple of efforts to reduce the salient, which they called the "hernia," but their attacks had proven so costly that both sides had eventually settled down and tacitly accepted the status quo. In mid-January 1918, the 1st Division moved into this sector, operating as a unit for the first time, relieving the French 1st Moroccan Division.

The 1st Division had no intention of allowing a quiet sector to remain so. Soon after its arrival in the line, on February 5, the new division commander, Robert L. Bullard, put out Instruction No. 1:

1. There are no orders which require us to wait for the enemy to fire on us before we fire on him; do not wait for him to fire first. Be active all over no-man's-land; do not leave its control to the enemy.
2. Front line commanders will immediately locate and report all places where there is a favorable opportunity for strong ambuscades and for raids on the enemy's lines and advance posts.[19]

The men of the Big Red One took that message to heart, and they began to plan for raiding the enemy's trenches. In this difficult art they were amateurs playing in a professional league. The Germans maintained special bodies of raiding troops called *Stosstruppen* (or *Sturmbataillonen*) for the purpose. Generally, a raid would be preceded by a short period of preparation by artillery and machine gun fire on the enemy trenches, machine gun positions, and artillery. Then these supporting fires would be placed so as to create a box within which the raid would be made. Under the cover of this "box barrage" the raiding party would proceed in small detachments, well rehearsed beforehand. They would pass through the enemy wire, into his trenches, and hope to knock out machine guns and seize prisoners.

Fortunately for the men of the 1st Division, the 1st French Moroccan Division, which they had replaced, was glad to provide them with expert advisers. After numerous conferences—the pace of activity was slow—the division planned two simultaneous raids, one to be executed by the 18th Infantry in the Remières Woods; the other, by the 16th Infantry, was to be directed toward the destroyed village of Richecourt. There was no shortage of volunteers, who were sent to the rear for rehearsals. The raid was planned for the morning of March 4.

After a week's delay, on the night of March 10–11, the American machine guns and artillery cut loose at 5:30 A.M. Four officers and sixty-one men swarmed through the trenches and reached the enemy's third line of trenches. No Germans were found; there were no casualties on either side. The same happened with the 18th Infantry at 5:30 P.M. that day.

Though no blood was shed, the division was happy to perfect their raiding procedures. Bullard's men conducted several more such raids, and by the time the 1st Division was relieved on March 21, it had suffered casualties of 143 killed, 403 wounded, and three missing.[20]

On April 1, 1918, the 1st Division was relieved on the Ansauville line by the 26th Division. The opportunity for the Germans to retaliate against the 1st was therefore gone. Nevertheless, the Germans began to probe with their assault teams and then, in the early morning hours of April 20, 1918, they conducted a large raid, the largest they had yet launched against the inexperienced American troops.

The town of Seicheprey, the most vulnerable point in the American lines, was the target. Heavy artillery, observed from the nearby Butte de Montsec, opened with hundreds of guns in a rolling barrage, and immediately behind it came the six hundred men of the *Stosstruppen* battalion. On the east, in the Remières Woods, came another thousand carrying heavy packs. All in all, the number of men engaged, including engineers, signal personnel, and machine gunners, came to 3,200 Germans, concentrated against about six hundred New Englanders.

The German reinforced raid was a conspicuous success. Their shock troops penetrated the American lines at points both east and west of Seicheprey, and the town fell soon thereafter. The four hundred American troops previously defending the town appeared to be doomed. Their telephone wires cut, the regimental headquarters was soon out of contact with the battalions, and runners trying to carry messages never arrived. The battalion commander, Major George A. Rau, held on with what he had left—cooks, bakers, and clerks among them—but could not immediately drive the Germans back out of the town. The French corps commander, Major General Passaga, arrived and attempted to issue instructions to the American brigade commander, Brigadier General Peter Traub.

By nightfall, everything was in confusion, to the French and to the Americans as well. The Remières Woods were reported lost, and the battalions were out of contact. In fact, the Remières Woods were not lost, and the Americans, guided by the French, began a counterattack the next morning. The Germans voluntarily withdrew, taking with them 136 American prisoners, after having inflicted heavy casualties. The raid at Seicheprey was history.

But not the repercussions. The Germans claimed a victory over the ignorant Americans. Those same Americans, however, believed that they had repulsed a major attack, and they expressed pride in their performance. At home Seicheprey was touted as a great victory, and used to support the Third Liberty Loan.[21] In the AEF, however, it was down-played. In his memoirs, Pershing dismissed it tersely, without endorsing any claims one way or the other.

> On the night of April 20–21, the Germans made a raid on the 26th Division in the vicinity of Seicheprey. . . . It came during a heavy fog and was a complete surprise to our troops, who were considerably outnumbered. The fighting in Seicheprey was violent, causing heavy losses on both sides. The town was taken by the enemy. The success of the raid may be attributed largely to the destruction by the German artillery of the divisional system of communications, which naturally resulted in some confusion in the division. Although cooperation among the units was difficult under the circumstances, it was finally established and the original front was reoccupied the following day.[22]

In fact, American troops had performed well despite their newness to combat. The 26th Division had gained some valuable experience. But the operations thus far had been mere baptisms of fire. The major actions were yet to come.

WHILE PERSHING'S divisions were undergoing their first combat experiences, the authorities in Washington were busy putting their own house in order. The time had come for General Tasker Bliss to retire as Army chief of staff, and Newton Baker was casting about for a replacement of his own choosing. A name that came to his attention was that of Major General Peyton March.

Peyton Conway March was an odd sort of Army officer. A West Point graduate from the Class of 1888, he was a little younger than Pershing and Bliss, but he was friends with them. Even so, he had never developed the social manners that were generally considered prerequisite for a successful military career; his style was ruthless and abrasive. That style had never held him back, however, especially when he had been called on to perform difficult jobs. His superior officers viewed him as a troubleshooter; the victims of his unyielding demands saw him as a hatchet man.

March's specialty was the artillery, and he was good at it. He had been selected as the division artillery commander of the 1st Division when that highly selected unit had sailed to France in June of 1917. In the early stages of training, the artillery brigade was separated from the infantry brigades, and the then-Brigadier General March was left much on his own, to train the 1st Artillery Brigade as he saw fit.

In that capacity March was ideally qualified. American units, trained in the United States on the American 3-inch gun, had to be taught to fire the French 75mm gun, the pride of the French Army and the weapon the Americans would use. Since the procedures for the two types of gun were different, March had to supervise the retraining of the Americans when they arrived in Europe.

March did so with his customary zeal and efficiency. He began by visiting the Fourth French Army, commanded by General Henri Joseph Gouraud, the "one-armed hero of the Dardanelles." He studied, he later wrote, "the handling of Field Artillery by a French Army, from headquarters down to the trenches." At Douglas Haig's headquarters he spent time with the British artillery commander as he went about his duties. He dined with Haig himself, unabashedly quizzing the Marshal on British use of artillery. He then visited General Sir Henry Horne, a fellow artilleryman, now in command of the British Fourth Army. He even visited Portuguese and Belgian troops serving with the British.[23]

Like so many in that first group of 1st Division officers, however, March was removed for other duties in early August of 1917. The position he now assumed was an even more important one: he was to be Pershing's Chief of Artillery for the entire American Expeditionary Force. Here he was happy, planning to make a major contribution in the techniques he knew best.

It did not last. About three months after assuming his new position, March received a message to report to Pershing at Chaumont. Pershing showed him a letter from Secretary of War Baker outlining the War Department's plans for the reorganization of the high command in the wake of Bliss's retirement as chief of staff, to occur on December 31, 1917. Baker asked if March would be available for that position.

March was in a quandary. He enjoyed duty with troops and military tradition has it that the best soldiers place service in a combat zone at the highest priority; it would be unbecoming to return home willingly even for such a spectacular promotion. At March's request, therefore, Pershing informed Baker that he was not available. When March heard soon thereafter that Major General John Biddle had been appointed as acting chief, he went back to work with a clear mind.[24]

On January 26, 1918, however, Pershing received a stronger letter from Baker:

Can General Peyton C. March be spared to return to this country as Acting Chief of Staff? If he can, direct his immediate return. I feel it urgently necessary to have him.[25]

There was nothing negotiable about that message. March had to go, though he later claimed that he felt "sick" at the prospect of leaving France. In preparation for his new position, he determined to see everything he could in France before leaving—not just artillery installations. He consulted Major General Francis J. Kernan, new chief of the Services of Supply, to familiarize himself with the organization of Pershing's line of communication; he visited General Bliss, who had now been designated permanent representative to the Supreme War Council; he consulted for a couple of hours with Brigadier General Charles Dawes on problems of local supply procurement. He spent some time consulting with Pershing himself. He left for the United States in February 1918, arriving in New York on March 2. Two days later he took over as acting chief of staff from General Biddle.

Congress would soon bestow on March the temporary rank of full general—four stars. March would quickly inject a new sense of urgency in the War Department General Staff. His appointment would also carry grave implications for the practically full autonomy heretofore enjoyed by General Pershing.

More importantly for the war effort, the key senior members of the American high command were now in place.

CHAPTER EIGHT

THE CALM
BEFORE THE STORM

BY EARLY 1918, Secretary of War Newton Baker felt that he had been running the Army from a desk in Washington long enough; he wanted to see things for himself. On February 20, therefore, he penned a letter to President Wilson asking permission to make an extended visit to France. His arguments were persuasive. He had been receiving repeated cablegrams and letters from General Pershing urging him to visit the American Expeditionary Force, and he wanted to make a personal inspection of ports, transportation, and storage facilities and camps of the overseas army. The reports from the officers of the Army, he concluded, convinced him that the only way to get a complete view of the situation was to make a personal inspection.

The President approved the idea enthusiastically, and Baker left Washington within a week. He arrived at Brest early in the morning of Monday, March 11, 1918, and was soon aboard a train for Paris. At the station to meet him were Ambassador William Sharp, Bliss, Pershing, and French officers representing Premier Clemenceau. Taken immediately to the Hotel Crillon, he devoted the next two days to making the rounds of necessary official calls.

Baker was in his element. In spite of his self-effacing manner when dealing with high officials and generals, he was a politician at heart, and the former mayor of Cleveland was basking in all the attention he was receiving. In a cable home to the President, he exulted,

It is most fortunate that my visit comes at this time. I am securing much important and helpful information and the efficiency of our cooperation will undoubtedly be greatly increased. I have spent two days in Paris and tonight I start a thorough inspection of the port terminal, transportation, supply, and storage systems, all of which will include about ten days.

He added that he would visit the British, French, and Belgian military headquarters "to gratify millions."[1] Baker's last phrase was probably written with tongue in cheek; nevertheless, he was enjoying the heady atmosphere.

Much was expected from Baker's trip. Although the War Department emphasized that his visit was a "purely military pilgrimage, without diplomatic significance," officials conjectured that, with the American troops holding "a constantly increasing sector of the battle lines," the wishes of the "Washington Government undoubtedly will have a greater weight than heretofore with allied chieftains." He was to confer at length with Pershing to get first hand "the judgment of that officer on all that is going on in France."[2]

There would be much to see in France. At the time of Baker's visit, the total AEF was only about half a million men, and only two divisions, the 32d and 41st,[3] had arrived to join the original big four that had spent the winter around Neufchâteau. Nevertheless, three divisions, the 1st, 26th, and 42d, were already fighting, so the Secretary could get all the taste of battle that he needed.

Pershing was amenable to Baker's desire to visit the front line troops, but his own preoccupation was to familiarize the Secretary with the vast and growing Services of Supply. For there, in the rear areas, was where the War Department could most effectively aid him. Pershing was determined to show as much of the Services of Supply as he could in the few days available.

The American Line of Communications in France, while far from complete in March of 1918, was well along in development. It was based on an extensive rail system that was already in place when the AEF arrived, but was being vastly improved by the Americans. New rail lines were being laid and Yankee railroad men were busy repairing worn-out French rolling stock. Pershing's requests, made nearly a year earlier, had been largely met by the French, and the rail net was being served by three port complexes.[4] One centered around St. Nazaire; one centered on Bordeaux; and the third was at La Rochelle and its subsidiary port, La Pallice.[5]

Pershing and Baker left Paris by train the evening of Tuesday, March 12, and in a whirlwind tour, Baker and Pershing visited the permanent port works of Bordeaux, the new berths at Bassens, and the St. Sulpice storage area, where "a network of railway sidings led to row after row of new storehouses being filled with property that required cover." They finished the morning with a walk through the base hospital, a large, thousand-bed installation that had scarcely been opened (American casualties had not yet been severe).[6] After luncheon in the luxurious Chapeau Rouge restaurant, the party went that afternoon to observe a large artillery camp of instruction and a remount depot, which at that time held only "a few hundred horses and mules."[7]

The next day Pershing showed the Secretary the progress that had been made at St. Nazaire. The French had allocated ten berths at that port for American use; thirteen vessels were being unloaded with supplies that day, all destined for the AEF. That afternoon, at nearby Montoir, the Baker party inspected the port area in an effective but informal manner, seated on benches aboard a completely unadorned flatcar. That port, Baker was told, had consisted only of marshes the previous October. Since then the ground had been filled in from dredgings and the whole area would soon allow forty large, or sixty medium-sized steamers to be unloaded simultaneously.[8] At Savenay they found a base hospital with several hundred patients, thus giving Baker a chance to speak to the wounded with words of cheer. Pershing noted with great satisfaction that the nurses were "especially neat and military."[9]

On March 15 the Baker-Pershing party arrived at Tours, which served as the headquarters of the Services of Supply. There Baker was able to speak to the assembled officers in the presence of their new commanding general, Major General Francis Kernan. Tours itself was only a headquarters, not a big supply depot.

At Tours, Baker was shown a delousing station, a mundane but extremely important installation. The problem of lice infestation was critical to morale. The biting little creatures, "cooties" to the troops, may not have been life-threatening, but they were certainly annoying to men with their lives at risk in the trenches. Pershing explained the procedures: when a man was relieved from the front he was required to shed his entire set of clothing, take a bath, and go through a delousing process. Then, presumably rid of the little pests for the moment, he was issued a new uniform. The plant at Tours was in the process of renovating and repairing what uniforms could be salvaged, thus lessening the amount of tonnage required for replacements. It was worth a savings of many millions of dollars, Pershing boasted.[10]

One of the most complete of the interior depots—the largest, in fact—was located at the town of Gièvres, on the railroad about 125 miles south of Paris. The component of men at this one depot alone was twenty thousand and, according to Pershing, it boasted 165 storehouses, with four million square feet of storage space. It could store two million tons of gasoline, 6,500 tons of fresh meat, and thirty days' supply of clothing and food for an army of two million men. Pershing was justifiably proud of this installation, and once again the party spent almost two hours observing it by flatcar.[11]

From Tours, the Baker party went to Issoudon, the home of the main Air Service School. Here General Benny Foulois joined the party to show them the depot and the school, pointing out that this was only one of fifteen where Americans were being given instruction. As Baker watched, many monoplanes and biplanes took to the air, one after the other, until there were soon a hundred in flight. Baker was happy to learn that each plane was being piloted by an American. A French officer on the spot was carried away with enthusiasm. "With all these machines we see in the air," he beamed to a receptive Baker, "we see no more than a tenth of what America has in this one school. You will soon have no need for French instruction." All this was welcome news to the Secretary of War of a country that had shamefully and parsimoniously neglected that branch of service, with all its potential.

Finally Baker and Pershing reached Pershing's Chaumont headquarters on March 18, after a full week. Baker professed himself delighted. He described for the general staff officers and the press how much he had seen during the time of his visit. He assured them of the importance of what they were doing. After a nod to Pershing's "vision, authority, and high organizing ability," he finished up with a rosy statement:

> While we are busy at home with our industrial preparations and training of troops, our hearts are transplanted to France. My visit has brought me a great uplift in spirit. As a boy takes apart a watch to see how it is made in order to understand the functions of its parts, I have been taking this army apart.[12]

PERSHING COULD NOT DEVOTE his entire schedule to playing host for Baker's visit. He had other things to do. For much of the next few days, therefore, the Secretary of War would be taken around to see the front line units by the AEF's chief of staff, General James Harbord. Before Baker and Harbord left for the front, however, Pershing wanted to show off the immense training area he was developing at the town of Langres, about twenty-five miles south of Chaumont, on the Marne. At that historic little town of about nine thousand people, Pershing had established a complex of schools designed to train Americans in the specialties they were expected to exercise at the front. One of the most important aspects of the school was the General Staff College, designed to teach officers much needed staff procedures far beyond the rudiments that could be taught at Plattsburgh back in the United States. The AEF schools around Langres were also instructing officers and men in hands-on military techniques: machine guns, chemical warfare, sapping and mining, flash and sound ranging, camouflage, tanks, balloons, grenades, searchlights, and even the use of pigeons.

Langres was supposedly a highly secret installation. Though considered one of the three most important cities in the AEF—Chaumont and Tours being the other two—its very name was never used. Violators of such secrecy were at least theoretically vulnerable to general court-martial. It was known only by the number of its Army post office—"APO 714." If the Germans became aware of Langres and its curriculum, so the reasoning went, they would benefit by learning the preoccupation of the Americans in training.[13]

There remained only one more visit for the Secretary, that to the front. To give Baker a representative sampling of soldier life, Harbord had selected the sector currently being held by the 42d Division. A reason for the selection was the fact that the Rainbow Division was already one of the more battle-hardened of the American divisions. An added bonus—important, one suspects—was that it included a battalion from Ohio, Baker's home state. Harbord made sure that the Ohio battalion would be out of the line when the Secretary arrived.

The next morning, March 19, Baker and Harbord breakfasted early in anticipation of their visit to the front, and they were off by 5:30 A.M. The first stop was the small village of Moyen, where Baker met with his fellow citizens of Ohio under the stars. Soon afterward they reached an advanced headquarters, from which Baker would go forward to inspect the trenches.

For a moment it appeared that Baker's trip to the front would have to be canceled. The road scheduled for his use was under heavy shell fire, and his hosts were unwilling to allow him to take the risk. He was determined, however, and when another, quieter route was mentioned, he eagerly insisted that they go ahead. He assented to wear a gas mask and to carry a regulation steel helmet, though he wore that uncomfortable head-gear for only a short time. Dismounting from the car while it was still out of artillery range, the party slipped and slid through the mud, entered a communications trench, and made their way up to the front.[14]

Even seeing the main trench line was not enough to satisfy the little Secretary, however. Over the protests of the members of the party, he made his way up forward to a listening post. There he conversed with the soldier on guard and, peeping over the parapet into No Man's Land, declaimed, "Now I am on the frontier of freedom." His words were dutifully reported to the press.

Baker's moment of greatest peril, it turned out, came on the return trip from the front lines. A German gunner spotted his vehicle and a 105mm shell burst less than fifty yards from it. The shell hit a dugout, and Baker was constrained with difficulty from running over to check whether any men were in it. His driver, however, "realizing the danger, opened the throttle and made his best speed until the danger zone was past."[15] Heroics were all well and good, but the canny driver had his own life on the line as well as that of the Secretary of War.

The rest of the trip to the front was less dramatic, but one vignette was memorable. Stopping at an American cemetery near Lunéville, Baker witnessed a funeral procession carrying the body of a Private Wilkinson, from Missouri, a signalman from the Rainbow Division. The wooden casket was being carried on the shoulders of Wilkinson's comrades, and a village priest was on hand together with the chaplain of one of the infantry regiments nearby.

Many others of the soldier's comrades were on hand, as well as a number of French soldiers and civilians, few if any of whom could have known him but who recognized him as one who had come to France to drive the hated Boche from their homeland. A French officer stepped forward and presented the fallen American with a posthumous Croix de Guerre, and just as the volleys were fired, a lone German airplane appeared. Antiaircraft batteries opened up. Harbord was content with the whole episode. "There was little lacking to impress the scene on the Secretary's memory," he wrote later.[16]

After leaving the front, Baker stopped by a hospital for a short visit with Captain Archibald Roosevelt, of the 1st Division. Roosevelt's luck had run out, and he had been severely wounded.[17] Baker and Harbord spent the evening at Ligny-en-Barrois, over the Heights of the Meuse.

Before returning to Chaumont, Baker wanted to make one more stop, Domremy, the home of Jeanne d'Arc, the Maid of Orleans, the Savior of France. Baker said little, but Harbord, the amateur historian, allowed his mind to wander. The Sainte's only request, he recalled, was that Domremy, her native village, should henceforth pay no taxes. The French King had accordingly declared, "There shall be no taxes paid in Domremy forever."

The edict lasted for 360 years, until the French Revolution displaced the Bourbon kings. Harbord noted with ironic amusement. "The Revolution came and Domremy has paid taxes ever since. *Vive la République!*"[18]

• • •

As Secretary Baker's visit to France was drawing to a close, Pershing's dream of consolidating American troops into a single fighting force, the First United States Army, seemed to be approaching reality. In addition to his six divisions (the original four plus the 41st and 32d), he expected the 3d Division to arrive in early April, bringing the total to seven,[19] or the equivalent of fourteen British, French, or German divisions. Shipments of troops were now accelerating, and the strength of the AEF was to reach 650,000 men by June 15.[20]

Once the First Army was organized, it would have need of subordinate headquarters, or corps, to exercise direct command over the American divisions. Since Pershing had only a few divisions in the spring, however, he decided to organize only one such headquarters for the moment, to be commanded by his deputy, Major General Hunter Liggett.

Pershing's order establishing I Corps was dated January 15, 1918; its headquarters was to be located at Neufchâteau, and Liggett was directed to exercise general command of the 1st, 2d, 26th, and 42d divisions. Liggett set about preparing not only to train them but to command them in battle.

It was not meant to come out that way—at least for the moment. Pershing's plans to organize his First American Army were predicated on a continuation of the relatively stable conditions that had existed for a long time on the Western Front. But that front was soon to be torn asunder by the first of several major German offensives that would change the primary preoccupations of the Allies from the matter of organization to that of survival. The Germans, led by General Erich Ludendorff, had been, for four months, planning otherwise.

Baker's visit had been made during the calm before the storm.

CHAPTER NINE

UNIFIED COMMAND AT LAST!

ON NOVEMBER 11, 1917, during the days between the Rapallo Conference in Italy and the first meeting of the Allied Supreme War Council,
First Quartermaster General Erich Ludendorff called a meeting of German General Staff officers at the town of Mons, Belgium. To an observer
accustomed to the military procedures of the Americans, British, or
French, the list of invitees to the conference would seem strange, because almost none of the top commanders of the German Army were in
attendance. The Kaiser was absent, as was Ludendorff's official superior,
Field Marshal Paul von Hindenburg. Even Prince Rupprecht of Bavaria,
commander of the northern group of armies, was absent, though the
meeting was being held in his own headquarters.

To the officers attending that meeting, however, its composition
conformed to the customs of the General Staff. Dedicated to maintaining
its own position, but faced with the propensity of the Kaiser to appoint
men of high position and influence to the large commands, the General
Staff settled for an arrangement whereby the Kaiser would appoint General Staff members as the chiefs of staff to the pretentious and lavishly
decorated titular commanders. By means of superior professionalism,
coupled with considerable tact and deference, the chiefs of staff could in
fact though not in name exert actual command of operations.[1]

Thus the list of men attending this meeting included Colonel Count
Friedrich von der Schulenberg, chief of staff to the Crown Prince; General Hermann von Kuhl, chief of staff to Prince Rupprecht; and such outstanding younger military brains as Lieutenant Colonel Georg Wetzel,
head of one of Ludendorff's staff sections.[2]

Ludendorff needed all the professional help he could get. Foremost in his mind was the question of Germany's plans for the military operations of the next year, 1918. A realist, he was aware that the Fatherland was now racing against time. True, the turmoil in Russia was such that he could count on moving divisions from the Eastern Front to the Western, but balanced against that advantage was the surprising buildup of American forces. The assumption that the U-boats could prevent the delivery of American troops had turned out to be false, and the number of Yanks in France would certainly grow dramatically. In short, Germany must win the war during the spring and the summer of 1918.

Having presented that line of reasoning to the assembled staff, Ludendorff solicited the opinion of every member present, regardless of rank. All spoke freely, confident that they were among a group in which they had already been accepted. All agreed independently that a great offensive must be launched. The question was, where?

Three sectors, Ludendorff later recorded, were considered as possibilities. One area was Flanders, the British zone, between Ypres and Lens. Another would be along the Somme River farther south, at the juncture between the British and French armies, specifically, between Arras and St. Quentin. A third area would be in the vicinity of Verdun, an area occupied solely by the French. To avoid a repetition of the costly and fruitless offensive of 1916, such an attack in this region would be made east of the Verdun fortress.

Whatever area was selected would have to promise decisive results as early as possible during the following summer. It would have to promise a reasonable chance of tactical success. By applying those criteria, Ludendorff and his lieutenants were able to narrow down the field.

Quickly they ruled out an attack against the British in Flanders. In the springtime, the dominating consideration would be the firmness of the ground to permit exploitation of success and resupply. In Flanders, around Ypres, the ground is virtually impassable until early summer. Verdun also was undesirable because of its hilly country and—far more important—even a huge success in that area would result in no appreciable strategic advantage.

That left only the option to attack on the Somme. That area would afford sufficient maneuver room to permit exploitation of tactical success without definite limit. "If this blow succeeded the strategic result might indeed be enormous," Ludendorff declared, "as we should cut the bulk of the English Army from the French, and crowd it up with its back to the sea."[3] At the end of the meeting, therefore, Ludendorff summed up his conclusions formally:

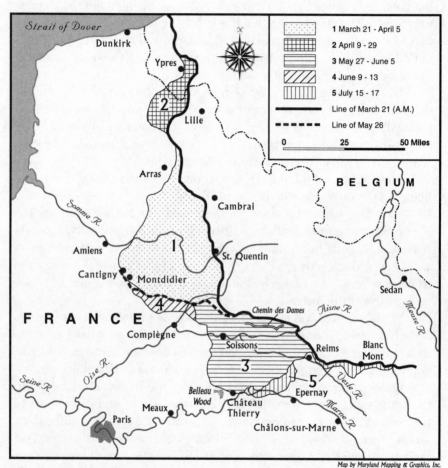

4. The Five Ludendorff Offensives.

Ludendorff's five offensives of the spring and summer of 1918 began on March 21 and continued until July 15. German failure to win the war by these offensives convinced him that, with the growing strength of the Americans, the war was lost.

The situation in Russia and Italy will, so far as can be seen, make it possible to deliver a blow on the Western Front in the New Year. The strength of the two sides will be approximately equal. About thirty-five divisions and one thousand heavy guns can be made available for *one* offensive; a second great simultaneous offensive will not be possible. Our general situation requires that we should strike at the earliest moment, if possible at the end of February or beginning of March, before the Americans can throw strong forces into the scale.

We must beat the British.[4]

The code name would be Michael.

LUDENDORFF'S PLANNING was, of course, dependent on assurances that the Russians would be knocked out of the war before early spring 1918. An impatient man, he was not content to sit by and await developments; he would take action to speed up the political process. In so doing Ludendorff was exceeding his purview as First Quartermaster General, but with some justification. A weak German government had placed him in a position to influence, if not dictate, overall governmental policy. A dramatic example of Ludendorff's political intrusions was his insisting that Kaiser Wilhelm initiate unrestricted submarine warfare early in February 1917.

Despite Ludendorff's demands, the peace negotiations between the Germans and Russians at Brest-Litovsk did not even begin until December 22, 1917, over six weeks after the meeting at Mons. Progress was going too slowly for Ludendorff's taste, and he blamed the German plenipotentiary at Brest-Litovsk, Secretary of State Richard von Kühlmann. Kühlmann, in Ludendorff's view, had underestimated the residual Russian will to resist the now overwhelming German military force. At the same time the plenipotentiary had appeared to be fearful of arousing the enemy's ill-will.[5] Early in January, therefore, Hindenburg and Ludendorff traveled to Berlin to urge Kühlmann in person to hasten the negotiations. They were disappointed; apparently the Kaiser had not inculcated the same sense of urgency in Kühlmann that the two generals felt.

Frustrated, Hindenburg and Ludendorff then secured an audience with the Kaiser himself. Perhaps overconfident of his position, Ludendorff spoke his mind bluntly, insisting that troops could not be moved away from the Eastern Front under existing conditions and that the negotiations must not be dragged out. The Kaiser, perhaps to his surprise, supported the peace negotiator, and Ludendorff was chagrined to learn that he had overstepped himself and "aroused the Emperor's disapproval."[6] Despite his overbearing ways, Ludendorff believed in the imperial system, and that rebuke came as a personal blow to him.

• • •

THE TREATY OF BREST-LITOVSK was signed on March 3, 1918, though only after some fighting had recommenced briefly in the middle of February.[7] Relieved, the First Quartermaster General was now free to move divisions to the Western Front.

Ludendorff did not wait for the conclusion of the treaty negotiations to begin training the troops that would participate in his great offensive. As this was to be Ludendorff's first offensive since he and Hindenburg had assumed command in the West,[8] he had a free mind to examine the tactics that had been employed up to this time. Quickly he concluded that the German Army needed a thorough revamping of its offensive methods, and he turned to the new "Hutier tactics."

General Oskar von Hutier, a cousin of Ludendorff's, had used, if not invented, the new tactics that now bore his name when his German Eighth Army had made a successful attack against the failing Russians during the previous September. He introduced several departures from previously accepted procedures. For one thing, the new tactics passed up the long artillery barrage, which customarily went on for several days, substituting a short but very severe preparation. A rolling barrage was to be followed closely by fourteen-man assault groups of *Sturmtruppen*— storm troopers—whose main weapons were not the time-honored rifles but light machine guns, automatic rifles, flame throwers, and light mortars. These assault groups were to thread their way between enemy strongpoints, leaving their reduction to following heavy units supported by attack aircraft.[9] Ludendorff decided to adopt these tactics, and all officers that could be spared from their other duties were sent to special schools to learn them.

In his memoirs, Ludendorff claims that he also studied the British tactics at the recent Battle of Cambrai, which Marshal Haig had launched under the immediate command of General Sir Julian Byng on November 20. At that battle a quarter million British soldiers had attacked the main German position along a six-mile front, their objective being to seize Cambrai itself. The action is best remembered as the first in which tanks were used in mass, a total of 324 British vehicles participating. The tanks made spectacular initial gains, breaking through the Hindenburg position on the first day.

In the final analysis, the British attack at Cambrai had been halted. There were several causes: the tanks broke down; the British were unprepared to exploit the unexpected success; the Germans resisted tenaciously; and time allowed the German commander, General Georg von der Marwitz, to bring in reinforcements. Since the attack had eventually been stopped, the lessons of the battle appear to have been lost on Ludendorff; the outcome caused him to underestimate the value of the new tank. His attitude stemmed partly from necessity, for Germany was far behind the Allies in the development of this new device. His requests that his units be provided with a certain number were never met; but, he smugly noted, "our attacks succeeded without them." Ludendorff was ahead of his time in one respect, however. Foreshadowing the German *panzer* divisions and the Allied armored divisions of the Second World War, he prophesied that "tanks are effective only in masses." [10]

With airplanes as well, Ludendorff was farseeing. Noting that airplanes had originally been intended only as an "auxiliary arm," he later wrote,

> these battle-flights were finally given important tactical tasks. Thus the air force gained a new field of activity of the greatest importance. The airmen, in the course of their duties, were not only reconnaissance troops who had to fight, they were not only bomb-carriers for destructive work far in the enemy's rear, but they had, like the infantry artillery, and all other arms, to take part in the fighting on the ground. Like the other combatant forces, they were a destructive arm in the great battle on land.[11]

Ludendorff also relied heavily on artillery, planning to support his storm troopers by firepower unprecedented even on the Western Front. Twenty to thirty batteries, about one hundred guns, were to be massed in spaces of only eleven hundred yards. "No man had ever credited such figures before," Ludendorff claimed, "still less had any one ever thought of the quantities of ammunition thrown upon the enemy." [12]

AT HIS HEADQUARTERS at St. Omer, British Field Marshal Sir Douglas Haig was well aware that Ludendorff was preparing an offensive; that view was shared by everyone. Haig did what he could to prepare, but he was very much concerned over whether he would be allowed to fight his own battle. The Supreme War Council, at Versailles, he feared, was going to tie his hands.

Haig had reason to be concerned. As originally conceived, the council was intended to be advisory only, without executive powers. When Colonel House had returned to Washington in mid-December 1917, he had no illusions as to its effectiveness in its current state of organization. "The Supreme War Council as presently constituted," he wrote the President, "is almost a farce." [13] French Premier Clemenceau and Prime Minister Lloyd George had come to the same conclusion, and they acted as if the Council enjoyed executive powers. They requested Haig to take several of his divisions out of the line and place them in general reserve, to be employed as directed from Versailles.

Haig resisted strongly. Such an action, he contended, would mean that those divisions would be employed by Foch, the French military representative. The British representative on the Council, Sir Henry Wilson, was personally hostile to Haig, and Haig believed Wilson was overly influenced by Foch. When Foch said the word, Haig wrote bitterly, Wilson would leap "like a lap dog." [14]

Haig finessed the Supreme War Council's "request" by acting on his own. He reached an understanding with his French counterpart, Henri Pétain, who also disliked the Council's decree, to provide each other with mutual support in case of any kind of emergency. Haig and Pétain had always worked well together, and Haig had recently consolidated their friendship by agreeing, albeit reluctantly, to take over twenty-five additional miles of front from the French. [15]

THE FRONT ALONG WHICH Ludendorff planned his Somme offensive ran generally north-northwest to south-southeast from the small town of Lens, near Cambrai, to the Oise River on the south. He planned to attack generally westward on a sixty-mile front, using three armies in the assault. His northern army would be the Seventeenth, commanded by Otto von Below, who had won such a spectacular victory at Caporetto the previous fall. In the center would be the Second, commanded by General von der Marwitz; on the left (south) would be the Eighteenth, commanded by Oskar von Hutier, who had been transferred from the Eastern to the Western Front. The objective was to strike at the British armies north of the Oise River and then, after penetrating the front lines, to wheel northward toward the British rear. If the attack proved to be successful, two Allied communications centers would fall—Arras, in the north, and Amiens, on the Somme, about fifty miles from the line of contact.

The main effort was to be made by Marwitz's Second Army, because the terrain along his front was the most favorable. Hutier's Eighteenth Army on the south would be impeded by the meandering Somme River, which looped in such a fashion that Hutier would be forced to cross it twice. The Second Army, on the other hand, had no obstacle in its path until it reached the Somme at Peronne, at which point the river turns abruptly westward. From there on Second Army could continue north of the Somme and wheel northward along good ground to Doullens. With

Doullens in German hands, Arras would be cut off from the rear. In the light of these terrain restrictions, Hutier's mission was limited to protecting Second Army's left flank.

Conceptually the first day's operations were to be directed tightly by higher headquarters. Once the enemy's positions were broken through, however, subordinate commanders would be on their own. The German Army, contrary to myth, was superb at decentralization.

Nothing had been left to chance. Ludendorff's total force consisted of 3,575,000 officers and men organized in 192 divisions. Sixty-nine of the 192 divisions were concentrated for the Michael attack, facing thirty-three British divisions, of which ten were out of the line in reserve.[16] German artillery pieces outnumbered British by two thousand heavy guns versus 976.[17] When the barrage began, 6,700 German guns, light and heavy, under the direction of Colonel Georg Bruchmüller, roared out along a forty-mile front between the Sensée River on the north and the Oise on the south.[18]

JUST BEFORE 5:00 A.M. on Thursday, March 21, 1918, the first units of Operation Michael jumped off.

The British front and back areas were deluged with poison gas shells. Though not all the Germans attacked at once, the whole front was moving forward by 10:00 A.M., protected from hostile observation by a dense fog. In many instances the German infantry hit the British positions before it had even been spotted. Both the outpost line and much of the forward zone were lost, though the British held on to the battle zone, the third defense line. The maximum German advance was eight thousand yards, but the British had no reserves with which to counterattack.[19]

At the end of the first day, Ludendorff decided to change his original plan. The reason was the unexpected success of Hutier's Eighteenth Army, on the south, which was hitting Sir Hubert Gough's Fifth British Army. Gough's men were occupying positions previously occupied by the French and he had been allowed insufficient time to organize them according to British doctrine. Furthermore, Gough's front was seriously overextended, and the heavy fog that covered the British front was especially thick on Gough's south flank along the banks of the Oise.

With long-range vision all but impossible, British gun positions, brigade headquarters, and telephone exchanges were soon of no use. Masses of German troops overran territory they had willingly given up and had denuded of trees and buildings in their previous withdrawal. Hutier's men had penetrated to a depth of nearly ten miles south of St. Quentin and the Somme. So successful was he, in fact, that his army captured some of the bridges over the Somme intact. In the north the penetrations were less spectacular, amounting to some three to five miles all along the front. Ludendorff accordingly decided to reinforce Hutier's success in the south, driving southwest across the Somme.

That night the Germans began to bring up their supplies and artillery for the next day's attack, while the British looked around to see what they had left. Though some of the bypassed British units were able to make their way back to their own lines, the situation was grave; British headquarters did not fully realize, at the close of that day, the extent of the damage their forces had incurred. Almost all of Gough's fifteen divisions had been destroyed as fighting units.[20]

ON THURSDAY, MARCH 21, the day that Ludendorff's attack was launched, General Pershing was just finishing his lengthy visit with Secretary of War Baker. The two had been invited to lunch by General Pétain, after which Baker planned to continue on to Field Marshal Haig's headquarters and from there leave for a trip to Britain. Unaware of any impending crisis, they took a staff car, bound for Compiègne. As the Americans approached Pétain's headquarters, however, they heard a loud roar above the noise of their automobile. No question about it; the roar came from massed artillery.

Pétain greeted his visitors cordially, and despite his obvious concern he kept the luncheon conversation light. Only after they finished eating did the French general brief his visitors on the situation of the war. In particular, he emphasized the informal arrangement he had made with Haig for the backup of the British in case of a major German attack. There was no doubt in Pétain's mind that that moment had come.[21]

Pershing returned to Paris after the meeting with Pétain and the next day, March 22, drove out to Versailles for a conference with Bliss. There he learned that the situation on Haig's front was even more serious than had been anticipated—the French government was rumored to be making preliminary plans to move to Bordeaux. To add to the panic, the Germans had set up a huge gun, with a range of seventy-five miles, and had begun lobbing shells into the streets of Paris.[22]

On Monday, March 25, Pershing motored back to Compiègne for another visit with Pétain, arriving there late in the evening. He was disturbed to observe that Pétain was a changed man, nervous and shaken. The impression was reinforced by the fact that Pétain had ordered his headquarters to prepare to move back to Chantilly. The British, Pétain told him, were admitting the loss of 150,000 men, and people were already leaving Paris.[23] It seemed to Pershing that Pétain no longer considered the informal accord he had made with Haig to be binding. The French general, Pershing thought, was now concerned almost exclusively with protecting Paris.

From Pétain's headquarters Pershing continued on to Haig's, where he found that the Field Marshal had reached the same conclusion regarding Pétain. The Frenchman, Haig believed, had abandoned any intention of honoring the agreement for mutual support in case of emergency. As the right flank of Sir Hubert Gough's Fifth British Army collapsed under the weight of the German attack, Pétain appeared to be deploying his newly arrived divisions facing northward, as if prepared to accept a rupture to develop between the two national forces. Haig now expected Pétain to do nothing more than set up a defensive line to protect his nation's capital.

Haig therefore took action. If he could not rely on Pétain, he would appeal to those in higher authority. On March 25, the day of Pershing's visit, he cabled London urgently requesting the Secretary of State for War, Lord Milner, to come to his headquarters at Doullens, accompanied by the chief of the Imperial General Staff, Sir Henry Wilson. At the same time he invited the high officials of the French government to join them. Both the British and French officials accepted.

ON MARCH 26, 1918, the British and French officials met at a conference that would turn out to be historic.[24] French President Raymond Poincaré chaired the meeting, but the men with the real power were Premier Clemenceau, Foch, and Pétain on the French side; and Milner, Haig, and Wilson on the British. The question was simple: what to do next?

Despite the rank and prestige of some of the visitors, it was Haig who took the initiative. Two important communications centers on his front had to be held, Arras in the north and Amiens in the south. Arras seemed to be in no immediate danger. There General Byng's Third British Army, well entrenched, was expected to hold. The critical issue was the fate of Amiens, on the Somme, almost on the boundary between the French and British forces. Since General Gough's Fifth British Army had crumbled in that area, Haig desperately needed Pétain to come to his assistance. Pétain demurred, remarking that the Germans would beat the British in an open battle and intimating that he would be content if Amiens itself could be saved. He was, in fact, concentrating on the railroad junction at Amiens at that moment.[25] At that exchange, Foch sided with Haig: "We must fight in front of Amiens. We must stop them where we are now."

That was enough for Haig. "If General Foch will give me his advice," he said, "I will gladly follow it."[26] Haig had been the strongest opponent of a French Commander-in-Chief for the Western Front, but with these words he had opened the door for the appointment of a Supreme Commander.

The others felt the same way. By the end of the day, the conferees from the two nations had agreed to a formula drawn up by Clemenceau:

> General Foch is charged by the British and French Governments with the co-ordination of the action of the Allied Armies on the Western Front. He will make arrangements to this effect with the two Generals-in-Chief, who are invited to furnish him with the necessary information.[27]

The French and British had attained unified command at last.

CHAPTER TEN

"I WILL NOT BE COERCED"

THE AGREEMENT to appoint Ferdinand Foch as Supreme Commander, made at Doullens, was highly significant, but time and circumstances had precluded the inclusion of the Americans in the structure of Foch's new command. Within days, however, that matter was cleared up. Pershing had been a strong advocate of a single command from the beginning. Securing President Wilson's agreement to place his force under Foch was never in doubt.

The extent of Foch's authority, however, was never well defined. It was one thing to grant Foch authority for tactical coordination; it was another to give him a say regarding Pershing's plans for an integrated American army. In that sphere, Pershing was far from docile. He was therefore disturbed when he received an ominous message from Newton Baker reporting on his meeting with the British Prime Minister on March 25:

> [Lloyd George] urges three proposals for your consideration; First, that our divisions in France be placed immediately in line to relieve French divisions for service elsewhere. . . . Second, that all available engineers troops be taken from Lines of Communication work and sent to the aid of British engineers preparing positions back of present line. Third, that infantry be sent first of the entire six divisions to be transported by the British. . . . We leave here tomorrow, Tuesday, at 7:30, for Paris.[1]

The Welshman never missed an opportunity! At least Pershing would be able to confer directly with Baker the next day. This new development had caused Baker to return to Paris.

On Tuesday evening, March 26, Pershing drove to the railroad station in Paris to meet the returning Secretary. While waiting for the train to pull in, he witnessed a scene that he described as "pathetic." Terror-stricken crowds from the French countryside were fleeing through Paris, many without knowing where they were heading. Pershing noted that this was the second time these people had been through this experience—the first had been four years earlier. He was touched, as he wrote later:

> War in its effects upon the armies themselves is frightful enough, but the terror and suffering that it causes women and children are incomparably worse. These thousands were leaving everything behind them, going to some distant part of their country to become, many of them, dependent upon their friends, others, perchance friendless and penniless, to live by charity as a burden to the community or to beg from door to door.[2]

That was as much philosophy as Black Jack Pershing could allow himself.

The following day, Wednesday, March 27, Pershing underwent a test of wills not only with his allies but with his fellow American officials. He was aware that Secretary Baker, in London, had been subjected to a great deal of attention from Lloyd George, still intent on getting American infantry assigned to British divisions. Tasker Bliss, aware that this would be the subject of the day's meeting of the Supreme War Council, invited Pershing to attend, and Pershing readily agreed.

The meeting convened in the Council Room at Versailles at 3:00 P.M. The atmosphere was gloomy; only the day before, General Pétain had issued a directive defining the mission of the French Reserve Army Group as to "close the route to Paris to the Germans and to cover Amiens," adding that this order "countermanded all previous instructions." That was hardly an optimistic backdrop.[3]

The purpose of this meeting, however, was long-range, and it is difficult to see how its results could have affected the current battle raging on the Somme. Under consideration—or reconsideration—was a proposal submitted by British General Henry Rawlinson, doubtless at the behest of the Prime Minister, that shipments of American troops to France be limited to infantry and machine gun units, to be incorporated into British divisions.

Pershing stated his position forcefully. The question, he insisted, had supposedly been settled in early 1918, with the so-called Six-Division Plan, agreed to between the British Secretary of State for War, Lord Milner, and Pershing. British shipping would carry six American divisions (150,000 men) to France, ninety thousand of them infantry; the rest would be artillery, engineers, and such other troops as to constitute rounded divisions.[4] The British proposal would involve the shipment of only infantry, something Pershing was not ready to commit himself or his government to do. In view of the present emergency, however, he would agree that the infantry of the six divisions be shipped first, regardless of divisional organization, but that the artillery, engineers, and other troops be sent over as soon as possible and, reunited with their infantry, constituted into divisions. This arrangement had been followed with the French, and Pershing called it "the safest and most rational plan."[5]

After some discussion, Pershing left the meeting. At that point Tasker Bliss, in an uncommon reversal of his usual uncompromising support of Pershing, said, "General Pershing has expressed only his personal opinion, and it is the military representatives who must make the decision." He then submitted a draft proposal that was essentially the same as the Rawlinson proposal, adding only that American infantry assigned to British units should come from troops delivered from the United States, not from those divisions serving already with the French. It was adopted as Collective (Joint) Note No. 18 at once.[6]

On the next day, March 28, Pershing and Baker received the shocking word of the Supreme War Council's Joint Note. Pershing was furious, and his irritation was doubled by the knowledge that Tasker Bliss had participated in it. The resolution was intended, Pershing believed, "to put the weight of the Supreme War Council behind the idea of maintaining Allied units by American replacements as a policy."[7]

Baker called Pershing and Bliss to discuss the problem. At the end, Baker sent a message to President Wilson. He supported giving "preferential transportation to American infantry and machine gun units in the present emergency," but he urged that Wilson add an amendment, saying that "such units . . . will be under the direction of the Commander-in-Chief of the American Expeditionary Forces and will be assigned for training and use by him in his discretion . . . in such a manner as to render the greatest military assistance, keeping in mind always the determination of this Government to have its various military forces collected, as speedily as their training and the military situation will permit, into an independent American army."[8]

Pershing could live with that arrangement—or at least he knew when he was beaten. Perhaps the seriousness of the situation had been imprinted on him. Whatever the reason, he was seized by an impulse, and on that same day he left Paris for Clermont-sur-Oise to see Foch in person.

Pershing and his aide made their way through the heavy truck traffic and found the pleasant French farmhouse that Foch was using for his headquarters. As he waited under a blooming cherry tree for Foch to appear, Pershing lapsed into one of his occasional contemplative moods. The place, he noted, was "quaintly picturesque and quiet, entirely undisturbed by the sound or sight of anything suggestive of war. Yet only a few miles to the northeast the French were at that moment making a furious counterattack against the enemy at Montdidier in one of the critical battles of the war."[9] At last he was invited to enter the farmhouse.

Clemenceau, Pétain, and other French officials were already there, being briefed on the current situation, which was improving slightly. The British had used thirty divisions and the French seventeen to stem the German onslaught of some seventy-eight, and by now it appeared that the British Fifth Army was getting back on its feet and that the lines would hold for the time being.

Pershing had not come for that conference, however, and when he asked to be alone with Foch, the others courteously withdrew to the yard. To Foch Pershing spoke his piece. The Americans, he said, were "ready and anxious to do their part in this crisis," adding that he was soliciting suggestions as to how they might help. Foch, visibly touched, took him by the arm out into the yard so all could hear. In halting French, Pershing made his dramatic announcement:

> I have come to tell you that the American people would consider it a great honor for our troops to be engaged in the present battle. I ask you for this in their name and my own.
>
> At this moment there are no other questions but of fighting. Infantry, artillery, aviation, all that we have is yours; use them as you wish. More will come, in numbers equal to the requirements.[10]

PERSHING'S DRAMATIC DECLARATION gave a great lift to everyone, especially the beleaguered French and British. It was doubtless a sincere offer, if impulsive, but it was primarily a gesture. By no means could it make an immediate contribution to the crisis facing the Allies on the Somme. Of the six divisions that Pershing had in France at that time, only the 1st was considered battleworthy. The Big Red One would be committed soon, but the presence of that single division would hardly turn the tide. The real issue, completely unresolved, had to do with those divisions yet to come.

To British Prime Minister David Lloyd George, these were subjects of a political, not a military nature, and he never let up in his ongoing appeal to President Wilson to ignore the views and recommendations of Pershing. He continued to urge sending American infantry and machine gun units to fill the vacancies in the British formations. The latest of these appeals had been made as recently as March 23, two days after the launching of Ludendorff's offensive, when the British ambassador in Washington, Lord Reading, paid a personal call on Wilson to urge him to "drop all questions of interpretation of past agreements and send over infantry as fast as possible." The situation was so critical, the British insisted, that "if America delays it may be too late." American troops should be brigaded with British and French troops. There was no time to wait while larger American formations were organized.

At that time Wilson appeared to agree. At the end of the meeting, he showed Reading to the door, placed his hand on the ambassador's shoulder, and said, "Mr. Ambassador, I'll do my damnedest." [11]

AT THE TIME of Pershing's offer to Foch, the first Ludendorff offensive had largely run its course. The Allies were now afforded the breathing space they needed to straighten out a matter of utmost importance, the specific powers entrusted to General Ferdinand Foch as Allied Supreme Commander. The agreement at Doullens had been too general—and had made no mention of the Americans. To iron out these essential details, the Supreme War Council met on April 3, 1918, at Beauvais, a small town forty-five miles north of Paris. Both Lloyd George and Clemenceau were present, along with their generals; the Americans were represented by Tasker Bliss. Pershing was invited to attend also.

Clemenceau, as chairman, opened the meeting and announced that its purpose was to "settle a very simple question" regarding the functions of General Foch. On the Premier's request, Foch explained that the powers conferred by the Doullens conference had been limited to coordination of the Allies while the action was on. It had been construed, he continued, to be "limited to the time the Allies were in action." Since the German offensive had now come to a halt, there was "nothing to coordinate." He requested authority to prepare for action and direct it. [12]

For once Lloyd George and Pershing were in accord. When Pershing made an eloquent plea for complete unity of command, the Prime Minister actually came over and shook his hand. Haig and Pétain, while unenthusiastic, agreed "in principle."

There was only one testy moment. Pershing insisted that the Doullens agreement, now strengthened by the Beauvais agreement, include the American army as well as the British and French. Pétain, possibly irritated by Pershing's aggressiveness, sniffed, "There is no American army as such, as its units are either in training or are amalgamated with the British and French."

Pétain had touched Pershing's raw nerve. Quickly he responded,

> There may not be an American army in force functioning now but there
> soon will be, and I want this resolution to apply to it when it becomes a fact.
> The American Government is represented here at this conference and in
> the war, and any action as to the supreme command that includes the
> British and French armies should also include the American Army.

There was really no problem. The Beauvais agreement, "confid-
ing in General Foch the strategic direction of military operations,"
was signed by all three nations. One important caveat was included,
however:

> The Commanders-in-Chief of the British, French, and American Armies
> will exercise to the fullest extent the tactical direction of their armies. Each
> Commander-in-Chief will have the right to appeal to his Government, if in
> his opinion his Army is placed in danger by the instructions received from
> General Foch.[13]

PERSHING HAD EVERY REASON to feel satisfied with that outcome. His
respite from problems regarding his command was short-lived, however.
On April 7, a War Department cable informed him of the Wilson-
Reading meeting that had taken place two weeks earlier. Since Wilson
had not informed the War Department of the outcome, the Americans
had learned of it only indirectly, through British shipping channels. It
came up with new numbers: it now assumed the American bottoms could
carry 52,000 troops a month, that the British could carry 60,000, and that
other sources, including Dutch, could carry an additional 8,000. That
added up neatly to 120,000 troops per month, but its wording seemed
suspiciously slanted. Lord Reading, it said, had "approached" the President about approving the dispatch of 120,000 infantry per month to Europe between now and July, all infantry and machine gun units. These
men were to be brigaded with British and French divisions. The outcome
of the recent controversy was therefore overridden. It ended with a
meaningless statement: "The President agrees that all possible measures
must be taken to insure maximum use of troop tonnage."[14]

Pershing and Baker were taken aback. How authoritative was this
message? Though it did not specify that Wilson had actually agreed to the
numbers proposed by Reading, the implication was clear that he had.
Furthermore, the message did not deal with the actual allocation of the
120,000 troops that were to be sent per month. It went far beyond any-

thing that had transpired before. The total numbers, from April through July, would come to 480,000 men; the previous agreements had dealt only with the composition of the first six divisions, or 180,000. To add to their chagrin, a visitor from the British War Office arrived at Chaumont with further details of the British interpretation of the Wilson-Reading meeting, which pictured Wilson as having approved the Joint Note No. 18 without Baker's caveat. Since the joint note "wipe[d] out all previous agreements,"[15] the British claimed, the only remaining question was the proportion of the American troops that should go to the British, French, and Americans, mentioned in that order.

Pershing was now thoroughly alarmed, but Baker, who was as unaware of the attitude of Wilson as he, backed him all the way. He did not want, Baker declared, for the British to get an exaggerated idea that this scheme provided a means by which their losses will be made up in the future. He went on to add, "I want no feeling of disillusionment when General Pershing calls for the troops entrusted to them for training."[16]

As a result of this understanding, the two Americans decided that sixty thousand American infantry and machine gun units should be brought over by the British in April and then should go to the British for training. However, the disposition of any troops other than those sixty thousand would be left for future decision—by Pershing.

The British swallowed this dictum but were disappointed, with much reason from their viewpoint. In order to provide half of the shipping for the movement of American troops, they were forgoing large cargoes of foodstuffs and raw materials, causing the British government to lower the rations of the civil population to "something not far above the starvation level."[17]

ON APRIL 9, 1918, German General Erich Ludendorff launched his second major offensive, this time in Flanders. Two German armies, the Fourth in the north and the Sixth in the south, hit the British lines on a thirty-mile front between Givenchy and Wytschaete. The town of Armentières, famous in song, fell on the first day, and a Polish division in the path of the Sixth Army on the south was virtually destroyed. The objective this time—no doubt about it—was to destroy the British Army in France, not just to separate it from the French. Sir Douglas Haig, in a dark hour, issued his famous "back to the wall" message the next day:

There is no other course open to us but to fight it out. Every position must be held to the last man. There must be no retirement. With our backs to the wall and believing in the justice of our cause each one must fight on to the end. The safety of our home and the freedom of mankind alike depend upon the conduct of each one of us at this critical moment.[18]

Haig's dramatic rhetoric, his most noted communication, may have inspired his troops to extraordinary efforts, but events proved the situation to be less serious than his wording implied. Ludendorff's army, like Haig's, was suffering from heavy losses, and though the offensive gained about twenty miles at its deepest, the British were able to defend successfully behind the Ypres Canal in the north and the Aire Canal in the south.

Yet the Allied leaders remained deeply concerned. Ludendorff, they reasoned, still had more resources to throw at them, and their reaction, as before, was to renew their demand for American battalions to bolster their thinned-out ranks. Accordingly, the Supreme War Council met at Abbeville on May 1, 1918, supposedly to discuss the shipment of American troops to France. Unexpectedly, it wound up as a test of the power of General Ferdinand Foch as generalissimo.

Foch's actual powers still remained vague, even after the Americans had joined in accepting him as their General-in-Chief at the Beauvais conference of early April. A vain, ambitious, but very capable man, Foch was determined to establish his authority in terms as broad as possible.[19] Did his purview extend only to the tactical coordination of national forces, or did it give him a right to intrude in the very composition of the national forces themselves?

Foch inserted himself into more than the coordination of Allied and American troop units, joining in the debate over the shipment of American troops and their disposal after their arrival in France. He did, in fact, go further than anyone had gone before, insisting that only American infantry and machine gun units would be shipped from the United States for a period of four whole months. (Despite the questionable interpretation of the Wilson-Reading meeting, all previous signed arrangements had applied solely to shipments for the month of May.)

At the outset, Prime Minister Clemenceau targeted in on the old six-division agreement, pointing out that it had been negotiated solely between the Americans and the British. The French, he complained, had not been consulted as to the disposition of the 120,000 men who were to be shipped over every month. He was not protesting the British-American arrangement for the month of May, he claimed, but he wished to receive the same number in June as the British had received in May. Lord Milner, who was speaking for the British, claimed that no allocation of American troops had been made for any month after May.

Pershing, predictably, disputed the assumptions of both the political leaders. He emphasized that no agreement currently existed "between [the American] government and anybody else that a single American soldier shall be sent to either the British or the French." But, he continued,

> There is in existence an agreement between Mr. Lloyd George and myself that six divisions shall be brought to France. Mr. Clemenceau will remember that I spoke to him about going to London to arrange for the shipment of American troops to France and that he approved.[20]

Clemenceau ignored the inconvenient fact that he had acceded to Pershing's consulting with Milner alone and now fell back on Foch's newly established authority. "The appointment of General Foch as Commander-in-Chief is not a mere decoration. . . . This post involves great responsibilities; he must meet the present situation; he must provide for the future. I accept what has been done for May, but I want to know what is intended for June."[21]

The complexion of the meeting had now changed. What had started out as primarily a quarrel between the French and British over their respective share of newly arriving American troops had become something larger, even more fundamental to the Americans. Pershing was now protesting in strong terms against the idea that any American troops at all would be assigned to either French or British formations. He insisted that such a scheme would delay, if not destroy, his chance for attaining his goal of a separate American army.

The French and British now closed ranks. Lloyd George, Clemenceau, and Foch all pleaded with Pershing to extend the troop transportation arrangements for May into June. Pershing fended them off, saying that he did not consider it necessary to make that decision at that meeting. Finally, Clemenceau played his trump. He called once more on Foch. In an impressive manner, the generalissimo declared,

> I am Commander-in-Chief of the Allied Armies in France and my appointment has been sanctioned not only by the British and French Governments, but by the President of the United States. Hence it is my duty to insist on my point of view. There is a program signed by Lord Milner and General Pershing at London. I ask to be made a party to this arrangement. If the Supreme Commander has nothing to say regarding such conventions, I should not hold the position.

Pershing was unimpressed. Foch's authority, he insisted, did not include the right to dictate arrangements regarding shipping of American troops. Foch, as he saw it, had been "put forward to force the kind of agreement they wanted." The French and British were ready to go, he concluded, "to any length to carry their point."[22]

And to some extent they were. The recriminations came to a climax when Foch presented his case in direct terms: "Are you willing to risk our being driven back to the Loire?" he asked.

"Yes," Pershing answered. "I am willing to take that risk."

The lines were drawn. Three Prime Ministers, one Chief of the Imperial British General Staff, and the Allied Commander-in-Chief leveled their fire on the lone General Pershing, using "all the force and prestige of their high positions." When they finally finished, Pershing pounded the table and announced, "Gentlemen, I have thought this program over very deliberately and will not be coerced." [23]

FORTUNATELY, time had been allotted for two days of meeting, and the meeting did not end on such a dramatic note. When the Supreme War Council met again the next day, both sides gave a little. The British somehow found shipping space to carry more than 120,000 American soldiers per month. They could find shipping space for another fifty thousand men, thus meeting with Pershing's requirements. Pershing therefore agreed that 120,000 American infantrymen and machine gunners could be sent, and he could use the additional fifty thousand spaces to bring the auxiliary troops he needed to round out the divisions he was forming. Everyone was satisfied.

As the political leaders and the generals prepared to leave Abbeville, General Foch, always generous, said to Pershing, *"Mon Général, nous sommes toujours d'accord."* [24]

Pershing appreciated this generous statement of goodwill, unrealistic as it was. But he knew that, despite the moment of euphoria, the issue of American troop deployment was far from settled.

CHAPTER ELEVEN

THE BIG RED ONE
AT CANTIGNY

BY MID-APRIL 1918, the time had come to commit American troops to battle in large numbers. All the heated discussions regarding possible "amalgamation" of United States forces into those of the French and British had centered on the Americans who would arrive in the future. All were agreed that the American divisions now training in France must soon enter the battle in full force. Pershing insisted that they do so as full American divisions, though of course assigned to the commands of French armies and corps.

After Pershing's dramatic offer of United States divisions at Clermont-sur-Oise in late March, he and Pétain conferred as to how to implement it. The 1st Division, they agreed, should be the one first committed, as it was the only division Pershing considered completely trained. The prerogative of selecting an area for the division's employment, however, fell within Pétain's purview, and he chose the sector of Montdidier, in Picardy, north of Paris, on the line where Ludendorff's First Offensive (Michael) had been stopped. The Big Red One, currently in the Anseauville sector, was replaced in April by the 26th Division, previously situated on the Chemin des Dames.[1]

The troops of the 1st Division, once out of the line, assembled in the vicinity of Toul,[2] and were soon on the road for their assembly area at Chaumont-en-Vexin, northwest of Paris. Most of the infantry traveled in the familiar forty-and-eight boxcars, and closed into the so-called Gisors area by April 8. The division was temporarily assigned to the French Fifth Army.[3]

On April 16, General Pershing drove out from Paris to speak to the men of the division as they were preparing to move up to the battle zone. He was happy to find the division commander, Robert Lee Bullard, largely recovered from an acute case of neuritis that had taken him away from duty for several days. He was surprised, however, at the extent of Bullard's rage against Major General Clarence Edwards, who commanded the 26th Division. The reason was Edwards's critical and uncooperative attitude in the recent relief.

Bullard's neuritis was probably unrelated to his anger against Edwards, but he had ample cause for complaint. Under the best of conditions, a relief under enemy fire is a difficult and risky operation, but this relief was more trying than necessary because Edwards made it so. Edwards was known by all to be difficult, and he lived up to his reputation. He had found fault with everything he saw, despite Bullard's extraordinary efforts to be unusually helpful and generous as his men turned over their sectors to their successors.[4]

By customary Army procedure, Bullard and his staff would have been required to answer each of Edwards's allegations one by one. Pershing, however, put that issue to rest at once. No admirer of Edwards himself, he simply said, "Drop it; don't spend your time on it."[5] For Bullard, that reassurance was enough.

Pershing, aware that the 1st Division would move out for the Montdidier area the next day, made sure to impress on the officers and men of the division how important was the task that lay ahead. After asking that all non-American officers be removed from the scene, he spoke to a representative group of officers and men. He was not an eloquent speaker, and Bullard noted his halting manner—full of "eh, eh, eh's." What he had to say, however, was serious:

> You are now to go against a victorious enemy under new and harder conditions. All our Allies will be watching to see how you conduct yourselves. I am confident that you will meet their best hope.[6]

The backdrop of Pershing's words of warning was General Erich Ludendorff's Second Great Offensive, still being conducted against the British between Ypres and Lens. Obviously, the 320,000 Americans in France could do little to help, especially since a third of them were assigned to duties with the Services of Supply. But with the danger that the British and French might be overcome, Marshal Foch and General Pétain had to make use of all resources available. This mission would be neither a training period nor window dressing. The 1st Division was now in serious combat.

• • •

THE 1ST DIVISION moved into position at Montdidier during the night of April 24, 1918, and by two days later had assumed complete charge of the area. Because of its size, it was relieving two French divisions, one of them a colonial division that had been badly mauled in the previous weeks of fighting. General Bullard was happy to be serving in the army of French General Marie Eugène Debeney, whom he regarded as a personal friend.[7] The French corps commander, General Vandenberg, Bullard described as "an older and very broken officer, but a fine soldier. . . . He had been shot in the leg and could hardly walk, and in the mouth and could hardly talk; but he was always very active and constructive. His earnestness, patience, and consideration obtained from Americans a prompt and willing response."[8]

It was well that the Americans found themselves in a harmonious atmosphere with their French allies, because they were facing tasks that would have been difficult for even the most experienced veterans. Since the Montdidier position had been occupied only very recently, it lacked those usual safety features that had been developed to minimize casualties from German artillery. The newly arrived Americans needed to dig communications trenches from the rear areas to the front lines, all the time exposed to German observation. The enemy's ability to take any moving target under controlled artillery fire made construction nearly impossible in daylight. Even when work was limited to hours of darkness, incoming shells resulted in a significant daily casualty list.

George Marshall, now a lieutenant colonel and still the G-3 of the division, was puzzled by the abnormally heavy volume of artillery fire going on between the two sides, considering that no infantry attack was under way. He was soon given an answer. The French, he was told, were responsible; their units in that sector had been so reduced by casualties that they had been relying on a continual, heavy artillery fire to discourage German probes.[9] It was only partly true. What the French and Americans did not realize was that Ludendorff was actually feeling out the lines. The German commander was seriously contemplating a continuation of his first offensive, Michael, westward through that area.

Marshall, as divisional chief of operations, felt a special need to familiarize himself with the terrain the division was occupying. But since daylight hours were dangerous for poking around within sight of the enemy, he hit upon a scheme to make such activities possible without excessive risk. His daily schedule would call for him to depart division headquarters at Ménil-St. Fermin at one o'clock in the morning and drive forward for about a mile. He would then leave his chauffeur hiding in a shell hole while he went forward and picked up a guide from whatever unit he was inspecting. After checking up on the dispositions of troops, which he could do in the darkness, he timed his arrival at the actual front to fall between dawn and sunrise. If he delayed until after sunrise, he would be forced to remain in a shell hole or a foxhole until darkness that evening would make it reasonably safe to return.[10]

It did not take long before General Bullard began to itch for some operation more active than mere defense, and he began urging General Vandenberg and General Debeney to give his division an offensive mission. His light and medium artillery had overcome their German counterparts, he claimed, and his men had gained the upper hand over the Germans.[11] Only in the use of poison gas were the Americans deficient. On May 7, Colonel Frank Parker, commanding the 18th Infantry, reported that the enemy had bombarded the village of Villers-Tournelle with both gas and high-explosive shells at a rate of fifty to one hundred a minute.[12] As a result, five hundred men of Parker's subsector had been evacuated as gas casualties. Spurred to action by that report, Bullard began to emphasize gas warfare, much as he disliked it in principle. Soon he felt that the Americans were catching up and, as Bullard put it, "we made [the Germans] also smell mustard."[13]

Early in May, after the division had been in the line for a week, General Bullard received orders to begin preparing to attack the heights extending to the north from Montdidier. The purpose of the attack would be to distract the Germans, who were expected to launch a new attack toward the Channel ports in the near future. The timing was to depend on the date that the expected Ludendorff offensive began. The 1st Division was to play the leading role, with a French division on either flank, and this operation was to signal a general attack by the entire Third French Army. Orders soon went out specifying the role to be played by each brigade and regiment, and work was redoubled in constructing the communications trenches to protect the telephone wires of the front line units.

This operation was being prepared on the assumption that the Germans would begin their new Flanders attack on the 18th of May. However, as that date approached, Allied intelligence services failed to pick up any evidence that it would actually occur. The French-American operation was therefore canceled.

The cancellation was disappointing to Bullard, and was disappointing to his superiors as well. The next day, May 19, General Pershing drove from Paris to Chantilly for the purpose of consulting with General Pétain on the prospect of assembling American divisions to form a separate

American army. Pétain was occupying a commodious private house in the forest, near that previously occupied by Marshal Joseph Joffre earlier in the war. As with his recent visit to Foch's headquarters, Pershing was struck by the beauty and quiet of the surroundings. They seemed, he mused with a touch of irony, to be "nature's protest against the horrors and other scenes of daily occurrence."[14]

If the surroundings were serene, however, Pétain was not. He refused to entertain Pershing's request; instead he came back with one of his own. His twenty-five French divisions, he said, needed reinforcement badly in order to maintain their numbers and their strength. Each needed two American infantry battalions, for a total of fifty. Furthermore, he wished these American battalions to remain with his French divisions until October! Pershing made a quick calculation and saw that acceding to Pétain's wishes would entail breaking up at least four American divisions, each of which could provide twelve battalions. This he considered completely unacceptable.

The two men did agree on one matter, however: that the Americans should make their presence felt on the Western Front by launching an attack—not merely a defense. The logical thing would be for the U.S. 1st Division to make an attack to straighten out the Montdidier salient by taking the town of Cantigny.[15] This would be a completely American operation, not part of an overall French offensive.

In view of the fact that the Americans were still inexperienced, Pétain and Pershing agreed that the objective should be an extremely limited one. It was to be conducted on a narrow front—narrow enough, in fact, that it would have to be executed by only a single infantry regiment. Informed of these conditions, General Bullard selected the 28th Infantry, of Colonel Beaumont B. Buck's 2d Brigade. The 28th was a logical choice, since it had recently relieved the 18th in the line facing Cantigny and was therefore familiar with the terrain. It was commanded by Colonel Hanson E. Ely, the division's hard-driving former chief of staff, in whom Bullard had complete confidence.

Even in a division whose roster of officers included many of the Army's select, Ely was considered a formidable warrior. A quarter century earlier, at six foot two and 220 pounds,[16] he had been one of West Point's first football players, and since then had lost none of his drive and stamina. He was also ambitious, and he had hounded Bullard to release him from the dead-end position of chief of staff and reassign him to a post where he could fight, receive recognition, and earn promotion. Ely was the man for a difficult assignment.

Ely attacked his new challenge with his usual energy. He had much to accomplish in the two weeks he had left to prepare his attack. When he received his orders, the 28th was in the line, and his first priority was to prepare new communications lines, since those that had been laid in preparation for the Montdidier attack would be of no use to men headed in a different direction. Again the men worked under cover of darkness, trying at the same time to avoid giving German intelligence convincing evidence of what was afoot.

Even more important, however, was the matter of instructing his troops in the tasks they were to perform in the attack. To facilitate that, Bullard relieved the 28th from its front line positions about a week before the attack and sent it to a training area in the rear. There, on ground similar to that which the regiment would cover in the actual attack, Ely trained his officers and men to follow a rolling barrage, which moved forward a hundred yards every four minutes. The shells were represented by men carrying tree branches. He stressed methods for keeping direction and rate of march and rehearsed the actions they would take once the objective had been seized—how they would quickly consolidate their new position to withstand the inevitable German counterattacks. On the last day of rehearsal, Ely included flame throwers with the front line units so that troops unfamiliar with that weapon would become accustomed to it. By the time they were finished, Ely seemed satisfied."[17]

From prisoners captured by advance patrols, Ely learned that he would be facing two German regiments, the 271st and the 272d, both regular German reserve units considered to be above average in quality. Their companies were down to only about 160 men each, which meant that the men of the 28th would be facing approximately equal numbers.[18] Lacking any appreciable preponderance in infantry strength, Ely therefore depended heavily on overwhelming fires and surprise. He was not disappointed, for the French were generous in providing an unusual degree of support: 250 artillery pieces, including some of large, 280mm caliber. He also had attached to him a group of twelve French tanks, a platoon of flame throwers, Company D, 1st Engineers, and certain aviation units.[19] The plan called for fire to open as of daylight to one hour before the jump-off, to allow registration and to cause damage to the German positions without giving away American intentions.

Two nights before the attack, a young engineer lieutenant, Oliver J. Kendall, went forward on a routine mission to distribute heavy intrenching tools along the front lines to a working party of fifty infantrymen. Unfortunately, he became lost in the dark and walked into a party of about ten Germans. An infantry lieutenant nearby succeeded in extricating almost all the engineers except Kendall himself, who was reported missing in action, together with all the engineer equipment. The incident caused the staff of the 1st Division considerable anguish. Kendall's probable fate was tragic enough—his body was found in a shallow grave after the war, his throat cut—but the fear was that his capture would telegraph American plans to the Germans. Kendall was known to have been carrying maps showing the troop dispositions to guide him in his mission. Quite possibly this episode could alert the Germans to the impending attack.[20]

ON THE MORNING of May 27, 1918, the eve of the planned Cantigny attack, a new development changed the tactical outlook dramatically. Erich Ludendorff launched his Third Great Offensive to win the war in 1918. In contrast to his other two, which had been directed toward damaging the French and possibly eliminating the British as a fighting force, this offensive was launched southward from the Chemin des Dames toward the Marne River. If successful, it could eventually threaten Paris, much as the first German drive had done in 1914. Pétain, justifiably alarmed, determined to concentrate all possible forces to meet it. Those forces understandably included the heavy artillery assigned to support the 1st Division attack on Cantigny. Most of the French artillery supporting Ely could remain for the duration of the attack itself, but it would then have to leave immediately.

This turn of events could very well have justified a cancellation of the attack on Cantigny, and arguably that was what should have been done. Even presuming that the attack was successful in seizing the town, the troops in that exposed position, lacking the support of the heavy pieces needed to suppress German artillery fire, would be subject to unmerciful retaliation while holding the position. General Pershing, however, insisted on sticking with his plan. It would go ahead, and the doughboys of the 28th Infantry would pay dearly.

Ely and his men moved into the front lines on schedule the evening of May 27, 1918. Because of their previous occupation of the sector, they were familiar with the ground. It was a compact area, only about fifteen hundred yards wide, about the same distance as that between the current front line and Ely's final objective, a few hundred yards beyond the town of Cantigny itself. As always in the attack, the various command posts were located well forward. Ely himself had taken position in a hole a couple of hundred yards southeast of the small Bois St. Elois, a patch of woods in the northern part of the sector and only about six hundred yards behind the front. Bullard took station in a basement in the ruined town of Villers-Tournelle, itself only a half mile from the front.

The direction of attack was almost due eastward. On Ely's left

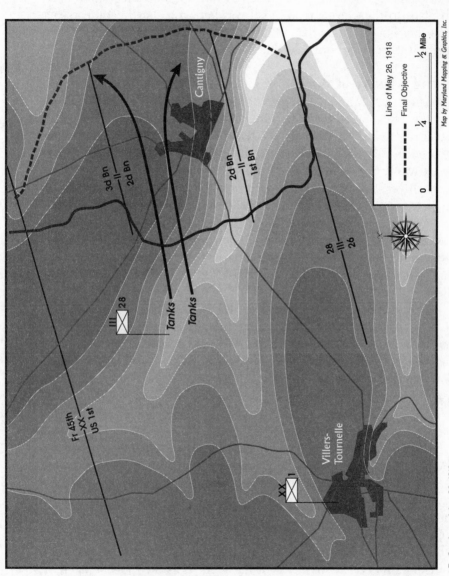

5. Cantigny, May 28, 1918.

Cantigny was a small battle involving only a single regiment, the 28th, of the 1st Division. Though the objective was seized easily, American casualties resulting from heavy German artillery fire were fearsome. The action was justified only for its morale effect, proving American capabilities in the attack

Map by Maryland Mapping & Graphics, Inc.

(north) flank was the French 45th Division, and on his right was the American 26th Infantry. The terrain his left was crossing was a fairly level, grassy plain between the American position and the village, but a sharp ravine a little farther to the south broke the level of the plain and extended around the southern portion of the town of Cantigny.[21]

The chain of command was awkward—a single line going from a regimental commander to a brigade commander to a division commander. That, of course, was brought about because only one of the division's four regiments was being employed. Other regiments would lend support, however. The 26th Infantry, to the south, was so located that its regimental commander, Colonel Hamilton Smith, could often see what was transpiring better than could Ely. The result was a collection of reports coming into division headquarters from all directions, though the operation was Ely's and Ely's alone.

Ely's scheme of attack was designed for a quick, violent charge, reflecting his confidence in quick success. To attain maximum speed in reaching the objective, he employed all three of his battalions abreast, holding out no major regimental reserve for maneuver in case of heavy resistance. Ely directed each battalion to employ three companies in the assault and keep its fourth company in reserve. Only the 2d Battalion of the 28th would actually enter Cantigny itself; the 3d on the left (north) and the 1st on the right (south) would bypass the town and dash straight to the regimental objective, a gentle ridge five hundred yards beyond the town. The attached French tanks would bypass the town on the level ground to the north, heading straight to the final objective. The assault on Cantigny placed all of Ely's eggs in one basket.

AT 5:04 A.M., MAY 28, Hanson Ely's command post at Bois St. Elois sent a terse message to Beaumont Buck's 2d Brigade: "Every element in position for the attack."

At 6:50 A.M. the 26th Infantry, also of Buck's brigade, replied, "First line went over led by tanks at 6:40."

Soon thereafter, by 7:21 A.M., the 28th reported, "Everything going well. About 20 prisoners so far. All front line bns. Connected by phone."

Ely's plan seemed to be working, and finally, at 7:24 A.M., Ely himself reported to Buck:

"Prisoners coming in, everything according to schedule. Nearly all of objective reached. Everything going fine. Hardly any casualties. Will keep you informed."[22]

Ely's report was accurate—not always the case in battle. His men had covered the 1,500 yard distance in short order, the flame throwers playing a major role in clearing out the cellars in the town. In the process, the men of the 28th were being exposed to their first sights of serious war. Lieutenant Clarence Huebner, destined to command the Big Red One in another war a quarter century later, was revolted to see a panic-stricken German scramble out of a cellar "just as I had seen rabbits in Kansas come out of burning strawstacks." Huebner watched as the man ran about fifteen yards and then, succumbing to his burns, keeled over dead.[23] Lieutenant Colonel J. M. Cullison, commanding the 3d Battalion, saw a German officer pretend to surrender but then throw a bomb at an approaching American lieutenant. The rest of the Americans showed the German and his forty men no mercy.[24]

With the town in American hands, Ely's men began consolidating the strong points on the ridgeline beyond it to protect it from counterattack.[25] The cost of the operation had been light, so far, by the standards of modern war: Marshall estimated between thirty-five and seventy-five casualties sustained by the 1st, against some 240 German prisoners.[26]

GENERAL PERSHING was on hand to witness the beginning of this attack, and his demeanor showed what a great personal stake he had in its success. He prized his favored 1st Division and was keenly conscious that its performance was being closely watched by the high-ranking French and British officers he dealt with. Even at the dramatic moment when the men went over the top, Pershing seemed strangely preoccupied. As they conferred in Bullard's command post, Bullard remarked that Pershing's mind was elsewhere, focused less on the action before him than on some aspects of his relations with the French. Like Bullard, Pershing took the success of the day's fighting almost as a matter of course, and he showed little glee at the ease with which it was accomplished.

At one point, he turned on Bullard almost angrily. "Do they [the French] patronize you?" he asked. "Do they assume superior airs with you?"

"No sir," Bullard answered quickly. "They do not. I have been with them too long and know them too well."

"By God! They have been trying it with me, and I don't intend to stand a bit of it." Bullard was convinced that Black Jack meant it.[27] Pershing was soon off, still preoccupied.

THE TIME WAS COMING, however, when Ely's men would have to pay the piper, and they needed every minute of the four-hour grace they were afforded to prepare for the expected German retaliation. With much of the reinforcing French artillery gone, the Americans lacked the heavy guns necessary to suppress those of the Germans. The concern, therefore, focused on German artillery more than infantry. The troops could do little about the heavy incoming rounds, but they could take action against attack by infantry. By 11:30 A.M., a report from the 28th Infantry indicated that they did not have long to wait. Anxious for any support they could get, one message pleaded, "Aeroplanes are needed on front." [28]

The counterattacks did not actually begin until the afternoon, however. By 2:14 P.M. the intelligence officer at headquarters informed Ely that "Individuals and small groups have been seen entering FOUNTAINE to number perhaps one or two hundred." [29] Fontaine was a small town on the road between Cantigny and Montdidier; it was therefore logical that the threat would come from that direction. Such enemy action would threaten Theodore Roosevelt's battalion of the adjacent 26th Infantry; more than just the 28th Infantry would participate in the battle.

In the meantime, incoming artillery was causing casualties, and Ely was becoming concerned. In one battalion, he reported, two companies had lost a third of their men, and one of them had lost all its officers. Another battalion had lost two captains killed, four officers wounded, and eighty men killed and wounded.[30]

At a little before 6:00 P.M. the heaviest blow fell. Two of Ely's battalions were falling back under heavy artillery and machine gun fire. He was committing two of the companies of the 18th Infantry that had been assigned to him. And now even the redoubtable Hanson Ely was showing signs of discouragement:

Unless heavy artillery can give us support it will be necessary to withdraw for entire front line is battered to pieces with artillery.[31]

Ely's request was a pipe dream; the heavy artillery had been moved to support the French to the southeast. But before the day was over Ely had reported the line straightened out. Losses had been heavy. Still Ely held.

With the shortage, if not lack, of French heavy artillery, German artillery fired freely. For seventy-two hours they poured shells on the American positions and launched repeated counterattacks. American light and medium artillery broke up all the German attacks, however; wire communications between front lines and artillery positions held up. Two German attacks were launched on May 29. Besides the men actually hit, many more Americans suffered severe shock from the impact of the near misses. The concentrated bombardment, George Marshall later wrote, "exceeded any experience [the men] were to have later on in the great battles of the war." [32] Still Bullard refused to relieve Ely's 28th Infantry. A relief under that heavy fire would be suicidal for the troops involved; furthermore, he thought it prudent to keep the rest of his regiments fresh in case the division should be caught up in the greater actions taking place to the east.

While the battle was at its height during the first evening at Cantigny, Bullard received a strange message from General Pershing. Only a few hours earlier the American Commander-in-Chief had seemed calm and reassured, almost indifferent regarding the action at Cantigny. Now he directed in most emphatic terms that the 28th must, under no conditions, quit the position it had taken. Bullard could only surmise that some of Pershing's French and British associates had expressed doubt regarding the Americans' ability to hang on to what they had won. [33]

Finally, three days after the attack, Ely's exhausted men were relieved by the 16th Infantry. The cost of their courage had been heavy: two hundred officers and men killed or missing, and 669 wounded. [34] Marshall himself later admitted that "The losses we suffered were not justified by the importance of the position itself." He added, however, that "they were many times justified by the importance of other great and far-reaching considerations." [35]

Robert Lee Bullard made even more extravagant claims:

> The German division that lost Cantigny was bitterly, almost insultingly reproached by its commander during his ineffectual efforts to make it retake the place in some half-a-dozen counterattacks. . . . They came and continued to come, these counterattacks—I thought they would never cease—but each failed under our steadfast, withering fire. Our men were in Cantigny to stay.
>
> Far, then, beyond the value of the place itself, and far beyond the size of the engagement, Cantigny was of import in its heartening of friend and disheartening of foe. It was a demonstration to the world of what was to be expected of the Americans. It was accepted by everybody. It took, I repeat, fully two months of felicitations from the Allies and as much observation of their rising spirits to make me realize this. [36]

WHILE THE MEN OF THE AEF were first proving themselves on the fields of France, the newly appointed Army chief of staff, Peyton March, was busily taking his "new broom" to the General Staff in Washington. March was in his element: ruthless, contemptuous of any established way of doing things, and energetic. In the measures he took to streamline the staff, he was backed to the hilt by Secretary Baker.

March's first action was to inject a note of urgency in the members of the staff. On arrival he soon asked his temporary predecessor, Major General John Biddle, what kind of office hours the staff kept. Biddle frankly admitted that he generally left the office around 5:00 in the evening and did not return unless some message from Pershing's headquarters in France made it necessary. March resolved to visit the staff that evening.

What he saw shocked him. The corridors were deserted, and nobody was present in the Acting Secretary of War's office. Outside the office of the Adjutant General March found piles of unopened sacks, with nobody there to open them. Only a single officer was on duty—he was in the code room.[37]

The next evening all the members of the General Staff were on duty, and until the end of the war every office stayed open all night. In a very short time, March later preened himself to write, "the piles of unopened mail sacks vanished."[38]

March thereupon set out to reorganize the General Staff in accordance with the procedures followed in all the leading armies of the world. Ironically, his new organization was based indirectly on the German. March had been a military attaché with the Japanese in Manchuria ten years earlier and there had studied the Japanese system, which in its own turn was based on the German system. No matter, so long as the system worked.[39]

March did other things. He raised the status of the intelligence function of the staff, an area of activity that had long been relegated to a minor status in the American Army. He established an Air Service, taking American aviation away from the Signal Corps and giving it an identity all its own. Finally, he established a Chemical Warfare Service, placing in charge of it Major General William Sibert, the man who had taken the 1st Division overseas but who Pershing believed lacked combat experience and presumably leadership.

Most of March's actions in Washington were necessary improvement, but of little concern to John J. Pershing at Chaumont. One obsession, however, was destined to cause trouble. Though March was junior to Pershing on the Regular Army promotion list, and though he had protested mildly about being sent back to Washington for his new position, he determined, once established in his new position, to be more than a rear echelon for the AEF. He was by law the highest ranking officer of the Army, which meant that Pershing, at least in theory, served under him. Secretary Baker, who saw no conflict in the two prima donnas' spheres of influence, gave the matter little attention. But legally, at least, he agreed to March's proposal to issue General Orders No. 80, 1918, which recognized March as the immediate adviser of the Secretary of

War on all matters relating to the military establishment. But then came the crucial sentence:

> The Chief of Staff by law (Act of May 12, 1917) takes rank and precedence over all officers of the Army, and by virtue of that position and by authority of and in the name of the Secretary of War he issues such orders as will insure that the policies of the War Department are harmoniously executed.[40]

To Pershing, who took himself very seriously, this gesture of defiance could not have been welcome.

CHAPTER TWELVE

THE 2D DIVISION
AT BELLEAU WOOD

GENERAL ERICH LUDENDORFF had not originally visualized his Third Offensive, launched across the Chemin des Dames on May 27, 1918, as an all-out effort.[1] He had intended it to be a gigantic feint, designed to draw French reserves eastward, away from the Arras region where they could support the British forces. Past experience had convinced Ludendorff that whenever a threat to Paris loomed, no matter how remote, the French would react strongly. He was again to be proven correct.

Ludendorff's original plan, therefore, was to take advantage of the French preoccupation with Paris, and to do so, he needed only to make a limited advance, from the Chemin des Dames southward across the Aisne River, stopping at the Vesle River, a distance of only about twelve miles. For that limited purpose he had selected an ideal area. For Ludendorff's twenty-five divisions to make any further advance, however, the Aisne-Marne region was far from ideal. It lacked an adequate system of north–south communications. Its railroad net depended entirely on an early capture of both Soissons on the west and Reims on the east. Furthermore, the region offered only two north–south roads worthy of the name. One led from Soissons and the other from Fismes, both terminating at Château Thierry, on the Marne. For those reasons, Ludendorff would be content to secure only his modest objective of the Vesle River.

When the attack jumped off, however, it met with unexpected success. The Chemin des Dames was being defended by only three French and two British divisions, sent to this supposedly quiet area for a rest. Five divisions were spread out over a fifty-mile front. Caught unaware, they were soon destroyed as fighting units. By the evening of the first day, therefore, General Max von Boehm's Seventh Army had already penetrated to the Vesle, seizing the towns of Braine, Bazoches, and Fismes. Ludendorff's original aims had already been reached.

The unexpectedly painless advance to the Vesle presented Ludendorff with a major decision. Should he halt his attack and turn again toward the critical Flanders area and the vulnerable junction between the British and French forces at the Somme? Doing so would probably promise the most decisive, immediate military results. But weighed against this was the military maxim of reinforcing success. And the psychological reward of threatening Paris might well balance the strategic advantages of the Somme offensive. The French were known to be tired and Ludendorff hoped they might sue for a negotiated peace if Paris were seriously threatened.

In the end Ludendorff decided to continue his offensive to the Marne, hoping to minimize the logistical inadequacy of the Aisne-Marne region by a quick seizure of the important rail centers of Soissons and Reims. With those cities secured, he would drive southward to the line of the Marne and then wheel westward toward Paris,[2] forcing the outnumbered French to fight in the open.

The decision brought immediate rewards. By June 3 Ludendorff's troops had seized a bridgehead over the Marne River east of Château Thierry, only fifty-six miles by road from Paris. The French had lost sixty thousand men as prisoners, along with 650 guns, two thousand machine guns, and vast quantities of other supplies, including aviation.[3] Worse than that, they appeared to be defeated psychologically.

ON MAY 30, 1918, General Pershing received an urgent request from General Pétain asking for American divisions to help stop the German tide. Pershing was more than willing to help, but his resources were limited. Most of his divisions were committed in quiet sectors. Of those not committed in the line, only the 2d and 3d Divisions were within a reasonable distance from the battlefield. The 2d was at Chaumont-en-Vexin, preparing to relieve the 1st, and the 3d was undergoing final training near Chaumont, south of Verdun. Pershing immediately sent word for both divisions to head in the direction of Château Thierry.

By the afternoon of May 31 the 7th Machine Gun Battalion of the 3d Division went into action along the south bank of the Marne River at Château Thierry, and by daylight the next day it had placed eight guns to defend the main wagon bridge over the river, and another nine guns to defend the approaches to the railroad bridge. By the end of the day, the infantry regiments of the 3d Division arrived and were deployed along the Marne for ten miles, eastward from Château Thierry to Dormans. Pershing later noted with satisfaction that the "conduct of the machine gun battalion in the operation was highly praised by General Pétain."[4]

The 2d Division, commanded by Major General Omar Bundy, was not far behind. Its orders to replace the 1st Division at Cantigny were rescinded, and it was now ordered to assemble at Meaux, a communications center about forty miles east of Paris, on the main road that ran between Paris on the west and Metz on the east. Once assembled at Meaux, the division was to await further orders.

THE 2D DIVISION (REGULAR) was the only one of Pershing's original four that had been organized in France rather than in the United States. Assembled from separate units in late October 1917, it had not been committed to quiet sectors until March of 1918. Its officers had not been among those handpicked by Pershing, as were those of the 1st, but they were capable men, some of them colorful.

Perhaps the weakest reed in the hierarchy of the 2d Division was the commanding general himself, Major General Omar Bundy. Bundy was a small, dapper man, a West Point graduate from the Class of 1883, three years ahead of Pershing.[5] He had fought against the Sioux in 1890 and had served creditably near San Juan Hill during the Spanish-American War and later against the Moros in the Philippines. Made a brigadier general in May 1917, Bundy had come overseas as one of the brigade commanders in the 1st Division before receiving command of the 2d Division. Though his record was good, Bundy was not a born warrior. An officer at Chaumont, in an official report, wrote during the latter stages of the 2d Division's training period that Bundy "appears to be trying to learn his duties as a division commander but gives no evidence of unusual ability for this position."[6] When the report was sent to Pershing, he ignored it.

Bundy's chief of staff, Colonel Preston Brown, was a different sort of soldier. Sharp-witted and pugnacious, he had once been accused, perhaps unjustifiably, of executing insurgents illegally in the Philippines.[7] But despite his sharp temperament, Brown was a capable officer and Bundy often allowed him to carry the brunt of negotiations with the French—and anyone else.

The 3d Brigade was commanded by Brigadier General Edward M. Lewis, a West Point classmate of Pershing's and described by Harbord as a "fine soldier."[8] His brigade consisted of two old Regular Army regiments, the 9th (Lieutenant Lud Janda's regiment) and the 23d. These regiments, like all designated as Regular at the time, were composed of volunteers. Those of the 3d came largely from northern New York, "leavened," in Harbord's words, "by a strong percentage of regulars." They needed more training, of course, but they were physically fit.[9]

The division's other brigade, the 4th, enjoyed a certain distinction in that it was a Marine, not an Army brigade. Its commander was Brigadier General Harbord, Pershing's late chief of staff. Anxious for field duty, Harbord had prevailed on his chief to release him from Chaumont to command this choice brigade when its commander, Brigadier Charles Doyen, USMC, had been found to be physically unfit for combat duty. If Harbord had worried about how the brigade would accept an Army officer to command it, his doubts were quickly dispelled. At the ceremony in which Harbord accepted command from Doyen, Colonel Wendell C. Neville, commanding the 5th Marine Regiment, gave him comforting assurances. The motto of the Marines, he said, was *semper fidelis*—"always faithful." Harbord could depend on them.

The 4th Marine Brigade could also depend on their new commander. Harbord was a large, impressive, rather pompous man, but one who recognized the value of showmanship. For some odd reason he always wore a French helmet rather than the American, which was a replica of the British. But he was always loyal to his Marine Brigade, taking its side in any controversy, even against his fellow Army officers.

It was not Harbord, or even the Marine commanders under him, that gave the brigade distinction, however. It was the nature of the two regiments of the brigade. The 5th Marine Regiment was comprised of old Regulars who had not been removed and scattered as had most Regular Army officers and men from their regiments. It was therefore the closest the American military establishment had to a truly Regular unit.

The 6th Marine Regiment was composed differently. Its officers were old-line Marine officers but its enlisted men had been recruited since America had entered the war. Nevertheless, it also enjoyed a privileged status. The Marine Corps accepted only volunteers in its ranks, and it was able to set exceptionally high standards for joining. Sixty percent of the men of the 6th Marines had attended at least some college, and their physical requirements were stringent. Admission to the Corps required a man to shoot at least a minimal score on the firing range before being admitted.[10] The brigade fit in well with the 2d Division, being the most Regular unit in a division that prided itself on being recognized as Regular.

THE 2D DIVISION received orders to move on May 30, as did the 3d, but its move to the Marne was delayed. The French high command had for a while been uncertain whether to use the 2d to relieve the 1st at Cantigny, as had originally been planned, or to send it to Château Thierry. By nightfall of the 30th, however, a decision had been made, and the infantry of the 2d Division were loaded up in trucks, bound for Meaux. Maybe they would defend that city, where the Ourcq River, flowing southward, joined the Marne. The artillery of the division, with its horses, went by railroad.

James Harbord was among the first to arrive in the new area, traveling ahead of his troops. At Meaux he received orders to assemble his brigade behind the Ourcq River. Those orders lasted only a short time, however. The situation was not so bad as had been imagined; the 2d Division would defend farther eastward.

By 4:30 A.M. on June 1, the first elements of the division began their march along the road eastward to Montreuil, a town about halfway between Meaux and Château Thierry, east of the Ourcq and north of the Marne. Ahead rode Harbord, passing through crowds of fleeing civilians going westward. He was distressed by the scenes about him:

> The streets were thronged by French officers and civilians. Every rod of the road was covered. All kinds of French units, artillery at a trot, straggling groups of infantry, lone engineers, Red Cross trains, wagons, trucks, which sometimes would congest and block the road for half an hour. . . . Hundreds of refugees crowded the roads, fleeing before the German advance. Men, women, children hurrying toward the rear; tired, worn, with terror in their faces.[11]

Shortly after 6:00 A.M., Harbord reached the town of Coupru, where the headquarters of the French XXI Corps was located. There he was welcomed by the corps commander, an old colonial officer named Jean De-Goutte, who greeted him cordially. He was glad to see the Americans, DeGoutte said through an interpreter, and then asked, "Where are your troops?" When he learned to his disappointment that Harbord commanded only one brigade, he contented himself with giving a rundown of the situation. "They have been pressing us since the morning of the 27th and have advanced over fifty kilometers in seventy-two hours," he said. "I know that your men need rest. Let them get something to eat. If it can be avoided, I shall not call on you today, but your troops must be ready to go into the line any time after eleven if called on."[12] Harbord, grateful, took his leave.

Soon after Harbord left DeGoutte's headquarters, General Omar Bundy arrived, accompanied by his chief of staff, Colonel Preston

Brown, and by Colonel Le Roy Upton, commanding the 9th Infantry Regiment. To Bundy, DeGoutte gave a more specific accounting of the situation. The German forces had just taken the town of Château Thierry, or at least the main portion, which lay north of the Marne. They had then turned westward along the Paris highway and had seized Hill 204, a prominence on the south side of the road west of Château Thierry. North of Hill 204, the enemy had also occupied the town of Vaux, then the high ground running northwest through Bouresches and Torcy. The situation was desperate: Hill 204, which dominated all the surrounding area, was only four miles from the place where they were conferring. Between that hill and their present location were only two depleted and exhausted French divisions. DeGoutte intended to send the American units into the battle one at a time, under French command, as he had done with the previous units.

The Americans protested vigorously, Preston Brown acting as spokesman. Such an employment of American troops, Brown declared, would lead only to catastrophe. He was convinced that one reason the French divisions had met defeat was the way they had been handled; their strengths had been frittered away by piecemeal commitment. Besides, only one American regiment, the 9th Infantry, was available, since the rest of the division was being strung out to the west on a single road. The men were tired and hungry, lacking artillery and machine guns, and carrying only one hundred rounds of ammunition per man. The best plan, Brown insisted, would be for the Americans to build up a secondary defensive line behind that of the French and then hold that new line as the French dropped back through.

DeGoutte, possibly too weary to argue, assented to Brown's plan. The 9th Infantry would take up a position facing eastward toward Château Thierry. But he still had his doubts. Anxiously he turned to Brown: "Can the Americans really hold?"

Preston Brown looked up from his map and indulged in a touch of heroic hyperbole. "General, these are American regulars. In a hundred and fifty years they have never been beaten. They will hold." [13]

AT ABOUT NOON that same day, June 1, Bundy sent for Harbord, Brown, and Edward Lewis, whose 3d Brigade was in the lead, to meet him at the Hôtel de Ville of Montreuil, about fifteen miles east of Château Thierry. As the group discussed the situation, a motorcyclist stepped in and handed Bundy a message from General DeGoutte. The enemy, it said, had seized an important position north of the assigned sector of the 9th Infantry, and the French general declared it "absolutely necessary" that the 9th avoid delay in getting into position. He also called on the 23d Infantry to be sent in on the left (north) flank of the 9th. All American troops were to be under the command of French General Michel, commanding the French 43d Division, until such time as the 2d Division should take over responsibility for the sector. DeGoutte assured Bundy that Michel would not move any of these regiments to any sector other than that he had specified.

Bundy was now forced to take action. He turned to Brown and ordered him to send in the 23d as requested. But Brown demurred; the 23d was behind the 4th Brigade on the only major road, temporarily unavailable. Bundy then turned to Harbord and said, "You will have to put in one of your regiments." Harbord also protested: his men had not slept during the entire night of May 30 and had spent the day of the 31st in buses, well into the night. He was willing to commit them, of course, but pleaded that their unit integrity be respected, that the regiments be allowed to go into action together, as a brigade. Bundy acquiesced: the 4th Brigade would occupy a line north of the Paris–Metz highway and the 3d Brigade would assume a defensive position on the right of the marines, to the south of the Paris–Metz highway.[14]

Making plans was one thing, but putting them into effect in a confused situation was another. DeGoutte's urgent message to Bundy had specified that the 2d Division advance forward to a line running from Azy on the Marne leftward to include Vaux in the center to the town of Gandelu on the left, a distance of about ten miles. The left (Marine) sector included both Belleau Wood and the important ridge line called Hill 142. If the Americans could not take positions that far forward, DeGoutte suggested a line running south of both Hill 142 and Belleau Wood, through Lucy-le-Bocage. Harbord selected the less ambitious line. When he reported to Bundy in the late afternoon of June 1 that his brigade was "in position," he meant the rearward line based on Lucy-le-Bocage rather than the line DeGoutte had drawn.[15] In the confusion, that may have been all that his men were capable of doing.

Despite the fact that the French were the only troops in actual contact with the enemy, many shells were falling on the 2d Division men, and their losses were considerable. Still the division struggled into line, the 3d Brigade on the right, the 4th Brigade on the left. As a temporary measure Harbord protected the Marine left flank by detaching a task force consisting of the 23d Infantry, under Colonel Paul Malone, with a battalion from the 5th Marines, the 5th Machine Gun Battalion, and a company of engineers, to the area of Champillon.[16] Once in place, the men of the 2d Division waited while the French fought a losing battle in front of them.

For three days they stayed in their foxholes, the shells still falling, until the regiments of the French 43d Division finally withdrew through American lines.

During the late afternoon of June 4, 1918, General Michel turned the sector over to the 2d Division. At the same time, he suggested that Bundy withdraw his troops to stronger positions in the rear. Bundy refused. He would counterattack to occupy Hill 142 and Belleau Wood.

The die was cast for a heroic tragedy.

BELLEAU WOOD

BY THE MORNING of Wednesday, June 5, the situation on the 2d Division front was simplified. The new French 167th Division, on Bundy's left, had moved into place and had taken over the sector previously held by Malone's 23d Infantry task force. The division sector ran essentially from Champillon to Lucy-le-Bocage to Triangle Farm to Vaux on the right.[17] The sector was divided into two distinct brigade sectors, with the 3d Brigade on the right and the 4th Brigade on the left. The boundary between them intersected the main line of resistance at Triangle Farm, in the center. With everything thus in place, both Bundy and DeGoutte considered it advantageous to push the Germans back and recover Bouresches and Belleau Wood, an operation they felt could be accomplished with little difficulty. Local attacks, presumed to be against light opposition, were set for the next day, June 6, 1918.

It so happened that both Bouresches and Belleau Wood lay in the left sector of the division, that of the 4th Brigade, and that brigade would therefore bear the responsibility for these first attacks. The first objective was Hill 142, which dominated the area. With that ridge in friendly hands, DeGoutte, Bundy, and Harbord believed it would be easy to occupy Belleau Wood. The town of Bouresches should then fall by itself. Bundy issued orders for the attack to Harbord on the evening of the 5th of June.

Neville's 5th Marine Regiment, on the left of the 4th Brigade, led off with the attack designed to take Hill 142, the town of Bouresches, and the western edge of Belleau Wood—all terrain features the Americans might have occupied with impunity four days earlier. The morning attack against Hill 142 was to be made by one battalion, and once that hill was seized, the attack against Bouresches and Belleau Wood was to be conducted by Neville's two other battalions, reinforced by part of a battalion from Colonel Albertus W. Catlin's 6th Marines.[18]

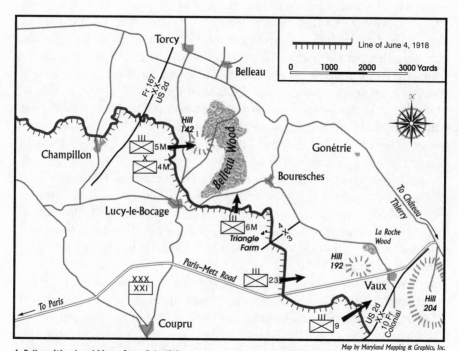

6. Belleau Wood and Vaux, June–July 1918.

Map by Maryland Mapping & Graphics, Inc.

These were actions of the 2d Division, in conjunction with the 3d Division's defense of the Marne farther east. The defensive phase of this battle was important in halting the third German drive. The attack to take Belleau Wood, however, though it has become a byword for sacrifice and heroism, was badly bungled, causing many unnecessary American casualties in the 4th Marine Brigade.

For some reason—possibly haste, possibly lack of combat experience—the forward companies had made very little reconnaissance of the terrain in front. One patrol from the 6th Marines, to be sure, had reported activity in Belleau Wood on the night of June 4, but Harbord and the others ignored that message, assuming that Belleau Wood, as the French had advised, was mostly unoccupied. Only the northeastern corner, the end farthest away from the point of attack, was believed to contain Germans.

The 1st Battalion, 5th Marines, attacked Hill 142 at 3:45 A.M. on June 6, despite the fact that two of the battalion's four companies and some of its assigned machine guns had not yet arrived. In addition, though the battalion commander had received instructions to move forward by infiltration, he sent his men in ranks, Civil War style, straight into enemy machine guns. Only by dint of speed and aggressiveness—coupled with heavy losses—did the marines take their objective. That they attained quickly, but then they were forced to beat off counterattacks for the rest of the day. The battalion lost nine officers and 325 men. One company lost all its lieutenants.

Harbord, in his command post, seemed satisfied, and that afternoon he and the regimental commander, Colonel Neville, turned their attention to the planned attack on Bouresches and Belleau Wood. One battalion would attack the forest from the west while two battalions, one detached from the 6th Marines, would attack the forest and the town from the south.

Again the attacking troops had to jump off before they were ready, and again the marines went forward lined up in rows, easy targets for German machine guns. The best they were able to accomplish, at a fearsome price, was to gain the edge of Belleau Wood. On the right, however, the 96th Company of the 6th Marines seized the town of Bouresches—the one clear-cut success of the day. On June 6, 1918, the 4th Brigade had lost 1,087 officers and men, 222 of them killed.[19]

The attack of the 4th Marine Brigade that June 6, 1918, had been a tragedy, a useless slaughter of valiant, dedicated men for minimal gains. But that was not the impression the outside world received of the action. The misunderstanding came about through an extremely odd set of circumstances.

Among the newspaper correspondents accompanying the 4th Brigade that day was the noted war correspondent Floyd Gibbons, who elected to accompany the Marine battalion attacking Bouresches and the southern edge of Belleau Wood. When the first reports of easy success came back, Gibbons filed a sensationalized piece describing what he had heard and sent it to Paris to be submitted to his newspaper through the Army censor, asking that the article be permitted to identify the Marines as the force in question. Censorship rules forbade the identification of units, despite the frustration of the various newspaper correspondents, who had been forbidden from identifying the unit at Cantigny. That policy might have applied here but for the tragedy that befell Gibbons. As soon as he had filed his story, Gibbons fell with a hideous facial wound that, among other disfigurements, removed his left eye.

The press censor at Pershing's headquarters, believing his friend dead, wished to pay him a final tribute. He argued that the Marines were an arm of service, not a unit. According to Harbord, he said something like, "This is the last thing I can ever do for poor old Floyd."[20] In the absence of both Pershing and his intelligence officer, the censor granted the request. Perhaps he was unaware that only one Marine brigade was in Europe, a sure unit identification.

The American public, hungry for news of American action in France, latched on to Gibbons's report with an outburst of enthusiasm. Avidly they swallowed the story of the ease with which American marines could defeat the enemy. Reports were lavish. On Thursday, June 6, 1918, the *Chicago Daily Tribune* blazoned, "U.S. MARINES SMASH HUNS GAIN GLORY IN BRISK FIGHT ON THE MARNE CAPTURE MACHINE GUNS KILL BOCHES, TAKE PRISONERS." The *New York Herald* carried headlines that read, "MARINES IN GREAT CHARGE OVERTHROW CRACK FOE FORCES."[21] The *Chicago Tribune* and the *New York Times* also carried inflated stories.

The reaction throughout the rest of AEF was one of anger and dismay. Admittedly, the 4th Marine Brigade richly deserved credit for hard, brave fighting, but such lavish praise for a single unit implied a criticism of the efforts of the others. Lieutenant Lud Janda, of the 9th Infantry, later expressed that feeling in a letter to his father. Noting that the 4th Marine Brigade took a press agent along with them, he complained that the practice was "against military etiquette." He added that "two regiments of Marines have received more notoriety than the whole A.E.F. simply because of the press agency."[22]

Unfortunately, the matter also brought out the petty side of certain high-ranking Army officers, especially in the 2d Division itself. Harbord, whose service with the 4th Marine Brigade had affected him deeply, complained bitterly that when Clemenceau visited the division in late June to "see the brave Americans who had saved Paris," Bundy invited two colonels of the 3d Brigade to share refreshments with him but the members of the 4th Marine Brigade learned of the occasion only the next day.[23] It was the Army that put the 4th Brigade in Belleau Wood. The brigade was commanded by an Army officer, Harbord, who probably committed it prematurely. Finally, it was an Army censor who cleared the story.[24] No question the incident was unfortunate; even Harbord called the Marine identification "unforgivable." Nevertheless, it had its bright side. It gave an incalculable boost to French morale.

THE AMERICAN AND ALLIED reaction to the news at Belleau Wood was of course quickly made known to the German high command, and Erich Ludendorff claimed to be unimpressed. His troops, he wrote, "remained masters of the [Marne] situation, both in attack and defense." He called the Americans "unskilfully led, attacked in masses, and failed."[25] But in spite of the First Quartermaster General's sniffings at the American performance, his Seventh Army commander, General Max von Boehm, took the action very seriously. Accordingly he issued a special order:

> An American success along our front, even if only temporary, may have the most unfavorable influence of the attitude of the Entente and the duration of the war. In the coming battles, therefore, it is not a question of the possession of this or that village or woods, insignificant in itself; it is a question of whether the Anglo-American claim that the American Army is the equal or even the superior of the German Army is to be made good.[26]

What that meant was a fight to the death over an insignificant hunting lodge with its surrounding woods.

The German 28th Division counterattacked on the morning of June 7, the day after the original attack by the Marine Brigade. By this time, Belleau Wood had already become a cause célèbre. That small woods, only a half square mile at most, had to be cleared, in the minds of all commanders, from Pershing down through Bundy, Harbord, and Harbord's regimental commanders.

On that same day Harbord declared that the attack would be continued. By now, however, he had come to admit that the wood was indeed occupied—and in strength—despite what the French had told him several days before. All day long on the 9th of June he pounded that small area with artillery, so strong that he reported to Bundy, "Artillery has blown the wood all to hell."[27]

Early on the 10th of June, Catlin's 6th Marine Regiment attacked due northward into the southern edge of Belleau Wood. At first things again seemed to go well. At 4:41 A.M. the battalion commander reported success; the artillery had indeed destroyed the woods. An hour later the regimental intelligence officer reported to Harbord that the action in the woods was "deemed finished." Harbord wished to relieve his troops, who were exhausted, dirty, and hungry, but first he determined to ensure that the woods were clear. But again he met disappointment. A battalion from the 5th Marine Regiment sent eastward to hit the western part of the woods discovered that the seeming success of the morning's attack had been a complete delusion. The woods had hardly been entered.[28]

The confusion continued, almost invariably with troops sent in too hastily, without sufficient preparation, with overly optimistic reporting. The woods were so thick that commanders had no idea how far they had penetrated, and even what direction they were going in. The brigade had suffered unreasonable losses in fine young manpower. After two weeks of fighting, beginning on July 1, the 4th Brigade had taken almost 50 percent casualties. The woods were filled with refuse, excrement, and, increasingly, putrefying corpses.[29] A single battalion had lost twenty-one officers and 836 men. Some relief came from the French, who took over the crest of Hill 142 on the left. But the 4th Brigade remained desperate for a rest.

On June 14 Harbord went to Bundy to make his plea for relief. His brigade, he said, had attacked on the 10th, 11th, and the 14th; they were worn out. The 3d Division, Harbord knew, was nearby. Further, the 7th Infantry was out of the line, available to take over the Marine sector. Bundy agreed and went to General Naulin, the new French corps commander.

The Frenchman, however, was unimpressed by the plight of the Americans, and was difficult to convince. Finally Bundy played his ace card. He was, he said, "prepared to exercise his seniority as ranking American officer in the Second and Third Divisions and to assume command of all American troops for such purposes as he saw fit."[30] Naulin, apparently not too sure of himself when dealing with these brash Yankees, finally issued orders for the 7th Infantry to relieve the Marine Brigade. Harbord, because of his familiarity with the area, was left to exercise personal command of the regiment.

The 7th Infantry went into their first battle under the worst of conditions. Not only were the troops inadequately trained, but they were given no time for preparation. In a memorandum, Preston Brown assigned the 7th Infantry to Harbord's command for a period of six days, one battalion of marines being relieved by a battalion of the 7th Infantry each successive night, beginning that same night.[31] At the same time Brown sent an order to the regimental commander directing him to designate a battalion to go into the trenches that night with two days' reserve rations per man, one hundred rounds of ball cartridges, gas masks, and other essential equipment. At the same time the regimental commander, accompanied by the battalion commander and his company commanders, were to report to 2d Division headquarters *at once.*[32] The regimental commander, presumably, was to ready his men and then be in two places at one time. Preston Brown was apparently suffering from fatigue himself.

IF JAMES HARBORD was expecting a great surge of energy from the relieving 7th Infantry, he was sorely disappointed. When the 1st Battalion entered the line, it began placing wire in the front of its position as protection against attack. Harbord rebuked the battalion commander severely. Asserting that the Americans had "nothing to fear" from the Germans, he directed the battalion commander to exert pressure "until those people are killed or driven out."[33] When the same battalion failed to take an objective two days later, Harbord blamed the "inefficiency of officers of the 7th Infantry and the lack of instruction of the men." He added that "the 1st Battalion [7th infantry] is untrustworthy for first line work at this time."[34]

Other accounts of the 7th Infantry performance are far more charitable than those of the irascible Harbord. None, however, throw accolades on its performance. The 7th Infantry had simply been committed before it was ready, in a very difficult situation.

HARBORD'S DISSATISFACTION with the 7th Infantry did not mean that he intended to coddle his marines. After the 4th Brigade resumed responsibility for its former position in the line, he assigned a battalion the task of clearing the northern portion of the woods by 10:00 P.M., June 23. The attack failed, and once again Harbord's deadline was reset. He pulled the 5th Marines back for the full day of June 24, during which he pounded the woods again with artillery—something he should have done eighteen days earlier.

At 5:00 P.M. on June 25, the 5th Marine Regiment attacked the northern portion of Belleau Wood once again. This time the artillery had done the job, and the German defenders began surrendering in droves. Late that night Harbord reassured Colonel Neville that there would be no counterattack. "You are in charge of the Bois de Belleau." The next morning the battalion commander who had made the attack reported the good news: "Woods now U.S. Marine Corps entirely."[35]

VAUX

WHILE THE 4TH MARINE BRIGADE was fighting its heartbreaking battles under less than superb leadership, the 3d Brigade, 2d Division, was also taking heavy casualties. Though not involved in fruitless attacks, it was fending off one German attack after another, in the process receiving continual artillery fire. The 3d Brigade had sustained nearly two thousand casualties during June, at the same time that the 4th Brigade was suffering five thousand. But despite its lighter losses the 3d Brigade was not content; it had gained no ground and had received neither accolades nor citations, intangible rewards that might partially have compensated for their losses.[36] Between June 21 and 24 a severe gas attack had cost the 9th Infantry 170 casualties.[37] If Bundy kept the 2d Division in the line longer than necessary—as Harbord accused him of doing[38]—he had much justification in terms of the morale of the 3d Brigade.

The attack to secure the town of Vaux, however, was neither a stunt nor an afterthought. When General Naulin had taken over command from DeGoutte on June 14, he had consulted with Bundy about an attack to fill one gaping hole in the line: the town of Vaux, with the critical Hill 204 to its right and Hill 192 and the La Roche Wood to its left. These terrain features were so located as to make a deep reentrant into the 2d Division's position. Bundy agreed on the need to conduct such an attack, but he secured permission to delay it until Belleau Wood was cleared— one major divisional operation at a time. Now that moment had come and with it the time to take those three objectives. That done, the German drive toward Paris could comfortably be considered at an end. So General Lebrun, commander of the French II Corps, issued an order two weeks later for the 2d Division to attack Vaux, the La Roche Wood, and Hill 192. The French 153d Regiment, 39th Division, would take Hill 204 on the right.[39]

The German forces defending this area were substantial but not daunting. The sector to be attacked by the Americans was called Sector Wald by the Germans, and it was defended by a single regiment, the 402d Infantry, of the 201st German Division. The 402d consisted of sixty-nine officers and a little over two thousand men. While experienced, the troops were riddled with illness and not considered as "high in martial spirit."[40]

The 2d Division at Vaux, unlike the situation at Belleau Wood, had time to ensure that the success of the attack on Vaux would not be left to chance. Fortunately, the new division intelligence officer, Colonel Arthur Conger, was highly qualified for his job, and he assembled information vital to the success of the attack:

Former residents of the town of Vaux, now refugees in back areas, were collected and brought to headquarters for interrogation; German prisoners and captured documents were examined. For the village of Vaux, a solid, stone-built place, detailed information was secured from French refugees; among these was the village stone-mason, who had worked in every house in the village. Diagrams were prepared showing every one of the eighty-two houses, with floor and cellar plans, the thickness of house walls, and dimensions of all garden walls. The location of all German troops and their defenses were carefully noted. This completed study was a little masterpiece; from it commanders of troops in the attack could assign in advance the task of their smallest units, with even more confidence than in a trench raid.[41]

In addition, the attack would be supported, as at Cantigny, by divisional artillery, reinforced heavily by larger calibers from the French. Twelve French batteries, including three batteries of heavy 155mm Corps artillery, would provide counterbattery and long-range fires.[42]

The attack jumped off at 6:00 P.M. on July 1, 1918. General Lewis's attack plan was simple. After the twelve-hour artillery preparation, each regiment, the 23d on the left and the 9th on the right, would attack along a one-battalion front, the 23d to take Hill 192 and the La Roche Wood. The sector of the 9th, on the right, included Vaux and extended to the eastern edge of La Roche Wood.[43] The town of Vaux, the Americans found, was virtually deserted; artillery fire had taken care of that. As a result, the town was cleared within a half hour and the troops soon occupied their objective, the railroad line to the east of town. By 8:30 P.M. the Americans were consolidating "a line running from Hill 192 east across the northern face of La Roche Wood to the railroad line north of Vaux to the viaduct on the right." Their right was tied in with the French 153d Regiment on Hill 204.[44] The operation had gone off without a major hitch.

The capture of Vaux brought an end to the operations of the 2d Division at Château Thierry. The fighting during that month of June 1918 had cost the 2d Division dearly—nine thousand casualties out of a total infantry strength of seventeen thousand. But, along with Cantigny, it had proved beyond question that the Americans would fight.

CHAPTER THIRTEEN

THE ROCK OF THE MARNE

"I will be in Paris by midnight of July 17, 1918."

—Kaiser Wilhem II

"Let 'em come!"

—Colonel U. G. McAlexander

THE AMERICANS had performed well in their first exposures to battle, but in the overall picture their contribution to halting Ludendorff's Third Offensive, and its threat to Paris, had been minor. Only the American 2d Division and the 7th Machine Gun Battalion of the 3d Division had participated among many French units. Actually Ludendorff's offensive had been stopped principally by logistical failure rather than military action. By early June 1918, the First Quartermaster General could not conduct even a respectable defense of the Aisne-Marne salient, let alone use it as a base from which to push on toward Paris. The two roads and the single railroad he had available to transport the tons of supplies his troops needed were totally inadequate.

Ludendorff therefore shifted his effort from the Marne to an area northwest of Château Thierry. His Fourth Great Offensive, called the Noyon-Montdidier offensive, sought to expand the salient south of the Retz Forest. Possession of that area would constitute a threat to Paris from the north, a threat even greater than that from the Marne Valley. Ludendorff launched this attack on July 8, only two days after the 4th Marine Brigade had begun its ordeal in Belleau Wood.

Like Ludendorff's Second Offensive in Flanders, however, the Fourth Offensive brought little by way of results. By now the German Army had suffered half a million casualties, of whom 95,000 had been killed and 32,000 had been taken prisoner. Supplies of corn and potato fodder from Germany were becoming scant, and the German ranks were being ravaged by an epidemic of flu.[1] Ludendorff's chances of all-out success were daily growing slimmer.

Yet Ludendorff believed he had strength for one more major attack. As the first phase of that offensive he would have to broaden his Aisne-Marne salient on the east by taking the major rail hub of Reims. He had tried to do so before and had failed. This time he would avoid making a frontal assault and bypass the city by attacking in two wings, one to drive southward from a point east of Reims; the other to cross the Marne between Reims and Château Thierry. If successful, that pincer movement would cut off and trap the French defenders, whose line had previously bent in front of his attacks but had never broken. With Reims in his possession, he would control the railroad running southwest to Château Thierry and would enjoy more elbow room.

Taking Reims, however, was only Ludendorff's minimum objective. There was always a chance, if things went well, that this Fifth Offensive might take Paris where all other efforts had failed. To strive for that prize, Ludendorff's best chance lay in seizing the valley of the Surmelin River, a modest stream that flows northward and empties into the Marne at a point several miles east of Château Thierry. The Surmelin Valley is the only gap in the east–west line of hills that runs along the south bank of the Marne. It was the only such gap capable of sustaining the operations of a modern army.

MARSHAL FERDINAND FOCH had been advised that the Germans were planning another offensive, but its exact place and time were unknown. As it turned out, Ludendorff had selected an area that was being defended by General Jean DeGoutte's Fifth French Army, a weak organization that consisted of only two Italian divisions, part of the newly arrived American 28th Division, the French 125th Division, and Major General Joseph Dickman's American 3d Division, on the extreme western flank. All of these units played their part in the defense, but it was Dickman's 3d Division that held the critical Surmelin Valley.

Joseph Theodore Dickman was hardly a picture book version of a combat soldier. At age sixty-one, he was one of the oldest members of the American high command, and his bulk and stolid appearance could well be misleading. A recounting of his military record sounds very much like those of the other generals. He had spent his early years as a cavalryman fighting Indians in the West, was cited for gallantry in the Santiago campaign, and later fought against the Filipino insurgents and in the China

Relief Expedition (1900). None of those tours of service would, in themselves, presage future distinguished service.

Dickman was, however, a thoroughly competent professional. He had graduated with honors from the Infantry and Cavalry School at Fort Leavenworth and was a serious student of the military art. He was said— a possible exaggeration—to have learned five foreign languages in order "that he might get the letter and the spirit of the various writings of European tacticians." At the same time he was known as "a staunch friend of the enlisted man."[2] Along with many others, he had been promoted to the grade of brigadier general in the Regular Army in May 1917.

When Dickman had first deployed his division behind the Marne near Château Thierry on May 30, he had organized his defense in depth, placing two of his infantry regiments along the Marne and holding two in reserve.[3] Later on, he moved his two reserve regiments forward so that all four were along the river. The 4th Infantry he placed on his left at Château Thierry, then the 7th, then the 30th, and on the division's right he placed the 38th. Then, for the rest of the month of June, the men of the 3d Division enjoyed relative quiet.[4]

Dickman's dispositions to meet the expected German assault were either very wise or very lucky, for the most critical and vulnerable portion of his line, which included the Surmelin Valley, was his right flank, an area whose defenders, the 30th and the 38th Regiments, were commanded by two exceptional soldiers.

The more colorful of the two was Colonel Ulysses Grant McAlexander, age fifty-six, who commanded the 38th Infantry. A West Point graduate in the Class of 1887, he was known as a difficult but capable officer, one of the few selected to sail with the 1st Division in June 1917. His independence of mind nearly terminated his future once the division had gone into training at Gondrecourt, when he was commanding the 18th Infantry. Ordered to send many of his key officers to the new AEF staff school at Langres, he refused to comply on the basis that he needed them for training his troops. He was relieved of command and reassigned to a routine position in the Services of Supply at St. Nazaire. He did not despair, however; he threw himself into his new duties with such zeal that his superiors reinstated him to the command of an infantry regiment, this time the 38th, of the 3d Division. Anyone attacking McAlexander's 38th Infantry would be dealing with a formidable antagonist.

Colonel Edmund Luther (Billy) Butts, commanding the 30th Infantry on McAlexander's left, was of a different mold. At age forty-nine he was one of the younger regimental commanders of the AEF, from the Class of 1890 in West Point. There he had excelled in athletics and military rankings but not in academics. Too young to participate in the Indian wars, he had also missed combat in Cuba and the Philippines. But he was an organization man through and through, respected by the officer corps and idolized by his troops. He was also on friendly terms with Ulysses G. McAlexander.

It was well that Butts and McAlexander were compatible, because their two-regimental front, guarding the Surmelin Valley, constituted a single tactical position. How to defend it was a difficult question, one that demanded the attention not only of the regimental commanders but of Dickman and even his French superiors as well. Here Dickman found himself at odds with General DeGoutte, commanding the sector. The mile-and-a-half front defended by the 30th and 38th involved two sizable hills back from the river, one located on either side of the Surmelin Valley. Near the river and in the forward section of the valley the ground was flat. Accordingly, a so-called "elastic" defense would be ideal in those circumstances.

Here Dickman ran into unexpected difficulties with his French superior, General DeGoutte, who ordered him to defend the riverbank in force, so that the Germans would be repulsed, as Dickman later recalled, by "Americans *with one foot in the water*."[5] DeGoutte's order was surprising, because the French Army had taken pride in their development of the elastic defense technique, which called for outposting the front lines lightly and placing the main line of resistance farther back, out of range of the enemy's artillery preparation. Nevertheless, DeGoutte insisted on a defense that was far from elastic.

Dickman had his own ideas. Noting that a bend in the Marne River in the sector held by the 30th included flat ground vulnerable to fire from the considerable heights to the west, north, and east, he doggedly followed his own judgment, outposting the river but placing his principal defenses on the heights. Partly to placate DeGoutte, he contrived to give the appearance of a compromise by slightly reinforcing his thinly held outpost line, especially at night. "At no time," he wrote later, did he do so "to the extent demanded by [DeGoutte's] order."[6]

Having decided to defy orders and conduct a defense in depth, Dickman conceded that the troops occupying the flat ground along the river and up the Surmelin would have to give way under pressure; a German penetration might actually go some miles. But the Surmelin Valley, Dickman reasoned, would ultimately be useless to the enemy unless all Americans were cleared from the heights on both sides.

On that assumption, he examined the terrain features that he would need to hold. Essentially they were two. On the west was a steep north–south ridge on top of which was the Bois d'Aigremont. On the east across the Surmelin Valley was the Moulin Ridge, of approximately the same height. Since he was assigning the Surmelin to the 38th, on the right, Dickman placed McAlexander's left flank at the Bois d'Aigremont, sharing that ridge with the 30th. Since Dickman considered the position of the 30th to be more difficult to hold than that of the 38th, he attached two of McAlexander's twelve infantry companies to Butts. McAlexander would now fight his battle with ten infantry companies, Butts with fourteen.

All in all, it was a strong position for an elastic defense, but it had one serious Achilles' heel: McAlexander's front would occupy only half of the Moulin Ridge. On his right flank would be the French 125th Division. Dickman and McAlexander were certain that the term "elastic defense," in the eyes of the 125th French Division, would mean a withdrawal sufficient to expose the 38th's flank.

McAlexander then studied the front he would defend. Four positions, he concluded, would be key to his defense, two of them temporary and two of them critical, to be held at all costs. The outpost line along the Marne River and the Paris–Metz road, about a mile and a half from the river, would fall into the first category.

For the dangerous but important task of defending the banks of the Marne in an outpost line, McAlexander chose Major Guy I. Rowe's 2d Battalion. The line, he decided, would not be held uniformly. To protect the approaches to the critical ridges to the rear, even the outpost line was to be stronger on the flanks than in the center. Thus McAlexander gave a narrow front to Jesse Wooldridge's Company G, on the left, so that it could take a position in depth.*

On the right flank of the outpost line, McAlexander placed E Company along the riverbank and backed it up with F Company, whose position unabashedly faced the French 125th Division. The fourth company of the 2d Battalion, H, was stretched out along the riverbank between G and E Companies.

The Paris–Metz road, the second delaying position, was to be defended by the 1st Battalion. Since the two companies attached to Butts had come from the 1st, however, its fighting strength was cut in half.

The two positions on the final line could be called "McAlexander's last stand," because he considered them to be all-important. One was

---

* Wooldridge placed only one platoon along the riverbank. His main line of resistance was located back about 350 yards from the riverbank, along an elevated railroad embankment, where he deployed two platoons. Since the embankment was nine feet high and too wide to defend from the rear, he placed one platoon in front of it and another immediately to its rear. The fourth he placed behind that on a spur track that jutted southeast into the sector. Wooldridge, *Giants*, p. 25.

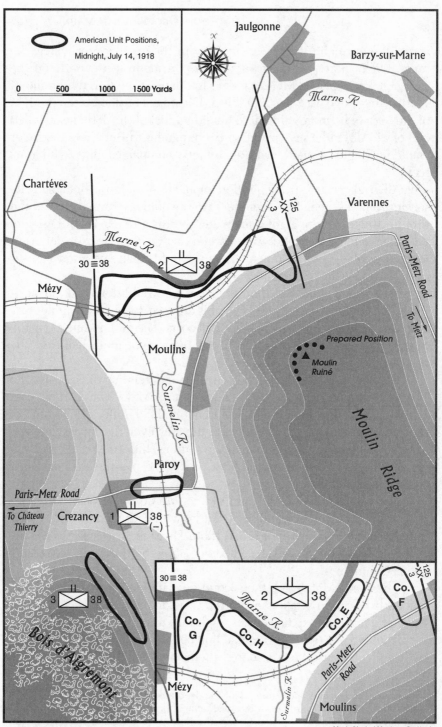

7. The Battle of Château Thierry, July 15, 1918.

This critical defense of the Surmelin Valley may well have saved Paris from Ludendorff's last attack. It earned the 3d Division, more specifically the 38th Infantry Regiment, the title of "Rock of the Marne." This map shows American positions before the German attack early in the morning.

located on the western ridge, near the Bois d'Aigremont. There he placed his entire 3d Battalion, consisting of four companies. On the Moulin Ridge, to the east, he prepared entrenchments at a place called Moulin Ruiné, halfway up the slope. The entrenchments at the Moulin Ruiné were prepared to defend in two directions: facing westward into the Surmelin Valley and facing eastward toward the French 125th Division.

McAlexander did not occupy the Moulin Ruiné at first—he had no troops to place there. That position would be occupied only if, as expected, the German attack broke through the first and second lines, in which case it would have to be defended with whatever companies of the 1st and 2d Battalions could make it back there from their initial positions.[7]

Neither McAlexander nor Dickman worried much about French reaction to the precautions the Americans were taking to protect the east flank, the French sector. If their prudent deployment caused resentment, so be it.

WITH HIS TROOPS IN PLACE, McAlexander waited impatiently for the attack to come. A warrior in every sense, he did not regard fighting as a mere facet of his military duties, as many were wont to do. Fighting was his obsession, and he inspired his 38th Infantry with a similar zeal down to the last man. He had no patience with the "live and let live" customs that had grown up over the years of futile trench warfare between the French and Germans, which called for killing the enemy only when active battle was joined. One of McAlexander's first orders reflected his aggressive attitude: "Don't let anything show itself on the other side [of the Marne] and live."[8]

He put that philosophy into practice personally, and if he had a weakness as a commander it was his habit of exposing himself too rashly to enemy fire. He constantly appeared at places he had forbidden others to go in order to study the terrain from all angles. He was constantly conferring with his company commanders on the front. He even went on individual sniping expeditions, armed with a Springfield .30 caliber rifle, shooting anyone who appeared on the German side fifty yards away. His theory of creating a regiment would sound pompous were it not so rigorously followed by the commander himself:

> Do you wish an invincible, unconquerable regiment? Then organize it, administer it, train it and fight it . . . with a pride that scoffs at danger. Inspire it with a soul of intrepidity and honor and make it to know that its defeat is impossible, that it may be killed but that it cannot be conquered.[9]

McAlexander's men were inspired with his spirit, but they abbreviated it to terms they could better understand: "Let 'em come."

PARTS OF TWO GERMAN DIVISIONS were in position to assault the American 30th and 38th Infantry Regiments: the entire 10th Division[10] and one regiment of the 36th. The other two regiments of the 36th Division, on the east, were to attack the French 125th Division.[11] The German timetable was precise: artillery preparation would begin at 12:10 A.M., July 15; pontoons placed in the water at 1:55 A.M.; first infantry crossings 2:10 A.M.; consolidation of bridgehead (behind railroad embankment) 2:20 A.M.; beginning of the rolling barrage, with infantry following, 3:50 A.M.[12]

Shortly before Ludendorff's offensive was scheduled to begin, the French Fifth Army received an unexpected bonanza: some German prisoners captured near Reims divulged vital information, confirming both the time and the place of Ludendorff's next planned attack. Accordingly, the Americans preempted the action. On the night of July 14, beginning at 11:45 P.M.,

> every gun on this side of the river blazed forth in an intensive bombardment which caused great havoc in the German masses forming up for the attack. The support trenches and other points where German troops would naturally assemble for the assault were so heavily shelled that some of their units had to be replaced before the attack began.[13]

AT 3:30 A.M., July 15, the German creeping barrage began. As expected, Wooldridge's G Company along the river was heavily attacked by the German 6th Grenadiers of the 10th Division. For an hour Wooldridge's front platoon held, supported by machine gun fire and automatic weapons fire from the 30th Infantry in Mézy on his left. But the enemy secured a foothold and wiped out nearly the entire platoon.[14]

Eventually the German infantry pushed through to the railroad bank in the rear. When the platoon defending the embankment was overcome, Wooldridge moved the next platoon up in its place. G Company was pushed back, but the Americans had exacted a fearsome price. Enfilading the German lines, Wooldridge's men cut down the enemy and gloated as they saw the units disintegrate, as Wooldridge later boasted, from "a soldier's maneuver into a military omelet." His company was never completely broken through.[15]

In the center, however, the Germans succeeded in crossing the river and driving southward up the Surmelin Valley. They also drove back the forward elements of the 30th Infantry, temporarily occupying Mézy on the river at the boundary between the two regiments.[16] To save what remained of his company, therefore, Wooldridge sent one platoon to counterattack the German position and to regain contact with some elements of the 30th Infantry. He then gathered a force consisting of his own remaining men and two platoons from the 30th Infantry—some two hundred riflemen all told—and retook the ruins of Mézy, resolved to hold his position to the last man. In three counterattacks Wooldridge's men captured nearly three hundred prisoners.[17]

At about 8:00 A.M. Colonel McAlexander received orders to counterattack with his entrenched 1st and 3d Battalions in order to restore the line between Mézy and Moulin—that is, across the Surmelin Valley. Only four of McAlexander's ten available companies had as yet been committed, but to leave his fortifications and attack across the valley in the face of overwhelming German numbers seemed too hazardous. He therefore ignored his orders and kept the 3d Battalion in place at the Bois d'Aigremont while also concentrating on building up the Moulin Ruiné position, as previously planned. The companies of the 1st Battalion, previously at Paroy and Crezancy, attacked in that direction, picking up a reported four hundred prisoners in the wake of heavy fighting.[18]

It was well for the Americans that McAlexander had dared to disobey orders. The French 125th Division, on the right of the 38th Infantry, fell back under the impact of the 5th Grenadier Regiment of the German 36th Division, and the enemy pursued southward with relative ease. The 38th Infantry faced the contingency it had prepared for, and McAlexander turned his troops to protect from that direction. At first he was successful. F Company, facing the French zone on the river, not only held its position but actually made a bayonet attack into Varennes. The river line was untenable in the long run, but the 2d Battalion had done its job in delaying and hurting the enemy. To do so it had paid a heavy price. Out of a total of thirty-two officers and 930 men, the battalion lost twelve officers and 461 men, nearly half its strength.[19] Its remnants fell back to the Moulin Ruiné, along with the survivors of the 1st Battalion.

McAlexander's situation was now desperate. His regimental front had been pierced to a depth of some four thousand yards, and the battered 38th Infantry now consisted of two islands of resistance, one at the Bois d'Aigremont on the west flank and the other at the Moulin Ruiné across the Surmelin on the east. He was now facing the enemy on three sides: the Marne, the vacated positions of the 30th Infantry on the left, and the area vacated by the French on his right. Nevertheless, he refused to withdraw. Instead he exercised what command he could over his two

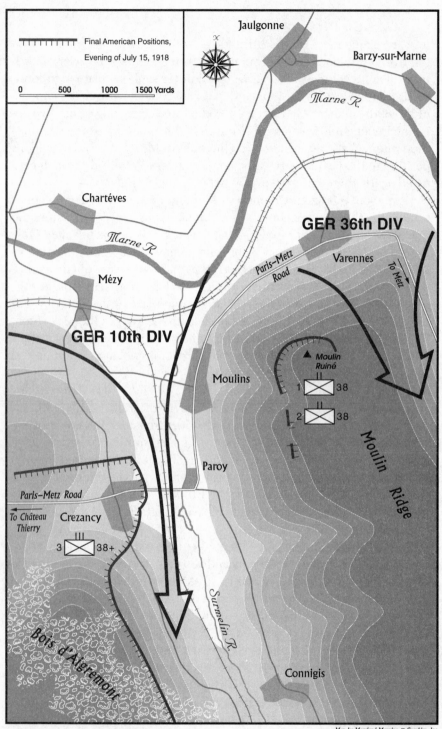

Final American Positions,
Evening of July 15, 1918

0   500   1000   1500 Yards

Jaulgonne

Barzy-sur-Marne

Marne R.

Chartéves

GER 36th DIV

Marne R.

Paris–Metz
Road

Varennes

To Metz

Mézy

GER 10th DIV

Moulin
Ruiné

Moulins

1 ⊠ 38

2 ⊠ 38

Paroy

Moulin Ridge

Paris–Metz Road

To Château
Thierry

Crezancy

3 ⊠ 38+

Surmelin R.

Bois d'Aigremont

Connigis

Map by Maryland Mapping & Graphics, Inc.

8. The Battle of Château Thierry, Evening of July 15, 1918.

By the end of July 15, 1918, very little was left of the 38th Infantry. Nevertheless, the heights of the Surmelin
were held on both the east and the west, thus halting the German offensive. Ludendorff had lost his gamble.

separated parts, and at 4:30 P.M. he even ordered his 3d Battalion and two companies of the 1st Battalion to move forward a few hundred yards to squeeze the German penetration between those positions.[20] The 3d Division artillery poured thousands of rounds on the exposed attackers.

Thus ended the action of the 38th Infantry on the 15th of July, 1918. The 30th had lost even more men, though in a less dramatic fashion. Together, the two regiments, the 30th and 38th, earned for the 3d Division the proud nickname of "The Rock of the Marne." Though fighting at the Moulin Ruiné continued throughout July 16, Ludendorff knew by the end of the 15th that his fifth offensive had failed. The doughboys could justly claim a major role in halting it.

IT HAD COME AT A PRICE. The 38th Infantry alone had lost nearly one fifth of its strength.[21] But they had "fought off two German divisions, captured prisoners from six different enemy regiments, and demolished the 1,700-man Sixth Grenadiers so badly that the German leadership could only find 150 survivors at day's end."[22] Evidence of the slaughter could be found in the anguished journal of Lieutenant Kurt Hesse, adjutant of the 5th Grenadier Regiment. While calling the action the "heaviest defeat of the war," he continued,

> Never have I seen so many dead men, never such frightful battle scenes. . . . The American . . . had nerve; we must give him credit for that; but he also displayed a savage roughness.
> "The Americans kill everybody!" was the cry of terror of July 15th, which for a long time stuck in the bones of our men. . . . Of the troops led into action on July 15th, more than 60 per cent were left dead or wounded, lying on the field of battle.[23]

The United States 3d Division went on to perform creditable service to the end of the war. When Joseph Dickman was promoted to command IV Corps, he was succeeded at 3d Division by Beaumont Buck, of Cantigny. Eventually Buck, also promoted, was succeeded by the aggressive Preston Brown, of the 2d Division. But the moment that made the 3d Division immortal in American military annals was its first, earning it the title of the "Marne Division."

CHAPTER FOURTEEN

SOISSONS—THE TURNING POINT

It is not often possible to say of wars just when and where the scales wavered, hung, then turned for good and all . . . but when, at half-past ten of the morning of July 18 . . . the Americans and Moroccans had carried the plateau that gave artillery command of the main highway from Soissons to Chateau Thierry, the war's great divide was topped.

—LIEUTENANT GENERAL HUNTER LIGGETT [1]

MAJOR GENERAL ROBERT LEE BULLARD, until recently the commander of the 1st Division, was enjoying the heady feeling of promotion. He had just been elevated to the position of corps commander following General Pershing's decision to begin organizing the American Expeditionary Force into corps.[2] Replacing Bullard in command of the Big Red One would be the loud, hard-driving, and ruthless Charles P. Summerall, previously division artillery commander.

Bullard's elation was tempered, however, by a severe touch of regret. He hated to leave his prestigious post as commanding general of the vaunted Big Red One. A corps command, while a step up the ladder, was a faceless position.[3] So Bullard sought solace in the unrealistic idea that he was not leaving the 1st Division entirely, as his newly organized IV Corps would include both the 1st and 2d Divisions.

Bullard had little time to indulge such thoughts, though, because he could sense that something big was in the air. To find out what was in the offing, he made his way to Tallefontaine, the place where he was to meet his new corps, a few miles north of Villers-Cotterêts. There he learned that something big was indeed about to happen. General Ferdinand Foch had decided to assume the offensive against the Germans, and the place he had chosen to do so was at the Aisne-Marne salient, created by Ludendorff's third and fourth offensives in late May and early June.

The main effort in reducing that salient was to be made on the west by General Charles Mangin's French Tenth Army, which was to attack from the Forêt de Retz (Forêt de Villers-Cotterêts, known to the Americans as the Retz Forest)[4] eastward to cut the main road and rail lines running from Soissons south to Château Thierry. Bullard's corps was to play a leading role. Understandably, Bullard's spirits were perked up by this heady prospect, and he was further elated to be serving under General Mangin, the "Fox Terrier with the clamped jaw." Mangin was one of the most aggressive of the French commanders, and unusually friendly toward the Americans.

FOCH'S PLAN to reduce the Aisne-Marne salient was no fly-by-night concept; it had been in the planning stage for weeks,[5] its execution delayed until he believed that Ludendorff's strength had been sufficiently dissipated. By mid-July, Foch had decided that the time was ripe, and on the 14th, the day before Ludendorff launched his short-lived fifth offensive against Reims and Château Thierry, he ordered Pétain to put it into motion four days later. Intelligence had predicted one more attack by Ludendorff, but Foch, optimistic as always, declared that the attack "would constitute an extremely efficacious method of defence."[6] Since placing troops into position and stockpiling supplies would require four days, the date was set for the early morning hours of July 18, 1918. That schedule was never altered.

Admittedly, Foch's Soissons offensive carried risk. During those four days of preparation between July 14 and 18, the several divisions involved would be on the road, moving to the assembly area of the Retz Forest. If things should go badly on other fronts during that period, those divisions might, in Foch's words, be "sorely missed." But he would take that chance. Foch, described as "a man of ardent spirit and unflinching will," was always in his element when attacking.[7]

Though Bullard now had responsibility for both the 1st and 2d Divisions, he could not instantly forget his concerns for the command he had just left, the 1st. The four infantry regiments, he knew, had been given time to rest; but the artillery had been left on the line to support the small French division that had replaced the 1st at Cantigny, and its troops were tired. Nevertheless, the division was attacking under conditions far better than those of the previous January in Lorraine. It was July, so the men were not facing bitter cold, and the once emaciated horses, thanks to steady care, could now be called "rounded out, fat, chubby," fit for harder work. Bullard took pride that his former division arrived at the Retz Forest "in good order on time."[8]

The 2d Division, Bullard's other American unit, was not so well off as the 1st. True, it was more experienced, for its battles at Belleau Wood and Vaux had involved the entire division, not a single regiment, but the experience so gained was more than offset by the losses suffered. Through the replacement system these had been made up in numbers, but the leaders lost at Belleau Wood could never be fully replaced. Further, the 2d Division had not been alerted to move to the Retz Forest as early as the 1st. Bullard was anxiously awaiting its arrival when, on the night of the 17th, its new commander, Major General James G. Harbord, reported in, bedraggled and highly upset.

Though promoted to major general six days earlier, Harbord had been left in the dark regarding his next command. Still temporarily assigned to the 2d Division, Harbord had secured Bundy's grudging permission to take a few days' leave in Paris. He left happily, anticipating some shopping for his wife and visiting with old friends from AEF headquarters. At lunch with Pershing, he received his first intimations that Omar Bundy would be leaving 2d Division, a prospect that might have given Harbord hope and even expectation of succeeding to command the division. But nothing was confirmed; he did not know what division he would be assigned to.

At that point, James Harbord was riding the crest of a wave, and his friends cheerfully indulged his already well-developed vanity. On Sunday evening, July 14, he was guest of honor at a dinner held in the Inter-Allied Club, once the home of Baron Charles Rothschild. Thirty guests were present, and the speeches, given by people who had seen the glittering headlines but not the grim reality of Belleau Wood, flattered him beyond reason.[9] Back in his hotel, however, he was brought forcibly down to earth by a midnight call from Colonel Preston Brown, still chief of staff of the 2d Division.

Harbord, Brown disclosed, had now been confirmed as the new commander of the 2d Division, and General Foch had called a meeting in Paris for the next morning. Harbord, as the new division commander, was expected to attend. Harbord instantly dropped his personal plans and alerted his aides. Together they left Paris early the next morning for 2d Division headquarters, located in the Château de Chamigny on the Marne. It was necessary, Harbord thought, to assume formal command of the division before returning to Paris for the meeting. There he learned that his division was to move to the Retz Forest and that he was to report to General Bullard.

It was then that Harbord's troubles began. Once back at the division headquarters, he discovered that the French high command, in his absence, had removed his divisional artillery to Betz, just southwest of the Retz Forest and near the Tenth Army headquarters of General Mangin. At the same time, the division trains had been moved to Lizy-sur-Ourcq, in the general direction of Betz but separated from the infantry. The next day, Harbord was informed, the four infantry regiments of the division were to move by bus to Marcilly, also close to Betz. However, those regiments were so dispersed around the countryside that Harbord had no idea where they were. Exasperated, he went ahead of the troops to Bullard's headquarters. Colonel Brown, as chief of staff, could round up the missing parts of the division.

Harbord was in a difficult position. He had not seen the terrain his division was going to fight over, and he was not yet sure where his infantry regiments were—or if they would arrive in time for the attack. He felt keenly that he was new to command. Still, he spurned offers from well-meaning French officers to write his division attack order, for there was a limit to how much patronizing he could endure.

Harbord's troops were experiencing troubles worse than humiliation, however. The soldiers and marines of the 2d Division were stumbling and sliding their way through the ancient forest preserve in the rain. They had been without sleep for two nights, and the roads were clogged with trucks, horses, and even tanks. In one instance, a horse stepped sideways in front of a marching marine, who had fallen asleep with his head pressed against the horse's flank.[10] Others fell asleep but kept marching. Once again, as at Belleau Wood, the division had been subject to confused direction from the French. Colonel Brown, a stickler for military punctilio, growled at receiving movement orders from a French captain, but he obeyed the order anyway.[11] Somehow, however, things fell into place. The 2d Division infantry, exhausted, made it to the line of departure the next morning with only minutes to spare.[12]

The men finally in place, Robert Bullard was faced with an agonizing decision. As the time for attack approached, he realized that the corps he was to command (now III Corps, not IV Corps) was incapable of functioning—"the newest thing I ever saw—except what the stork brings," he wrote later. Its officers and men were unfamiliar with each other and with their duties, and the short time remaining before the attack would be totally inadequate for him to organize them so they could "function as a corps."[13] His troops would come under the French XX Corps, commanded by French General P. E. Berdoulat.

Bullard therefore decided, based on the contingent authority Pershing himself had given him, that his two divisions should go into the Soissons attack as divisions "in a French corps, already on the ground, with its orders and plans all ready."[14]

It was a sensible thing to do. It was also courageous. Bullard knew that Pershing would be disappointed to see his hopes for an operational American corps delayed. And Pershing did not take disappointments lightly.

BERDOULAT'S XX FRENCH CORPS, with headquarters at Retheuil, was now scheduled to make the main effort of Mangin's attack, which was in turn the main effort of Foch's July offensive. For this task he had been assigned five divisions, the 1st and 2d United States Divisions, the 1st Moroccan Colonial Division, and the French 58th and 69th Divisions.[15] For the attack he planned to use the two American divisions and the Moroccans in the first line, and the two French divisions following in the second line.

They made a powerful combination. The American divisions were large, well-led, and enthusiastic.[16] The Moroccans were veteran troops, described as "warriors of all the races of the earth—Negroes, Moroccans, Canadians, Spaniards, Americans, Chinese, and Senegalese," including remnants of the old French Foreign Legion. They were also old friends of the 1st Division. It was the Moroccans, seven months earlier, that the 1st Division had relieved in far-off Lorraine, and the Americans knew their quality as soldiers. It was a source of satisfaction to Bullard to note that the Moroccans had heard of the fighting spirit of the Yanks and were now greeting them warmly as reliable comrades, not as pupils.

Berdoulat's scheme of maneuver reflected the French policy of making maximum use of the new American divisions. The area in which his corps was to operate consisted of a plateau shaped like a rough square, seven miles to a side, cut by many steep ravines. His corps mission was to attack from the western face of this square and drive eastward to cut the Crise Ravine, through which ran Ludendorff's main artery, both road and rail, between Soissons and Château Thierry. The 1st U.S. Division was located in the north, the most favorable terrain; the 2d Division in the south was also on good ground. Berdoulat placed the Moroccans in the center, where a formidable ravine at St. Pierre-Aigle, with the Bois de Quesnoy behind it, virtually forbade attack. That meant that the Moroccans would have to wait until the initial attacks of the Americans,

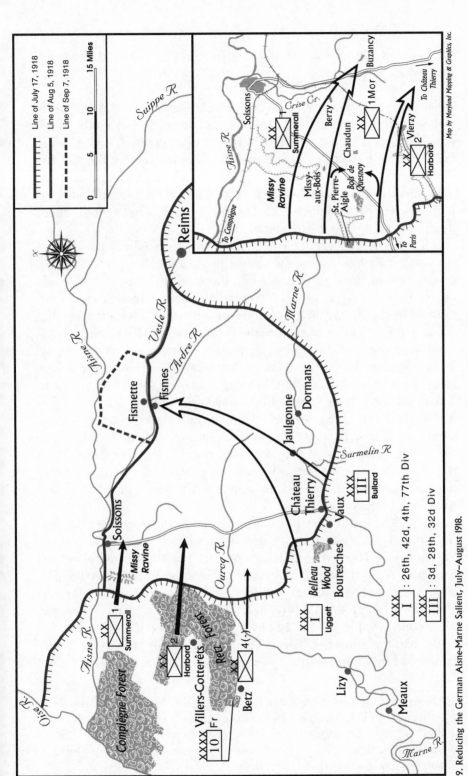

9. Reducing the German Aisne-Marne Salient, July–August 1918.

Marshal Foch's plan for reducing the salient created by Ludendorff's third offensive, which had been launched on May 27, 1918. The main effort was made by the U.S. 1st and 2d Divisions and the French 1st Moroccan Division. Other American divisions, notably the 4th, 28th, and 32d, also attained valuable battle experience.

especially the 2d Division on the south, could drive forward and pinch the obstacle out.[17]

THOUGH THE FRENCH WERE STRONG in artillery, the attack was made without a formal preparation. The rains and mists had hidden the Tenth Army's concentration in the Retz Forest. A few minutes before H-hour, however, the French let loose with heavy counterbattery fire and the heretofore sporadic German artillery fire was silenced. The neutralizing of German artillery gave Bullard some comfort, though he still reflected that "artillery fire is not what kills men; it is the machine guns." Those deadly weapons were still in operation.[18]

The battle, Bullard would later claim, was essentially won in the first day's attack. By 8:00 A.M. of the 18th of July the 1st Division had made a penetration of about three miles into the German lines, and the main enemy defenses were broken.[19] Nevertheless, the attacking troops did not find the battle easy: it took five days for the 1st Division to cover the remaining seven miles to capture the town of Berzy-la-Sec, whose commanding position effectively cut the Soissons–Château Thierry highway. The main obstacle was the fearsome Missy-aux-Bois Ravine, about four miles behind the original German lines, a ravine so steep that American counterbattery artillery was ineffective against German guns shielded in it.[20] When the 2nd Brigade reached that ravine, they were forced to clear it out, foot by foot. In addition, as the division approached Berzy-la-Sec at the end of the third day,[21] the plateau narrowed, restricting maneuver so that the town became a virtual fortress. By July 24, after a week of fighting, the 1st Division crossed the Soissons–Château Thierry road and seized the heights of Buzancy.

The 2d Division, on the south, had heavy fighting after the first penetration was made. Its problems began when it reached the level of the plateau and turned north to join up with the Moroccans behind the St. Pierre-Aigle Ravine. By the time all these units met, they had become disorganized. Soldiers, marines, and Moroccans were intermingled. However, progress was rapid from then on, and by the evening of the second day, July 19, the 2d Division had reached the point where it could take the Soisson–Château Thierry road under artillery fire. Harbord then sent an impassioned plea to French General Berdoulat:

I desire to insist most strongly that [my division] should not be called on for further offensive effort. Due to the congestion of the roads through the Forêt de Retz, the regulation of which was not under our control . . . the troops in the fighting line of the division have many of them been without water or food for over twenty-four hours.[22]

Throughout these days the fighting was brutal, and the American units, in common with all troops relatively new to combat, who require a great deal of personal leadership, lost an inordinately high proportion of its officers. In one instance a battalion, a major's command, was being commanded by a sergeant—and commanded well.

The highest ranking officer killed was Colonel Hamilton Smith, the commanding officer of the 26th Infantry, 1st Division. Ironically he met his death after the main operation had ended. By July 25, the end of the campaign, all of Smith's field officers had been either wounded or killed, and Smith was himself acting almost as a platoon commander. While conducting some of the officers of the 15th Scottish Division around the area in preparation for a relief, he detected a German machine gun emplacement nearby. Taking a few minutes to direct a unit to reduce the machine gun nest, he exposed himself and was cut down, dying instantly. Smith's death, the regimental history noted, "brought gloom and a grim determination to avenge."[23] Every battalion commander of the 26th Infantry was a casualty, and the 3,500 man regiment, a colonel's command, had been taken over and directed smoothly by a captain with only two years of service in the Army.[24]

Despite the high casualties, the units performed admirably, and when the 1st and 2d Divisions were withdrawn, they left in good order. The 1st Division had taken 3,800 prisoners and sixty-eight field guns, in addition to cutting the Soissons–Château Thierry road.[25] The price, however, had been high. In three and a half days, the 2d Division sustained 4,300 casualties, about half the number it had lost during the three weeks of fighting in Belleau Wood. The 1st Division lost even more, some 6,900 officers and men.[26]

THOUGH THE FRENCH XX CORPS of the Tenth French Army executed Foch's main effort in reducing the Aisne-Marne salient, its success did not mean that the salient immediately evaporated. Many thousands of determined German troops remained throughout the area, and they were going to fight wherever there was a strong defensive position; they were not disposed to turn tail and run. American divisions participated in other French corps, and for the first time in the war an American corps directed troops in battle.

Major General Hunter Liggett, whose I Corps headquarters had been training ever since early in 1918, was finally about to take it into the active chain of command. The troops under its command were located in the Belleau Wood area, where the 26th Division had replaced the 2d. Liggett had established his headquarters at La Ferté-sous-Jouarre, a town about halfway between Meaux and Château Thierry, on June 18, and when Foch's Aisne-Marne offensive was launched on July 18, I Corps commanded both the 26th and a French division in the attack. It was a first, soon joined by Bullard's III Corps, once it had been whipped into shape.

The axis of attack for I Corps was southwest to northeast, from Belleau and Château Thierry toward Fère, about eighteen miles away, with a final objective of Fismes, on the Vesle River. Next to Soissons and Reims, Fismes was the most important town in the salient. That action was also important; it quickly made veterans of some new American divisions, particularly the 28th (Pennsylvania) and the 32d (Wisconsin).

CORPORAL CHESTER E. (ZEB) BAKER, a soldier in Company F, 112th Infantry, 28th Division, had been in France for only three months. On July 15 he saw his first serious combat. Baker was a twenty-five-year-old National Guardsman, who had served with a unit of the 28th on the Mexican border in 1916 and 1917 but had not seen any action. Now he was undergoing the first shock of battle.

Near Queue Farm, on the left of the 3d Division, Baker caught his first glimpse of the face of war. There his outfit had undergone heavy shelling in the first stages of the counterattack that began on July 18. According to Baker, he and his comrades were nearly "unmanned":

> We saw ambulances overturned, their cargoes of wounded men—some still on their stretchers—now beyond all help. Tanks, twisted and useless, sat silent with their crews hanging dead from the tops of them; field artillery, battered into useless junk, their firing crews bloated corpses in the hot sun, the stench . . . the overwhelming stench that made us fight to keep our gorges down, and, most horrifying of all the clouds of vultures circling in the azure sky over the battlefield . . . props in a morality play about the futility of war.[27]

The 28th Division, whose red "Keystone" shoulder patch would soon be nicknamed the "Bucket of Blood," was teamed up with the 32d ("Gemutlichkeit") Division from Michigan and Wisconsin in attacking up the Château Thierry–Fismes road. This road, though secondary to that running from Soissons to Château Thierry, still constituted a substantial supply route for the German shock troops that Ludendorff was trying to maintain in the Aisne-Marne salient. The Americans of the 28th met only light resistance at first since the 32d Division had been carrying the bulk of the fighting. On August 6, however, the 28th Division arrived within sight of Fismes, most of which was already occupied by troops of the 32d Division. The 32d Division men welcomed their relief warmly.

The first assignment of Baker's 2d Battalion was to finish clearing out Fismes, which sat on the south side of the Vesle River, across from Fismette on the north. To do so, they were ordered to search through "every tiny nook and corner, to rout out any lingering Germans." Senses alert, Baker dodged from doorway to doorway, looking.

As Baker made his way through the streets of Fismes, he was startled to hear the strains of music coming from a large, half-ruined brick house, with only part of its roof left. Fascinated, he entered into the wide central hallway and looked through a double door into a large parlor. There stood a great piano, undamaged, with a mud-spattered, bewhiskered young soldier seated before it, playing some piece of unfamiliar classical music. Beside the musician stood another soldier, rapt as was Baker. "There was something nearly sacred," Baker later recorded, "about sounds so beautiful rising to the heavens in the midst of terrible devastation."

The young pianist finished, and Baker burst into applause. The musician stood and bowed "as if he'd been in the Metropolitan Opera House." Then after a bright smile, he went back to his playing, switching for Baker's benefit to a familiar old hymn, "In the Garden." Baker was overwhelmed with emotion:

> I felt tears trickling down my cheeks as I silently said the words I'd loved to hear my mother sing, along with the music: "and He walks with me, and He talks with me, and He tells me that I am His own . . ." Never, never, before or since, have the words had such meaning to me. Never had I felt such dependence on my Maker.

Baker never saw the pianist again—he never learned the lad's name.

Once more out in the street, the young Pennsylvanian was brought back to the grim task at hand. There in the public square a couple of his comrades were examining something mysterious. Baker joined them and saw a "huge, round marble pillar, one of four which supported the porch of the magnificent city hall," lying across the street. Sticking out from beneath the pillar was the khaki-clad arm of a doughboy, still clutching its rifle. A little further on lay a dead German soldier with an American bayonet, its rifle still attached, protruding from his breast. Beside the German corpse lay another American, his probable killer. Baker presumed that the American was "the owner of the rifle, who'd evidently been shot or killed by flying shrapnel before he could draw out the bayonet."[28]

Baker's company stayed in Fismes two days, awaiting the moment to cross the Vesle River into Fismette, on the other side. The Vesle was only a few yards wide, a stream by American standards, but it was unfordable, and the single bridge crossing it had been demolished by retreating German engineers. For the men of the 28th it was a time of suspense; they had a feeling that the German force was on the run, and they wanted to follow up their advantage. Nevertheless they had to wait until American engineers, often working under fire, could replace the regular bridge with a pontoon bridge.

On August 8, Baker's company started across the pontoon bridge, protected by the fires of the 109th Machine Gun Brigade. Soon they found that German artillery had the bridge in range. Incoming fire hit several Americans, and when Baker instinctively paused to help one, a voice came from the rear, "Keep going, keep going, the medics will get them." Feeling guilty, Baker hurried on.

After some fighting on the Fismette side of the river, Baker found himself still confused about where the Germans were and where the Americans were. An old German civilian, hit in the neck by a random rifle shot, came running out into the street, shouting "Kamerad! Kamerad!"

Just then Baker heard another shot ring out. The old man's knees buckled, and he sprawled headlong, still yelling in fright. The shot had been fired by one of F Company's new replacements, a boy who appeared to be not over sixteen, his face white from terror. The boy did not stop, but pumped round after round into the old man's dead body. Baker could not condemn the boy; the saying around F Company was that there are only two kinds of soldiers: the quick and the dead. Nevertheless, he surmised that the boy would see the aged man's face in his dreams for the rest of his life. The old man reminded Baker of his own father.

As the fighting continued, Baker found himself standing beside a young American officer, looking over a group of German dead and wounded. Suddenly one of the wounded men rose and fired a pistol at the officer, who responded instantaneously, blowing away the man's lower jaw. The officer turned away, trying to find an English-speaking officer among the German prisoners. Having found one, the American ordered his prisoner to accompany him on an inspection of the German wounded. A noise interrupted him; the man whose jaw had been shot off showed that he was still alive, the lower half of his face missing except for his tongue. The expression in the man's blue eyes would, in Baker's words, "have made an angel weep." The man's pleas were all too eloquent, and Baker tapped the pistol at his side. The man nodded frantically.

Baker drew his pistol but could not fire it. Just then a sergeant came running up toward him. "Shoot the poor devil!" he shouted. Baker could still not pull the trigger. The sergeant gave him a furious look and screamed, "You damned, yellow-bellied coward!" He then drew his own pistol, put it to the man's head, and pulled the trigger.[29]

The taking of Fismette did not end the Aisne-Marne campaign, but further offensive action northward was soon suspended by order of Marshal Foch, who settled for a line north of the Vesle but short of the Aisne. Important objectives beckoned elsewhere, and the German gains from Ludendorff's five offensives had been essentially erased. American participation in the reduction of the Aisne-Marne salient was major— 300,000 men, suffering fifty thousand casualties.[30] And as George Marshall later put it,

> The entire aspect of the war had changed. The great counteroffensive on July 18 at Soissons had swung the tide of battle in favor of the Allies, and the profound depression which had been accumulating since March 21st was in a day dissipated and replaced by a wild enthusiasm throughout France and especially directed toward the American troops who had so unexpectedly assumed the leading role in the Marne operation. Only one who has witnessed the despair and experienced the desperate resolution when defeat is anticipated, can fully realize the reversal of feeling flowing from the sudden vision of a not too distant victory.[31]

GENERAL PERSHING was now close to realizing his goal of a separate American force. Several American divisions had proven themselves in battle, and two American corps—Liggett's I Corps and Bullard's III— had functioned well. Two such corps placed together would constitute an army. Armed with that argument, the American general left Chaumont on July 24 to attend a meeting at the headquarters of Marshal Foch to present his case. Haig and Pétain were also present with certain staff officers. Pershing brought a small group, headed by his G-3, Colonel Fox Conner.

The meeting, in contrast to some others in recent memory, was full of good feeling and confidence. Ludendorff's fifth offensive had been stopped cold on the Marne, and the Aisne-Marne salient, which jutted down into the Allied positions, was just being rendered untenable. "It was the general opinion," according to Pershing, "that every advantage should be taken of this fact and that the Allies should continue their attacks with as much vigor as possible."[32]

Pershing was enjoying an aura of newfound success. He might not yet be fully accepted as a coequal by the other generals—he was still too new and his men were still too untried—but he possessed a trump to all their aces: the American Expeditionary Force now numbered 1,200,000 men and was increasing in strength at the rate of 250,000 a month.[33] The

French and British had been fighting for years, and possessed the edge in experience and organization, but they had drained their countries' manpower. Pershing controlled the only force that was growing stronger every day.

In view of the moral and material advantages the Allies now enjoyed over the Germans, Foch proposed three new limited offensives in preparation for greater efforts later. The first two were of little interest to Pershing: offensives to free the Paris–Avricourt railroad in the Marne region and the Paris–Amiens railroad in the west. The third, however, affected him directly: "The release of the Paris-Avricourt railroad in the region of Commercy by the reduction of the St. Mihiel salient by the American Army." This last action, Foch concluded, would bring the Allies within reach of the Briey region and permit Allied action between the Moselle and the Meuse.[34] That was music to Pershing's ears. Foch's plan had recognized an American "Army" and at the same time had assigned it a mission!

That same day, still at Foch's headquarters, Pershing arranged with Pétain for Hunter Liggett's I Corps, in the Marne region, to be expanded to four American divisions, two in the line and two in reserve. Further, Robert Bullard's III Corps was to be placed in line next to that of Liggett, the two adjacent corps forming an army on that front. He also visualized a second American army being formed in the St. Mihiel sector. Pershing returned to Chaumont and lost no time in issuing a formal order creating the First Army, to take effect on July 24, 1918. Its headquarters for the moment would remain at La Ferté-sous-Jouarre.[35]

Events were moving rapidly, however. Between July 24, when Pershing had issued his general order, and August 10, when it was to go into effect, the role of the Americans was modified. Foch had decided to halt the Aisne-Marne offensive, so plans to expand the American force in the Marne region were disbanded. For the moment, no second American army would be created. Instead the Americans would be organized into only a single army, the First, and Pershing himself would command it.

Pershing had now assumed two positions: that of Commanding General, American Expeditionary Force, and of Commanding General, First United States Army. The arrangement was awkward, and events would call its wisdom into question. Pershing, however, had the feeling that until he had actually commanded a field army in combat, he would never be able to achieve true equality of status among his Allied colleagues. Yet it would surely be impractical, as well as unacceptable to him, to have anyone installed over him at Chaumont as Commanding General of the AEF. So for the moment he would hold down both jobs.

On August 10, 1918, Pershing motored from Chaumont to La Ferté-sous-Jouarre to take formal command of the First Army and to give instructions for its headquarters to move to Neufchâteau, near Verdun. There it was to begin preparation for the attack on the St. Mihiel salient. General Robert Lee Bullard, Colonel Hamilton Smith, Corporal Chester Baker, and countless others had purchased the American right to equality with their European allies in the Great War.

BOOK THREE

THE AEF FIGHTS INDEPENDENTLY: ST. MIHIEL AND THE MEUSE-ARGONNE

President Woodrow Wilson *Library of Congress*

Colonel Edward House. Though House's title of "Colonel" was only honorary, it was respected. A trusted confidant of President Wilson's, House was given heavy responsibilities despite his total lack of portfolio. He reveled in his power but exercised it well. *Library of Congress*

Left, Secretary of War Newton D. Baker
National Archives

Below left, General Tasker Bliss. The model of a learned soldier, Bliss was for a brief time chief of staff of the United States Army, but his stellar service was given later, as the American member of the Supreme War Council. *U.S. Army Military History Institute*

Below, General Peyton C. March. After serving as General Pershing's chief of artillery until early 1918, March was called to Washington to be chief of staff of the United States Army because of his recognized abilities and ruthlessness. Insufficiently appreciated by others because of his abrasive manner and his physical awkwardness, March performed gargantuan service for Secretary Baker, who never underestimated his contributions. *Library of Congress*

The Draft Lottery. Secretary of War Newton D. Baker, blindfolded, drew the first draft number to be called up: Number 258.   *National Archives*

Below left, Major General Leonard Wood. Wood, onetime Army chief of staff, was a strong advocate of military preparedness along with his friend, former president Theodore Roosevelt.   *U.S. Army Military History Institute*

Below right, Colonel Theodore Roosevelt. Proud of his service in the Spanish-American War, in retirement former president Theodore Roosevelt preferred the title of "Colonel." He was an early and passionate advocate of preparedness for war; his criticisms of the Wilson administration's conduct of the war went beyond the limits of loyal opposition.   *Library of Congress*

General John J. Pershing. This photo of the Commanding General of the American Expeditionary Force was probably taken after the end of the war. *U.S. Army Military History Institute*

Major General James G. Harbord. Originally General Pershing's chief of staff, Harbord was briefly commander of the 4th Marine Brigade and the 2d Division, as well as Commanding General of the Services of Supply. *U.S. Army Military History Institute*

French Premier Georges Clemenceau *Library of Congress*

Marshal of France Joseph Joffre

George Creel. This master propagandist was specifically charged by President Woodrow Wilson with selling the war effort to the American public. *National Archives*

Theda Bara. The prominent motion picture actress—one of the many recruited by George Creel—is shown here at a rally selling Liberty Bonds. *National Archives*

David Lloyd George. Prime
Minister of Great Britain, he
succeeded Herbert Asquith in
December 1916. His antagonism
toward Field Marshal Sir Douglas
Haig did much to bring about
both the Supreme War Council
and the establishment of the
office of Supreme Commander,
which was to be occupied by a
Frenchman, Marshal Ferdinand
Foch. *National Archives*

Field Marshal Sir Douglas Haig.
As Commander-in-Chief of
British forces on the Continent,
Haig came under criticism for
alleged profligacy in spending
British lives in hopeless attacks.
Nevertheless, his fighting spirit
was needed on the bogged-down
Western Front. *National Archives*

Marshal Ferdinand Foch. A corps commander in the early days of the Great War, Foch rose to the position of chief of staff of the French Army. When the Allies finally agreed on the need for a Supreme Commander, Foch was the logical choice. Always optimistic and aggressive, Foch was accused of being too much under the authority of Clemenceau, but he undoubtedly performed a service by keeping the "Tiger" in some sort of restraint. *Imperial War Museum*

Marshal Henri Pétain. Commander-in-Chief of the French forces after the fall of Nivelle in April of 1917, Pétain was a realistic, generous ally to the Americans and a mainstay to Pershing when the Americans felt beset by Foch and Clemenceau. *Library of Congress*

Kaiser Wilhelm II of Germany. This photograph shows why the Kaiser provided an ideal target for Allied and American propagandists. Note that the Dove of Peace atop Wilhelm's headgear is itself wearing a crown. *Imperial War Museum*

German High Command. A posed photograph shows Field Marshal Paul von Hindenburg, Kaiser Wilhelm II, and First Quartermaster General Erich Ludendorff planning strategy. *National Archives*

Destroyer and transport. This was the beginning of a convoy to carry troops and supplies across the North Atlantic. *National Archives*

Major General Pershing lands at Bordeaux in June 1917 *National Archives*

Yanks arriving in England   *Imperial War Museum*

Yanks in church, November 11, 1918. Though not of the same young men, this photo, with its somber, hollow-eyed worshipers, presents a dramatic contrast to the jubilant arrivals in the photo above.   *Imperial War Museum*

Major General (later Lieutenant General) Hunter Liggett. Liggett, as Pershing's second-in-command, was commander of I Corps at Soissons, St. Mihiel, and the Argonne. Later he was commander of the First Army, succeeding Pershing. *National Archives*

Brigadier General Douglas MacArthur. He is shown as commander of the 84th Brigade. Though the uniform is more formal than MacArthur's usual garb in combat, the nonregulation soft cap is in evidence. *National Archives*

Colonel George C. Marshall
National Archives

Lieutenant General Robert L. Bullard. Bullard was commander of the 1st Division in its first actions at St. Mihiel and Cantigny. He was later commander of III Corps and finally commander of the Second U.S. Army. *U.S. Army Military History Institute*

Major General John L. Hines. Hines was General Pershing's adjutant in the Mexican expedition, and the first American officer since Stonewall Jackson to command successively a regiment, a brigade, and a corps. He later succeeded Pershing as chief of staff, U.S. Army. *National Archives*

Colonel (later Major General) Hanson E. Ely. This photo, taken after the war when Ely was a major general, reflects the grim determination for which he was known. *National Archives*

Major General Joseph T. Dickman. Dickman was commander of the 3d Division at Château Thierry; later commander of IV Corps; then I Corps; and finally commander of the newly organized Third U.S. Army.   *National Archives*

Major General Charles P. Summerall. Summerall was divisional artillery commander of the 1st Division, later commander of the same division, and finally commander of the V Corps in the Meuse-Argonne.   *U.S. Army Military History Institute*

Major General John A. Lejeune, USMC. Lejeune, though a Marine Corps officer, had close affiliations with the Army, being a member of the Army General Staff before the war. He was ideal to command the 2d Division, with its noted 4th Marine Brigade.   *National Archives*

Above left, Brigadier General Ulysses G. McAlexander. As commander of the 38th Infantry Regiment, 3d Division, he earned it the title "The Rock of the Marne" with his action east of Château Thierry.   *U.S. Army Military History Institute*

Above right, Lieutenant (later Major) Lud Janda. Twenty-one-year-old Ladislav Janda, Company M, 9th Infantry, 2d Division, rose to command his battalion by war's end. Janda is in the middle in this photo taken just after St. Mihiel.
Courtesy of Mrs. Dot Beard

Lieutenant Colonel George S. Patton, Jr. An ambitious and farseeing young pioneer in tanks, Patton is shown here beside a French Renault tank, the mainstay of his 1st Tank Brigade.   *U.S. Army Military History Institute*

Above left, Brigadier General Fox Conner. This artillery officer became General Pershing's operations officer (G-3) and lifelong friend in later years. *National Archives*

Above right, Brigadier General Benjamin Foulois. Benny Foulois was General Pershing's chief aviation officer in Mexico when this photo was taken in 1916. Less flamboyant than his more-publicized subordinate Billy Mitchell, Foulois's good sense had a great deal to do with the success of American aviation in the First World War. *National Archives*

Below, Preston Brown and Bertie de Chambrun. The occasion for this photo of two very different men is puzzling. Preston Brown was a combat soldier—chief of staff of the 2d Division, later commander of the 3d Division. Colonel Bertie de Chambrun in civil life was Marquis Jacques Adelbert de Chambrun. Descendent of Lafayette and friend of the Americans, Chambrun was assigned by the French to be a liaison officer with Pershing's headquarters. *National Archives*

Above left, Brigadier General William (Billy) Mitchell. Chief aviation officer for the First Army at St. Mihiel and the Meuse-Argonne, Mitchell was an intrepid, outspoken airman and a passionate advocate of air power. *U.S. Army Military History Institute*

Above right, Lieutenant Frank Luke. Known as the Balloon Buster, Luke was the man Rickenbacker considered the best pilot of all. He did not survive the war to rival Rickenbacker, however. *National Archives*

Rickenbacker with his plane. Captain Eddie Rickenbacker, a former race-car driver, became the leading American air ace with twenty-six kills. All airplanes used by the Americans were French. *National Archives*

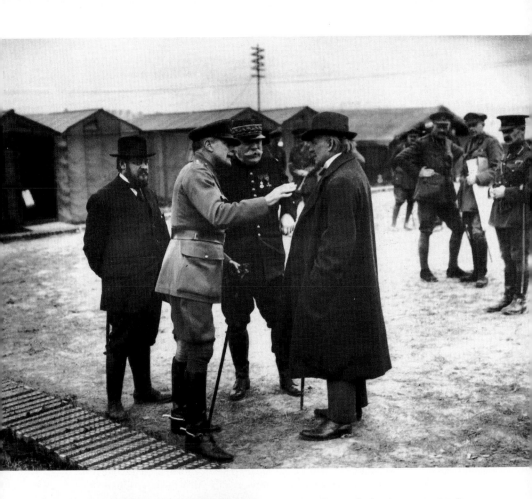

Haig, Joffre, and Lloyd George. No love was lost between the aristocratic Haig and the British Prime Minister. This photo of a conference seems to show a confrontation between them, with French Marshal Joffre as a witness. *Imperial War Museum*

Brigadier General Charles G. Dawes. Dawes, a businessman in civilian life, was in charge of supply procurement from French sources. He was later vice president of the United States under Calvin Coolidge. *Library of Congress*

Stretcher-bearers, Vaux. The capture of Vaux by the 3d Brigade, 2d Division, on July 1, 1918, was carried out quickly and methodically. Like all other actions, however, it had its price. *National Archives*

A chaplain performs his duties. Chaplain (Lieutenant) Finnel of the 124th Machine Gun Battalion identifies the dead of the 33d Division, Meuse-Argonne. *National Archives*

Barrage balloon. These cumbersome devices were invaluable for observation, particularly for artillery adjustment. *Imperial War Museum*

A section of the Hindenburg Line
Imperial War Museum

Gas masks. These were samples of the various kinds of gas masks used by the Western Allies.
National Archives

The 7th Machine Gun Battalion, 3d Division. The first American unit to go into action to stop Ludendorff's Third Offensive, it arrived at Château Thierry on May 31, 1918. *University of Kansas*

Traffic jam at Esne. Traffic jams such as this one on the supply route supporting the attack on Montfaucon materially slowed the rate of American resupply and convinced Clemenceau—at least for a time—that the Americans were incapable of handling their logistical problems. *National Archives*

Foch and Pershing. This photo, showing the strain in the faces of both men, was taken on the 30th of August 1918, the day of their most serious and vitriolic confrontation. *National Archives*

Pershing and Summerall. This photo was taken when Pershing inspected the 1st Division between Soissons and St. Mihiel. *U.S. Army Military History Institute*

American 37mm gun in action. This standard photo, usually identified with action in the Argonne, shows a 37mm gun, not a machine gun, but it is often erroneously identified as such. *National Archives*

Pershing and Baker with nurse. This visit occurred in March 1918 during the visit of Secretary of War Baker to the base hospital at Savenay. Pershing was especially pleased by the military appearance of the nurses. *Imperial War Museum*

Ruins of Montfaucon *National Archives*

Major Charles Whittlesey, commanding
the 1st Battalion, 308th Infantry, 77th
Division, was awarded the Congressional
Medal of Honor for his heroism with the
Lost Battalion in the Argonne Forest.
National Archives

A message via carrier pigeon   *National Archives*

French couple and Yankee guests. This photo taken late in the war shows two Americans from different units. It was probably staged; however, American soldiers were often housed in the barns of French farmers, and scenes like this occurred often. *National Archives*

Varennes from across the Aire   *National Archives*

Hospital in a ruined church   *National Archives*

Singing in a ruined church
National Archives

German machine gun nest. Comprising a substantial crew, these machine gunners were usually willing to make themselves sacrifices for the Fatherland. *Imperial War Museum*

Dead German machine gunner. German tactics in retreat called for a delaying force of machine gunners, whose role was virtually suicidal. Americans erroneously reported that some machine gunners had been chained to their weapons. *National Archives*

British heavy tank in barbed wire   *Imperial War Museum*

Troops of Company I, 368th Infantry. They are shown at the Four de Paris, at the western base of the Argonne Forest. The "Colored Regiments" were attached to the Fourth French Army to protect the left flank of Liggett's I Corps. Note the French helmets.   *National Archives*

Prince Maximillian von Baden. A liberal Junker
generally referred to simply as Prince Max, he was used
to try to secure easy terms for Germany at
the end of the war. *Imperial War Museum*

Ceremony for Marshal Pétain *Imperial War Museum*

General Erich Ludendorff. Though he adopted the strange title of First Quartermaster General of the German Army, Ludendorff was virtual dictator of Germany from late 1916 nearly to the war's end. His departure was a requisite for a peace with the Allies.
National Archives

General John J. Pershing. Pershing cut an impressive figure in the Victory Parade in Paris following the Armistice.   *National Archives*

ST. MIHIEL—
DRESS REHEARSAL

VICTORY WAS NOW IN THE AIR. Only five months earlier, in March 1918, defeat had seemed to loom as Ludendorff's first offensive was launched along the Somme River. The Allies had survived that offensive, and under the new generalissimo, Ferdinand Foch, they had dealt with each successive offensive with increasing success. But it was only in mid-July, with the defeat of Ludendorff's last effort and the passing of the initiative to the Allies at Soissons, that victory seemed assured. Most people continued to think in terms of a war's end in 1919, but some dared to hope that it could come sooner. In any event, the Americans would play a major role.

To make a significant contribution to victory in 1918 or to play the dominant Allied role if the war stretched to 1919, Pershing and the other members of the AEF knew they had to create more than just a group of combat divisions, or even of corps. Their goal was to establish a balanced fighting force, and to do that they needed a logistical system capable of keeping up with the supply requirements of one or more field armies. By the summer of 1918, Pershing was well aware that his problems in building a logistical base were far from solved.

Pershing had long been searching for ways to build up the status of his logistical organization. He had tried, for example, to enhance the prestige of Major General Francis Kernan by redesignating his command from the Lines of Communication to Services of Supply. That renaming was, however, only a cosmetic change, and it had done little to improve the situation. Kernan had been doing a conscientious job, but Pershing had sensed that he was in over his head.

The shortcomings of the SOS were no secret. Visitors from Washington, who included inspectors, congressmen, and others, had reported to Secretary Baker and Chief of Staff March that the ports under American control were functioning inadequately. Ships were being unloaded only at a snail's pace, and when supplies had been landed on the docks, they were not leaving by rail and truck as rapidly as they should. Stocks were accumulating, and near chaos threatened.

Though Pershing was aware of his logistical problems, he was still jarred when he received a long, detailed message on the subject from Secretary Baker. Although the letter was couched in conciliatory terms and covered many subjects, its main point stood out clearly against all the persiflage. Baker and President Wilson both desired, it said, "to relieve you of unnecessary burdens, but of course to leave you with all the authority necessary to secure the best results from your forces." Noting the growth of the AEF, plus the fact that the Americans would be playing a larger role in the battles on the Western Front, the letter surmised that the fighting would "necessarily take more of your time, and both the President and I want to feel that the planning and execution of military undertakings has your personal consideration. . . . The American people think of you as their 'fighting General.' "

To free Pershing to attend to the "military part" of his task, Baker's letter proposed a drastic solution. Major General George W. Goethals, currently Quartermaster General in Washington, could be sent to assume command of the SOS. Goethals, who enjoyed tremendous prestige as the builder of the Panama Canal, could not, of course, be relegated to a position inferior to that of another commander. Therefore,

> Such a plan would place General Goethals rather in a coordinate than a subordinate relationship to you, but of course it would transfer all of the supply responsibilities from you to him and you could then forget about docks, railroads, storage houses, and all other vast industrial undertakings. . . . I would be very glad to know what you think about this suggestion.[1]

Pershing's private reaction on receiving that message has never been recorded. However, he rejected the concept unequivocally. No commander will voluntarily relinquish authority over his means of supply—in four years of fighting neither the British, French, or German armies had ever resorted to such an arrangement. Fortunately for Pershing, his prestige with the people of the United States was such that when he sent back a definite protest, he heard no further word about it.

Nevertheless, something had to be done and done soon. Almost automatically, Pershing turned to his favorite officer, Major General James Harbord.

• • •

HARBORD WAS RELAXING at lunch that July 25, assured that his 2d Division had fought well in the recent Soissons campaign. His troops were now back in a rest area, rejuvenating themselves. He was therefore not unduly alarmed when, during the meal, he received a phone call from Chaumont ordering him to report to Pershing at once. Within fifteen minutes he left by car for the five-hour trip, passing through Meaux, the town his disorganized 4th Brigade had passed through on the way to Belleau Wood only six weeks before. On the way he conjectured idly on the possible subject of the conference. Perhaps Pershing wished to discuss the status of training of the 2d Division. Or possibly, Harbord dreamed, Pershing was ordering him back to Chaumont "out of the goodness of his heart," so he could take a little rest and visit with his old associates.[2]

Harbord, however, was in for a surprise. Hardly had the two men exchanged salutations when Pershing revealed the reason for the summons. He was planning to make some personnel changes in the Services of Supply, he said. He intended to remove Kernan and appoint someone else in his place. Harbord was his choice, and he had delayed bringing the matter up until the 2d Division's role in the Soissons campaign should be complete. Pershing then went into detail, describing the overall setup and the problems with the SOS and asked Harbord if he would be willing to so serve.

Although commanding the SOS was a vital job, the request was still a blow to Harbord. He was happy at the 2d Division and was proud of its success at Soissons. He had permitted thoughts of eventual corps or even field army command to creep into his mind. But first and foremost he was loyal to Pershing, so when he asked permission to delay a final answer until the next morning, there was little doubt in the mind of either man. He would do what Pershing asked.

In accepting the position the next morning, Harbord had one earnest request. He asked that Pershing accompany him on a tour of the various ports being used by the SOS so that the commanding general could explain the circumstances of Harbord's new appointment. As Harbord later described it, "Someone had to be along to explain my being there. It had not been the habit to reward successful commanders of troops in battle by sending them to the SOS."[3]

When Pershing agreed, Harbord hurried back to the Château of Droiselle, his command post, to turn over command of the 2d Division to Brigadier General John A. Lejeune, USMC. Harbord had been in command of the division for only two weeks.

For all his troubles with the SOS, Pershing was happy to be finally organizing the First American Army. He was also content with the sector of the front line that Foch had assigned him, the St. Mihiel salient. The Americans were familiar with the area—some of Pershing's divisions had received their first taste of combat in that quiet zone—but more important, Pershing saw great possibilities for dramatic, decisive action there. Once the St. Mihiel salient was reduced, the American First Army would be well established across the Meuse River and could attack northward and eastward toward the all-important city of Metz and the railroad that ran through it. The seizure of Metz would force the French and British to recognize the Americans as having made a major contribution to the final victory, now anticipated. Pershing began to take steps to put this plan into motion.

He established his new headquarters at La Ferté-sous-Jouarre. After conditions in the Marne sector had quieted down, and Foch had decided to suspend further offensives, Pershing suggested shifting all the American divisions, along with First Army Headquarters, to the St. Mihiel region. Foch readily acquiesced.

Foch dealt in general terms, principles, but it was Pétain to whom Pershing looked for practical cooperation. At Pétain's headquarters on August 9, the two generals took stock of the units the French could make available for the St. Mihiel operation. Much to Pershing's satisfaction, Pétain promised "to do everything in his power to furnish whatever [the American First Army] might require." That evening Pershing gave instructions to the newly established First Army staff to prepare for movement to Neufchâteau.[4] (It was soon moved forward to Ligny-en-Barrois.)

PLANNING COULD NOW BEGIN, and much of the load fell on the shoulders of Lieutenant Colonel George Marshall, formerly operations officer of the 1st Division, who had been called for service in the operations division of Pershing's staff at Chaumont. Unfortunately for Marshall, he was now being penalized for his conspicuous success as an operations officer. Bullard had already selected him to command one of the division's four regiments, a full colonel's position. Instead he would remain at staff work, even if on a higher level.

More important to Marshall, however, was the wrench of leaving the comrades he had come overseas with, had shared hardships with, and had learned with. "Never again," he wrote later, was he to know that "comradeship which grows out of the intimate relationship among those in immediate contact with the fighting troops. Whatever else was to happen to me—in that war or in the future—could be but a minor incident in my career."[5]

Marshall's duties at AEF headquarters required a complete reorientation of his thinking. In the 1st Division he had been intimately involved in concrete matters directly concerned with the mission and the welfare of the troops—feeding, clothing, training, marching, and fighting. "Their health and morale was a daily issue; their dead and wounded a daily tragedy."[6] At GHQ he would be involved instead with such matters as ocean tonnage, ports of debarkation, construction of the AEF's supply line, methods of training on a grand scale, the problems of securing artillery and tanks from the Allies, especially the French—and the complicated relations with those two nationalities.

After his first meeting with Brigadier General Fox Conner, his new boss, Marshall knew why he had been summoned. Not only had he developed a reputation as a planner, but he was intimately familiar with the St. Mihiel area from his early days when the 1st Division had been assigned there as part of its introduction to combat. Seicheprey, the scene of the notable German raid on American lines three months earlier, had been the sector of the 1st Division for weeks.

Much had happened since those early days, however, and as Conner showed Marshall the record of the historic July 24 meeting between Pershing and Foch, the younger officer realized the extent to which the entire aspect of the war had changed. The great counteroffensive at Soissons on July 18 had "swung the tide of battle in favor of the Allies, and the profound depression which had been accumulating since March 21 was in a day dissipated and replaced by a wild enthusiasm throughout France."[7]

Immediately Marshall began planning the reduction of the St. Mihiel salient with what forces were available. At that time, the AEF consisted of only nineteen divisions, of which about half were serving with French and British corps. That left a total of only six American divisions and one French division for the effort. With that relatively modest force he planned to employ four divisions in the assault and three in a follow-up role.

The St. Mihiel salient, a strange bulge in the lines, was shaped like a right triangle. The longer leg ran north–south between Verdun and the town of St. Mihiel. The base, or shorter leg, ran east–west between St. Mihiel and Pont-à-Mousson, on the Moselle River. With only four divisions to employ in the assault, Marshall lacked the force to hit both legs of the triangle. He therefore planned to attack only the southern side, along the east–west line from St. Mihiel to Pont-à-Mousson. If sufficient force were later to become available, he would also hit the north–south leg, which ran through the hilly, wooded highlands called the Heights of the Meuse.

Marshall completed his plan on August 6, only to learn from Conner three days later that three additional divisions had become available, raising his total force to ten, making possible a new, more ambitious plan. Hardly had Marshall finished that one, however, when Conner informed him on August 13 that the total number had been raised to fourteen.[8] Eventually sixteen American and six French divisions would participate in the attack. So Marshall's concerns now switched from a paucity of force to a shortage of space in which to concentrate the new divisions and support them.[9]

Though Marshall always gave his very best to whatever was his task at hand, general staff duty was not what he really preferred. His spirits were therefore raised one day when Major General John Lejeune, the commander of the 2d Division, came into his office with an exciting offer, for him to take command of the 23d Infantry, in the 3d Brigade—if he could shake himself free from his duties at AEF headquarters. Marshall was enthusiastic, and his hopes were high when Lejeune and Preston Brown went into Conner's office to discuss the idea; his hopes ran even higher when he received word from Conner to pack up his belongings. His spirits fell when he learned his destination. He was not going to the 2d Division, but to Neufchâteau, where he would be the operations officer of the newly formed First Army.

Stoically, Marshall made the trip. On reporting to the First Army chief of staff, Hugh Drum, he learned that much planning had already been done—in parallel with his own.[10]

THE MISSION of the American First Army, despite the elaborate preparations, remained open to debate almost up to the minute the St. Mihiel attack was launched. On August 30, the day Pershing assumed responsibility for the St. Mihiel sector, he received a visit at Ligny-en-Barrois from Marshal Foch and his chief of staff, General Maxime Weygand. After the usual exchange of greetings Foch disclosed the purpose of his visit: he visualized a complete change in plans for the employment of the American First Army.

The Germans, Foch said, had been thrown into disorder by the recent Allied attacks, and in order to deny them a chance to rest and refit, he planned for the British to continue attacking toward Cambrai and the French toward Menile. The entire German position in France and Belgium constituted a great salient, against which he planned to attack in a converging maneuver. He desired the Americans to participate by constituting the right wing of this converging force. Reducing the St. Mihiel salient, and following it up by operations east of the Meuse, would not

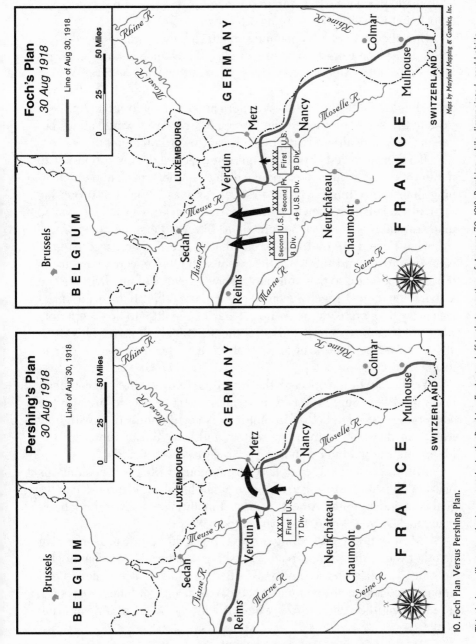

Pershing's Plan
30 Aug 1918

Line of Aug 30, 1918

0   25   50 Miles

Brussels

B E L G I U M

Sedan

LUXEMBOURG

Verdun

Reims

Metz

Nancy

Colmar

Mulhouse

G E R M A N Y

XXXX
First U.S.
17 Div.

Neufchâteau

Chaumont

F R A N C E

SWITZERLAND

Rhine R.

Moselle R.

Meuse R.

Aisne R.

Marne R.

Seine R.

Moselle R.

Rhine R.

Foch's Plan
30 Aug 1918

Line of Aug 30, 1918

0   25   50 Miles

Brussels

B E L G I U M

Sedan

LUXEMBOURG

Verdun

Reims

Metz

Nancy

Colmar

Mulhouse

G E R M A N Y

XXXX
First U.S.
6 Div.

XXXX
Second Fr.
+6 U.S. Div.

XXXX
Second U.S.
8 Div.

Neufchâteau

Chaumont

F R A N C E

SWITZERLAND

Rhine R.

Moselle R.

Meuse R.

Aisne R.

Marne R.

Seine R.

Moselle R.

Rhine R.

Maps by Maryland Mapping & Graphics, Inc.

10. Foch Plan Versus Pershing Plan.

This dual map illustrates the issue at stake in the Pershing-Foch standoff in their meeting of August 30, 1918. Pershing, while disappointed, could abide shifting the American effort from an eastward to a northward direction, but he insisted on keeping the American First Army intact; Foch's plan would have split the Americans into two armies, with a French army in between them.

contribute. He was willing for Pershing to make the St. Mihiel offensive, but to restrict it to an attack against the southern face only. Such a cutback would permit the transfer of a number of American divisions to participate in his planned converging offensive.

Specifically Foch was planning an attack between the Meuse River and the Argonne Forest, to be executed by the French Second Army reinforced by a few American divisions. West of the Argonne, Foch visualized a French-American attack to be launched a few days after the preceding one. On the right, an American army would attack on both sides of the Aisne; on the left the French Fourth Army would attack between the Americans and the Souain Road (toward Mézières).[11]

Pershing bristled. Foch, he quickly concluded, was proposing to minimize the St. Mihiel operation, which the Americans had been planning almost since their arrival in France. Far worse, Foch was proposing to break up Pershing's newly organized American army by taking away so many divisions as to leave a mere shell. Bitterly, Pershing complained, "Marshal Foch, here on the very day that you turn over a sector to the American Army, and almost on the eve of an offensive, you ask me to reduce the operation so that you can take away several of my divisions and assign some to the French Second Army and use others to form an American army to operate on the Aisne . . . leaving me little to do except hold what will become a quiet sector after the St. Mihiel offensive. This virtually destroys the American army that we have been trying so long to form."

Foch doubtless expected that reaction, and he threw out a challenge. Did Pershing, he asked, have an alternative way to execute the converging operation he had in mind? Pershing did indeed: to withdraw American divisions from other sectors and give him a front with the Meuse on his right but extending "as far west as possible."[12]

The discussion was long and acrimonious, with Foch pushing his plan and Pershing refusing to abandon either his planned offensive or his goal of an independent American army. Finally an exasperated Foch demanded, "Do you wish to take part in the battle?"

"Most assuredly," Pershing replied, "but as an American army and in no other way." After a short pause, Pershing countered. "Marshal Foch," he said, "you have no authority as Allied Commander-in-Chief to call upon me to yield up my command of the American Army and have it scattered among the Allied forces where it will not be an American army at all."

"I must insist upon the arrangement."

"Marshal Foch, you may insist all you please, but I decline absolutely to agree to your plan. While our army will fight wherever you may decide, it will not fight except as an independent American army." Pershing then produced a letter from President Wilson giving him authority to insist on just that point.

By this time both men had risen from the table. Foch wrapped up his maps and the meeting broke up without agreement. Pershing thought, despite the confrontation, that Foch really desired to support an American army but had fallen under the influence of others.[13]

The next day Pershing wrote Foch a lengthy memorandum, mostly a recap of the arguments he had previously put forth. The note, however, included a concession that eventually would solve the impasse: the American Army could, Pershing thought, execute the full-scale attack on St. Mihiel and then continue in another direction without pause. At this point he had in mind the Belfort-Lunéville sector to the south. This proposal represented a drastic departure from Foch's plan, but the offer to execute an additional mission after St. Mihiel at least showed some flexibility.

Pershing now sought the backing of Pétain, and on the same day that he sent his memorandum to Foch he went to Pétain's train at Nettancourt. In Pétain Pershing often found an ally and a source of ideas, and this day was no exception. Both generals, though subordinate to Foch, were agreed that while the Supreme Commander had the right to determine the strategic use of either army, "the details were solely the province of the Commander-in-Chief of the army concerned."[14] Furthermore the French commander agreed that splitting the American forces was a bad idea, though he sided with Foch in opposing extended operations eastward across the Meuse. To meet both Foch's and Pershing's basic needs, Pétain declared himself agreeable to passing the entire front from the Moselle to the Argonne Forest to the Americans. He was not optimistic regarding the success of an attack northward between the Meuse and Argonne, however; he thought that Montfaucon was about as far north as the Allies could reach in 1918.[15]

When Marshal Foch called a meeting at his headquarters on September 2, the sparring continued, but in a more conciliatory atmosphere.[16] When Pershing proposed that the Americans participate in both the St. Mihiel operation and later the northward attack between the Meuse and Argonne, Foch agreed, even conceding that the Meuse-Argonne attack could be postponed to assure American participation. He set the date for the American First Army to jump off in the Meuse-Argonne on September 26—a space of a little less than two weeks after St. Mihiel.

The American commander had achieved his basic goals in securing Foch's agreement to his all-out attack against the St. Mihiel salient and to maintaining the First Army intact. But to secure that conclusion he had paid a fearsome price, just how fearsome neither he nor anyone else realized at the time. The most immediate aspect had to do with the burden he was placing on his staff. He had committed Marshall and others to the nearly impossible task of planning the reduction of the St. Mihiel salient and then, without a pause, to moving some 600,000 men, 2,700 guns, and all their equipment by three roads over a distance of sixty miles, all in the hours of darkness. Within the next twenty-four days, his staff had to plan for "two great attacks on battlefields sixty miles apart." [17]

More important was the price Pershing had called on the American soldier to pay. To keep the American Army intact, the largely inexperienced Americans would have to attack a veteran, professional enemy through the most difficult terrain on the Western Front.

CONFLICTING VIEWS regarding troop employment aside, Pershing could not complain about Allied, particularly French, cooperation. Though the Allies considered the St. Mihiel offensive to be mainly a sideshow, they recognized its importance from a morale standpoint. The French were particularly generous in providing air support. A total of 1,481 aircraft were placed under Pershing's command, all of which—with the exception of the British night bombers—were of French manufacture. Many of the pilots would be French. It was to be the largest concentration of air forces up to that time on the Western Front. [18]

These aircraft were assigned to Pershing as commander of the First United States Army, and he in turn delegated day-to-day operational control to the First Army aviation officer, Colonel Billy Mitchell. Despite his faults, Mitchell was a great organizer and intrepid flier, [19] and his operations order illustrates his zeal and thoroughness. The first mission he assigned his command was to keep enemy aircraft from crossing the front lines and learning of American intentions, especially while the operation was being organized before the battle. On the night preceding the attack, his planes were to hit targets in the enemy rear, especially aerodromes, railroad crossings, and bridges. On the day of the attack, deep patrols would break up enemy air formations, conduct surveillance, and "if the infantry signalling is efficient," launch strafing attacks on enemy machine guns and reserves. Assuming that the German position would then be broken, he directed his pilots to take advantage of the vulnerability of a retreating army. Mitchell intended his air force to execute a plan designed for "facilitating the advance of the ground troops but spreading fear and consternation into the enemy's line of communications, his replacement system and the cities behind them which supplied our foe with the sinews of war." [20] St. Mihiel would be a precursor of the employment of air power in the future.

DESPITE MITCHELL'S EFFORTS to keep the skies over the battlefield free of German planes, total secrecy was impossible. As troops began moving and as rumors began flying, the fact of an impending offensive in the St. Mihiel region could never be hidden. For one thing, American soldiers talked too much. German agents abounded in Lorraine, and everyone, including the civilians, knew that something was afoot. Pershing and his staff therefore set about to confuse the enemy as to the location of the next blow, which the enemy knew was coming. For that task Pershing made use of the unwitting services of his friend, Major General Omar Bundy.

When Bundy was removed from command of the 2d Division and placed in command of the VI Corps, he had no idea that his headquarters was really a dummy. Properly backed up, it could be useful in confusing the enemy. Pershing and his staff set out to convey the impression that the American First Army would be employed in the Vosges Mountains, south of the St. Mihiel salient, where the front line ran a short way west of the famed Belfort Gap. Bundy, not privy to the fact that this was a ruse, was instructed to plan for his corps to attack on a thirty-mile front to seize the area of Mulhouse-Belfort as a passageway into the Rhine Valley. He was sent with a small staff to reconnoiter the area.

Along with Bundy went Colonel Arthur Conger, that expert intelligence officer who had done so much to make the 2d Division's attack on Vaux a notable success. Conger was aware of the nature of his current mission, even though Bundy was not.

Conger checked into an expensive hotel in Belfort and began directing a series of "visible clues" to fool the Germans. For the benefit of enemy air reconnaissance, Conger employed two old tanks in creating an elaborate group of tracks to be picked up by enemy aerial observation. Fox Conner, at AEF headquarters, directed radio stations to fill the air with bogus messages. Conger then left a bogus message to be picked up in his hotel room.

A professional at the intelligence and counterintelligence game, Conger knew that no competent enemy spy would ever believe a message left out in the open. He therefore used a new piece of carbon paper to make two copies of a spurious report which he assiduously sent back to General Pershing. He then dropped a single piece of crinkled carbon paper in the wastebasket and went down to the hotel bar for a drink. When he eventually returned to his room, he found to his satisfaction that the carbon was gone.

The Belfort Ruse was effective, at least up to a point. The Germans, rightly considering any operation to clear the Belfort Gap a foolish idea, still did not completely discount the possibility that the Allies, whom they considered stupid, could try such a thing. As a result, German villages around the nearby Altkirch were evacuated, and fortresses defending the Rhine River were reinforced with additional artillery. Munitions dumps were moved rearward. The local people were fooled more than were their generals; burgomeisters had difficulty in quelling panic among the vulnerable elements of their populations. The hoax remained secret for a time between Pershing, Conger, and a couple of other officers at AEF. Bundy played his part well; he never disclosed the point at which he discovered that he had been a cat's paw. Certainly he never complained about the unconventional role he had been forced to play.[21]

BY SEPTEMBER OF 1918 the attack on the St. Mihiel salient had lost much of its strategic importance. In mid-1917, when the Americans were first planning the location of their sector, it had seemed almost obvious. Each nation was fighting its own battle, and eastern France was the region least vital to either the British or the French. Since that region fit in with Pershing's planned logistical support, and since the Longwy-Briey iron region was so important to Germany, it made an excellent mission for the new American army. But with the appointment of Foch as generalissimo, the efforts of the Allied nations were being coordinated in a way new to the war. Foch was now planning to reduce Germany's penetration into northern France and Belgium by main attacks on the flanks (British and Americans) and by executing holding attacks in the center (French). That plan made the logical direction for Pershing's attack northward toward Sedan and Mézières, not eastward from Verdun to Metz. His AEF would have a vital role on the east flank of the great pincer movement.

Nevertheless, there were strong reasons for going through with the St. Mihiel offensive even after its strategic significance had faded. One was morale. The Americans were organized and ready for this attack, divisions deployed, and supporting forces—artillery, aircraft, and tanks—in place. It was geared to be an easy victory—something important for new troops. Its cancellation would be discouraging. In addition, the existence of the salient at the Americans' right rear, if not eliminated, would be a constant worry as the Yanks attacked northward in the Meuse-

Argonne. There was every reason to conduct the attack, even as a dress rehearsal for the main campaign, to come two weeks later.

The German defenses in the St. Mihiel salient were heavy and elaborate, consisting of two lines. The forward line was called the Wilhelm Defense Zone, and it ran from Pont-à-Mousson on the east to include the town of St. Mihiel itself, a distance of about forty miles, then northward up the Heights of the Meuse to Grimaucourt, just southeast of Verdun.[22] The Wilhelm position was about five miles deep, manned by seven mediocre divisions, totaling 23,000 actual front line troops, with two divisions in reserve. Pershing's intelligence staff estimated that Ludendorff could reinforce the position with two additional divisions in forty-eight hours.[23]

The second line was called the Michel Line, a heavily fortified portion of the Hindenburg Line. It actually ran along the hypotenuse of the right triangle, from Preny on the southeast to Etain on the northwest, a nearly straight line of about fifty miles. In contrast to the lightly held Wilhelm Line, the Michel position was heavily built up.

Ludendorff had never regarded the Wilhelm Line as one of vital importance. It had been held for four years primarily because the Allies had made no serious attempt to blunt it after a costly and unsuccessful effort to do so in 1915. So long as the salient could be occupied at low cost, he had kept it because it constituted a buffer, with the added bonus that it constituted a constant source of concern to the French, into whose side it stuck.

The time had now come, however, for the Germans to evacuate the Wilhelm Line and pull back into the Michel. Ludendorff's intelligence services had detected much movement of American troops behind the southern face of the St. Mihiel salient, and the recent German defeat at the hands of the British at Amiens dictated a shortening of his lines.[24]

Accordingly Ludendorff conferred with the local commanders in the area. Not surprisingly, he found them reluctant to give up the forward position without a fight, arguing that it was desirable to hold "because of the industrial areas behind it." But Ludendorff was adamant, and the local commander, General Max von Gallwitz, ordered the evacuation on September 8, 1918.[25] The Americans were unaware of this, of course, and Pershing's men went about preparing for the assault as if it were to be defended by the Germans to the last man.

Conceptually, Pershing's plan of attack was directed only against the German forward line, the Wilhelm. On the left of the southern face, Dickman's IV Corps (1st, 42d, and 89th Divisions, west to east) was making the all-important attack. The 1st Division was to attack from Seicheprey, at about the middle of the front, and its objective, to be reached in

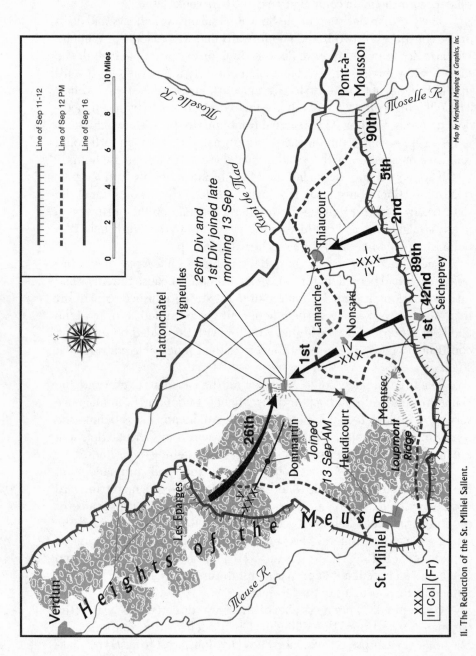

II. The Reduction of the St. Mihiel Salient.

This action, made easy by overpowering force, was performed creditably by the First U.S. Army, and began the long and costly process of building it into a smooth-running machine.

two days, was the small town of Vigneulles, about twelve miles to the German rear. At Vigneulles the 1st Division was to join up with troops from the 26th Division, of Cameron's V Corps, coming down from Mouilly,[26] on the western face. On Dickman's right, the I Corps (2d, 5th, 90th, and 82d Divisions, west to east) was to attack to secure the final line of Regniéville-Thiaucourt-Vigneulles.[27] The nose of the salient was expected to collapse when the flanks were assaulted, allowing the French II Colonial Corps, part of First Army, to occupy the town of St. Mihiel with little effort. It was considered fitting to allow the French to retake the town since it had languished under German rule for four years. The operation was to be supported by a total of three thousand artillery pieces, the "largest concentration ever made to that date."[28] From Pershing's point of view, the operation must allow no possibility of failure.

As was the case at both Cantigny and Soissons, the main effort of this attack would be executed by the 1st Division, as it drove toward the town of Vigneulles. The terrain in which it was operating was rolling, and it included one serious obstacle, the towering strongpoint of Montsec, from which German observers could call down lethal artillery fire. It was a strong position, and it would be expensive in lives—and useless—to attack it frontally. Pershing's planners, therefore, opted simply to bypass it. Montsec was just outside the zone of the 1st Division, and Summerall planned on smothering it with smoke and allowing it to fall of its own weight after the trap between the 1st and 26th Divisions had been closed. Another terrain feature to be reckoned with was a stream called the Rupt de Mad, a sometimes fordable waterway that had to be spanned.

Summerall expected progress to be rapid despite those obstacles, and he therefore attacked in line—that is, all four regiments abreast. Such a formation got the most troops forward in a hurry but downgraded his own ability to react to battlefield changes. Summerall held only one battalion, from the 26th Infantry, plus the 1st Machine Gun Battalion, as his divisional reserve. Since he regarded his left flank, toward Montsec, as his dangerous point, he left the 1st Brigade (16th and 18th Infantry Regiments) intact. The 26th Infantry, which provided the reserve, was on his east, or right flank. The 2d and 3d Machine Gun Battalions he distributed evenly among the regiments. For artillery support, the Big Red One was reinforced to bring the divisional total to 120 75mm field guns, forty 155mm howitzers, and eight 8-inch howitzers, a powerful wallop.[29]

The objective for the 1st Division on September 12 was a German position in the vicinity of the towns of Nonsard and Lamarche, about nine miles ahead of the line of departure and a little over halfway to Vigneulles. There were three other interim phase lines, however, the first one being to secure a crossing over the Rupt de Mad, in front of Seiche-prey. The Germans were not expected to defend any of these positions heavily, and the chief difficulty would be in crossing the bands of barbed wire, both German and American. The American bands were clipped the night before the attack, with safe lanes marked with white tape, but the troops were largely on their own in penetrating the German positions. The British heavy tanks, though originally promised, were declared not available, and the four-hour artillery preparation was not expected to clear a path. Nevertheless, morale just before the attack was high.

PLANNED FOR MONTHS, the St. Mihiel offensive turned out to be an anticlimax in execution. At 1:00 A.M., September 12, 1918, the artillery from the First U.S. Army began a heavy barrage all along the front. At 5:00 A.M., according to schedule, the fires lifted in accordance with what was now an established procedure, one hundred yards advance every four minutes. Then came the surprise: the Americans found the barbed wire on their front remarkably easy to cross. The German wire had been in place for years, and it was therefore old and rusty, easy to break down. Some Americans tossed chicken wire on top of the entanglements, thus tamping it down.[30]

The losses were light, and by a little after noon, the infantry troops of the 1st Division found themselves on the line of Lamarche and Nonsard, the day's objectives. Dickman, at IV Corps, sent word to move on to the second day's objective. At the end of the day, the 18th Infantry, on the division's left, was two miles beyond the day's objectives, and patrols had been sent ahead to locate Heudicourt, to the west, where elements of the 26th Division were expected.[31]

The 26th Division was well chosen to be the other main player of the St. Mihiel salient. It was one of the two American divisions available to Major General George Cameron for his attack from Les Eparges that early September morning. In contrast with the attack on the southern face of the salient, however, those units on the Heights of the Meuse were faced with dense forest. The lead elements of the 26th headed toward St. Remy, Dommartin, and Hannonville on a frontage only as wide as a single road. They were favored with exceedingly light resistance, however, and by 2:00 on the morning of September 13, the lead troops of the 26th entered Vigneulles. Patrols pushed on, and by dawn had made contact with the French 39th Division at Heudicourt, only five miles north of Montsec. Later in the morning they joined up with the 1st Division for a more substantial juncture. The St. Mihiel salient was closed.

The German front gave way but in good order. On the right of the 1st Division Menoher's 42nd Rainbow Division kept pace, crossing the Rupt de Mad early and winding up even with the 1st. The 89th, on the right of the 42d, also crossed the Rupt de Mad, and together with the 2d took the major town of Thiaucourt. The 5th and the 90th protected Liggett's right flank. All divisions wheeled northeast, and pushed up to Ludendorff's Michel Line, without making any effort to penetrate it. By the evening of September 13, Pershing could begin removing troops from the St. Mihiel salient and sending them toward the Meuse Argonne.

By the cruel accounting of modern war, the two-day battle of St. Mihiel involved only light casualties. Yet seven thousand Americans were killed or wounded during the two days of fighting. In a way it was a vast maneuver, a dress rehearsal for the grueling battles yet to come. But a great rehearsal it had been, and it is highly doubtful if the American Army could have been organized and rehearsed in any other way. Tanks and airplanes had been used in numbers heretofore unknown to Americans. New divisions had experienced at least a taste of combat.

The event had produced memorable sidelights, for both the great and the humble. One young officer, humble in rank only, was the irrepressible Lieutenant Lud Janda, commanding Company M of the 23d Infantry, 2d Division, who wrote home five days after the attack:

Dear Folks:
   Came out this time almost without a scratch. Had a peach of a time.
   Got into position 4 hours before H hour. Artillery opened up a fine bombardment and at a few minutes before time to go over we went along the trench waking the men up. (The boys are peculiar—nothing seems to phase [sic] them.)
   When the moment arrived, over we went scrambling and tugging our way through the barbed wire (my clothes are a sight, leggings torn to ribbons) accompanied by the rattle of Fritz's typewriters. Kept going on and finally ran him back a few kilometers thereby breaking his trench system, with its highly-organized positions and abundance of barbed wire. (My hands are pretty well infected.)

Janda had suffered difficulties he did not emphasize to the folks at home. A bomb had gone off right next to him, leaving him stone deaf. But he had no concern about whether he would regain his hearing. And he could communicate by writing and sign language.[32]

Janda was a veteran, who by now had learned to take things in stride. St. Mihiel was, however, an exciting experience to a young replacement, Lieutenant Maury Maverick, who had just reported to the 28th Infantry,

1st Division. Maverick, a brash Texan from an influential family, was a man who seemed to relish living up to his last name. He never missed a chance to ridicule the war in general and his own role in particular. His insouciance sometimes got him into trouble, but he performed his duties conscientiously.

As the first day's battle approached, Maverick found himself in charge of the ammunition train of his battalion. Though in command, he had little idea of what he was supposed to do. He had been given no orders, not even a map. His sole consolation was that he had a horse to ride. When the First Army jumped off in the early morning hours of September 12, the infantry battalions of the 28th went forward so rapidly that Maverick and his command could not keep up. Trying to bring his ammunition train forward to find the rifle companies, he found his way blocked by congested traffic. Telling his men to stay where they were, he left the main road and struck out cross-country to find a way forward.

Suddenly Maverick found himself face-to-face with a band of German soldiers. So frightened was he that he nearly fell off his horse, expecting to be "shot full of holes." His first day of battle, it flashed across his mind, would be his last!

Maverick's life was probably saved by the fact that many Germans, at least in that sector, were thoroughly discouraged with the war and had little stomach to fight. To his amazement, therefore, nobody shot him. The enemy—he counted twenty-six of them—dropped their guns and raised their hands in surrender. "Kamerad! Kamerad!" they shouted as they inched closer to the befuddled American. At a respectful distance they stopped. An officer stepped forward and in bad English pleaded with Maverick to save the lives of his men. By now, Maverick later wrote, he began to feel "very brave and patronizing."

Maverick had a job to do, and he tried to get rid of his new captives. Pointing to the rear, he shouted, "Beat it!" But they would not "beat it." Making themselves understood, they said that if he turned them loose they would be shot by other Americans. By now completely over his fright, Maverick now looked on his captives as only pitiful. Two of the younger Germans were crying. Maverick's pride, which had succeeded his fear, was now transformed into "brotherly love." He acceded to their pleas.

Maverick led his captives back to the main road, some of them marching so close to him that they seemed like "a pack of hunting dogs with a huntsman." One soldier even offered him a piece of sausage. When they finally came upon a larger group of prisoners marching to the rear, Maverick was able to turn his charges loose. Knowing no German, he dismissed them with a terse "Allez!" The leader saluted him stiffly and clumsily, but gratefully.

The wry Maverick later mused to himself about his incident:

> If I had ridden back on my horse, having him curvet and prance, and had shouted that I had captured twenty-six Germans, I could have gotten a crowd together, made a record of it—and have gotten a batch of medals. Since my uncle was in Congress, there would have been no limit.[33]

Maverick's time would come later. St. Mihiel was only his introduction to infantry combat.

Despite the quality of the opposition the Americans faced, legends grew from the St. Mihiel offensive. One had it that two prominent generals of World War II, Douglas MacArthur and George Patton, met briefly on the battlefield, exchanged a few words, and went their ways.

Secretary of War Newton Baker was also on hand to witness the product of his efforts in action. And from Washington President Wilson sent a cable to Pershing:

> Accept my warmest congratulations on the brilliant achievements of the Army under your command. The boys have done what we expected of them and done it the way we most admire. We are deeply proud of them and of their Chief. Please convey to all concerned my grateful and affectionate thanks.[34]

Most remarkable of all, however, was the reaction of Pershing himself. Talking with his intelligence officer, Brigadier General Dennis Nolan, Black Jack confided that "the reason for the American triumph lay in the superior nature of the American character. Americans were the product of immigrants who had possessed the initiative and courage to leave the Old World . . . to make a mighty nation out of a wilderness. Americans had the willpower and spirit that Europeans lacked." The American soldier, he went on, with military training equal to that given a European, "was superior to his Old World counterpart."[35]

Those words seem strange to a modern-day American, but a key to Pershing's makeup is the fact that he believed them. The next few weeks would give him time to reconsider his views on the matter.

CHAPTER SIXTEEN

THE RACE AGAINST TIME

ST. MIHIEL was widely acclaimed as a great success for the AEF,[1] but Pershing, despite his general satisfaction, could allow neither himself nor the nearly two million men in his charge any time to rest and savor victory. The far greater challenge of the Meuse-Argonne lay before them.

Pershing's men would soon be paying a price for the concessions he had yielded to Foch as the price of keeping the American Army intact. He had agreed to launch a major campaign in formidable defensive terrain with inadequate time to prepare, a combination that would inevitably bring hardships on his men. But for the immediate moment his problems were logistical, how to move an army sixty miles, complete with supporting artillery, ammunition, and supplies, in the space of only two weeks. The burden of planning the movement fell on the staffs, and especially on the young operations officer of First Army, Colonel George Marshall.

The task was staggering. At the outset Pershing and his staff conceded that it would be impossible to move the divisions that had fought at St. Mihiel up to the Argonne in time. The artillery, however, would have to make the switch. That meant the displacement of about two thousand guns and 600,000 tons of supplies and ammunition. A single division's artillery, seventy-two guns, would occupy about ten miles of road space.[2] The total artillery to be moved would require three hundred miles of road. In addition, nine hundred trucks were needed to move the infantry of a single American division.

The problem was exacerbated by the fact that the bulk of the matériel to be moved was located on the southern, not the western, face of the former St. Mihiel salient. Nearly all of it would have to cross the Meuse at St. Mihiel and then move northwest of Bar-le-Duc before turn-

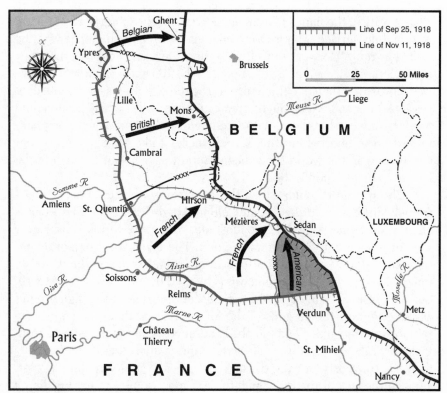

12. Marshal Foch's Plan for the Final Offensive.

Map by Maryland Mapping & Graphics, Inc.

This map shows the American role in the Meuse-Argonne. Considering the growing strength of the AEF, the American role might appear minor. However, the Meuse-Argonne territory was vital to Germany because it protected the railroad line that supplied at least the southern half of their front line troops.

ing northward. The road net was extremely limited. All traffic would have to travel over three muddy roads that were in desperate need of maintenance. Those same roads were also being used by French troops moving from the Belfort region across the rear of the U.S. First Army to join the French Fourth Army on its western flank. To preserve secrecy, all movements would have to be conducted during the hours of darkness.

Fortunately, the French had experience in this type of troop movement, and to cope with it they had created a single office, concentrating all authority in the hands of a single individual. The Chief of the Military Automobile Service, Major Doumenc, made up in competence what he lacked in rank. He worked well with the Americans, and together they made compromises that fit the needs of both armies. If Marshall gave way more often than one might expect, he did so with his eyes open; concessions on small issues might create the goodwill by which one could win large concessions later. With Doumenc's help, American troops were moved up in line behind the French successfully. Marshall later wondered "how in the world the concentration was ever put through in the face of so many complications."[3]

The terrain through which the Americans were to attack was extremely difficult, so difficult that Colonel Hugh Drum, the First Army's chief of staff, once called it "the most ideal defensive terrain I have ever seen or read about."[4] Drum had a point. The First Army area of operations consisted of a north–south corridor, a shallow valley about twenty miles wide. Its right (east) flank was protected by the unfordable Meuse, but the Germans still occupied the adjacent portion of the high ground across the river (the Heights of the Meuse). From that dominating terrain the enemy enjoyed ample observation posts and gun positions from which to rake the eastern half of the American sector. The left (west) flank of the corridor was defined by the elevated Argonne Forest. Though the lack of roads through the Argonne would protect Pershing's force from a major ground counterattack, the Argonne, like the Heights of the Meuse, provided the enemy with a series of ideal artillery positions and observation posts. Between the two heights the Germans could place carefully directed long-range artillery fire almost anywhere in the zone.

From the beginning, Pershing and Foch thought of the American objectives in different terms. Early in September, Foch's order to the First Army called on it merely to break the so-called Kriemhilde position, from Brieulles-sur-Meuse on the east to Romagne-sous-Montfaucon to Grandpré on the west. With the main German position breached, Pershing was to continue in the direction of Buzancy and from there farther northward to Stonne. The Buzancy–Stonne line would outflank the line

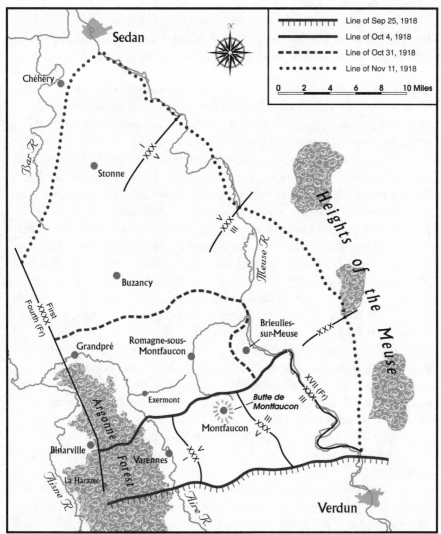

13. The Meuse-Argonne Campaign.

Map by Maryland Mapping & Graphics, Inc.

This map covers the entire American campaign in the Meuse-Argonne region. The initial attack fell short of General Pershing's hopes, which called for seizing the Romagne area in two days. However, once that line was eventually taken, the rest of the attack went into an exploitation phase.

the Germans had assumed along the Aisne River between Vouziers and Rethel (not shown in the map).[5] In other words, Pershing's mission, in Foch's view, was largely to facilitate the advance of the French Fourth Army on his left (west).

Pershing was quite willing to accept those objectives, but they fell far short of the grander scheme he had in mind, to drive toward Mézières and its more famous but less important neighboring town, Sedan, about twenty miles beyond the Aisne. Both are situated on the Meuse, which flows northward at Verdun but then bends westward; it afforded Pershing protection on his right flank at first but, as it crossed over his front farther northward, became an obstacle. Mézières and Sedan were about twenty-seven miles north of Pershing's line of departure.

To reach Mézières and Sedan Pershing's army would have to fight through rolling country that included at least three ridgelines on which the Germans had organized defensive positions. The first was the east–west Etzel position, which was only five miles north of the line of departure. In the middle of this ridge stood Montfaucon (Mount of the Falcon), a very strong position. The next German defensive position was the ridgeline identified by the town of Romagne, about four miles north of Montfaucon. This Kriemhilde Line, mentioned in Foch's September order, was part of the main German position that the Allies loosely termed the Hindenburg Line. A third line, the Barricourt Ridge, was less heavily fortified than either Montfaucon or Romagne, as it represented the last-ditch German defense south of the Meuse, a position that the Kaiser's troops never believed they would be called on to defend.

It would be a mistake, however, to visualize these lines as single entrenchments. The heavily rolling country, which resembles the Shenandoah Valley, provided many alternate (switch) positions, thus giving any single "line" considerable depth. A soldier fighting on a switch position would have no idea as to whether he was attacking the main position or not.[6]

A final feature of the Meuse-Argonne Valley was the Aire River, a northward-flowing stream that essentially defines the eastern edge of the Argonne Forest. As it flows north, the Aire gradually bends westward, eventually joining the Aisne River just beyond Grandpré. Fortunately for the Americans, the Aire was fordable in many places.[7]

The Germans had been defending this territory ever since 1914, and the lines had changed very little since then, despite the sanguinary fighting on both sides of the Meuse during the siege of Verdun in 1916. In the four years of occupation, German construction teams had not only made the positions strong, they had also made the troops who occupied the area as comfortable as possible. Five miles north of the line of contact in the Argonne Forest sat the *Abriz der Kronprinz,* one-time headquarters of the Crown Prince of Bavaria when he was in command of the area. Other positions lacked the marble and the crystal chandeliers that adorned the *Abriz der Kronprinz,* but many of the concrete bunkers and pillboxes were well protected and comfortable. To supply their elaborate defenses, the Germans had run narrow gauge railroads into the area to dumps very close to the front. Numerous bunkers, observation posts, machine gun emplacements, and artillery positions had been laid out at leisure by thoroughly professional engineers. The Germans expected to be there to stay.

Their confidence in the strength of their position in the Meuse-Argonne, however, had caused them to neglect it in recent years. Some of the barbed wire entanglements had rusted through, as they had at St. Mihiel. More important for the Americans, the area was lightly held. American intelligence estimated that only five German divisions were currently manning the extensive defenses as of early September in 1918. Because the American First Army's secrecy measures had been successful, German intelligence could provide no convincing evidence to induce Ludendorff to reinforce the area. Ludendorff, in fact, had been expecting the Americans to follow up the St. Mihiel attack with an offensive eastward to Metz and the Briey iron region, as Pershing had always advocated.

The German ability to reinforce the Meuse-Argonne area, however, was a cause for great concern. Within twenty-four hours, according to Pershing's staff, the enemy could augment the Meuse-Argonne front with four new divisions. In another twenty-four hours they could bring in two more. Nine more could arrive in seventy-two hours. Thus in five days the German total could reach twenty divisions, a daunting force when manning strong defenses.[8]

Under those circumstances, Pershing would have to move rapidly if he hoped to break the Kriemhilde Line before the arrival of German reinforcements could make the American loss of life unacceptable. In the light of Pétain's pessimistic remark that Pershing would be lucky to take even Montfaucon by Christmas, it seemed to be an unpromising prospect. Nevertheless, Pershing decided to take the chance. He ordered the First Army to advance ten miles by the end of the first day, taking Montfaucon and attacking the Kriemhilde position before the Germans had a chance to reinforce. It was a desperate gamble, but Pershing believed that he had no other choice.

For maximum speed Pershing decided to employ nine divisions in the assault, organized in three corps. Each corps would hold a fourth division in reserve. In addition, Pershing kept out an army reserve of six divisions. On such a narrow front, large-scale maneuver in the attack was out of the question; all divisions would drive straight ahead. Pershing might have preferred to use even more divisions, but his logistical support was strained enough as it was.

Pershing's corps commanders—Robert Bullard, George Cameron, and Hunter Liggett—were officers with good records but very little experience at corps level. Of the three, Hunter Liggett, commanding I Corps on the left, had the best organized staff, having assumed command in early 1918. Both Liggett and Bullard had gained some practical experience as components of French armies in the reduction of the Soissons salient. George Cameron, commanding V Corps, was therefore at a relative disadvantage. Cameron had been elevated to corps command from the 4th Division only in time for the short campaign at St. Mihiel.

For some inexplicable reason, Cameron's V Corps, saddled with executing the army's main effort against Montfaucon,[9] was given three inexperienced divisions. And within V Corps itself, the division slated for the all-important assault on Montfaucon was the 79th, quite probably in the worst condition of any unit in First Army. Its commander, Joseph Kuhn,[10] was a respected officer, but the division itself had been continually robbed of all its experienced soldiers and NCOs in order to provide replacements for other units. Nor had the 79th completed the training that most other divisions received before going into the line.

Bullard's III Corps, on the right, fared better. Of Bullard's divisions, the 4th was a regular outfit, and it had acquired some combat experience fighting under the French at Soissons. The other divisions, the 80th and the 33d, were new but satisfactory. In addition, Bullard's mission was the least challenging of those facing the corps commanders.

Liggett, whose I Corps was on the left, was faced with the complicated mission of reducing the Argonne Forest. He would be hampered by the Aire River, which flowed generally in the direction of his attack and therefore restricted the movement of troops across his front. He was also annoyed by the fact that no recognizable terrain feature defined his left boundary with the French Fourth Army—the boundary was a mere line on a map. As a partial compensation, Liggett had been given two of the First Army's veteran divisions, the 28th (Pennsylvania National Guard) and the 77th, a National Army division from New York. His third assault unit was the 35th, a National Guard division from Kansas and Missouri. His main attack, to be conducted along the west bank of the Aire to flank the Argonne from the east, he assigned to the 28th, and the task of entering the Argonne at its base he assigned to the 77th. The least difficult mission, or so Liggett thought, he gave to the 35th, to attack northward east of the Aire.

AS THE TIME FOR THE ATTACK neared, each corps commander was faced with a different set of problems.

General Robert Bullard, whose III Corps was slated to attack on First Army's right, had already proven himself, though he had not participated in the St. Mihiel offensive. In early September he was still embroiled in the Soissons operation under French command. But when Pershing set about to unite his army, Bullard's corps was removed from the French command and sent eastward.

Bullard knew nothing about what was afoot as he prepared to leave. He sensed that something was in the air, however, because of Pershing's unwonted absence from his command post. Pershing had always made a point of visiting Bullard whenever possible, but during early September those visits had ceased. For the first twelve days of the month his absence was easily explained by the St. Mihiel campaign, then under way, but that campaign was now over. But instead of coming to see Bullard, Pershing had simply sent him orders to report to First Army headquarters, at Ligny-en-Barrois.[11] Bullard went ahead on September 6, leaving the rest of his headquarters to follow him.

When Bullard arrived at First Army headquarters, he found that nobody paid any attention to him despite the fact that he was a major general. Unconcerned, Bullard later noted that everyone was "tremendously but suppressedly busy,"[12] because there was so much to do, and it had to be done out of sight of enemy aircraft reconnaissance. As a result, Bullard asked no questions and learned no more than his simple instructions: his III Corps was to proceed to Souilly and he was to report personally to General Hirschauer, whose Second French Army was holding the future American front in the Meuse-Argonne.

As Bullard motored up the road between Ligny and Souilly, he was conscious that this route was known by the French as the "Sacred Road," the lifeline that had saved Verdun from the great German attack in 1916—and all of France in the process. But Bullard was a sardonic man, who had little time for such concepts. Though he conceded that the French might have been right in giving that supply route credit for saving Verdun, he viewed the term "sacred" with some amusement. The somewhat mystical aura of a mere road made him contemplate "how Frenchmen in their own minds fasten upon a single thing as pivotal." Musing on the "dramatic nature" of the French, he concluded that "they hang success or failure upon a single thing, which failing, all is lost."[13] Bullard considered himself an authority on the French mind.

Souilly, though damaged, was a comfortable town, and Bullard found it much to his taste. It was the center of a mighty cantonment of troops, and he was pleased to be billeted in the very house that General Pétain had occupied during the crucial Verdun battle of two years before. He did not have long to enjoy his surroundings, however, for First Army revealed plans to use Souilly for its own headquarters, and he soon received orders to move III Corps headquarters forward. Bullard transferred his staff to Rampont, a town so close to the front lines that German artillery was able to reach it. For its protection, he located his headquarters behind a bluff, thus making it acceptably safe. Still he remained in the dark as to what was going on, though it was obviously something of importance. With J. J. Pershing, as Bullard termed the American commander, it would happen "without announcement."[14]

Bullard soon learned the situation when he was given the general outline of the imminent attack by one of Pershing's staff officers. At the same time he was given a specific mission: his headquarters was to act as the receiving station for all the divisions being sent up from the rear by First Army. Units soon began arriving as rapidly as they could be moved; at one point Bullard noted with a touch of pride that he was directing "more than half a million men."[15] He was in complete charge of placing the units in locations where they could readily move up and relieve their corresponding French units in the line, but in places where they were concealed from enemy observation.

It was a ticklish assignment, because it depended on the way the troops behaved. Their going into position secretly was a "hard duty," as Bullard put it. He was well aware that quiet demeanor and self-discipline were not strong American characteristics and that enforcing discipline would be a test of each unit's training. Although he was generally satisfied with the way the various units met the challenge, their performance was far from uniform. The way in which the troops kept themselves concealed and observed the orders of secrecy was "in direct proportion to the discipline and the training of the divisions to which they belonged." Bullard went even further. According to his observations, he noted, their later performance in battle corresponded "in exact proportion to the thoroughness of their training and the amount of their experience in contact with the enemy."[16]

Major General Hunter Liggett's challenge was far more difficult. On September 21, 1918, his I Corps assumed responsibility for the corps sector on the left of First Army. At his headquarters at Rarecourt the next day he received his orders for the attack, which were to be carried out on the morning of the 26th. In order to prepare thoroughly, he made a point of befriending General Hirschauer, still commanding the French Second Army sector, and found the Alsatian the very soul of cooperation. From Hirschauer Liggett learned every detail he could regarding the ground. He then took his three assault division commanders—Robert Alexander of the 77th, Charles H. Muir of the 28th, and Peter E. Traub of the 35th—over the ground with Hirschauer's guidance.

Liggett's analytical mind studied the terrain carefully. The Argonne Forest itself, he later wrote, was a "long and narrow wood running roughly north and south and not unlike, in shape and position, Manhattan Island. It was bounded on the west by the headwaters of the Aisne and on the east by the Aire River, a small stream flowing into the Aisne at Grandpré, on its eastern shore. Between the two streams were a succession of ridges, some of them as much as 750 feet above the river valleys, all heavily wooded and divided by ravines and gulches with sides too steep for a foothold." The Germans held only the northern half of the Argonne Forest; they had been stopped at this point in 1914. Liggett did not underestimate the problems attendant to the Argonne:

> The region was a natural forest besides which the Virginia Wilderness in which Grant and Lee fought was a park. It was masked and tortuous before the enemy strung his first wire and dug his first trench. . . . The underbrush had grown up through the German barbed and rabbit wire, interlacing it and concealing it, and machine guns lurked like copperheads in the ambush of shell-fallen trees. Other machine guns were strewn in concrete pill boxes and in defiles. On the offense tanks could not follow, nor artillery see where it was shooting, while the enemy guns, on the defense, could fire by map. . . . Patently it would be suicidal to attack such a labyrinth directly; it must be pinched out by attacks on either side.[17]

There was one bright spot, though small in the face of Liggett's obstacles. The Germans had considered the Argonne Forest so easy to defend that they had garrisoned it only with middle-aged men of a Wurttemburg Landwehr division.[18]

HUNTER LIGGETT, quite properly, thought in broad tactical terms, but the close-up view of what was happening on the ground was far different. Corporal Chester Baker, of Company F, 112th Infantry, 28th Division, was one who later recollected events vividly. Baker and his comrades of the Keystone Division left their positions at Fismes, on the Vesle River, with somewhat mixed emotions. They felt relief at being removed from the front, but since they had gone through so much at Fismes, they had developed a proprietary attitude toward the area. In a way they regarded the campaign as incomplete, for the Vesle was one river short of the Aisne, where Ludendorff had begun his third offensive in May. The Pennsylvanians had always felt that, along with the Norsemen of the 32d, they were obliged to restore the original line. From the experience in the Aisne-Marne sector Baker and his compatriots had come to think of themselves as true veterans.

Nevertheless, since Marshal Foch had decided to halt that counteroffensive back in early August, and since Pershing was busy consolidating all available American divisions into his own army, it was only logical that the 28th be withdrawn from the Aisne-Marne sector. So in early September the men of the 28th left the Fismes sector and marched eastward through a driving rain, bound for some unknown destination. After a long and rough ride by truck they reached the town of Blesme-Haussignnemont on September 13, the second day of the battle of St. Mihiel.[19]

At last the men of the 28th settled down in the vicinity of the little town of Les Islettes, south of Varennes,[20] awaiting their turn to move up to the front. Because of the need for secrecy, the Americans would relieve the French on the night before the attack—the night of September 25, 1918.

On the night of the 24th, as the men of the 28th Division were settling into their assembly positions, the division commander, Major General Charles Muir, moved his command post from Les Islettes to a point only two miles behind the lines and made an unexpected tour of the front. The men watched as he gazed contemplatively at countless squirrels as they played among the foliage of the great trees. His men viewed their general with "widespread curiosity." The average soldier, one of them noted, "knows as little of a division commander as of the Grand Llama of Tibet. Frequently he cares as little too."[21]

The following night, Baker's F Company moved up behind the lines and the men were given a few hours to catch some sleep. As darkness descended, the American artillerymen in the Argonne cut the wires that had held the sawed-through trees in front of their gun positions. When they finished removing the trees that had hid them, fields of fire opened through which to shoot.[22]

At 11:00 P.M. a signal gun barked, and in an instant the gunners of all artillery pieces pulled their lanyards. At that moment, what the soldiers called the "million dollar barrage" began. The infantrymen were roused out of their fitful slumber by "all hell breaking loose," the doughboys somewhat irritated that the artillery had failed to notify them before-hand. The noise was so great that even Baker and his fellow "veterans of the Marne" were rattled, to say nothing of the new replacements.

They had not long to wait. Soon they gathered their equipment and fell in along the road, which was jammed with wagons and trucks haul-ing ammunition to the front. Frenchmen, newly relieved from their trenches, tried to make their way to the rear. The animals complicated the congestion. Too often the troops had to stop and help the horses and mules pull the wagons free of boggy places. Sometimes they were told to clear the sides of the roads from barbed wire.

At one point Baker and his men were forced to duck under the long-barreled guns firing at the front, a test of both eardrums and courage. Suddenly a new recruit threw down his rifle and went screaming to the rear.

"Grab that yellow son-of-a-bitch!" the sergeant yelled.

A truck suddenly appeared, carrying an officer. The vehicle's driver slammed on its brakes to avoid hitting the fleeing recruit. The officer jumped out, grabbed the boy with both arms, and yelled to the sergeant to let the matter drop: "I'll see that he gets to a hospital."

As Baker moved on, he thought to himself that "the kid was only giv-ing way to the impulse we all shared." Even the sergeant who had ex-pressed such contempt for the boy, he thought, "was doing so to squelch his own fear demon."[23]

Baker's company reached the position vacated by the French some-time after midnight. The men lay under cover watching the American ar-tillery shells exploding on enemy positions, occasionally cheering when a shell hit a German ammunition dump. Baker was eating a piece of French hardtack when the order came:

"All right, let's go," shouted the captain.

The battle for the Meuse-Argonne had begun.

CHAPTER SEVENTEEN

MONTFAUCON— OMINOUS VICTORY

The troops were tired when they went into the fight. They had been held in the woods with wet clothes and wet feet for a week or more, made a long march before going in, without any sleep, and went over the top after having been under our bombardment for several hours. For green troops it was quite an ordeal.

—Colonel William H. Oury, commanding the 314th Infantry

The doughboys of Pershing's First U.S. Army were facing an awesome task. Pershing had never deviated from his original goal of driving all the way to the formidable Kriemhilde Line the first day of the attack, and his Order No. 20, issued on September 20, made that perfectly clear. "General Instructions for the Attack" specified:

> The advance will be pushed with great vigor. The American Army Objective will be reached during the afternoon of D-Day. The penetration thus made in the hostile third position will be exploited during the night of D/D+1.[1]

Achievement of that ambitious objective was dependent on capturing the Butte of Montfaucon, the hill standing squarely in the center of the army's zone of action. The Butte, not to be confused with the town of Montfaucon at its foot, was not a towering eminence. It stood only about three hundred feet above the floor of the valley. Its location, however, gave it overriding importance; it lay about halfway between the Heights

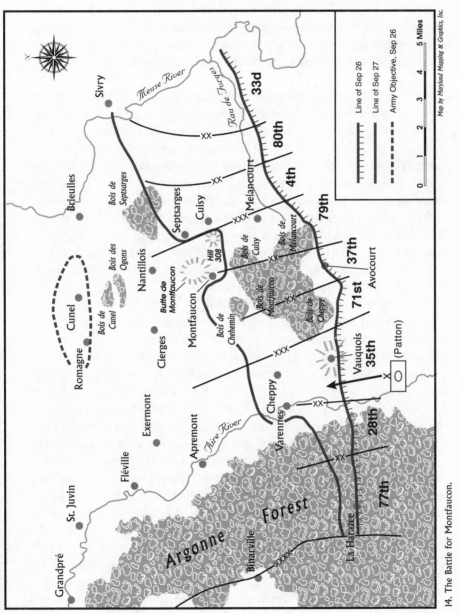

Map legend:

———————— Line of Sep 26
———————— Line of Sep 27
— — — — Army Objective, Sep 26

0 1 2 3 4 5 Miles

Map by Maryland Mapping & Graphics, Inc.

14. The Battle for Montfaucon.

This map shows the action of September 26, 1918, in which Pershing's hopes for a quick and easy victory were dashed. The line at the end of the day fell far short of the Army objective: Cunel-Romagne. It even fell short of taking Montfaucon.

of the Meuse on the east and the Argonne Forest on the west. The outposts atop its crest gave German artillery excellent observation for accurate fire adjustment, thus transforming the Meuse-Argonne Valley from one twenty-mile corridor to two corridors of ten miles each.[2] The town of Montfaucon was also a significant road junction. One road ran from the town center in a northwest direction to Romagne; another ran northeastwardly to Briuelles. These were two of Foch's three original objectives.[3]

Though Pershing's plans made the V Corps drive on Montfaucon the First Army's main effort, they did not provide V Corps with the degree of support normally assigned to such important missions. It was not a question of available infantry troop strength. On paper, Pershing had plenty of divisions available.[4] There were two reasons, one realistic and one mistaken. The realistic consideration lay in the nature of the terrain. V Corps would have to cross a series of thick woods, most of them small, surrounded by a rolling plain that was badly broken up by streams, gullies, and the scars of previous fighting. That ground would be difficult to fight across. Worse, its nature would hinder Pershing's efforts to construct a road net across it capable of supporting a fast, sustained drive. And it would be unfavorable ground for the use of tanks, weapons that were becoming a significant factor in tactical planning.

The second reason why V Corps did not receive more support was the mistaken belief that the seizure of Montfaucon, General Pétain's warning notwithstanding, would be easy. That misconception explains many other seemingly illogical decisions in First Army's planning.

As a result of these assumptions, Brigadier General Samuel Rockenbach, Pershing's senior tank officer, had early recommended to First Army that, since the most favorable operating terrain for tanks would be the narrow valley of the Aire River, he should attach the weaker of his two brigades (forty tanks) to V Corps and assign Lieutenant Colonel George Patton's far stronger brigade (142 tanks), to Liggett's I Corps, whose sector included the Aire Valley.[5] Ultimately, after Montfaucon and the heights around Romagne were taken, the line of the Aire River would become the axis of the army's main effort because it led to Grandpré, where the Aire River met the Aisne and cut off the northern approaches to the Argonne Forest. Beyond Grandpré the zone of I Corps continued northward to Pershing's ultimate objectives of Sedan and on to Mézières on the Meuse.[6]

Artillery support for First Army was less of a problem because it was strong enough to support all three corps satisfactorily. Pershing had 2,775 artillery pieces of all calibers, and his conventional artillery was to be supplemented amply by the use of poison gas. Tactics for such poison gas varied across the front. Since the XVII French Corps, on the right (eastern) bank of the Meuse was not scheduled to attack, Field Order No. 20 called for persistent gases, such as mustard, to be used on the German artillery positions atop the heights across the river. In the areas where American troops would advance, only nonpersistent gases, which would quickly dissipate, could be used. Priority targets for gas attacks were the Argonne Forest, the Bois de Montfaucon, the Bois de Chehemin, and the Bois de Septsarges. Gas bombardment was to cease four hours before the attack commenced.[7]

The amount of air support available was disappointing. Though the Meuse-Argonne campaign greatly surpassed the St. Mihiel operation in size and difficulty, First Army's allocation for this action was only 821 airplanes, in contrast to nearly 1,500 available for the lesser St. Mihiel campaign. The St. Mihiel had been the only operation being conducted on the Western Front during the two days of the attack. When the Americans launched the Meuse-Argonne offensive, the British were attacking to take Cambrai, the Flanders group of armies (British and Belgian) were attacking across the Lys, and the Fourth French Army was moving against the Aisne River position on Pershing's left. All needed air support.

ATTACK OF SEPTEMBER 26, 1918

THE TROOPS of the American First Army went over the top at 5:30 A.M. on September 26, meeting only light resistance at first. A dense fog, which limited visibility to about forty feet, drastically reduced casualties from aimed German rifle and machine gun fire. On the other hand, the fog created confusion, even more than usually follows an attack. Despite the fog, American artillerymen went ahead with the smoke barrage originally planned, unnecessary as it now was. Some of the troops mistook this smoke for an enemy gas attack, and in their struggle to don gas masks many lost contact with one another. In addition, the plans for the officers to lead their troops by compass went awry because the steel fragments embedded in the ground from previous battles interfered with the accuracy of the compasses. As a result, units became separated even more than usually would be the case in an infantry attack. However, once control was regained, the doughboys moved forward swiftly—for a while.

OPERATIONS OF III CORPS

ON THE EAST, Major General Robert Bullard's III Corps encountered few problems. Its mission, to protect the right of the V Corps as it attacked Montfaucon, was limited by the topography. Since the Meuse-Argonne Valley is more of a triangle than a square, the III Corps sector, in its lower-right-hand corner, found itself attacking obliquely toward the river. At least that was so for the two right-hand divisions. Thus Bullard's right division, the 33d (Illinois National Guard),[8] reached its final objective on the Meuse within a few hours, where it dug in behind the railroad track that ran down the west bank of the Meuse. The same was true for the 80th, on the left of the 33d. This division of North Carolinians had a somewhat longer distance to cover, but by the close of the day they had also taken their position on their objective further north on the Meuse, behind the same railroad track as the 33d, and tied in with them on their right.

Bullard's left division, the 4th, was faced with a more difficult task. Unlike the other two divisions, the objective assigned to the 4th lacked a definite obstacle, such as a river, where it would stop. Rather than drive to the Meuse and defend there, the 4th was ordered to continue northward, protecting the right flank of General Joseph Kuhn's 79th Division as it drove toward Montfaucon. Maintaining liaison with the 79th across a corps boundary would prove to be a problem.

The 4th was, however, an excellent choice of unit for this difficult task. It was a regular division, formerly commanded by General George Cameron, whose performance had warranted his elevation to command of the V Corps. Its present commander, John L. Hines, was an even more experienced combat officer. He had been Pershing's adjutant in Mexico two years earlier, and had come overseas commanding the 16th Infantry Regiment in the 1st Division. Later commanding a brigade in the 1st, he had been elevated to the command of the 4th Division because of his superior performance at Soissons. The 4th Division lived up to its promise; in the course of the first day's attack it drove ahead six miles, passing Montfaucon on its left, and consolidated a defensive line on the forward slope of the Bois de Septsarges. Bullard and his men felt considerable satisfaction at the end of the day, though they knew full well that the day's action had been only the first of many difficult ones to come.

OPERATIONS OF I CORPS

AT I CORPS HEADQUARTERS on the west of First Army, Hunter Liggett sat down to play a game of double solitaire. He could do nothing to affect the battle, so he had developed the habit as a way of occupying his mind during the first couple of hours of an attack.[9] In the course of the 26th of

September reports indicated that his I Corps troops had done well. Predictably, his left-hand division, the 77th, made the least progress, because it was advancing into the nearly impenetrable Argonne Forest. Since the German defenses in the Argonne were lightly manned, however, the New Yorkers were able to advance almost uniformly along their front for a mile and a half, slower than their comrades on the right but at least making some progress.

The Pennsylvanians of the 28th Division, attacking on the right of the 77th, were saddled with a complicated problem in coordination. Their left-hand regiment, assigned a sector in the Argonne Forest, could not advance much faster than could the 77th Division on the left. Their right-hand regiment, however, was attacking in the relatively open country of the Aire Valley, and its progress was much more rapid. In the course of the first day the 28th went nearly five miles, taking the half of Varennes that lay west of the Aire and continuing on another mile and a half.[10]

The 35th Division (Kansas and Missouri National Guard) formed the right flank of Liggett's corps. Its front included one challenging obstacle, the Butte de Vauquois, with its honeycombs of tunnels and gun positions from the Verdun battle. Wisely, the 35th bypassed the butte on both sides. Once cut off, the German garrison surrendered without more than token resistance. The division then went on to take Cheppy, in the valley of the Ruanthe Creek, and pushed on, taking over four miles.

TANK ACTIONS IN SUPPORT OF I CORPS

THE FIRST DAY'S ACTION of I Corps was noteworthy for a reason unrelated to the actual ground gained: it served as one of the first major testing grounds of the fledgling American Tank Corps. It was not a test of American equipment; all the tanks were French, most of them small, two-man Renaults. Its significance lay in the fact that for the first time Americans were conducting tank warfare under difficult conditions. Lieutenant Colonel George Patton, whose name would later be so closely associated with tank warfare, headed the effort.

Patton, aged thirty-two, was a dedicated, almost fanatic cavalry officer, who only thirty months earlier had protested passionately when Pershing had decided to pursue Mexican bandit Pancho Villa into Mexico without taking along the traditional cavalry sabers. Patton had made a name for himself in the Mexican expedition as an aggressive, flamboyant officer. A favorite of Pershing's both for professional and personal reasons,[11] he had come to France as one of the general's aides. Once exposed to the fighting in France however, Patton had quickly realized that the day of the traditional horse cavalry was gone, thanks to the introduction of weapons such as the machine gun. He requested and received Pershing's permission to leave the staff and join the new Tank Corps.

Patton embraced his new arm wholeheartedly, regarding it as a successor, even an extension of the old cavalry. That concept ran counter to the thinking of most infantry commanders, who regarded the new weapons only as mobile pillboxes. The future would prove that the tank would perform both functions: independent action and infantry support. Patton was a pioneer in all its uses. His main contribution would be in promoting the tank's independent role. His single day of combat in the Meuse-Argonne was significant.

Patton's 1st Tank Brigade, attached to Hunter Liggett's I Corps for the attack up the Aire Valley, was a powerful unit. Besides its total of 142 small six-ton French Renaults it also included a few of the heavier French Schneiders.[12] Logically, the two types of tanks were grouped separately. The more numerous Renaults were split into two battalions of three companies each; the remaining Schneiders were grouped together as a very small battalion.

On September 21, five days before the attack, Patton visited the headquarters of I Corps and there submitted a lengthy plan for the use of his tanks to the chief of staff, Colonel Malin Craig. The most important aspect of that plan was its basic concept, which called for the tanks to be concentrated rather than dispersed among the infantry. Presaging armored warfare by years, Patton visualized using tanks as an exploiting force, fanning out and wreaking havoc in the enemy rear once a penetration of the enemy's line of resistance had been accomplished.

This plan for the deployment of his unit was unconventional and possibly reflected a desire to keep his tanks under his own command. His brigade was ordered to support both the 28th Division, on the western side of the Aire River, and the 35th, on the eastern side. At first glance, such a mission would call for the assignment of one assault battalion to each of those divisions, so neither battalion would be split by the Aire River. Patton, however, recommended another scheme. Since the flat ground to the east side of the Aire Valley provided about double the maneuver room as that on the western, he planned to form his battalions in column, with the lead battalion deploying one company on the west bank of the Aire and two on the east. His stated reason for so doing was to place the command of the entire vanguard, on both sides of the river, in the hands of his highly trusted second in command, Major Sereno Brett. Conveniently, that method of deployment kept control of the follow-up battalion as a powerful reserve in Patton's own hands. If the plan was questioned, Patton's scheme was approved at I Corps headquarters.

Though under the titular command of Pershing's senior tank officer, General Samuel Rockenbach, Patton overshadowed his chief much as Douglas MacArthur, in the 42d Division, overshadowed his chief, General Menoher. In both cases, it was a personal style that set them apart. Rockenbach kept his headquarters back at Souilly with First Army, the reasoning being that he could best control his units from the rear. Rockenbach was sincere, and he instructed his subordinates to do likewise. He had, in fact, chastised Patton during the St. Mihiel campaign for his habit of leaving his command post to go out with his troops. Patton tried to comply with Rockenbach's desires—there was nothing insubordinate about him, at least in theory. So when the First Army attacked in early morning of the 26th of September, he stayed at his forward command post (whimsically code-named "Bonehead") at Les Côtes de Forimont for as long as his impulsive nature would allow.

It was not long before Patton's patience ran out, however, and he took a group of a dozen officers and men on foot toward Boureuilles and Varennes, following the treads of the tanks that had gone before him.

At first very little seemed to be happening. Patton spotted some of his tanks, stopped to talk with their commanders, and kept going. He also picked up bands of infantrymen going to the rear, claiming that they had become lost from their units in the fog. Giving the men the benefit of the doubt, Patton ordered them to join his party, which soon grew to nearly a hundred men.

Eventually Patton and his party reached a point between Varennes and Cheppy, at a place where a narrow gauge railroad bed crossed the road. There they came under heavy machine gun fire. Patton ordered his men into the safety of the railroad bed and began searching for ways to bring some of his tanks from the rear to silence the German machine guns. (The two messengers he sent to the rear never returned.) Patton finally went back himself, determined to discover the problem. Immediately he saw what it was. His tanks were stymied behind a wide ditch because the single crossing place was blocked by a Schneider tank unsuccessfully trying to cross. Artillery shells were coming in and all of Patton's men were hiding, either in the ditches or inside the tanks themselves.

Despite the warnings and protests of his men, Patton personally exposed himself to the fire while he directed often very reluctant work crews to get the tanks across the ditch. It was not easy to do so. Patton resorted to hitting one man on the head with a shovel. He might have killed him. He never knew.[13] Miraculously Patton was successful in crossing the ditch. Also miraculously, he himself was untouched. "To hell with them," he muttered. "They can't hit me." The tanks went forward and Patton and his men followed on foot. Soon, however, the incoming machine gun fire became so severe that everyone, even Patton, flattened out on the ground.

At that time Patton experienced a vision, which he recorded nine years later:

> Once in the Argonne just before I was wounded I felt a great desire to run. I was trembling with fear when suddenly I thought of my progenitors and seemed to see them in a cloud above the German lines looking at me. I became calm at once and saying aloud, "It is time for another Patton to die" called for volunteers and went forward to what I believed to be certain death. Six men went with me; five were killed and I was wounded so I was not much in error.[14]

Patton never expressed regret over the deaths of the five men who had volunteered to follow him.

Patton was down with a wound in the leg and five men were dead. The only man untouched was Private First Class Joseph T. Angelo, Patton's orderly, who stayed by his side under heavy machine gun fire. Finally, after a considerable time, some of Patton's reserve tanks came by and silenced the German machine guns. Patton, still conscious, continued to direct the movements of his tanks until he was sure that Major Brett had formally taken over the command of the brigade. Even then Patton insisted on being taken to the headquarters of the 35th Division to report before being sent back to an evacuation hospital.[15]

Patton had been wounded without ever having been in a tank during the fighting. But he had used his weapons as he saw fit—as a concentrated force. Major Sereno Brett, who took over, commanded the 1st Tank Brigade for the rest of the campaign. Unfortunately for the Americans, however, the strength of the brigade was rapidly reduced by enemy action and mechanical breakdowns. It played only a minor role in the overall fighting in the Meuse-Argonne.[16]

THE ATTACK OF V CORPS ON MONTFAUCON

THE ATTACKS of the I and III Corps on the flanks were going well for Pershing's army, but those were secondary efforts to the attack of General George Cameron's V Corps to seize Montfaucon in the center of the line.

On that operation, followed by a continuation to seize the Kriemhilde position before the Germans could reinforce it, lay Pershing's hopes of a quick and easy victory. Unfortunately, because of considerations beyond his control, Cameron pursued this all-important mission with one hand tied behind his back.

Besides the modest amount of tank and air support he was receiving, Cameron was also hampered by the choice of the 79th Division, on his right, as the unit to make the attack on Montfaucon. As noted earlier, the 79th was one of those units that had suffered the worst kind of abuse at the hands of higher authorities when it came to personnel. Several times its ranks had been stripped to provide replacements for other divisions. As a result, it was largely made up of untrained troops, 60 percent of its infantrymen and 50 percent of its artillerymen having donned the uniform after May 25, 1918, only four months earlier.[17] In addition to the lack of training and experience, its two infantry brigades were going into battle without the organic divisional artillery regiment, which was still being trained elsewhere. Coordination between the infantry and the artillery units supporting it was thus rendered extremely difficult.

The division commander, Major General Joseph Kuhn, was also inexperienced in commanding infantry troops. Kuhn was a capable, highly respected officer, who had stood at the top of the Class of 1885 at West Point, had been an observer in the Japanese-Russian war of 1904–1905, and had been chief of the Army War College Division of the General Staff in April 1917, when French Marshal Joffre had visited Washington. But Kuhn's field service had always been with the engineers, particularly in construction work and "river and harbor" duty. He was a fine officer but he was no warrior in the mold of Hanson Ely or U. G. McAlexander.[18]

Despite the width of the division's zone—three thousand yards—General Kuhn decided to attack Montfaucon in a column of brigades, Brigadier General William Nicholson's 157th leading and Brigadier General Robert Noble's 158th following. Such a formation kept maximum control in Kuhn's hands, since it provided him with a brigade in reserve to deploy after battle was joined. On the other hand, it made the task of the 157th, in the lead, doubly difficult because it forced Nicholson to supervise activities across the entire three thousand yards (nearly two miles). A frontage of half that length would have been difficult enough! Nicholson did not quarrel; he deployed his brigade with Colonel Claude Sweezey's 313th Infantry on the left (west) and Colonel William Oury's 314th on the right.

The sectors of Nicholson's two regiments were very different, a fact that made coordination between them all but impossible. Sweezey's

313th Infantry, on the left, was to pass through the eastern extremes of a large wooded mass, a forest so large that its various parts were given distinctive names. The first portion of the forest was the Bois de Melancourt; later, a half mile beyond, lay the Bois de Cuisy. To add to the confusion, the eastern edge of the wood mass was uneven, so Sweezey's attack route would take him out of the Bois de Melancourt, but to reach the Bois de Cuisy, only about a mile from the Butte of Montfaucon, he would have to pass across the open ground known as the Golfe de Montfaucon.

Oury's sector, on the other hand, crossed open terrain all along its path. About a mile beyond the line of departure, it would encounter the small town of Melancourt.* Since Oury had the advantage of a road leading from Melancourt to Montfaucon,[19] his route was considered easier, even though it would be open to enemy fire nearly the whole way, passing under Hill 308 and the town of Cuisy on the right. Planners at division and corps had correspondingly considered Sweezey's route through the woods on the left to be the more difficult, and their phase lines reflect that they expected little progress from the 313th.[20]

Once the attack was under way, the 313th Infantry, on the left, found resistance so light at first that by 8:00 A.M. Sweezey reported that his forward troops had reached the far end of the Bois de Melancourt. He was now facing the Golfe de Montfaucon, beyond which lay the Bois de Cuisy.[21] At that point, however, trouble began to brew. The 79th Division headquarters lost contact with Nicholson's 157th Brigade headquarters, and the 157th Brigade, in turn, lost communications with Oury's 314th Infantry. Nicholson, as brigade commander, was forced to choose between keeping in touch with division headquarters and keeping control of his regiments. Quickly, he decided to stick with the 313th. He moved his brigade command post to a point right behind Sweezey's lead battalion in the Bois de Melancourt, out of contact with both division headquarters and the 314th Infantry, on his right. He decided to stay with what he considered the most promising attack.

On the right, Colonel Oury's 314th Infantry also advanced without difficulty at first. Then, after losing touch with Nicholson, Oury moved forward on his own initiative, taking the town of Melancourt by 10:00 A.M. As his regiment passed Melancourt, however, the fog lifted and both lead battalions found themselves under heavy enemy machine gun fire. Pinned down, they called for artillery support, but none came. Lacking in heavy weapons of their own, even the one-pounder 37mm gun, which

---

* Not to be confused with the Bois de Melancourt, in Sweezey's sector.

was fairly effective against machine guns, the infantrymen of the 314th began to feel very much alone. They dug in to defend.

In the meantime, despite the confusion, General Kuhn and his staff at 79th Division headquarters misinterpreted the lack of information as evidence that all was going well. As early as 10:40 A.M. Kuhn reported to General Cameron at V Corps that the front line ran from the north edge of the Bois de Montfaucon in a northeasterly direction. Such a line would have put even the Butte of Montfaucon in American hands. Cameron's V Corps headquarters, delighted, passed the report to First Army at Souilly. But the information was utterly false.

Melancourt was about as far as the 314th Infantry of the 79th Division went that 26th of September, with the exception of a small but important action. Oury made a serious effort to push forward to clear out some enemy that the 4th Division, in its steady drive to Septsarges on its right, had bypassed.[22] With help from the 4th Division, Oury might have taken the Butte de Montfaucon, but no such help was forthcoming. General John Hines, commanding the 4th, was unsuccessful in securing permission from III Corps to come to Oury's aid. Boundaries were considered sacrosanct.

One more attempt to take Montfaucon was made that day. Prodded by 79th Division headquarters,[23] Sweezey's 313th Infantry made a final effort, crossing from the Bois de Cuisy and actually occupying the town of Montfaucon for a short time. However, he could not hold. Lacking artillery support and suffering from enemy artillery and machine guns, Sweezey pulled his regiment back to the Bois de Cuisy, where they dug in for the night.

Although the 79th had advanced some five miles on September 26, it had fallen about a mile and a half short of its first objective, Montfaucon.

ON THE EVENING of September 26, German General Max von Gallwitz evaluated the results of the day's fighting. The American effort had shown inexperience on every hand. Well aware that Pershing's more experienced divisions were still located in the St. Mihiel region, he was still suspicious that the Meuse-Argonne attack might be nothing more than a diversion from the Americans' real effort. Nevertheless, he ordered new reserves into that area. Content with the situation, Gallwitz entered into his record, "On the 27th and 28th, we had no more worries."[24]

SEPTEMBER 27, 1918

AS NIGHT FELL on September 26, General Joseph Kuhn realized that he had failed to live up to Pershing's hopes, if not his expectations. It was a troubling situation for Kuhn, who was well aware that his own career was on the line. Pershing, he knew, would ignore any excuses for failure, no matter how valid. Obstacles such as poor roads, untrained officers and men, and lack of supporting arms did not impress him. Failure such as this would mean only one thing in an officer: an absence of sufficient aggressiveness. His own case, Kuhn knew, would be no exception.[25] The wording of the message he received from V Corps around midnight left no doubt about that:

> Commander in Chief expects the 79th to advance to positions abreast the 4th Division in the vicinity of Nantillois.[26]

To Joseph Kuhn, that order meant that he would have to act and act fast. Studying the approaches to Montfaucon, he concluded that he would have to concentrate first on the left, where Sweezey's 313th, on what had turned out to be the best avenue, had met with greatest success. He was also concerned about the murky situation of the 4th Division, III Corps, on his right. He had received word that the 4th Division had been ordered to take Nantillois, northeast of Montfaucon, and to do so had been given authority to cross into the territory of the 79th, and was even authorized to go behind Montfaucon to get there. Kuhn could not, he believed, conduct an attack in that questionable area for fear of touching off a fight with friendly troops, or at least hitting them with his artillery fire.[27]

To continue toward Montfaucon, therefore, Kuhn decided to reorganize his division; he would now attack with two brigades abreast, giving priority to the 157th on the left. Kuhn sent for the commander of the 158th Brigade, General Noble, at around midnight and ordered Noble to take command of the 314th and 315th Infantry Regiments. He was to move them to the right of the 157th Brigade and make contact with the 4th Division at Nantillois. Noble was given a written order at 1:15 A.M. and told to take action at once. Noble said he understood and departed.

Having accepted his written orders, Noble realized that in the darkness he had no idea where the 315th was now located. (The 316th, it turned out, had moved off to the west, taking position behind the 313th.) So Noble sent out staff officers to locate his units and called a council of war to meet at 7:00 A.M. General Kuhn, however, did not wait for Noble to report. He went to see the situation for himself, finding Noble at the

158th Brigade headquarters at 6:00 A.M. (In the meantime, Kuhn had passed the 315th by the road, apparently doing nothing.) When he asked Noble what he had done thus far, the brigadier had no action to report. Kuhn relieved him on the spot and replaced him with Colonel William Oury, commanding officer of the 314th.[28]

By late morning, September 27, 1918, the 79th Division had found a semblance of order. It was formed with two brigades abreast; fire support in the form of machine guns and a one-pounder cannon had become a reality. As planned, the main effort against Montfaucon was conducted by Nicholson's 157th Brigade on the left. By noon Colonel Sweezey reported that he had taken the Butte de Montfaucon.[29]

General Kuhn greeted the success with exasperation rather than joy. On seeing Nicholson for the first time, he burst out, "Where the hell have you been? What do you mean by breaking liaison with me?"

Nicholson was not to be browbeaten: "I've been taking Montfaucon! That's where I've been."[30]

GENERAL PERSHING had lost his gamble. The Germans, once satisfied that the Meuse-Argonne was the main American effort, began reinforcing rapidly. By the end of the first day, September 26, four German divisions had entered the Meuse-Argonne Valley. By September 30, six more German divisions had arrived.[31] Nevertheless, Pershing ordered the attack continued. By September 29 his army had pushed forward to an average of eight miles. There his forward momentum ceased.

For the first time in the World War, American troops would now be forced to retreat. The 35th Division had pushed forward by the 29th of September to a point across the Exermont Valley, which joined Chehéry with Cierges Ridge. There they ran into a strong German position; in point of fact it was a switch position of the Kriemhilde Line. The Germans counterattacked that day, and the members of the 35th were forced back across the valley. Other assault divisions were likewise exhausted and depleted. Pershing ordered a halt in the attack. It was time to wait for the veterans, now on the road from St. Mihiel.

By taking Montfaucon in a day and a half, the Americans had done better than Pétain had predicted, and by that criterion they had scored a great victory. But that victory had fallen short of Pershing's need to take not only Montfaucon, but Romagne as well, in the course of forty-eight hours. Now the Germans could reinforce their defenses and turn Pershing's hopes for a quick exploitation into a battle of attrition. It was a victory, but an ominous one.

CHAPTER EIGHTEEN

ARGONNE

GEORGES CLEMENCEAU, the Tiger of France, was in the habit of taking an auto tour on Sunday afternoons. Moreover, as the Premier of his country, he was unaccustomed to being denied access to places he wanted to visit. So he thought it completely proper to appear unannounced at Pershing's Souilly headquarters on Sunday, September 29, intending to visit Montfaucon. He had heard that the Crown Prince's luxurious command post on that butte had survived intact and he wished to visit it.

Pershing attempted to dissuade Clemenceau. The roads, he protested, were in no condition for anyone to travel into the battle zone. But Clemenceau insisted. When the Premier threatened to go ahead on his own, Pershing reluctantly agreed to accompany him.

What Clemenceau saw dismayed him. As Pershing had predicted, the roads were jammed with trucks and animals, men struggling to maintain some sort of order and get men and matériel forward. Great 155mm guns, whose weight the roads could never carry, were tearing ruts into already torn-up ground. Part of the congestion was caused by elements of the 1st Division, en route from St. Mihiel. In many places, traffic was at a standstill.

As a result, Clemenceau never came close to seeing Montfaucon. For the moment, as long as he was with Pershing, he masked his fury behind a facade of geniality, but the Frenchman was now convinced that the Americans were unfit to operate as an independent command.

Clemenceau was overreacting to his disappointment. Pershing was all too aware of the chaos in his army's rear area, that the task before him and his men would be difficult and costly, the result of his having lost his race against time. Nevertheless, he had no intention of halting his offensive while he brought order out of chaos; his American superiors would

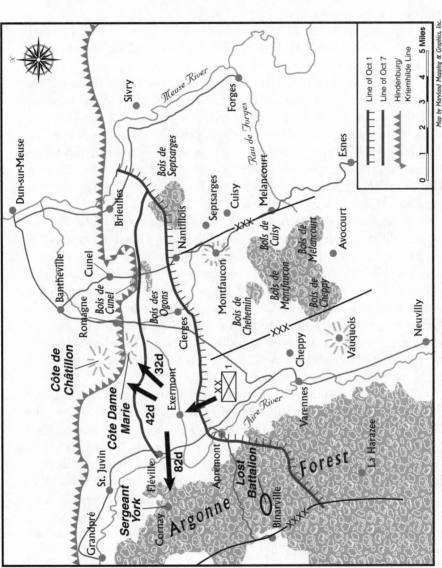

15. The Action at Exermont and the Clearing of the Argonne.

Hunter Liggett's action in bypassing the impassable Argonne on the east and cutting off the German defenders at Cornay was probably the most imaginative action by the Americans during the war. It encompassed two sagas, that of the Lost Battalion, of the 77th Division, and the exploits of Sergeant York, 82d Division.

Map by Maryland Mapping & Graphics, Inc.

never stand for that, and it would run counter to his own nature. On October 1, 1918, therefore, Pershing ordered the First U.S. Army to resume the attack northward to take the ridge of Romagne-sous-Montfaucon, which he had originally hoped to be assaulting on the first day in the Meuse-Argonne campaign.

Pershing had by now brought in some of his more experienced divisions. Those in Bullard's III Corps—the 4th, 80th, and 33d—were left in place. But Pershing removed all three of Cameron's divisions in V Corps. The 79th, so badly mauled in the attack on Montfaucon, he replaced with Beaumont Buck's 3d Division; the 37th was replaced by William Haan's 32d, the veterans of Fismes; and the 91st was pulled back into corps reserve. Those changes left V Corps with only two divisions, the 3d and 32d. At the same time Pershing relieved that corps of responsibility for taking Romagne Heights, specifically the Côte Dame Marie and the Côte de Châtillon. Those prime objectives could be approached indirectly from the southwest, by Liggett's I Corps.

To perform the gargantuan task of securing a foothold on the Romagne hill mass—or at least to initiate the effort—Pershing committed his Praetorian Guard, the 1st Division, in place of the 35th Division, which had been driven back from that position on September 29.[1] That hill mass lay north of the Exermont Ravine, and the German trench line in that area was actually a switch position of the Kriemhilde Line itself. Gallwitz had counterattacked so fiercely on September 29 because an American success in that area would have exposed the Heights of Romagne, west of the Andon Creek. The town of Romagne itself, which lay in the valley of that creek, was unimportant.

To the east of Andon Creek stood the Heights of Cunel, hillocks that dominated the area from Romagne to the Meuse. The effort to take Cunel was assigned to Bullard's III Corps. The objective of Cameron's V Corps was even more limited, the Bois de Chauvignon. To that end, First Army's Order No. 33, issued on October 1, set a boundary that gave Bullard the town of Nantillois as well as the road running from Nantillois to Cunel. Cameron was to have exclusive use of the road that ran from Montfaucon to Cierges, thence north toward the town of Romagne. In a situation where resupply and movement of artillery was at a premium, roads took precedence over high ground.

IN THE DAYS between the halt and the resumption of the advance, the American high command had been conducting serious, even anguished reviews of what had gone wrong in the operation against Montfaucon. There were many factors, but prominent among them was the breakdown of liaison between the 79th Division of V Corps and the 4th Division of III Corps on its right. The 4th Division had driven on past Montfaucon without turning westward to assist its beleaguered sister division. Order No. 33 therefore included the following admonition:

> (X) (2) . . . Corps Commanders within their own corps and by mutual agreement with adjacent Corps Commanders will insure cooperative flanking maneuver between adjacent divisions and brigades. The personal attention of Corps Commanders will be given to this feature of the attack.

Other problems needed to be straightened out as well. One was the tendency of soldiers under fire to huddle together, to bunch up, a natural though dangerous human instinct. The other was the coordination between infantry and artillery:

> (3) Division commanders will give their personal attention to the formation of their infantry in depth and to insure that this depth is employed, not to thicken advanced lines but to pass through advanced lines or for maneuver to the flanks. The mixing of units by the constant reinforcing of the advance lines will be provided against.

> (4) Special step[s] will be taken by Corps and Division Commanders to insure close liaison between the advance infantry line and its supporting artillery. Artillery information officers will accompany the advance infantry line for this purpose.[2]

H-Hour was set for 5:30 A.M., on October 4, 1918.

THE RESULTS of the renewed attack were again disappointing, especially in the eastern portion of the American line. The 4th Division of III Corps took three days to capture the Bois de Fays, only one mile ahead of the line of departure. In V Corps the 3d Division pushed forward but was unable to take the Bois de Cunel. The 32d took Cierges. These were all minimal gains by some of Pershing's best divisions, local successes only.

Once more staffs at all levels began analyzing the problems. The major fault, they concluded, lay not with ineptness on the part of the divisions themselves but in the volume of enemy artillery fire that was raining down from the Heights of the Meuse. Up to that time Pershing had limited the mission of the French XVII Corps, on the Heights of the Meuse, to keeping the enemy "busy by demonstrations."[3] He now reconsidered, and on October 5, 1918, he ordered the French corps to attack along a five-mile front with five divisions, four French and one American.[4] German artillery east of the Meuse would now have a new preoccupation, to protect the front on their own side of the Meuse. If Pershing ever had second thoughts about his original orders, he did not express them.

THE ADVANCE EAST of the Meuse would be slow, but more immediate action could be taken against the Argonne, to the west, the area of Hunter Liggett's I Corps. Action in that area was dramatic; in fact, the operations there between October 2 and October 7 have left the two most vivid stories of the campaign, the ones by which it will be remembered. They are the stories of the "Lost Battalion" and of Alvin York.

Pershing's order of September 29 to suspend operations had not applied to the attack in the Argonne Forest; the 77th Division was ordered to keep pushing ahead to silence the German guns located in the Argonne at the first possible moment. German artillery there was having such an effect on the Americans in the Aire Valley that one officer at First Army feared that their effect would force the Americans to pull back south of Montfaucon, even back to the original jump-off point.[5] The guns had to be eliminated, and efforts to reduce their hiding places in the Argonne Forest by attack up both sides of the forest were not working. So General Robert Alexander's 77th had to keep pushing.

The conditions in the Argonne were different from those anywhere else on the front. The forest was as thick as Belleau Wood, but many times larger. If, as Liggett thought, the forest resembled Manhattan in size and shape,[6] the Americans were beginning on 14th Street. The density of the forest meant that cohesive action between units was impossible; even most of the infantry's supporting weapons were of little use. The Argonne battle therefore degenerated into a series of small unit actions, in which each battalion fought its own little war. No ground, once taken, could be given up. As General Evan Johnson, commander of the 154th Brigade, put it: "Any ground gained must be held. . . . If I find anybody ordering a withdrawal from ground once held, I will see that he leaves the Service."[7]

Such admonitions, while not ignored, were taken with a grain of salt by most officers. One officer who took Johnson at his word, however, was Major Charles W. Whittlesey, commanding the 1st Battalion of the 308th Infantry in Johnson's brigade. Whittlesey had already demonstrated his determination to abide by them. During the advance to the regiment's present position, the 1st Battalion had been cut off by a German infiltration from the west; the regiment of the 92d Division, attached to French units on his left, had failed to keep up. In that "first trap" his men had gone for three days with little or no food, and they were already tired by the time the rest of the regiment had caught up with them. Nevertheless, since some resupply had been possible, Whittlesey's battalion had not been relieved when friendly troops made contact; instead it was ordered to keep its place in the line.

The advance of the 77th was resumed on October 2, two days before the rest of the First Army was scheduled to jump off. Whittlesey's 1st Battalion was in the vanguard, despite his protests. His direction of attack led his battalion up a valley in the direction of Charlevaux, north of Binarville. Soon General Johnson, realizing that Whittlesey's battalion was lacking a company, sent three companies from the 2d Battalion, under Captain George G. McMurtry, to reinforce him. Somehow a company from the 307th Infantry also joined him. Whittlesey therefore commanded a force of seven depleted rifle companies and parts of two machine gun companies. His total at the start was about 670 men.[8]

As Whittlesey's composite battalion moved north, it found a gap in the German line caused by the temporary movement of enemy troops elsewhere. Whittlesey pushed forward and reached his assigned objective on the road leading from Binarville on the west to Apremont on the east. The day was drawing to a close, and he had lost about ninety men pushing through the gap. He placed his command in a ravine south of the road, on the east side of the gully he had been following, where his men would be relatively safe from incoming artillery during the night. He was out of contact with the units on his flank, but that was common in that tangled forest.

Early the next morning, Whittlesey's men began receiving heavy German mortar fire. Becoming uneasy about his open flanks, he sent Company E, now down to about fifty men, back toward the rear with a request that Johnson send his two remaining companies up to join him. A little over an hour later, eighteen men struggled back into his perimeter; they had been ambushed. The Germans had strung wire defenses between Whittlesey and the rest of the 77th Division, and the 1st Battalion was now cut off. Whittlesey sent off the first of his six carrier pigeons reporting his whereabouts.

The second pigeon, released the following morning, October 4, carried a report that Whittlesey had lost 222 men, eighty-two of them killed. His machine gun crews were down to five, manned at half strength. He had only three enlisted medics with him, and they were running out of bandages. Based on that report, General Alexander sent the two companies that Whittlesey lacked; they failed after two tries, each reduced to the size of a platoon.[9]

October 5, the third day of the ordeal, would be the worst. Becoming desperate to silence the mortars and machine guns hitting his position, Whittlesey sent a pigeon requesting artillery support. The shells came in—right on top of his battalion. One platoon was wiped out from the "friendly" fire, and after a couple of hours, Whittlesey had become desperate. He sent his fourth pigeon, pleading, "Our own artillery is dropping a barrage directly on us. For heaven's sake stop it!" Unfortunately the soldier tending the pigeons was nervous, and he allowed a bird to get away without the message. The next pigeon was Whittlesey's next to last, affectionately named Cher Ami. Cher Ami, it turned out, was as frightened as were the soldiers. It flew straight up and perched shivering on a branch of a tree. Whittlesey and the pigeon keeper were therefore forced to expose themselves by throwing stones at the bird. Finally it left for home through the incoming artillery fire.[10]

The next day American artillery fire began to come in on the enemy. The prospect of an immediate German attack was diminishing, and the chief threats to the men of the battalion would now be fatigue, hunger, and thirst. Efforts to combat those enemies were futile. American airplanes spotted Whittlesey's position and attempted to drop supplies. The food, ammunition, water and medicines fell into German hands, and the Americans were forced to hear the Germans enjoying the bonanza while they continued to suffer.

The worst cause of suffering was the thirst. A clear brook flowed only fifty yards from Whittlesey's elongated position, in which the troops were huddled against the hill. Some men tried to make it down the precipitous hill to fill canteens. Few if any survived. Whittlesey then took a drastic step: he posted guards to shoot anyone attempting to sneak down and fill canteens.

Through it all, the men of the 1st Battalion, 308th Infantry, held on, partly out of numbness and resignation to death but also because of the inspiration given them by their two leaders, Whittlesey and McMurtry. Both officers were wounded—McMurtry's swollen knee had been festering for days from a shrapnel wound—but both defied danger by limping and staggering among the men, from foxhole to foxhole, assuring them that help was on the way. After four whole days of siege, they were down to 245 effectives and one pigeon.

WHILE WHITTLESEY'S beleaguered men were enduring their ordeal, events were taking place seven miles to the east that would eventually bring about their rescue. It was not to come from the efforts of their own division in the Argonne Forest but from their comrades across the Aire.

On the night of September 30–October 1, the 1st Division had moved into the lines formerly occupied by the 35th Division. The Big Red One had suffered heavy casualties at Cantigny and Soissons, and had lost a few men at St. Mihiel, but their spirit remained high, thanks to their professional leadership, and they had worked out procedures to develop mutual confidence between units. The 6th Field Artillery, for example, had always supported the 1st Brigade (16th and 18th Infantry Regiments). The 7th Field Artillery had teamed up with the 2d Brigade (26th and 28th Infantry Regiments). The 5th Field Artillery was kept in general support of the whole division.

In the distribution of machine gun companies also, unit association had become routine. Each infantry battalion had its own machine gun company through attachment of companies from the divisional machine gun battalions.[11]

The frontage the division occupied extended about four kilometers, from the Aire River eastward to Eclisefontaine. The eastern portion of the divisional area extended along the Apremont–Eclisefontaine road, but the west part slanted southwestward to Baulny. Almost immediately upon taking over this sector the 1st Division pushed the west portion of the line forward to occupy the Apremont road for its entire length. The 1st Brigade was on the left (west) and the 2d on the right (east).

During the night of October 2, as Charles Whittlesey was first settling into his position, the 1st Division sent out combat patrols to learn the nature of the enemy. What they found was not encouraging. The enemy was obviously there in force, and many patrols were ambushed or caught in machine gun fire. The front of the 1st Brigade was occupied by the German 5th Guards Division, and prisoners taken from that unit reported that they had orders to fight to the last man. The 2d Brigade was facing the 52d German Division. Both, according to 1st Division intelligence, were "fresh, first-class divisions."[12]

The terrain over which the 1st Division was to attack was about as difficult as it could get. The left flank of the 1st Brigade sector ran along high ground above the north–south Apremont–Fléville road, which ran along the Aire, and was open to the raking fire of German guns in the Argonne Forest.

First the troops were to seize a hill mass called the Montrebeau, on which the Chaudron Farm hillock occupied about a mile square. Beyond that hill about a mile was the more formidable Montrefagne, the point of a nose leading northeast to an even more formidable position, Hill 272. To get from Montrebeau to Montrefagne, the troops would be forced to cross a steep cross-compartment, the Exermont Valley, along which ran the east–west Exermont road. General Summerall's plans for the first day called for seizing both Montrebeau and Montrefagne, plus most of the distance to Hill 272. Nobody would have assigned such a mission to any division but Pershing's best.

FIRST DAY, OCTOBER 4

THE ATTACK of the 1st Division jumped off on schedule, at 5:25 A.M. The tanks, which had been held back to prevent signaling the imminence of the attack, immediately joined the lead ranks. The 1st Brigade, following their rolling artillery barrage and utilizing what swales they could to protect them from fire from the Argonne, attacked over the ground that had once been occupied temporarily by the 35th Division. The sight of American corpses, wounds bandaged, left out to die by the Germans, enraged the Americans, inspiring them to take additional revenge. There was also evidence of the carnage that had befallen the various patrols sent out two nights earlier. Despite heavy fire from all directions, the 1st Brigade took its first objective, the northern edge of the Montrebeau, by 7:00 A.M. A half hour later the 2d Brigade was on its first objective also, despite heavy resistance.

After a half hour to pause and regroup, the 1st Brigade continued its attack across the Exermont Ravine, headed for the heights beyond. Elements of the 16th Infantry, along the main road, entered the town of Fléville. The cost was high. The 3d Battalion, 16th Infantry, had crossed the line of departure that morning with twenty officers and eight hundred men. By the time it had secured its second objective it was down to two officers and 240 men. And fire continued from the west. The nearest friendly troops on the left were two kilometers to the rear.[13]

To the right of the 16th Infantry, other regiments had made less progress. But orders were for each infantry unit to push forward on its own, and artillery support had decentralized to create four independent regimental combat teams of infantry and artillery. Despite the fact that the 18th was halted at Beauregard Farm just across the Exermont Ravine, and the 28th at La Neuville-le-Compte Farm to its right, the front remained continuous.

The tanks proved to be a great help in reducing German machine gun nests. Forty-seven of them had started the day with the division, one company with the 1st Brigade, two companies with the 2d Brigade, and one company in reserve. Yet so fierce was hostile fire that only three tanks remained at the end of the day; 84 percent of the tankers were casualties.[14]

THE SOLDIERS ON THE GROUND saw the operation from a different perspective. Lieutenant Maury Maverick, of the 28th Infantry, for one, has left a vivid account of the Exermont attack.

After his easy capture of twenty-six frightened Germans at St. Mihiel, Maverick had undergone a sobering baptism of fire as his regiment, part of the 2d Brigade, had pulled into line at Exermont four days earlier. While Maverick was conferring with his company commander, Captain Frank Felbel, they heard a shrieking noise, then a dull explosion. Suspecting gas, they quickly donned their masks. Groping in the dark, Maverick stumbled over the body of a dead American. When he removed his mask, Maverick winced; the man stank. He was probably one of those men of the 35th Division who had been killed three days earlier. The next morning, in position, Maverick was jarred by the burst of a shell close by. One man was dead; another lost a leg and both arms. Maverick was buried in dirt. He was afraid to move for fear that he would "fall to pieces." But he was unhurt.

As Maverick's company was preparing to jump off at 5:30 A.M. four days later, on October 4, he could hear the various lieutenants shouting at their men. "God damn it, don't you know we're going over the top at five thirty-five?" On the German side there was only silence, a vacuum. Maverick began to hope that the enemy had retreated. When they jumped off on schedule, however, they discovered that the Germans, at least a rear guard of machine gunners, were still there. Forewarned by the American shouting, they could not have been surprised at the timing of the attack.

The Germans were veterans; most of the Americans were not. But the Yanks advanced bravely into the barrage of steel and fire, and their ranks dwindled fast. Of a company of two hundred, half were dead or wounded within a few minutes. Captain Felbel was one of the dead.

Maverick took command. When he counted the survivors, he found that the company had not a single sergeant left. Three of the four platoons were commanded by corporals; the fourth was commanded by Private Quinn, recently reduced for being absent without leave, but a veteran soldier. Maverick recorded his confusion:

At this moment of five-thirty-five, everything happened that never happens in the story books of war. We literally lost each other. There were no bugles, no flags, no drums, and as far as we knew, no heroes. The great noise was like a great stillness, everything seemed blotted out. We hardly knew where the Germans were. We were simply in a big black spot with streaks of screaming red and yellow, with roaring giants in the sky tearing and whirling and roaring.[15]

Still Maverick and his men—what was left of them—pushed ahead. His walking stick did him no good; when he came to a ditch, he fell in it. Still there was nothing to do but keep going. Maverick later recalled holding his head down so that any shell fragments would hit his steel helmet, only to discover that he was not wearing a helmet at all. He borrowed one from "a poor fellow who had no further use for it." It was too small, but there was no shortage of dead Americans who had no further use for their helmets.[16]

On they went. Then a shell burst over Maverick's head, and a piece of it tore out part of his shoulder blade and collarbone. On the ground but still conscious, Maverick was amazed that it seemed less than five seconds before a Medical Corps man was dressing his wound. He looked for the runners who had been with him a minute before. "The two in the middle had been cut down to a pile of horrible red guts and blood and meat, while the two men on the outside had been cut up somewhat less badly but no less fatally."

Still Maury Maverick stayed with his company, for the simple reason that there was nobody else to take over. He found four more runners and kept going. After an hour, however, he had lost so much blood that he was getting weak. He could carry on no longer—though he could still walk. He turned the company over to Private Quinn and headed for the rear.[17]

SECOND DAY, OCTOBER 5, 1918

IN THE COURSE of the first day's fighting, only the 16th Infantry, on the left of the 1st Division zone, had attained its objective, crossing the Exermont Ravine and gaining a foothold on the hill mass across. Elsewhere the division had crossed the Exermont Ravine from Montrebeau and Eclisefontaine and secured footholds on the long, thin hill mass beyond but had fallen short of taking Montrefagne, which was simply the nose of the ridge line running northeast up to Hill 272.

On the second day, therefore, the division's first object was to bring the other three regiments, to the east of the 16th, into line with the 16th. The second objective was to take Montrefagne, and then Hill 272. After that it would continue another mile to seize the Côte Maldah.

As it turned out, only the first objective for the day was accomplished, plus the seizure of Montrefagne, which had nearly been accomplished the day before. At tremendous cost, the 18th, 28th, and 26th Regiments, from west to east, fought ahead about a mile so that the line, as of the end of the day, ran (west to east) from Fléville–Ariétal Farm, into the Bois de Moncy. Only the barest of footholds had been taken on the Hill 272 mass. But the Argonne Forest, to the west, had been flanked.

AT HIS HEADQUARTERS in Floriment, Major General Hunter Liggett, in whose I Corps the 1st Division had been fighting, saw an opportunity to exploit the division's gains. In spite of the fact that the division had not attained all the ambitious goals set for it, its advance from Apremont to Fléville had opened the enemy's east flank in the Argonne. Between those two towns the Americans held the right bank of the Aire and the Germans the left. But the Americans held the initiative.

On the evening of October 5 Liggett blocked out a plan that he submitted to First Army for approval. He would commit his reserve, the 82d Division, from the area just taken by the 1st Division, to attack westward across the Aire, behind the German troops in the Argonne. If successful, the attack would force the enemy to evacuate the Argonne Forest. It would save Whittlesey's Lost Battalion and relieve the 1st Division of the heavy shelling it was still receiving from German artillery west of the Aire.

Liggett's plan was not without risk. By hitting the German rear in the Argonne, he was also opening his own right flank to possible German counterattack from the north. The crossing points of the Aire were problematical; no Americans knew exactly where they were. So Liggett ran into resistance from fainter hearts. At his own headquarters, only his chief of staff, Malin Craig, supported his plan. The French officers attached to his headquarters were unanimously opposed to it. But after Liggett secured the approval of Hugh Drum, chief of staff of the First Army, and then of General McAndrew, chief of staff at Chaumont, Liggett considered it authorized, and he was willing to take the chance. The plight of Whittlesey and of the 1st Division made it all worth the risk.

THE ATTACK OF THE 82D Division lacked the full weight that Liggett would have liked. The bulk of the division was in corps reserve, a considerable distance from the action, and it could not be ready, as a whole division, for some time.

Fortunately for the Americans, one regiment of the 82d, the 328th Infantry, under Colonel Frank Ely, had been attached to the 28th. Liggett immediately sent it to the rear of the 1st Division, on the right bank of the Aire, south of Fléville. Some guides, though not nearly enough, were available.

Early in the morning of Monday, the 7th of October, several companies of the 328th Infantry forded the frigid waters of the Aire River and deployed to cut the north–south road running through the Argonne through Cornay. To secure that town they were forced to scale the steep sides of Hill 180 and, further south, Hill 233. At the same time a brigade of the 28th stormed Hill 244[18] and took the adjacent one-street town of Châtel Chéhéry. The Americans had turned the German flank in the Argonne.

With the loss of that road and the prospect of reinforcing troops from the 82d cutting off their rear, the German command realized that their position in the Argonne had become untenable. They began a hasty withdrawal, and between the morning of the 7th and the 9th they evacuated as much as five miles along the western reaches of the forest. In the south, the 77th Division resumed its attack to the north.

ON THAT SAME MORNING of October 7, Charles Whittlesey's Lost Battalion was entering its fifth day isolated in the Argonne Forest. All efforts to resupply by air had failed, as had all the attacks launched in his direction by the rest of the division. Like many others of Whittlesey's men, Private Lowell B. Hollingshead had given up all hope of surviving this ordeal. He was slightly wounded and weak with hunger. Above all his other desires, even survival, was a yearning for rest and food.

At about 10:00 A.M. an unfamiliar sergeant crept over to the foxhole where Hollingshead and several of his buddies were huddled. Major Whittlesey, the sergeant said, had called for eight volunteers to infiltrate out through the German lines and report the situation of the battalion to their comrades a few miles south. Hollingshead volunteered immediately. He did not know the sergeant, nor did he know what company he was from, but he was impelled by one driving thought, the "desire for food and anything that would help me secure it." [19]

Soon the small patrol was heading south, protected by a light fog and mist. The men crossed the small Charlevaux Creek, some stepping, some wading. In such a dangerous situation none dared stop to drink, thirsty though they were. Stopping to rest for a moment in the protection of a thicket, the men hoped they had broken free. To add to their hope, they had one man, a full-blooded Indian, to act as their guide. They placed their trust in him.

The Indian managed his charges well, stopping periodically to allow them to rest in their weakened condition. Finally, however, he stopped and raised his hand; danger lay ahead.

Then it happened. The patrol found themselves right in the middle of a spate of machine gun fire, and Hollingshead saw little spurts of dirt kicking around them. He lost consciousness and sometime later awoke to find himself looking down the long barrel of a German Luger. The officer holding the weapon was half smiling, half sneering. Hollingshead threw his hands up and muttered "Kamerad." The German, a handsome fellow, then broke into a broad smile. Looking around, Hollingshead discovered the fates of his comrades; four of them, including the Indian scout, were dead. The rest were wounded. Hollingshead's wound in the leg was the least serious.

The next few hours were a relief for the famished doughboy. In the tent of an interrogation officer he refused to talk, but the officer appeared to accept his reluctance. Hollingshead was generously fed and allowed to rest. He identified the officer as Lieutenant Heinrich Prinz, a German who had lived for some time in the United States.

Soon Prinz gave up on interrogating Hollingshead and went across the tent to a typewriter and began typing out a message. He asked Hollingshead if he would take the message back to his commanding officer. The soldier agreed if he could be given time for a little rest. He then dozed off.

Eventually Hollingshead felt a tap on the shoulder. "If you are going to get the message back before dark you must start now." Hollingshead indicated that he was ready. One of the German captors gave him a cane; another tied a white cloth to the end of it. Conducted out of the German position blindfolded, Hollingshead was suddenly alone with a single guide. The guide led him down a road and removed the blindfold. Both men smiled and shook hands. A few minutes later Hollingshead was in the presence of Whittlesey, who immediately began reading the message.[20]

The message was courteous. It described Hollingshead's conduct in glowing terms, calling him "quite an honorable fellow, doing honor to his Fatherland in the strictest sense of the word." Conceding rather generously that Hollingshead was carrying the message "very much against his will," the message got to the point. It urged the American commander to "surrender with his forces, as it would be quite useless to resist any more, in view of the present conditions." Then:

> The suffering of your wounded men can be heard over here in the German lines, and we are appealing to your humane sentiments to stop. A white flag shown by one of your men will tell us that you agree with these conditions.[21]

Whittlesey never bothered to reply. It was not worth the effort. He deduced from the tone of the message that the Germans were finished and that the note was an act of desperation.

That evening elements of the 77th Division broke through the German lines and relieved the Lost Battalion, or what remained of it. Only 191 of Whittlesey's original 670 men were able to walk out of their position.

THE SAGA OF THE LOST BATTALION was one of the stories that have become legend as the result of the actions in the Argonne in early October 1918. The other was the unbelievable exploit of Corporal, later Sergeant,

Alvin C. York. The two incidents were related indirectly, because York's feat was part of the envelopment of the German position in the Argonne, which in turn contributed to the relief of Whittlesey and his men.[22] Neither man was a member of what might be considered the elite formations of the AEF.

Ironically, York had registered for the draft as a conscientious objector to war, for although he was an expert hunter and woodsman from Wolf Valley, Tennessee, he was also an elder in the Church of Christ, which subscribed to the words in the Bible forbidding killing. His mother and the congregation of the church protested his going into uniform when he was called by the draft. At Camp Gordon, Georgia, however, his company commander convinced him of the righteousness of the American cause by quoting scripture. York entered the Army as an infantryman, assigned to the 82d Division. He had no ambition for advancement, and despite his obvious leadership abilities, he had been promoted only to the grade of corporal when the division was committed in the Argonne.

By the morning of October 8, the 328th Infantry, on the left of the 82d Division, had penetrated the Argonne only about 1,500 yards, holding Hill 223. That morning it was ordered to continue the attack westward to seize the Decauville Railroad a little over a mile away, thus cutting a major German line of retreat. York's platoon, on the extreme left of the attack, was commanded by Lieutenant Harry M. Parsons, a former New York vaudeville actor. The platoon having run up against a machine gun nest, Parsons sent Sergeant Bernard Early, with fifteen men, to reduce it. York was one of them.

Under the cover of a heavy morning mist, Early and his men made their way undetected to the rear of the machine gun nest. They fixed bayonets and were preparing to charge the German position when they stumbled on a battalion field headquarters, where three German officers were studying a map and various other soldiers were resting. At one volley, the entire group threw their hands in the air in surrender.

Immediately the German machine gun crew, realizing what had happened, turned around and began spraying both Early and his prisoners, all of whom hit the ground. That burst wounded Early and two others, killing six. York, untouched, immediately assumed command of the seven remaining Americans.

At this point, Alvin York began his own private little war. Ordering the other doughboys to guard the prisoners, he hid in a secluded position and began picking off the Germans, one by one. An expert rifleman, and firing at close range, he missed only one; the rest he killed. Always hoping to end the killing, he shouted "Come down" between shots. At one point a German lieutenant and six men charged York's position. Now down to using a service pistol (so he later claimed), he killed every one.[23]

Seeing what had happened, York's prisoner, the German major, offered to arrange the surrender of all the gun positions, even though York was still vastly outnumbered. The German suggested a route that he said led to the American lines but York's backwoods sense of direction said otherwise. He placed the major up front, and, his service pistol in the small of the major's back, he pointed him in the other direction. As the strange group approached each machine gun position, the German officer would call out and the gun crew would join York's group of prisoners. By the time they reached the lines of the 2d Battalion, the number had grown to 132 enemy. The number that York had actually killed was never determined, but was probably around twenty.[24]

The heroism of Alvin York, subsequently promoted to Sergeant York, was of course only one incident in a large battle. However, the American Battle Monuments Commission *Guidebook* gives the incident much credit: "Largely on account of York's exceptional coolness, skill with firearms, bravery, and leadership his regiment was able to continue its advance on this day."[25]

The episode carries another aspect, however. Alvin York's astonishing feat was made possible in part by growing German demoralization. German soldiers, no matter how professional, knew at last that their cause in the First World War was lost.

By October 10, only three days after the 82d Division crossed the Aire River, the German Army had evacuated the Argonne.

CHAPTER NINETEEN

FEELERS FOR PEACE

> *The generals read [the Kaiser and his ministers] a re-*
> *port that proved how imminent was catastrophe. Graf*
> *von Waldow, a Prussian minister, said "It only remains*
> *to blow our brains out." . . . Prince Max hesitated to*
> *open negotiations in these conditions, but the Kaiser*
> *told him, "We didn't call you in to make difficulties for*
> *the generals."[1]*
>
> —MARC FERRO

WHEN PLANNING the gigantic Allied attack to be launched in late September 1918, Marshal Ferdinand Foch called it the "Greatest of All Battles." He had every reason to call it that, because the power of the Allied attack was the greatest of any in history up to that moment.

Eight Allied armies were to converge on the weakening Germans. On September 26, the Americans and the French Fourth Army were to attack on the east in the general direction of Sedan and Mézières. The next day the British First and Third Armies were to launch an offensive eastward in the direction of Cambrai. On September 28 the Flanders group of armies, Belgians and British, was to attack between the Lys River and the sea. The next day the Fourth British Army and the First French Army on the Somme were to attack in the general direction of St. Quentin–Cambrai.[2] The coordinated offensive had two related purposes. One, of course, was to damage the fighting power of the Kaiser's armies irreparably. The second was to convince the German high command that the war was lost.

In his office atop the Hôtel Britannique in Spa, First Quartermaster General Erich Ludendorff felt the impact of the Allied offensive as soon as it was launched. A catastrophe for Germany, he realized, was in the making; to limit its consequences the German government must attain an armistice. The remaining power of the German Army would be the Kaiser's last asset in any peace negotiations, and it must be saved for that purpose. An armistice must be attained without a moment's delay.

It was Saturday, September 28, 1918, when Ludendorff actually reached that conclusion. Two days earlier the Americans had hit the Meuse-Argonne front in a strength he had not anticipated, proving indisputably that they would fight and fight hard. The British, in the west, had reached the heights above the St. Quentin Canal between Cambrai and St. Quentin; the French had already crossed the canal farther south.[3] To top it off, reports had just come in confirming that Germany's Balkan ally, Bulgaria, had collapsed and sued for peace.

Ludendorff had been coming to this conclusion step by step. As early as July 15, when the last of his great offensives had failed east of Château Thierry, he had conceded that his gamble to win an all-out victory had failed. The next blow had come on August 8, the day that elements of the German Army had refused to fight at Cambrai. He admitted to a colleague the following day, "We cannot win this war any more, but we must not lose it."[4]

That period of despondency was only the beginning for the mercurial Ludendorff. Periodically new shocks would come along to devastate him. By mid-September, just before the American offensive at St. Mihiel, a military physician had been much concerned about Ludendorff's "erratic ways, marked by vicious outbursts of temper, restless nights broken by angry telephone calls to individual commanding generals, on occasion too much drinking, and crying spells."[5]

Ludendorff had been able to recover from these episodes, continuing to invent a new rationalization to fit every situation. On this day, however, his anguish was acute, and some witnesses claim that during the afternoon he suffered "a genuine fit, foaming at the mouth and collapsing on his office floor."[6] Yet by the end of the day the First Quartermaster General had managed to pull himself together. At 6:00 P.M., his mind made up, he left his office and descended the stairs to the next floor, to the office of Field Marshal Paul von Hindenburg, where he outlined his conclusions bluntly. The situation being beyond redemption, Ludendorff said, their "one task now was to act clearly and firmly, without delay."[7]

Hindenburg listened to Ludendorff's analysis of the situation and then, perhaps to Ludendorff's surprise, answered that he had come to the same conclusion that very evening. The two were not prepared for a humiliating surrender, however. Not yet thoroughly beaten, they visualized an armistice as a temporary agreement that would allow the German Army to evacuate the occupied territory in an orderly manner, permitting it to resume hostilities on the German border. The German Army would give up the territory it occupied in France and Belgium, but the generals had no intention of abandoning any territory in Eastern Europe.

It was a difficult moment for Hindenburg and Ludendorff. Though their names had been associated with the greatest German victories of the World War, that time was long past. Their duty, Ludendorff said dramatically, required them to sacrifice their luster to advocate measures to avoid the worst for Germany.[8] He did not expect to be called to account for having been less than candid with the German government, even the Kaiser, about the true conditions on the Western Front. Yet for a year, as the dominant force in the German government, the "Duo," as Hindenburg and Ludendorff were called, had told the German civilian government just what they chose. Even now they were still blaming the civilian government for Germany's defeat.

The next day the Duo shared their misgivings with the political echelons of the German government. Foreign Minister Paul von Hintze happened to be at Spa that day, and after having talked frankly with the two generals, he hurried back to Berlin. There he would disclose this new development to Count von Hertling, the seventy-five-year-old Chancellor, who had been in power since October 1917.

The next day, the Kaiser summoned the Duo back to Berlin to participate in what was pompously referred to as an "imperial conference." At that gathering, the Kaiser was forced to face facts he had previously avoided. They were still lightly sugarcoated. Some of Ludendorff's bravado returned, and he painted Germany's prospects in the most optimistic possible light. If an armistice could be attained with Germany's armies still intact, he claimed, the German armies might be able to fall back to the border defenses to rest and reorganize. Under those conditions, they could avoid a "shameful peace."[9]

The important decision resulting from that meeting was political, however, even though it stemmed from Hindenburg himself. When the conference began, Hindenburg proposed that Chancellor Hertling be replaced immediately and a parliamentary form of government established. Of necessity, the new cabinet should include the despised Social Democrats, whose new strength and aggressiveness made it impossible to exclude them any longer. To make the new government acceptable to the Allies, it should be made known that Hindenburg and Ludendorff had been stripped of their privileged status. No longer would they be allowed to dominate the civilian government. The Duo would now be truly subordinate to the new Chancellor, whoever he would be.

With these changes in place, the Duo went on, the government should ask American President Woodrow Wilson to arrange an armistice and preside over peace negotiations on the basis of his Fourteen Points, which he had set forth the previous January. Only by those means, the two soldiers declared, could a Bolshevik revolution be averted. The Kaiser, seeing this ploy as the only way to save his throne, readily agreed.

On October 2, 1918, the changes agreed to between the Kaiser and his generals became reality. Prince Maximillian von Baden was called to Berlin and persuaded to accept appointment as Chancellor of Imperial Germany. Prince Max, as he was called, was an odd choice, for the position he was taking called for a strong man, which he was not thought to be. He was, however, almost the only acceptable candidate. He enjoyed a royalist heritage, but he was by instinct a democrat, "known for his democratic tendencies and belief in the need for an early peace," qualities that made him acceptable to most Social Democrats,[10] the party most likely to head the future German government.

In the course of the negotiations, however, Prince Max showed a resolve that may have surprised the Kaiser and his generals. On being informed of his prospective appointment, he resolutely set down two necessary conditions: 1) that henceforth Parliament and Parliament alone would have the right to declare war or make peace, and 2) that any control the Kaiser still retained over the German Army or Navy would cease.[11] Only if these conditions were met would he serve. The Kaiser accepted those terms, and Prince Max began his duties without delay.

The new Chancellor soon discovered why Hindenburg and Ludendorff had been so anxious to establish a strong, democratic civilian government. At another imperial council, held that same afternoon of October 2, Hindenburg repeated his demand for a truce within forty-eight hours, but he wanted the civilian government, not the Army, to make the overtures. Prince Max demurred. The German Army, he argued, could prevent the Allies from invading the Fatherland for many months. If it could not, then the new Chancellor challenged the German Army to raise the white flag in the field. Hindenburg refused outright. Neither the Army nor the civilian government of Germany was willing to serve as the instrument of surrender; both wished the other branch of government to bear the onus.[12] No decision resulted.

Prince Max set out at once to broaden the base of his government. On October 3, 1918, the day after assuming office, he introduced two Socialist deputies into the government. Perhaps to his surprise, the Socialists agreed with the military: an immediate armistice was essential. Finally convinced, Prince Max informed the Reichstag the next day of the need for peace. Calculating that President Woodrow Wilson would be more inclined to generosity than either the British or the French, he sent a message to the President asking for peace based on the Fourteen Points:

> The German Government requests the President of the United States to take in hand the restoration of peace, acquaint all belligerent states with this request, and invite them to send plenipotentiaries for the purpose of opening negotiations. It accepts the program set forth by the President of the United States in his message to Congress on January 8 and in his later addresses, especially the speech of September 27,[13] as a basis for peace negotiations. With a view to avoiding further bloodshed, the German Government requests the immediate conclusion of an armistice on land and water and in the air.[14]

On Saturday, October 5, President Wilson was in New York to attend a concert. As he sat in his suite in the Waldorf-Astoria, the phone rang, and Colonel House answered. While Wilson and the others waited, House recorded a call from Army Intelligence, taking Prince Max's message word for word, and reading it back to the President.

Wilson was not surprised, because previous reports from the Western Front had alerted him to the possibility of a German collapse. When House finished reading, Wilson turned his head and said, "This means the end of the war." But it was not that simple. Though Wilson was impressed by the directness of the German message and was inclined to open negotiations right away, his press secretary, Joseph Tumulty, protested that no message could be believed so long as the Kaiser remained in power. Wilson was irritated at first because he felt bound to consider any German offer that accepted his proposals of peace.[15] Though he considered Prince Max a "sort of parlor liberal," he believed that the German Reichstag would now be so independent of the Kaiser as to justify dealing with it. On second thought, however, the President conceded that his strong desire to begin negotiations at once was restrained by the danger of offending his allies. He was also aware that public opinion would be strongly against the German proposal, seeing it as a trap.

Wilson set to work to define his position. He set to work with the help of Colonel House and Secretary of State Lansing, and together they produced draft after draft of a reply, some reversing the positions they had taken before. He finally decided to send a message that would concede nothing but at the same time avoid slamming the door on future negotiations. He also determined to send House to Paris to represent him in any peace negotiations.[16]

It took Wilson four days to respond to the German request, and when he did on October 8, he answered through Secretary of State Lansing. Lansing's tone was cautious; it was one thing to put forth lofty principles such as the Fourteen Points but another to implement them. Since the German approach to the Americans was obviously calculated to attain gentler peace terms than might be expected from the French, British, and Italians, Wilson had to be cautious. He must ensure that Germany would not be able to drive a wedge between the Allies on one hand and the associated Americans on the other.

Most importantly, Lansing's note specified that peace negotiations could never begin "so long as the Armies of [the Central Powers] are on [French and Belgian] soil." He also demanded to know whether the German Chancellor was "speaking merely for the constituted authorities of the empire who have so far conducted the war."[17] The implication was obvious: Wilson would not deal with the Kaiser.

Four days later Prince Max sent Wilson the required assurances, saying that "The present German Government, which has undertaken the responsibility for this step toward peace, has been formed by conferences and in agreement with the great majority of the Reichstag. The Chancellor, supported in all his actions by the will of this majority, speaks in the name of the German Government and the German People." The message also "assumes" that the governments of the French and British "also take the position taken by President Wilson in his address."[18]

THE GERMAN EFFORT to secure an easy peace based on Wilson's idealistic Fourteen Points never had a chance. Even if Wilson and the American people had been more receptive to this overture, the governments of Britain, France, and Italy had no intention of allowing Wilson to speak for them. On October 7, three days after Wilson received the first German dispatch, the Prime Ministers of the three European Allies met secretly in Paris. Technically, since they were meeting outside their official capacities as members of the Supreme War Council, American representation was unnecessary to their deliberations. More likely, the omission of an American presence was unintentional. Colonel House had not yet left Washington to join them, and General Tasker Bliss, the American military representative, was sick in bed with a bad cold. Clemenceau had the courtesy to ask Bliss his views, and from his bed the general replied that, in the absence of instructions from his government, he was in favor of "unconditional surrender."[19]

The meeting of the Allied leaders took only a day, and its conclusions were concise: at the very least the Germans would be required to evacuate Belgian and French territory and immediately cease submarine warfare. The military representatives of the Supreme War Council also came up with a set of elaborate and draconian conditions for a cessation of hostilities. So harsh were they that Bliss, in his sickbed, refused to sign them. They were too radical for him to accept without instructions from his government.

The next day, Bliss sent a letter to Secretary Baker, who was on the way home from a visit to France. In it he expressed doubts about the Supreme War Council's document. "It may be," he began, "that Germany feels beaten to such a degree that she will accept such conditions as a precedent to an armistice, but I doubt it." It was not, he went on, "an armistice in the ordinary sense of the word. It looks to me as though it were intended to say, 'We will not treat with you on the terms of President Wilson's fourteen propositions or on any other terms. Surrender, and we will then do as we please.' " As Bliss saw it, that was the message the Allies wanted Wilson to send to the Germans.[20]

In Washington, President Wilson backed off from any detailed discussion of an armistice. On October 14, Lansing sent Germany a message bowing out of any negotiations over conditions for an armistice. Those, Wilson advised, were matters that had to be left to the judgment of the military advisers of the American and Allied governments. The note demanded a suspension of the submarine war campaign, made reference to German brutalities in their conduct of the war in the West, and gave no assurances that the French and British governments subscribed to the terms of President Wilson's Fourteen Points.

WHEN TOLD of the President's message, Ludendorff was badly disappointed. "Wilson," he complained, "gave us nothing." Germany now faced the question of choosing between fighting to the end or submitting to terms of unconditional surrender. His recommendation was a compromise. Germany would send another note emphasizing that a peace must be "honorable" but at the same time continue fighting. After all, Ludendorff concluded, "Part of war is luck, and luck may come Germany's way again."[21]

There matters stood as John J. Pershing's AEF was seizing the important positions of the Kriemhilde Line in the Meuse-Argonne.

PERSHING KNEW LITTLE of the exchanges passing back and forth between the governments. He was aware, of course, that something was going on, but his government's negotiations had nothing to do with his current military task of clearing the Meuse-Argonne region and cutting the railroad line at Sedan. Pershing determined to continue as if he had heard nothing of them. He would, however, be affected by the reactions of French Premier Georges Clemenceau, who found the communications between Wilson and the Germans highly disturbing. At about the time of Wilson's exchanges with Prince Max, Clemenceau began a series of attacks on Pershing and his conduct of the Meuse-Argonne campaign. Perhaps the timing was coincidental, but it carried the suspicion of politics. In any case, the virulence of his campaign against the American commander was remarkable.

Ever since his failed effort to visit Montfaucon on September 29 (at which Pershing described him as "pleased with our progress"), the French Premier had been railing in private against the American lack of progress and apparent breakdown of logistical organization. Pershing's first inkling of Clemenceau's displeasure occurred on October 3, when General Maxime Weygand, Foch's chief of staff, visited Souilly with a new proposal for the employment of American divisions.

Foch's new scheme involved narrowing the American sector and inserting the French Second Army between Pershing's present territory and the French Fourth Army, which was bogged down west of the Argonne. The American divisions in place would remain where they were, but they would be transferred to the command of the French Second Army. Such an arrangement would leave Pershing a command—the territory on both sides of the Meuse—but in essence, it called for splitting his forces in half and taking one of those halves away from him.

Pershing rejected the idea outright, characterizing it as "similar to the one of August 30th, which had been so firmly opposed that I thought the matter settled once and for all." Furthermore, Pershing suspected that Clemenceau was behind the proposal. "As Chairman of the Supreme War Council," he later wrote angrily, "Clemenceau had been granted no authority to issue directions to the Allied Commander-in-Chief [Foch]." [22] Weygand left Souilly with nothing settled.

During the weeks following that episode, Clemenceau continued to fume. He even approached Colonel Edward House when the American emissary arrived later in October, citing his (Clemenceau's) version of the sorry condition of Pershing's Army. He also drafted a letter to Foch, parts of which were so vitriolic (against Foch as well as the Americans) that French President Poincaré dissuaded him from sending it. Nevertheless, Clemenceau refused to drop the matter. On October 21 he wrote Foch a letter that, while toned down from the previous draft, still held the generalissimo responsible for Pershing's "continued intransigence." He referred to Pershing's "invincible obstinacy," by which the Americans had "won out" against Foch and his immediate subordinates.

The French Army and the British Army, without a moment's respite, have been daily fighting, for the last three months, battles which are using them up at a time when it is impossible for us to reinforce them immediately with fresh effectives. These two Armies are pressing back the enemy with an ardor that excites world-wide admiration but our worthy American Allies, who thirst to get into action and are unanimously acknowledged to be great soldiers, have been marking time ever since their forward jump on the first day; and in spite of heavy losses, they have failed to conquer the ground assigned them as their objective. Nobody can maintain that these fine troops are unusable; they are merely unused. . . .

When General Pershing refused to obey your orders,[23] you could have appealed to President Wilson. For reasons which you considered more important, you put off this solution to the conflict fearing that it would bring reactions of a magnitude which you thought it difficult to gauge. I took the liberty of differing with you. . . .

If General Pershing finally resigns himself to obedience . . . I shall be wholly delighted. But if this new attempt to reconcile two contrary points of view should not bring the advantageous results you anticipate . . . it would then be certainly high time to tell President Wilson the truth and the whole truth. Indeed, neither you nor I have any right to conceal it from him.[24]

Though Clemenceau's letter was not immediately made public, his attitude was apparent to all. Rumors began flying around the American community in Paris that Clemenceau had ordered Foch to fire Pershing—something he obviously had no right to do. Word even reached Newton Baker, who was reported to have snorted, "It will be a long time before any American commander would be removed by any European premier."[25]

Foch handled Clemenceau's tirades with masterful tact. He disagreed with the Premier's letter because, as he put it, he felt he had "a more comprehensive knowledge of the difficulties encountered by the American Army" and he therefore did "not acquiesce in the radical solution contemplated by Monsieur Clemenceau." He did not, however, meet the Premier head-on; instead he offered his own solution to the problem.

On October 23 he sent Clemenceau a letter with a table showing the disposition of American divisions. Pershing had a nominal forty-three divisions in France, but thirteen of these were either in the process of debarking or were undergoing training at bases. That left the American commander with thirty combat-serviceable divisions. Of these thirty divisions, Foch went on, eight were serving with the French armies and two, in the American II Corps, were serving with the British. That left only twenty divisions under Pershing's direct operational control. Viewing those twenty as one "category" and the ten with the British and French in another, he declared that,

> I count on maintaining these two categories [and upon] varying the proportion between the two according to circumstances, increasing the 10 and diminishing the 20, whenever operations being prepared permit it. It is by manipulation of this sort that I expect to diminish the weaknesses of the High Command, rather than by orders.

Still, Foch promised little hope of carrying through with those subtle manipulations. From time to time he would issue orders, he said, but he admitted that even he, despite his official position, may not perhaps be in a position to have them executed. Foch then confronted his political chief with a courageous defense of Pershing's conduct of operations:

> There is no denying the magnitude of the effort made by the American Army. After attacking at St. Mihiel on September 12th, it attacked in the Argonne on the 26th. From September 26th to October 20th its losses in battle were 54,158 men—in exchange for small gains on a narrow front, it is true, but over particularly difficult terrain and in the face of serious resistance by the enemy.[26]

Foch's letter failed to satisfy Clemenceau; in fact in his later writings he seems to be more irritated with Foch than with Pershing. However, Foch's tact prevailed, and nothing serious came of this fracas between allies. It faded into the background in the light of the hard fighting that occurred in the last weeks of the war.

But machinations between enemies and allies in the national capitals could not cloud the fact that there was still much fighting to do.

CHAPTER TWENTY

FIRST ARMY COMES OF AGE

WITH THE CLEARING of the Argonne forest in early October, Pershing's First U.S. Army had overcome a major hurdle. But despite all the casualties suffered in this second assault, the main German line of resistance, the Kriemhilde, had not yet been reached. Even the formidable defense line behind Exermont Ridge that had been breached at such great cost was only an offshoot of the main line. The Kriemhilde remained essentially intact.

Anxious to lose no time in breaking the German position, Pershing ordered the attack continued without respite. Since the Romagne Heights, the key to the position, lay in the zone of the V Corps, he switched the 1st Division, which had a foothold on that hill mass, from Liggett to Cameron. The change was easily effected; Pershing simply moved the boundary between corps westward. The 1st Division, now under Cameron, would continue attacking toward the Romagne Heights.

The Big Red One, however, was nearly spent. In the course of a week, from October 4 to October 11, 1918, the division had suffered 7,500 casualties, about 1,800 of them killed,[1] the heaviest losses taken by any division in the Meuse-Argonne campaign. For the first time the division's apparently indestructible organization was coming loose. So when the lead elements of the division reached the outermost barbed wire of the Kriemhilde Line, it was relieved by the 42d (Rainbow) Division.

The Kriemhilde, that portion of the Hindenburg Line that ran through the American sector, consisted of a snaky trail running through heavily rolling country. On the east, it began north of Brieulles, on the Meuse. Since Brieulles sits in a cup surrounded by hills, the Kriemhilde extended westward along the northern rim of the cup, forming a sort of horseshoe, enclosing the Bois de Fays. It then swung directly westward and ran south of the Bois de Cunel and the town of the same name, then westward across the valley of the Andon Creek, back up to the heights of Romagne-sous-Montfaucon.[2] From there it turned somewhat northwest to a ridge protecting the road center of Landres-et-St. George, then westward to include Champigneulle, winding up at the Bellejoyeux Farm.[3]

The western part of the line, from Landres on, lay just behind the Aire River, which bent and flowed westward to join the Aisne north of the Argonne. The need to fight in that sector was always a source of deep regret for Hunter Liggett, who had recognized its significance even when he was sending the 82d Division to cut off the northern part of the Argonne. Had he been able to send a whole division, or even a full brigade across the Aire on October 7, he could easily and cheaply have taken Grandpré, the Bois de Loges, and Champigneulle, all of which had been lightly defended at that time.[4] But he had lacked the necessary troops at that time and now, much to his chagrin, his men would have to pay dearly for the same prizes.

The Kriemhilde was a strong position, on which the Germans had been working for years. Though called a line, it was actually an elongated honeycomb of entrenchments, a stretched-out maze that forced the attacker to cross multiple trenches in order to penetrate it. In addition to the depth of the defenses themselves, the rolling ground enabled a defender to organize one strongpoint after another. A single position, such as Cunel Heights, would not only be difficult and costly to take; its seizure would not necessarily jeopardize the defense of the next hillock. The battle, therefore, could not be decided by any single master stroke. Whether Pershing liked it or not, reducing Kriemhilde would be a matter of attrition: bodies for territory.

ON THE RIGHT OF FIRST ARMY, Major General Robert Lee Bullard's III Corps had continued to enjoy smoother sailing than had the other two corps. True, Bullard was engaged for a few days at Brieulles, Bois de Fay, and Bois des Ogons, but those were minor problems compared to Montfaucon, Exermont, and the Argonne. From his relatively comfortable vantage point, viewing the plight of his fellows, he was almost smug. It seemed to him, he later wrote, that the rest of First Army was nearly at a standstill, making small gains at the cost of heavy losses. These problems he attributed in his sweeping way only partially to the difficult ground, trenches, barbed wire, and machine guns. He explained the army's slow progress on the failure of the infantry to follow closely enough behind their leading artillery barrages. The American consumption of artillery, he observed, was "enormous."[5]

At a quiet moment, Bullard took a little sightseeing trip into the V Corps sector to his left. He had heard of the ancient city of Montfaucon (or what was left of it), and he wanted to see for himself. It was not far out of his way; his own 80th Division had moved into a position just to the north of it.

What he saw on the butte was remarkable. General Joseph Kuhn, commanding the 79th Division, was ensconced in a "wonderful house serving as headquarters and observatory." It had previously served as a headquarters for the Crown Prince of Germany, the sight that had been denied to French Premier Clemenceau on his fateful auto trip a week earlier.

Despite the luxurious headquarters, however, Montfaucon was not a pleasant place. The butte, which Bullard described as a "veritable aerie," had been denuded of vegetation, and from three sides—the north (Romagne), the east (Heights of the Meuse), and the west (the Argonne)—German artillery was taking it under heavy fire. Even rats had to hide in their holes, he remarked, and the various staff officers were "dodging about like a band of thieves hiding from the police." Bullard did not stay any longer than necessary.[6]

Bullard was by nature a front line soldier. Not only did he habitually keep his command post far up to the front, but he was unusually active in inspecting his front line units. That he did, as did most other officers in the AEF, on horseback. One evening, on return from such a ride, an aide met him with startling news: "You have been appointed to command the Second Army, with headquarters at Toul." General John Hines, he was told at the same time, would be coming to III Corps to replace him. General Pershing soon arrived to convey the news officially. When the Commanding General mentioned the subject, almost offhandedly, Bullard was "too much moved to talk." He asked no questions. He simply shook hands with his chief and left. He had been in command of III Corps in battle for only two weeks.[7]

Pershing had been considering a reorganization of the AEF ever since the St. Mihiel campaign, when it first occurred to him that he would soon have more divisions than a single army commander could handle. He had deferred organizing a second army, however, until he was satisfied that he had adequately launched the First Army in its attack up the Meuse-Argonne corridor. By the end of the first week in October, the moment had arrived. He would organize the Second U.S. Army and step up to assume the role of army group commander, on a par with both Haig and Pétain. It was a necessary move, possibly overdue.

Delighted in his new role, Bullard was sent off in grand style as he left III Corps headquarters, bound for Toul. Brigadier General Billy Mitchell, by sheer coincidence, had been planning a major air raid in that vicinity for some time, and his chosen target was a massive concentration of German troops located at Damvillers, across the Meuse and about seven miles from Bullard's headquarters. Mitchell planned to "smash their concentration, blow up their ammunition dumps and burn their supplies."[8]

Mitchell secured the ready cooperation of the French, and Americans all along the front were treated to the sight of 322 French Breguet bombers, flying at an altitude of twelve thousand feet. Mitchell was enraptured by the sight of the bombers flying in V formation, protected on each side, above, and below by small single-seater pursuit planes. The second squadron followed the first squadron by only a minute. All eighteen planes of each squadron dropped their bombs at once. Mitchell and the others on the ground could hear the "terrific explosions and detonations." An estimated sixty German planes attempted to interfere, but not one Allied plane was lost behind enemy lines. Together with a British raid conducted that night, it was, Mitchell gloated, the "greatest amount ever put over in a single day during the war."[9]

The bomb load, counting French, British, and Americans, came to only eighty-one tons of bombs. But Mitchell could foresee the future:

> Think what it will be in the future when we attack with one, two, or three thousand airplanes at one time; the effect will be decisive.[10]

HUNTER LIGGETT, Bullard's counterpart at I Corps, was less emotional than Bullard on learning that he would take over command of First Army from Pershing. When Pershing personally divulged the ill-kept secret during the evening of October 10, Liggett's mind wandered to other things. What occupied his thoughts most, he later wrote, was somebody's suggestion that the war might be brought to a victorious close before the end of the year. Such a prospect had never crossed Liggett's mind; all American planning had been predicated on a major campaign to be executed in 1919. On a personal note, Liggett was sad to be leaving the people of his corps headquarters, with whom he had been working throughout 1918. He was satisfied, however, to turn I Corps over to the competent Joseph Dickman.

The next day, while waiting for Dickman to arrive at I Corps headquarters, Liggett received another phone call from Pershing, this time asking his advice. Pershing had just returned from visiting General George Cameron, commanding V Corps, and he had found that officer worn out from the fight at Montfaucon. No specific complaint had been leveled against his performance, but Cameron declared himself exhausted. At his own request Cameron was returned to the command of the 4th Division, which he had commanded before. Who, Pershing asked, would Liggett recommend to replace Cameron? Liggett asked for an hour to think it over.

At the end of the hour Liggett called his chief, as promised. There were only three men that he would consider, he said. One was Summerall, at the 1st Division; one was McAndrew; and one was Harbord. Pershing agreed. Only one of the three was a possibility, however. Neither Harbord, at Services of Supply, nor McAndrew, Pershing's chief of staff, could be spared. Major General Charles Summerall, known to be an aggressive, hard-driving officer, was therefore named to the command of V Corps.[11]

On the night of October 12, Dickman arrived, and Liggett motored down to Souilly, headquarters of First Army, his future command. Invited to dinner on Pershing's private train car, Liggett could see that Pershing was absorbed in his own thoughts. The reason soon came out. Marshal Ferdinand Foch had been asking why the Americans were not advancing as fast as the French and British on the other fronts.

All those present at dinner were enraged at Foch's query, for there was no question in anyone's mind as to the answer. The Germans had now brought forty divisions into this vital Meuse-Argonne territory, to a front that had been occupied by only five at the beginning of the campaign. On learning of Foch's complaint, Liggett was particularly indignant, because he was sure that Foch knew the underlying cause as well as they.[12]

Though Liggett had arrived physically at his new headquarters, he was in no hurry to assume command. A new attack was under way, an attack that he had not planned. And he wanted a chance to reconnoiter the fronts of the V and III Corps, ground outside the zone he knew so well. He assumed formal command of First U.S. Army four days later, on October 16, 1918.

PERSHING'S MAIN EFFORT for the attack to be launched on October 14 fell once more to V Corps (now Summerall's), situated as it was on the rough plateau between Montfaucon and Romagne Heights. The area of high ground between the town of Romagne, on Andon Creek, and Fléville, on the Aire, was about eight miles wide and controlled the road net that bottlenecked through Landres and from there eventually to Buzancy farther off to the northwest. That area was favorable for the attack because it was far from the German guns on the Heights of the Meuse; those in the Argonne had been eliminated. The Heights of

Cunel, east and south of Andon Creek, were also important, but any attack against them would have been conducted under the noses of the German guns on the Heights of the Meuse; further, the roads they controlled led primarily to the Meuse. That secondary attack fell to Hines's III Corps. The principal mission of Dickman's I Corps, debouching from the Argonne, was to protect the left flank of V Corps by pushing to the Aire River.

Summerall's V Corps front included two important terrain objectives: the Côte de Châtillon on the left, just short of Landres; and the Côte Dame Marie on the right, overlooking the town of Romagne. Summerall was to take those positions with two of the best divisions available, the 42d to attack the Côte de Châtillon and the 32d to take Côte Dame Marie. The latter attack, on Côte Dame Marie, would be assisted by the 5th Division, of III Corps. Once the 5th had taken Cunel Heights it was to assist the 32d.

The 32d Division, from Minnesota, had fought well at Fismes in the Soissons campaign, but it was generally considered to be in poor condition to launch a major attack, because five thousand of its infantrymen were largely untrained replacements. (The division had lost seven thousand men in the Aisne-Marne.) Placed in the line between the 42d on the left (west) and the 5th on the right, the 32d was not expected to do much more than hold the line in front of Côte Dame Marie while the 42d and the 5th enveloped the hill from both sides. Such a plan underestimated the 32d and its commander.

General William Haan, commanding the 32d, pushed forward at the base of the ridge line and, though his troops sustained heavy losses, he sent forward a battalion of the 126th Infantry, which found a gap in the German belt of wire. When his men were unable to take advantage of that gap because of heavy machine gun fire, the battalion commander sent a party of eight men to silence it. Using all weapons including rifle grenades, the men eliminated the machine gun position and the 32d pushed forward. By the 14th of October the Côte Dame Marie, the key position of the Kriemhilde Line, was in American hands.[13]

Pershing was elated. "Unstinted praise must be given the 32d Division," he later wrote. "Notwithstanding heavy losses, the 64th Brigade (Edwin B. Winans) on October 14 captured Côte Dame Marie, perhaps the most important strong point of the Hindenburg Line on the Western Front. The town of Romagne and the eastern half of the Bois de Romagne were also taken by this division on that day."[14]

DESPITE THE CRITICAL IMPORTANCE of the action at Côte Dame Marie, that at Côte de Châtillon has been given a more dramatic place in history, because its chief historian was a master publicist, Douglas MacArthur. But despite MacArthur's penchant for hyperbole, his accomplishments were indeed remarkable.

On the night of October 11, with his brigade settling into their new front line positions, MacArthur was busy completing his plans for the attack on that hill. Unexpectedly, he received a visit from Charles Summerall, the corps commander. The evening was wet and black, and MacArthur saw instantly that Summerall was tired and worn. So MacArthur gave him a cup of blistering hot coffee.

Suddenly Summerall came awake. "Give me Châtillon, MacArthur," he said abruptly, "or a list of five thousand casualties."

MacArthur was startled but as always up to the occasion. "All right, General. We'll take it, or my name will head the list."

Summerall left without further word.

The next day MacArthur went on reconnaissance and by the time he was finished he believed that he had identified a pattern with German defenses. The enemy had organized a strong defense in the front but weak on the flanks. Even the deep belt of wire entanglements petered out at the end. He decided to envelop the German left (east) flank, his two regiments abreast. They jumped off the next morning.

It was not an easy fight. Attacking in small units, crawling and sideslipping forward through rain and hail of machine gun bullets, MacArthur's men took Hill 288 that first night, then took Hill 282 the next day, and skirted Hill 205 to take La Tuilerie Farm. But still the Châtillon stood before him.

As dusk fell that second day, a battalion of the 167th Infantry and a battalion of the 168th moved out abreast through a gap in the barbed wire. As MacArthur described the action:

> The two battalions, like the arms of a relentless pincer, closed in from both sides. Officers fell and sergeants leaped in to take command. Companies dwindled to platoons and corporals took over. At the end, Major Ross had only 300 men and six officers left out of 1,450 men and 25 officers. That is the way those gallant citizen-soldiers, so far from home, won the approach to final victory.[15]

MacArthur had not kept to the rear while the attack was going on. So far up front was he that he was later recommended for the Congressional Medal of Honor. Pershing's staff at Chaumont downgraded the decoration to the Distinguished Service Cross. In his *Reminiscences* MacArthur claims to have been satisfied. Others bear witness that he was not.

• • •

A MORE MODEST HERO was Lieutenant (acting Captain) Sam Woodfill, of the 5th Division, attacking on the right of the 32d. Woodfill, a sergeant in the Regular Army and a veteran of the Philippine Insurrection, had been promoted to officer rank in the Army Reserve. He was a superb shot and an outdoorsman, but he made no pretensions to military prowess. He had been in command of his company for only a few days before the final attack at Romagne, his company commander a casualty as of October 10.

When Woodfill's regiment jumped off on the morning of the 13th, he soon found himself under fire from German machine guns from three directions. In a shell hole still carrying wisps of American poison gas, he spotted three guns firing across the turnip patch that he and his company were to cross. One was in a church tower; another was in the loft of a barn, and the third was in the brush up ahead. From his shell hole he took careful aim, first at the position in the tower. From two hundred yards he put five shots from his Springfield into what he hoped was the aperture. On the fifth shot the German position was silent. The enemy position in the barn was easier. On his first shot he killed the luckless sniper, whose automatic weapon gave away his position.

The brush ahead was more difficult, and Woodfill could discern at least five different gunners trying to kill him. Six men he shot in the head, and when he charged the position, he saw a seventh figure, an officer, also apparently dead. Knowing that he had fired only six shots, Woodfill was puzzled until the officer leapt up and seized his rifle. Woodfill downed him with a pistol bullet through the heart. By now some of Woodfill's men had caught up with him, and onward they pushed, in one instance being forced to crawl through foot-deep mud in a woody ravine. In the second position, his pistol jammed with the mud, Woodfill was forced to kill his victims with a pickaxe.

Woodfill and his men had penetrated the middle of the Kriemhilde position. When the rest of the regiment caught up, he was evacuated. The regimental surgeon feared that the effects of the gas would bring on pneumonia, but Woodfill survived. He returned to the grade of sergeant after the war.[16]

Elsewhere along the line, the First Army attack ground ahead slowly, methodically, and at great cost. On the west, Dickman's I Corps, whose progress was tied to that of V Corps on his right, made slow and painful progress. The 82d Division, still part of I Corps, had crossed the Aire River and captured St. Juvin on the north bank, but west of that town the American lines crossed the river in few places. Most important, they were still a mile short of the strong positions at Champigneulle and Bellejoyeux Farm. East of the Meuse River, the French XVII Corps had advanced several miles since its jump-off on October 8 but was still short of Sivry. The First Army attack was therefore halted on October 17, only a day after Liggett took command.

THE PAUSE HAD COME none too soon, because the First Army needed reorganization. When Liggett made his survey of his future command, he found what he mildly called "signs of discouragement" among both men and officers, as the number of stragglers bore out. The number of men absent from their units, according to Liggett, came to about 100,000 in the Meuse-Argonne region alone.[17] The men were not all cowards. Liggett, who understood the American soldier well, later described the situation:

> The Meuse-Argonne was a battle fought under lowering, misty skies in a country so rough and tangled that men without a natural instinct of direction were astray the moment they lost sight of their nearest neighbor. . . . Troops moved by dead reckoning of pocket compasses, as ships in a fog. Having gone astray through no fault of their own, the men were not unduly concerned about how soon they got back to their commands; the most brief escape from discipline is sweet.

Liggett was not so naive as to put all skulkers into that innocent category, however. There were others that he called "thirty-third-degree brothers in the ancient order of AWOL, men who had shirked every possible duty from the day they first reported at camp." Harking back to the Civil War, he called them "coffee coolers." He cited another writer who observed,

> A real adept skulker or coffee boiler is a most interesting specimen, and how I remember the coolness with which he and his companion—for they go in pairs—would rise from their little fires on being discovered, and ask most innocently, "Lieutenant, can you tell me where the Umpteenth Regiment is?" And the answer, I am sorry to say, was too often, "Yes, right up there at the front, you damned rascal, as you well know." Of course they would make a show of moving, but they were back at their little fire as soon as you were out of sight.[18]

Others bore out Liggett's observations. The various inspectors general sent out by First Army headquarters came in with reports that varied with each unit, depending on the amount and nature of the fighting it had undergone, its degree of success, and the quality of its leadership. All were agreed, however, that many men were missing without authorization from their units.

One division inspected closely at this time was the 5th, which had been heavily involved in the taking of the critical Cunel Heights. The two infantry brigades of this division, plus the machine gun organizations, had gone into the line on October 12 with 12,224 men. Ten days later that strength had been reduced to 7,350, for a loss of nearly 40 percent. Casualties, including killed and wounded, had been reported as about 3,600, which meant that nearly 1,300 were unaccounted for. Some of the missing, but not many, had been evacuated as sick from the flu.

The case of the 5th may have been unusual. As the inspector reported, the 5th Division had received a whopping 3,044 practically untrained replacements; three companies of the 11th Infantry were commanded by officers of two weeks commissioned service. In some cases, both officers and men had arrived so recently that they did not know each other. The absentee problem was so severe that the commander of the 9th Brigade had used his staff to round up stragglers. On the first afternoon of battle, the inspector reported, a hundred malingerers had been taken out of shell holes close to the front line. A few days earlier, another inspector had reported the officers and men of the 5th were "jumpy" and estimated the number of stragglers from the division at 2,500.[19]

Other inspectors had different things to report. One officer, inspecting the 35th Division immediately after it had been driven back from Exermont in early October, was concerned with standard military discipline as a sign of its condition. Reporting on the 128th Machine Gun Battalion, he wrote,

Their billets are dirty, showing evidence of not having been inspected today. Dirty straw was strewn around the floor and there was a general unkempt condition. The kitchens were dirty, stoves dirty, kettles unpolished, dirt on the ground and outside the kitchens.

Of the 138th Infantry, he wrote,

This regiment has done nothing in two days. On Oct 6 at 9:30 the men had not gotten up. They had not been cleaned or washed up, there was defecation all around the camp and near the kitchens, rifles and Chauchat automatics had not been cleaned but were lying out in the rain rusting, and the animals were not groomed.

Regarding the general morale of the division, the inspector said,

The men are in good spirits but have wretched discipline. They do not salute. They make no attempt to clean their clothing or to keep buttoned up. . . . On the march their march discipline is wretched.

Not all the reports were so unfavorable. The 137th Infantry received credit for having attempted to clean up both rifles and men. The artillery was given credit for good march discipline. "The drivers, when halted, would dismount, and organizations were kept closed up with some attempt at keeping intervals between batteries."[20]

Such a report may tell us more about Colonel Baer, the inspector, than it does about the 35th Division at that time, for the reports of most divisions were far less critical. Reports of the 4th Division, for example, indicated unusual fortitude. The men there had been taking heavy losses and had gone ten days without shelter and with only one blanket per man. Yet the division commander insisted that the men could go another ten days without breaking. The 4th was superbly led and had enjoyed much success.

The inspectors covered many subjects other than morale, discipline, and straggling. Much space in their reports was devoted to levels of supply, shortages of equipment, and other administrative matters. They fell prey, however, to becoming too enthusiastic in their jobs. Living in relative comfort at Souilly and coming up by day to inspect troops under miserable conditions, they became emotionally involved with those who were undergoing great hardships. In particular, they tended to ask officers and men for recommendations as to supply needs, replacements, and even recommendations on tactical and strategic matters.

Finally, Brigadier General Hugh Drum, chief of staff of First Army, had had enough. Exhibiting little of Liggett's sympathies, he wrote a harsh memorandum on October 20. Citing comments that had been noticed by the Army commander, he pointed out some of his own complaints:

(a) Nearly all these reports cover the shortage in transportation and animals. The existence of this shortage is well known to higher authorities and all possible steps are being taken to meet the same. It is therefore unnecessary for the inspectors to continue their reports in this connection.
(b) The question of replacements needed for the various divisions is also known to higher authorities. It is therefore unnecessary for inspectors to investigate this question.

(c) From the reports received in this office and from the knowledge as to the number of days a division has been in the front line, and the amount of fighting it has carried on, this office is able to judge the division's condition as to fatigue and endurance.

(d) Some of the reports received indicate that inspectors have investigated tactical situations and have even gone to the extent of asking the views of division commanders and their subordinates as to the possibility of executing certain tactical missions. Investigation along these lines is entirely beyond the jurisdiction of inspectors.

It was undesirable, Drum wrote, that inspectors should attract the attention of commanders to the hardships of their troops. "Public investigations of this nature," he wrote, "have a tendency to create in the minds of the troops, not only a desire but a feeling that they should be relieved and that replacements should be sent to them."[21]

Such was the condition of the First Army as it prepared for its attack in late October. What to do about it? A set of "Combat Instructions" issued by Pershing on October 12 probably had little or no effect. These began by observing that American forward lines tended to hesitate at times when enemy opposition was weak, thus losing the advantage to be gained by a vigorous advance. It warned against allowing enemy machine guns to hold up an advance. Machine guns should be neutralized by smoke, 37mm guns, and artillery, if necessary. It called the attention of all junior officers to the official publication, "Combat Instructions," and admonished them to study its provisions.[22] Pershing, too, seemed to be showing the strain of combat.

NEVERTHELESS, THE OVERALL SITUATION was highly favorable to the Americans and their allies. In the face of crumbling enemy resistance, the First Army was rapidly coming of age, its staffs functioning well, and its supply and communications lines better organized. Units were being brought up to strength.[23] Hunter Liggett's assumption of command of the army had assured the undivided attention of a master tactician, a man not concerned with politics and broader issues. From mid-October to the last of the month he personally supervised the First Army attacks in a series of small efforts designed to improve its position to launch an all-out effort.

The stage was set to end the war.

CHAPTER TWENTY-ONE

THE WINDUP

In the autumn of 1918 there were no troops in Europe, besides the Americans, who could have forced their way through the fortified vastness of the Argonne Forest. . . . The battle of November 1 and 2, 1918, is the greatest feat of arms ever performed by an American Army. The plan was purely American, and the tactical execution was the climax of the American fighting spirit.

—JOSEPH T. DICKMAN[1]

BY THE END OF OCTOBER 1918, the German forces were reeling under the impact of Allied offensives from the North Sea to the Moselle. British attacks in the north were threatening Brussels. In the Meuse-Argonne, General Pershing's First United States Army—strictly speaking Hunter Liggett's First Army—had punctured the vaunted German Hindenburg Line at its two most critical points, Côte Dame Marie and its lesser sister, Côte de Châtillon. American heavy artillery had now reached the heights from where it could fire on the Sedan–Mézières railroad, thus isolating the German armies in the southern half of the Western Front. If the attacks could be continued for another ten days, Colonel George Marshall estimated, "about a million German soldiers in front and to the west of us would either have to surrender or disperse as individuals."[2] True, the doughboys were exhausted from the long advances of the previous week, but they were still pushing on to close to the left bank of the Meuse.

Though Pershing knew that the enemy was defeated, he had no intention of giving quarter; the situation called for increasing the pressure, not relaxing. He admonished his troops to further efforts:

Now that Germany and the Central Powers are losing, they are begging for an armistice. Their request is an acknowledgment of weakness and clearly means that the Allies are winning the war. That is the best of our reasons for our pushing the war more vigorously at this moment. . . . We must strike harder than ever. Our strong blows are telling, and continuous pressure by us has compelled the enemy to meet us, enabling our Allies to gain on other parts of the line. There can be no conclusion to this war until Germany is brought to her knees.[3]

Though the date for this final, crushing offensive was set for October 28, 1918, Liggett learned from General Gouraud of the Fourth French Army on his west flank that the French could not be ready until the first of November. Liggett therefore delayed his final offensive to comply— no hardship for him.

The attack would be conducted almost entirely by the First Army despite the organization of Robert Bullard's Second Army to the east of the Meuse. When Bullard left III Corps on October 12 and motored down to Toul by way of Souilly, he found the Second Army far from ready to fight. His staff was not organized,[4] and the army was completely lacking in artillery and engineers. Bullard set about to remedy these deficiencies quickly, because he expected to be ordered to attack soon. He had no idea in what direction he would be sent, toward the Briey iron region or Metz, but he never questioned Pershing. As always, Bullard expected the Commanding General to divulge plans at his own convenience.

In the meantime the new Second Army commander drove his subordinates unmercifully to get prepared. By the end of October 1918, his command had reached a strength of 176,000 American troops, organized into three corps but with only five divisions.[5] The command and support structure could obviously absorb many additional divisions and Bullard expected to receive them soon. But no orders came from the AEF to participate in the first phases of the forthcoming attack, to be launched on November 1. This would be completely a First Army operation.

BY THIS TIME the First American Army, under Hunter Liggett, had come of age. Its strength was over a million men, including 135,000 French troops.[6] The army's supply situation was getting under control, and the various commanders and their staffs had done much to learn their jobs. Aside from the 500,000 infantry fighting strength of First Army, its air arm had greatly improved. By now Billy Mitchell's air command was proving its worth by providing intelligence, protection from enemy aircraft, and an effective means of attacking enemy artillery positions. The airplane was no longer a novelty; it made a real difference whether one side or the other enjoyed air supremacy in a given sector.

Pershing used his air arm in a limited manner compared to the wide-ranging role the Air Force later adopted: his planes, he insisted, were there to render direct support of ground troops. Some of the airmen would have preferred to devote more effort to fighting the enemy air force, including destruction of German airfields, but Pershing's word stood, and he took pride in the progress the American airplanes had made in improving coordination between air and ground elements. He later claimed personal credit for that accomplishment; it was by his decree that all pilots were required to spend a certain amount of time serving with the infantry; thus could the aviators come to better understand the ground commander's problems.

Tank support was another matter, however. Liggett's original tank strength of 189 small tanks had been reduced to sixteen as of November 1.[7] Fortunately for the Americans, that loss did not mean vulnerability to German armor; Marwitz had none in the Meuse-Argonne region. Nevertheless, the shortage cost the Americans lives, for the tanks were proving themselves to be the only way to avoid direct, suicidal assault on machine gun nests. The lack of tanks was far more important to Pershing and Liggett than to Marwitz.

LIGGETT'S PLAN for November 1 was remarkably similar to that followed by First Army back on September 26: it visualized a frontal attack with divisions in line, commanded by the same three corps: Dickman's I Corps on the west (left), Summerall's V Corps in the center, and Hines's III Corps on the east (right). As with the earlier plan, the main effort was to be made by V Corps in the center, this time by the western division, Lejeune's 2d Division, to which all the surviving tanks of the army were assigned.[9]

Liggett visualized three phases for the offensive. The first was to be the assault of November 1, which was to gain the Barricourt Ridge and reach the general line of Aincreville, west of Hill 243, the northern edge of the Bois de Barricourt, and the center of the Bois de la Folie.[10] On that same day, III Corps was to take Brieulles-sur-Meuse, which had previously been left unoccupied by both sides. On the western flank, none of I Corps was to move ahead except the 80th Division on the right, which was to protect the left flank of V Corps's 2d Division. If all went well, the Bois de Bourgogne, on that corps' front, would be empty of the enemy at the end of the day.

The second phase of the attack was to be an exploitation of the gains

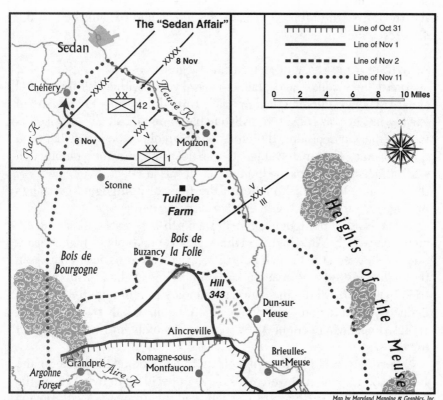

The "Sedan Affair"

Sedan

Chéhery

Bar R.

6 Nov

Meuse R.

8 Nov

42

1

Mouzon

Line of Oct 31
Line of Nov 1
Line of Nov 2
Line of Nov 11

0   2   4   6   8   10 Miles

Stonne

Tuilerie Farm

V XXX III

Heights of the Meuse

Bois de Bourgogne

Buzancy

Bois de la Folie

Hill 343

Dun-sur-Meuse

Aincreville

Romagne-sous-Montfaucon

Brieulles-sur-Meuse

Grandpré

Aire R.

Argonne Forest

Map by Maryland Mapping & Graphics, Inc.

16. Exploitation – The End of the War.

The last phases of the war, including the embarrassing Sedan Affair. Pershing and his troops had accomplished their mission.

made on November 1. Liggett did not expect the Germans to be able to put up any appreciable resistance after the first objectives were attained; their artillery positions would be overrun and their last defensive positions would be gone. He expected to reach the Meuse River above Sedan in one continuous drive.

The third phase, which was to take place at the same time as the latter part of the second, would be a crossing of the Meuse River at Dun-sur-Meuse in order to eliminate those last German artillery positions on the Heights of the Meuse.[11] That operation should be launched on the 4th of November.

AS THE SINGLE ARMY COMMANDER, Liggett's position was somewhat awkward; he was like the captain of a naval vessel with a visiting admiral aboard. Though Pershing had officially turned over direct command of First Army, he was constitutionally unable to relinquish all control of its tactics. Tactical decisions, therefore, were largely made jointly between the two men. Fortunately Liggett was not vain, and the combination worked satisfactorily for the limited time it was in effect. In one phase of the planning, the ticklish matter of the Bois de Bourgogne, Pershing's prestige with the Allies was needed to carry the day.

The Bois de Bourgogne, in reality a north–west extension of the Argonne beyond the Aire, had, as in the Argonne, been split by higher headquarters between the French Fourth Army and the American First. As in the earlier instance—a matter that Hunter Liggett had unsuccessfully tried to get corrected—the national boundary ran through thick woods, defined by nothing on the ground and on the maps only by an arbitrary, straight line, giving neither Army sole responsibility for the reduction of the forest.

Pershing and Liggett, with their staffs, had studied the matter of the Bois de Bourgogne and were eye-to-eye in deciding to bypass it on the east, cutting it off further north, as they had the Argonne. A fast-moving force could drive up the road that ran from Grandpré, along the eastern edge of the woods, finally reaching Boult-aux-Bois, on the boundary between the two armies and north of the bois. If the French on the west could meet the Americans at that point the Germans would have to evacuate the forest or find all their troops surrounded. Pershing and his staff were satisfied with that approach.[12]

THE ATTACK WENT OFF almost exactly as Liggett had visualized. By the end of the first day all the objectives he had designated had been taken and the enemy was in full retreat. That evening he received a message from Pershing's headquarters congratulating him on his advances but questioning why the left two divisions of I Corps, in the Bois de Bourgogne, had not advanced. Liggett answered that they had not been ordered to advance. By the next day they would move forward with no enemy in front of them. On November 2 the troops of I Corps moved out, some in motor trucks, to regain contact with the enemy. There was no opposition along the entire I Corps front.

Other corps pushed forward at the same pace. By November 3 the 2d Division of V Corps had made a spectacular pencil-like thrust northward to La Tuilerie Farm, only two miles from the heights overlooking the Meuse. Hines's III Corps, on the right, had driven forward six miles along the Meuse. The next day, November 4, the 5th Division crossed the Meuse.[13] Pershing's mission had been accomplished.

THE SEDAN AFFAIR

BY THE AFTERNOON of November, 5, 1918, Colonel George Marshall, operations officer of First U.S. Army, had every right to feel good. The AEF had performed well and had attained success, even earning the praise of Foch and Clemenceau for its recent advance. Marshall realized that he had played a significant role in that success. He did not realize, however, that he was about to become involved in an embarrassing episode that would cast a temporary pall over the recent American triumphs, an incident that came to be known as the Sedan Affair.

As the troops of First Army drove forward to close on the Meuse, they unilaterally assumed as their ultimate objective the historic town of Sedan, only a few miles away. Under normal circumstances, such an ambition would be reasonable enough, even though the town lay physically just outside the American First Army sector. These were not, however, normal circumstances, for Sedan, as the Americans failed to realize, was immensely important to the French. It was in that otherwise insignificant town that French Emperor Napoleon III had been captured by the Prussians in the humiliating War of 1870, the outcome of which had cost the French, among other things, the provinces of Alsace and Lorraine. Some of the unthinking American fervor to take Sedan had been caught—and encouraged—by the Commanding General himself.[14]

At 4:00 P.M. that November afternoon, Brigadier General Fox Conner, operations officer at Pershing's AEF headquarters at Chaumont, strode into Marshall's office at Souilly. At first the visit appeared to be routine. Marshall outlined the tactical situation, which had now been reduced to the question of whether the troops of the First Army were too exhausted to continue throughout the night. Almost casually, he pointed out that the Americans of I Corps, on the left, were headed directly for Sedan. Conner and Marshall knew that Marshal Foch, the day before, had specified that Sedan lay in the sector assigned to the French Fourth Army. The French, however, were far behind the Americans, leaving Hunter Liggett's left flank hanging in the air. Crossing the boundary— with proper permission and coordination, of course—just might be justified.

But Conner went even further: "It is General Pershing's desire," he told Marshall, "that the troops of the First Army should capture Sedan, and he directs that orders be issued accordingly." Marshall, taken aback, protested mildly, but in the light of Pershing's specific instructions, he called a stenographer and dictated a memorandum for Dickman at I Corps and Summerall at V Corps:

Subject: Message from the Commander-in-Chief.
1. General Pershing desires that the honor of entering Sedan should fall to the First American Army. He has every confidence that the troops of the 1st Corps, assisted on their right by the 5th Corps, will enable him to realize this desire.
2. In transmitting the foregoing message, your attention is invited to the favorable opportunity now existing for pressing our advantage throughout the night.[15]

Conner approved the memorandum and told Marshall to issue it immediately. Marshall, as he later recorded the episode, was skeptical but found his questioning fruitless. "This is the order of the Commander-in-Chief, which I am authorized to issue in his name," Conner said. "Now get it out as quickly as possible."[16] Marshall continued to drag his feet, however, because neither Liggett nor Chief of Staff Hugh Drum had been given an opportunity to see the order for themselves. He therefore proposed a compromise. He would wait until either Liggett or Drum should return to headquarters. If neither returned by 6:00 P.M., he would personally transmit the order by telephone to the corps commanders concerned. Conner, satisfied, left the matter in Marshall's hands.[17]

Marshall spent the rest of the afternoon telephoning the chief of staff's office every ten minutes. Finally, just before the witching hour of 6:00 P.M., Drum returned. The chief of staff saw no difficulties in the order, but he added a crucial sentence. Recalling how the seizure of Montfaucon had been delayed a day because the 4th Division on the right of the 79th had been imprisoned behind its boundaries, he added, "Boundaries will not be considered binding." [18] Marshall issued the order immediately after leaving General Drum's office.

Joseph Dickman, in whose I Corps sector the operation was to be conducted, was totally confused when Marshall's message came in. He assumed, of course, that Pershing had come to some agreement with French General Maistre regarding the crossing of the boundary into the French zone, a theory reinforced by Colonel Walter S. Grant, Marshall's assistant, who arrived in person and confirmed the order. At 7:00 P.M. Hugh Drum himself phoned in the same message. All this ran counter to word received from Lieutenant Blanquet, the French liaison officer at Dickman's headquarters, who got word somehow that General Pétain, in the vicinity, was "very much worried" about the Americans encroaching into the French sector. [19]

Matters were quickly taken out of Dickman's hands, however, because his counterpart at V Corps, Charles Summerall, showed no qualms at all. Instead Summerall apparently saw a glittering opportunity for the 1st Division, which he had once commanded, to wind up the war in a flash of glory. It was easy for Summerall to put his plans in effect; the 1st was out of the lines in V Corps reserve. Without consulting Dickman, Summerall ordered the division westward toward the Army boundary and Sedan. He showed no concern that this movement would place the 1st Division in a precarious position in front of the advancing French Fourth Army and across the rear of the 42d Division, nearing the Meuse. The move was made, though many bone-weary members of the Big Red One collapsed en route (it was reported that a few had even died of exhaustion). Supply lines of the 42d were torn up.

By the morning of November 7, complaints began pouring in from all quarters. Maistre telephoned Liggett in person and stated that the "progress of the [French] 40th Division is slowed up and rendered almost impossible by the presence of American troops on the road north of Chehery." [20] General Menoher, commanding the 42d Division, was less courteous. "The situation here as between the 1st and 42d Divisions intolerable. Urgently recommend that orders from 1st Army be issued to straighten matters out." [21]

At least the fiasco provided a touch of comic relief. Men from the 1st Division burst into the command post of the 42d Division and "captured" Brigadier General Douglas MacArthur, who was about to assume command of the 42d, as he stood at a planning table with some of his staff.

MacArthur was amused—or at least he pretended to be amused—but if so he was the only one. Everyone became angry and began blaming everyone else. Most furious, not surprisingly, were the French high command. General Gouraud protested violently to Hunter Liggett, who quickly sent a message to Summerall:

> The Army Commander directs that troops of the 5th Army Corps be withdrawn from the zone of advance of the 1st Army Corps. Report when this is accomplished.[22]

Liggett also went forward to Dickman's headquarters to see the situation for himself. It was the only time, he later wrote, that he lost his temper.[23]

By the time the countering orders were made, Colonel Theodore Roosevelt's 26th Infantry, 1st Division, had reached a woods several miles northwest of Chéhéry. There he received orders to withdraw. Soon the 26th was back in I Corps territory, and a semblance of order was restored. The French had the honor of retaking Sedan, and the humiliating capitulation of forty-eight years earlier was avenged.

The inevitable investigation of the bizarre incident was ordered but pursued only halfheartedly and with no results. Even Liggett and Dickman, the two officers most angry at Summerall's action, expressed admiration for the performance of the 1st Division in the unfortunate project.[24] For his part, Pershing passed it off. The war was almost over, and the culprits were Pershing's favorites: Charles Summerall, the 1st Division, and Pershing's own staff. Above all, Pershing had to realize that the original concept of taking Sedan had been his own.

THE AMERICAN FIRST ARMY had succeeded in cutting the Sedan–Mézières railroad, but General Pershing intended to continue fighting until the last moment of the war. Accordingly, he ordered the 2d and the 89th Divisions, from Summerall's V Corps, to cross the Meuse and take the towns of Autreville and Mouzon on the east bank. The crossing was to be executed on November 9. The reason for undertaking such a risky, if minor, operation is not clear; the 5th and 32d Divisions, of III Corps, had crossed the river at Dun-sur-Meuse and Brieulles farther south and they had enlarged the bridgehead to a depth of over ten miles, cutting a major road on the Woevre Plain at Jametz. If further attack eastward were ever ordered, that road would be the main axis of advance. Never mind that success; the attack of the 2d and 89th would go ahead anyway.

Crossing the river was not easy. All the efforts of V Corps to establish a bridgehead during November 9 and the daylight hours of November 10 were to no avail. German artillery quickly destroyed the bridges, with considerable and useless loss of American lives. Finally, on the evening of

November 10, two battalions of the 5th Marine Regiment, 2d Division, were able to sneak across the river by foot bridges under cover of darkness. One of those who crossed was Elton E. Mackin, 67th Company, 5th Marines.

Mackin was something of a novelty among his comrades because of his apparently charmed life. He had been with the 5th Marines since the second day at Belleau Wood in early June and had survived heavy fighting at Soissons, St. Mihiel, and Blanc Mont. He had been decorated for valor four times, earning the Distinguished Service Cross and two Silver Stars from the Army as well as the Navy Cross. He was among the very few men left from the company he had joined over five months earlier. The rest of the men were replacements, some coming from unlikely units such as the Military Police Company of Paris.[25] But veteran though he was, Mackin was still subject to the dangers and fears of any new recruit; it took only one bullet to kill a veteran of many battles.

The nighttime crossing over the Meuse was frightening for veteran and rookie alike; the foot bridge was covered by sporadic bursts of German machine gun fire. But Mackin and his men made it across and began to wend their way up the hills. Suddenly they heard a loud crash, followed by some cries from men drowning in the river. The bridge had been hit by German artillery, and the few troops who had made it to the east bank knew they were marooned. A moment of panic swept over Mackin and his fellows, but their company commander quickly took charge and ordered all men to lie down flat. Fortunately, the Germans did not realize that some Americans had crossed the river; the shells were hitting behind Mackin's small group, sweeping the engineers on the far shore behind them.

The original plan to overrun the German artillery positions was now out of the question, and the 67th Company was forced to take a desperate measure. So on orders from the company commander they formed a single file and headed southward on the river side of the hill, masked from the Germans, to find a spot of safety on the high ground. Soon they found a grassy trace of sunken road that served as a shallow breastwork, screened by brush. There they attacked, showing no mercy despite the lateness of the hour. As Mackin later wrote it, in the darkness "men met us there, rising from the ground in quick surprise and greeting us with guttural questionings before they died."[26] Some Germans escaped, however; Mackin and his comrades now knew that their presence was known to the enemy. They settled down to prepare for the worst, making "the place their own" while they awaited daybreak.

Once the Germans were aware of the 67th Company's location, the plight of the Americans became precarious. German artillery fire rained down. The marines withstood a couple of halfhearted German counterattacks, but the 67th Company found it necessary to pull back, even withdrawing its listening posts.

During one lull, Mackin's eyes wandered up to a place where his friend Woody Wilson lay sprawled on the high shoulder of a bank. Wilson was alert, looking down the sight of his rifle, bayonet fixed. Wilson was a "pudgy, fattish fellow," known for his congeniality and joking. Like Mackin, he had been with the regiment ever since Belleau Wood. At the moment, however, Mackin feared that Wilson was in a dangerously exposed position, visible to the enemy in the flares that were lighting the battlefield. Before Mackin could warn his friend, however, a shell hit close by and a fragment broke Wilson's leg above the knee. His comrades had difficulty in stopping the flow of blood.

Finally Mackin and the others were able to carry Wilson to a place where he was lying comfortably in a ditch, wrapped in blankets. During all this time, Wilson lay "grinning and kidding in the glow of the Very lights [flares] at men who loved him." Another shell hit. Wilson died, still trying desperately to talk to his friends through his pain. He was one of those whom Mackin mourned,

> So many men died that night, short hours away from Armistice. They had held on to hope in spite of everything.[27]

ON THAT SAME EVENING of November 10, 1918, Hunter Liggett made his plans for the next day. He had no orders or intentions to hold up along the present line. The attack would be pressed the next day, eastward toward Briey and Metz.

CHAPTER TWENTY-TWO

THE RAILROAD CAR
AT COMPIÈGNE

IN LATE OCTOBER 1918, while the First U.S. Army prepared to launch its final assault from the Kriemhilde position and the Second U.S. Army began preparation to attack toward Metz, the British had reoccupied the entire coast of Belgium, and the French were trying to protect Haig's right flank on the south. Marshal Foch was now ready for the final assault on the shaky German Army, "whose exhaustion," in Foch's words, "increased every day."[1] President Wilson had made it clear that he would not discuss peace terms directly with the German government. That move greatly eased the problems of the political leaders in Paris, though they had no intention of allowing Wilson to represent them in any case.

The European political leaders—Clemenceau, Lloyd George, and Orlando—while reserving the power of deciding whether or not to grant an armistice, needed military advice on such matters as the state of the troops, the efforts they were still capable of, and the conditions under which they could safely halt their operations without losing the benefit of their recent victories. In early discussions the term "military counselors" had been used, and it would be natural to assume that these "counselors" would be the military members of the Supreme War Council. Foch, however, made no such assumption. On October 16, two days after Wilson's note to Prince Max, he wrote to the council:

The phrase "military counselors," already frequently employed in the course of previous conversations, is ambiguous and demands elucidation. As a matter of fact, the only military counselors qualified to deal with the conditions of an armistice are the commanders in chief. They alone are responsible to their governments for the safety of their armies and the conditions under which hostilities should be resumed in case of rupture. They alone are thoroughly informed as to the state of their armies and of the enemy forces confronting them.[2]

The political leaders assented to Foch's position, and Foch called a meeting of the three Commanders-in-Chief at his headquarters at Senlis on Friday, October 25. While all commanders were enjoined to speak their piece, their views were not binding on Foch's recommendations to the Supreme War Council. Nevertheless, the more agreement he could achieve among the Generals-in-Chief, the stronger his position would be in dealing with the political leaders.

As Pershing sat down at the table with his counterparts—the ebullient Foch, the dapper, confident Haig, and the outwardly stolid Pétain—he felt slightly uncomfortable, aware that his American forces had not yet proved themselves in the eyes of his colleagues. Aside from Foch, who had come to recognize the worth of the Americans, Pershing was the only man in the room who was aware of how much his troops had accomplished by way of breaking the Kriemhilde portion of the Hindenburg Line while at the same time honing their staff procedures and improving their supply situation. Regardless of that supposed disadvantage, however, Pershing intended to speak his mind with full authority. He knew he had President Wilson behind him.

All the participants in the meeting knew its purpose, of course. Foch, however, insisted on beginning with a formal declaration. "You are doubtless aware," he began, "that the Germans are negotiating for an armistice through the intermediary of the American Government, and declare themselves ready to accept the Fourteen Points of President Wilson as a basis." He had called the group together to ascertain their views as to the armistice terms that would "render Germany powerless to recommence operations in case hostilities are resumed."[3]

Haig, despite his outward imperturbability, proposed surprisingly lenient terms for an armistice, terms he believed the Germans would readily accept. The enemy, he said, was "defeated" but far from "disintegrated," still capable of withdrawing to a shorter front and making a stand against equal or greater forces. The Allies, he continued, were becoming exhausted. The French and British armies were each short about 250,000 men, and no replacements were available. As to the American Army, it was "not yet organized, not yet formed, and had suffered a great deal on account of its ignorance of modern warfare."[4] Given that situation, Haig insisted that the Germans should be required to evacuate all occupied territory in Belgium and France, including Alsace and Lorraine. They should restore all the rolling stock they had seized in France and Belgium, and they should repatriate all inhabitants of occupied territory.[5] Those terms did not sound like those imposed by an alliance that considered itself victorious.

Foch was far less conciliatory to the Germans than was Haig. First of all, he disagreed with Haig's contention that the German Army was "not defeated." It had been "pounded every day for three months . . . losing on a front of 400 kilometers." Since July 15, he went on, the German Army had lost more than 250,000 prisoners and four thousand guns. He described it as "physically and morally, thoroughly beaten."[6]

Foch then turned to the Allied armies. Conceding that they were "not new," he insisted that "victorious armies are never fresh." The question was relative; the Germans were far more exhausted than were the Allies. As to the Americans,

The American Army is a young army, but it is full of idealism and strength and ardor. It has already won victories and is now on the eve of another victory; and nothing gives wings to an army like victory.[7]

Pétain spoke next. While agreeing with Foch that the German Army was beaten, he believed it unnecessary to disarm it formally. If the Germans were required to evacuate all occupied territory quickly, they would be forced to leave the bulk of their matériel behind. Rolling stock was something else, and Pétain proposed that the Germans be required to turn over five thousand locomotives and 100,000 freight cars. The Germans should also be made to evacuate the left bank of the Rhine, not only that portion that ran between Germany and Alsace, but that portion that ran through Germany as well. The Allies should establish bridgeheads over the Rhine at Mayence, Coblenz, and Cologne.[8]

Foch then called on Pershing, who, after agreeing with Foch and Pétain regarding the condition of the German Army, set forth a group of proposals similar to those of Pétain. He added one further requirement, however: "Surrender of all U-boats and U-boat bases to the control of a neutral power until their disposition is otherwise determined."

Haig immediately balked. "That is none of our affair," he declared. "It is a matter for the Admiralty to decide." Pershing insisted, however. His forces were operating three thousand miles from home, he said, and the German submarines still constituted a menace to American sea communications. Foch backed Pershing. "The suggestion of General Pershing regarding submarines," he said, "seems to me a reasonable one and his demand well founded."[9]

The conference ended with Haig refusing to modify the stance he had taken. Foch asked each attendee to submit his individual proposals in writing, but he felt no obligation to seek a compromise with the three military chiefs. Instead, he drafted a set of military terms of his own that closely resembled those proposed by Pétain, with Pershing's addition of the provision on submarines:

1. The immediate evacuation of lands unlawfully invaded: Belgium, France, Alsace-Lorraine, and Luxembourg, and the immediate repatriation of their inhabitants.
2. Surrender by the enemy of 5,000 cannon, 30,000 machine guns, and 3,000 *Minenwerfer* [trench mortars].
3. Evacuation by the German Army of all territory on the left bank of the Rhine; occupation by the Allies of bridgeheads on the right bank . . . at Mayence, Coblenz, Cologne, and Strasbourg, and the creation on the right bank of a neutral zone twenty-five miles wide running east of the river.

The terms also included delivery of five thousand locomotives, 150,000 railway cars, and 150 submarines. The German surface fleet was to be withdrawn to its Baltic ports and the naval blockade of Germany was to continue "during the period fixed for the fulfilment of the above conditions."[10] He carried these terms back to Versailles the next day.

WHILE MARSHAL FOCH WAS MEETING with his commanders at Senlis, Hindenburg and Ludendorff were also holding meetings, some of which were considerably less pleasant. Their troubles were very real. President Wilson's third message to Prince Max, delivered on October 23, presented a direct threat to them. "The Government of the United States," it began, "cannot deal with any but veritable representatives of the German people, who have been assured of a genuine constitutional standing as the real rulers of Germany." And then the clincher:

If [the United States Government] must deal with the military masters and the monarchical autocrats of Germany now . . . it must demand not peace negotiations but surrender.[11]

That declaration of Wilson's went much too far for Hindenburg and Ludendorff. Since they, along with the Kaiser, were the targets of Wilson's ultimatum, their only recourse to stay in power was to continue the fight. Accordingly, the Duo, without consulting their political superiors, sent a message to the German Army that called for continued resistance:

Wilson's answer is a demand for unconditional surrender. It is thus unacceptable for us soldiers. It proves that our enemy's desire for our destruction, which let loose the war in 1914, still exists undiminished. . . . Wilson's answer can thus be nothing for us soldiers to continue our resistance with all our strength. When our enemies know that no sacrifices will achieve the rupture of the German front, then they will be ready for a peace which will make the future of our country safe for the broad masses of our people.[12]

Hindenburg and Ludendorff did not inform the Kaiser of that message until the next day, and when they did so, they were disappointed at his reaction. The Emperor said little and then, showing the extent of his desperation to keep his own position, referred the Duo to the Chancellor to present their case. Members of the government, having received word of this message to the Army, were irate, seeing it as totally contrary to the government's policy. The Duo could hardly expect a cordial reception from Prince Max.

At the Chancellor's residence that evening, Prince Max was ill—or at least pretended to be. In his absence he was represented by the vice chancellor, Friedrich von Payer, along with the Minister of War and a small retinue of military officers. Ludendorff launched into a passionate tirade against the spread of Bolshevism and of the Bolshevik threat against officers. He likened Germany's situation to that of Russia, pointing out that the Kaiser was still the chief of the Army, and in the process referring to the Army's "honor."

Ludendorff was dealing with the wrong man. Payer was a practical Swabian, from southern Germany, no Prussian. He was known to show no deference to the military, and he was unmoved by references to the Army's honor. He was aware of the uproar in the Reichstag over Hindenburg's message to the Army and was also aware that Prince Max had declared that he would resign if Ludendorff were not removed.[13] After a long meeting of two and a half hours, Hindenburg and Ludendorff left discouraged. Ludendorff could say only, "There is no hope. Germany is lost."[14]

The next morning, October 26, Ludendorff resigned. He wrote his letter in his office at 8:00 A.M. and an hour later presented it to the Field Marshal. Hindenburg urged his lieutenant to withdraw it, and for a while Ludendorff relented. Soon, however, word came in that the Kaiser wished to see Ludendorff alone at Bellevue Castle. The interview was, as the First Quartermaster General later recalled it, a grim experience:

The Emperor seemed wholly changed. Speaking to me alone, he spoke especially against the army order of the evening of the 24th. There followed some of the bitterest moments of my life. I said to His Majesty that I had gained the painful impression that I no longer had his confidence and that I accordingly begged most humbly to be relieved of my office. His Majesty accepted my resignation.[15]

THE NEXT MOVE TOWARD A PEACE was now up to the Allies. The Supreme War Council, sitting in Versailles, had before it the German request for an armistice, and it must now decide whether to accept. If so, on what terms? On the first question, there was very little difference; nearly everyone agreed that the requested armistice should not be denied. The Allies and Americans were near exhaustion. And despite the macabre game of attrition the Allies had been forced to play, humanitarian considerations were on everyone's mind. Only one man dissented. John J. Pershing, believing that he possessed more authority than had actually been granted him, wrote from a sickbed, where he was down with a mild case of flu,

I believe the complete victory can only be obtained by continuing the war until we force unconditional surrender from Germany, but if the Allied Governments decide to grant an armistice, the terms should be so rigid that under no circumstances could Germany take up arms again.[16]

Pershing's message had no effect. Colonel House was dismayed when he read the message because the question of granting an armistice, as differentiated from specifying terms that would defang Germany, was considered political, outside the general's purview. Nevertheless, House transmitted it to the other members of the council, all of whom at least acted appalled. In Washington, Baker and Wilson agreed with House, and Pershing barely escaped receiving a letter of reprimand.

Far more typical of the military viewpoint was that of Ferdinand Foch. When asked about the advisability of granting an armistice, he put it aptly:

Fighting means struggling for certain results. If the Germans now sign an armistice under the general conditions we have just determined [at Senlis], those results are in our possession. This being achieved, no man has the right to cause another drop of blood to be shed.[17]

Haig, Foch, and Pétain were all in favor of an armistice, whatever their disagreements about specific terms. Even Bliss broke with Pershing. When asked, he harked back to history. "We should have to go back to the days of Rome or earlier to find a civilized nation refusing even to discuss terms upon which fighting might cease. It would be unheard of to say: 'No, we haven't killed enough of you, there are some towns we want to burn.' "[18]

BY OCTOBER 26, Colonel Edward House arrived in France, vested with complete authority to represent President Wilson. He carried no governmental portfolio, but he had served in this capacity on the Supreme War Council before; nobody questioned his authority. Indeed House was deferred to, occupying a place of honor directly across the table from the council chairman, Clemenceau. His first days in Paris were hectic with formal calls and meetings with influential men who desired his ear. Edward House was at the crest of his career.

When the formal talks of the Allied council began on October 31, the members soon realized that the matter of armistice terms for Germany was easily decided, because Foch's memorandum on the subject seemed reasonable. But Germany was only one of the nations the Allies and Americans were fighting. There remained the Austro-Hungarian Empire, Turkey, and Bulgaria, who had fought on the side of the Central Powers. Worse, the nations who were on the winning side had grown to an alarming number. Japan and Romania were among the more important. What nations should be represented at what meetings? Outsized meetings would be hopelessly cumbersome. (Edward House commented wryly, "Everybody wants to make a speech.")[19]

The big four—Britain, France, Italy, and the United States—eventually found a way to steer what was going on without appearing to. Every morning representatives of those countries, who called themselves the "steering committee," would meet in Paris informally. They rotated the place of meeting—the home of Clemenceau, House's apartment, or other locations. In the afternoons the smaller countries would be admitted in plenary sessions.

WHILE THE ALLIES and Americans were debating at Versailles, the structure of the German nation was disintegrating. On October 27, Vice Chancellor Friedrich von Payer went before the Reichstag and pleaded for peace. The Germans "could not take it amiss," he said, if the rest of the world had certain doubts that the Germans sincerely wanted peace. "What we need," he went on, was an "unequivocal, honest, and straightforward policy. . . . We have no use for anyone in the Government who still favors a peace of force more than a peace of justice."[20]

Prince Max, in complete agreement, then took steps to dismantle the mechanism by which Ludendorff had long guided public opinion, the

War Press Department. To make sure that daily communiqués were issued by responsible members of government, he designated Vice Chancellor Matthias Erzberger to take charge of the department.[21]

Germany's position was made more desperate a few days later when Austria signed an armistice on November 4 with the Italians at the Villi Guisti, near Padua, Italy. (Several days earlier the Hungarians had split off from the Dual Monarchy.) Germany now stood alone. The loss of the questionable fighting power of the Austrians was not critical, but Germany could not continue without the oil supplies that had flowed through Austro-Hungarian territory from Galicia and Romania.[22] Germany's plight was rapidly becoming hopeless.

On November 5, President Wilson sent a message to the government of Germany. Over the signature of Secretary of State Robert Lansing, it contained a critical sentence:

> I am instructed by the President to request you to notify the German Government that Marshal Foch has been authorized by the Government of the United States and the Allied Governments to receive properly accredited representatives of the German Government and to communicate to them terms of an armistice.[23]

UNREST WAS NOW SHAKING the German homeland. On November 7, as an indication of the disillusionment of the German people with the war, twenty thousand deserters from the German Army dared to band together and march through the streets of Berlin.[24] More serious, the Bolsheviks, having overthrown the Russian government, were now presenting themselves as an alternative to the Kaiser in the ruling of Germany. Their membership was small but aggressive. On November 8 the Reds seized control over parts of the German Navy. A Workmen's and Soldier's Council took over the German sea bases—Kiel, Wilhelmshaven, Helgoland, Borkum, and Cuxhaven—joined by the U-boat men in the revolt. The German Army managed to suppress the uprising,[25] but the German Navy would never take to sea again in the war.

IN THE EARLY MORNING hours of November 7, Marshal Foch, at Senlis, received a message from the German government:

> The German Government, having been informed through the President of the United States that Marshal Foch had received power to receive accredited representatives of the German Government, and communicate to them conditions of an armistice, the following plenipotentiaries have been named by it:

[Matthias] Erzberger, General H. K. A. von Winterfeldt, Count Alfred von Obendorff, General von Gruennel, and Naval Captain von Salow. . . . The plenipotentiaries request that they be informed by wireless of the place where they can meet Marshal Foch.[26]

Foch had been waiting for this message, and he immediately sent a wireless in reply. The German delegation was told to approach Allied lines along the Chimay–Fourmies–La Chapelle–Guise road, where a temporary cease-fire would be ordered, effective at 3:00 P.M. that day. That done, he left Senlis aboard his special train, bound for the woods northeast of Compiègne, where the German emissaries were to present themselves. His party was small. He took General Maxime Weygand, along with some aides and interpreters. Since the British Royal Navy needed representation, he had previously invited the First Sea Lord, Admiral Sir Rosslyn Wemyss. Foch's train arrived that evening, expecting to meet the Germans the next morning.

Making a rendezvous was not to be that easy. The conditions of the roads along the front were so bad that, after detours, the German delegation arrived at the appointed place in the French lines only at 9:00 P.M. that evening, and finally reached the designated woods at 7:00 A.M. the morning of the 8th. Foch announced that he would receive them two hours later.

Foch did nothing to make the defeated Germans comfortable. First he demanded to see their credentials. Erzberger, Obendorff, and Winterfeldt duly complied. Foch announced the members of his delegation and directed everyone to take his predesignated place at the conference table.

Foch also made clear to his visitors which party represented the victors and which the vanquished. What, he asked them, was the purpose of their visit? When Erzberger replied that they had come to receive the proposal of the Allied powers looking to an armistice, Foch said that he had none to make. When a confused Erzberger asked what would be the conditions of an armistice, Foch said that he had no conditions.

Erzberger now produced and read President Wilson's last message empowering Foch to make the armistice conditions known, using that as a basis for the meeting. Only then did Foch stop playing: "Do you ask for an armistice? If so, I can inform you of the conditions subject to which it can be obtained."[27] Erzberger thereupon asked for the armistice. Foch was satisfied, and at his bidding, General Maxime Weygand read the principal paragraphs of the armistice terms agreed to at Versailles.

The Germans gave no indication of their reaction to the armistice terms but asked that military operations be suspended immediately. Foch refused. Erzberger then described the disorganization prevalent in the German Army and cited the incidents occurring in Germany that had been leading to a spirit of revolution. He cited the threat of Bolshevism, into the sphere of which he feared Germany might fall. He also hinted that the scourge of Bolshevism might even spread to Western Europe.

Foch remained adamant. The disintegration in the German Army, he declared, was common to all beaten armies. As to the threat of Bolshevism in Western Europe, the respective governments would find means of defending themselves against the danger.[28]

Finally the Germans asked for an extension of the period during which their government would be able to consider the armistice terms. Foch declared that he possessed no authority to grant an extension; the time limit had been set by the "Allied and Associated governments" at 11:00 A.M., November 11, 1918. The only concession he made was to allow the Germans to use his wireless to notify their Chancellor that terms were coming by courier—and add that their request for suspension of hostilities had been turned down. Foch also arranged for safety measures for the courier. The message was sent at 11:30 A.M. on November 8.

The delegations then spent an uncomfortable two and a half days in each other's company, holding informal "informational" conferences. On the 9th the German delegation handed Weygand a text entitled "Observations on the Conditions of an Armistice with Germany." Foch considered these observations as the "arguments of the day before," not worth recording.[29]

By the night of November 10, 1918, time was running out. Erzberger sent a note to Foch advising him that the German government had not yet sent an answer to their terms but, as a means of reassurance, that "The plenipotentiaries have already taken steps looking to have instructions sent to them as quickly as possible." During the evening a note came to the woods at Compiègne from the German government accepting the conditions.[30] It only remained to decipher a long telegram from Hindenburg and to sign.

At 2:05 A.M., November 11, 1918, after certain formalities, the armistice was signed. Germany accepted all the terms laid down by the Allied and Associated Powers. It was to take effect at 11:00 A.M., November 11, 1918.

WHILE THE NEGOTIATIONS were concluding between Foch and the Germans, Pershing was not letting up in pressing ahead. He entirely concurred with the instructions the generalissimo had sent out to all commanders on the 9th:

> The enemy, disorganized by our repeated attack, retreats along the entire front.
>
> It is important to coordinate and expedite our movements. I appeal to the energy and the initiative of the Commanders-in-Chief and their armies to make decisive the results obtained.[31]

First and now Second Armies had continued the attack, even after receiving word at 6:00 A.M., November 11, that the armistice had been signed. The 89th Division (V Corps) occupied Stenay that morning, Pouilly-sur-Meuse and Autreville were taken, and the 2d Division expanded its bridgehead across the Meuse.[32] Men like Elton Mackin's friend Woody Wilson were dying and being maimed even after the armistice agreement had been signed.

As the appointed hour approached, Pershing faced a large wall map disconsolately. He was unrepentant in his view that the armistice was a mistake. As the eleventh hour of the eleventh day of the eleventh month of 1918 arrived, he was heard to mumble,

> I suppose our campaigns are ended, but what an enormous difference a few days more would have made.[33]

CHAPTER TWENTY-THREE

THE END OF THE AEF

Somewhere in the Argonne, music broke out in the Ger-
man lines and, from their trenches "like a jack-in-
the-box," troops jumped out and ran toward the front
line opposite. "Kamaraden! Kamaraden!" they cried in
their broken French, "la guerre ist fini!" They sang.
There was joy in their faces. "My word," wrote a French
witness, "they seem happier than us, these conquered
men." And he added: "We are all today of the same per-
suasion, we are all the same men, men finally delivered."

—GREGOR DALLAS [1]

WHEN THE ARMISTICE finally arrived, the reaction of the men on the front was one of mixed relief and disbelief. The slaughter of the previous years and months had come to an end. Most of the men justifiably rejoiced. Others did not know what to do. Their reactions were personal and defy broad description, but Thomas Johnson, a newspaper reporter, made a good effort:

> For most of them, dirty and dog-tired in body and spirit, it was something unnatural, almost incredible. They stood up in trenches and cold wet foxholes, stretched themselves, looked about in wonderment, while, so close often that a stone would hit them, other figures stood up, too and stretched themselves. They were gray-clad, and had been enemies, whom our men had tried to kill, lest they themselves be killed. [2]

TO PAUL CULBERTSON, of the American Field Service, the Armistice represented only the beginning of a tragic month. Three days earlier his close friend Arthur Brickley had contracted a case of the influenza that was ravaging soldiers and civilians alike in the Western World. Brickley, a Harvard aristocrat, was a fellow ambulance driver, and over the course of a year serving together the two young men had become close. Brickley was a little older than Culbertson, and he had served as an inspiration for the younger man. Off duty he had helped Paul with his French lessons, had played the piano in a nearby girls' school, and had encouraged Culbertson to dream of the day when he, like Arthur, might attend Harvard.

At first Brickley's case of flu was thought to be mild. As each day progressed, however, his condition worsened, and he became desperately sick. Paul could do nothing but hope and pray.

Brickley died on December 7 after an illness of over a month. With his death, Paul Culbertson lost all interest in attending Harvard.[3] Later he recovered from his grief and attended law school before taking up a career as a Foreign Service officer. He died at age eighty-one, sixty years after the Armistice.

To GEORGE S. PATTON, now recommended for promotion to the grade of full colonel, November 11 was a quiet day. He was at the hospital in Langres, nearly recovered from the leg wound he had suffered in the first hours of the Meuse-Argonne campaign. Patton was personally disappointed that the war had come to a close, since he had been in battle only five days, including those at St. Mihiel.[4] He observed the past by writing a poem dedicated to Captain Matt English, an officer who had been killed while serving in Patton's brigade. As to the future, he consoled himself in the certainty that another war would come. With that in mind, he spent his time writing a theoretic analysis on the problems of coordination between tanks and infantry.

MAJOR GENERAL JAMES G. HARBORD, commanding the Services of Supply at Tours, received the news of peace with jubilation. He ordered his band to form up in front of the French headquarters at Tours and play "La Marseillaise" and then "The Star Spangled Banner." He ordered the band to parade up and down the rue Nationale playing "the liveliest and cheeriest airs in its repertoire." Afterward he left for Paris to join General Charles Dawes for dinner and theater.[5] After he retired from the Army, he had a successful career in industry and remained Pershing's confidant for the rest of their lives.

THE ARMISTICE found Sergeant Chester E. Baker in the hospital with a case of mumps. Until the announcement was made official, he had regarded the talk of an impending armistice with skepticism. He was principally worried that his regiment, the 112th Infantry, 28th Division, might go over the top toward Metz without him. But then at 11 A.M. on November 11, he recorded, the Armistice was signed. "It was over. Thank God it was over."

Baker was embarrassed that he had ended his war service sick in the hospital, and his greatest wish was to share the moment with his comrades. He longed "to clasp the hands of the men [he had] marched with, suffered with, fought with all these months. But never mind, it was over."

Then, immediately after the first blush of relief, all of the men asked one question, the same question as Baker: "When will we be going home?"[6]

The answer to that question would lie in the hands of General John J. Pershing. The commander of the AEF took the Armistice in stride. To him it meant merely a change from wartime duties to the still onerous responsibilities of peacetime. Since Pershing had been living in relative comfort and exposed to little physical danger, his changes in circumstance, and his reactions, were less immediate than those of the front line troops. But his was the ultimate responsibility for preventing his Army from degenerating into a mob.

Once word of the Armistice was confirmed, Pershing issued a general order exhorting his men not to relax their discipline, while paying tribute to the men who had done the fighting.[7] He then drove to Paris and then Senlis where, by the direction of the President, he bestowed the Distinguished Service Medal on Marshal Ferdinand Foch. Pershing and his party returned to Paris in the afternoon "to find pandemonium." He met with Premier Clemenceau, and, previous difficulties forgotten for the moment, they fell into an embrace.[8]

Along with Pershing, Army Chief of Staff Peyton C. March would have much to do with the final disposition of American troops. For him the cessation of hostilities offered no respite. March had been annoyed by Pershing's insistence on planning for a 1919 campaign even after everyone realized that the war was ending. As late as October 30, in fact, Pershing sent March a message expressing concern over the supply of rifles for 1919. Two days earlier he had asked that 350,000 men be sent to France in January 1919.[9]

In the face of these unrealistic demands, March had acted on his own. He stopped the shipment of men to France on November 1, ten days before the Armistice. On the morning of November 11 he canceled all draft calls.[10] He then set about reversing the military machine that had been sending trained men overseas, and devoted the entire energies of the War Department to the work of demobilization. By January 4, 1919, he later wrote, the United States had demobilized over 700,000 men; by early February over a million.[11]

The bulk of Pershing's two million men were sent home as quickly as shipping could be obtained to carry them. Not all could leave at once, however. A force of 240,000 men would be required to occupy the American zone and the bridgehead over the Rhine at Coblenz, at least during the period of the peace negotiations at Versailles. After some shuffling of divisions and renumbering of armies, Pershing established the Third U.S. Army, under Major General Joseph Dickman. Assigned to it would be six divisions, four Regular and two National Guard, organized into two corps.[12] On November 15, at Ligny-en-Barrois, the army was formally organized and Dickman assumed command. Two days later advance elements crossed the Armistice line, with the French Tenth Army on its right and the French Fifth on its left. The 2d Battalion, 39th Infantry, 4th Division, arrived at Coblenz on December 8, 1918.[13]

They were the exception. The bulk of the AEF never saw the zone of occupied Germany; Dickman's Third Army included only a little over a tenth of the two million present in France at the Armistice. During the month of November 1918, over 26,000 men were shipped home; the number jumped to about 100,000 in December. In June, nearly 350,000 men were returned.[14]

BACK IN WASHINGTON, President Woodrow Wilson made a drastic decision: he determined to be the first United States President ever to leave the country while in office.[15] Up to this time he had allowed his alter ego, Colonel Edward House, to sit in the Supreme War Council, but the task of convincing Clemenceau, Lloyd George, and Orlando to create a peace treaty featuring his Fourteen Points could not be delegated. As members of his delegation he chose Secretary of State Robert Lansing, Colonel House, and that erudite warrior, General Tasker Bliss. Wilson, Lansing, and House left New York aboard the SS *America* in early December 1918.

On December 14, the slow-moving ocean liner docked at Brest amid an "unprecedented" welcoming party. When Wilson arrived in Paris the celebrations were said to be larger and more enthusiastic than those that had welcomed the Armistice seven weeks before. Signs along the streets gave notice of the faith people were putting in this American idealist to assist in making a treaty that would ensure a lasting peace.

Wilson spent a month conferring with staff, heads of foreign delegations, and military leaders. At one point he made a trip to Britain to visit

King George V and Queen Mary. It was not until January 18, 1919, that the peace delegates met in the Hall of Mirrors in the Palace of Versailles. It would be a dictated peace. With the signing of the military armistice, Germany had in fact surrendered unconditionally. Since the United States and the Allies were free to dictate any terms they wished, they set no place at the conference table for the defeated powers.

To the Americans of the AEF all this meant very little. Their main interest lay in the amount of time it would take to sign a treaty. Only after the signatures were affixed could their official status as belligerents come to an end.

On June 28, 1919, the Treaty of Versailles was signed, and the Americans had no further reason to keep a large force in Europe. The Third Army at Coblenz, now down to 110,000 troops, was redesignated as the American Forces in Germany, commanded by Major General Henry T. Allen. By September only a tenth of those remained. The American Forces in Germany would stay until 1923.

THE CREATION, training, supplying, and employment of the AEF had been a remarkable feat. From a force of only 200,000 officers and men of the Regular Army and National Guard in April 1917, America had raised an army of over four million, of whom about half had crossed the Atlantic. Twenty-four Yankee divisions had been employed in active combat, and they had comported themselves so well that they were given some of the most difficult tasks on the Western Front. True, most of the tanks, artillery, and airplanes they had used were of French manufacture, but with shipping at a premium—and with the French producing the best equipment on the Allied side—shipping priority was wisely devoted to men, not equipment.

The Americans had also created their own Services of Supply, and its figures are impressive. During the nineteen months of American participation, seven and a half million tons of shipping were sent from the United States to France. This tonnage included nearly 1,800 locomotives of the hundred-ton type, nearly 27,000 standard gauge freight cars, and nearly fifty thousand motor trucks. Some seventy thousand horses and mules were shipped overseas.[16]

There had been a price to pay. Americans had lost 53,500 men from battle deaths alone, most of them in a period of about six weeks. Deaths from other causes, mostly disease, were even greater: over 63,000. Of the nonmortal wounds, many of the 204,000 were debilitating.[17] These casualties, while heavy, were small compared to those of America's allies. The British had suffered about 900,000 men killed; France about 1.35 million. Germany and Austria together had lost nearly three million dead. The worst losses had been sustained by the Russians. One million seven hundred thousand Russians had lost their lives between 1914 and 1917.

ON WEDNESDAY, SEPTEMBER 10, 1919, the 1st Division, U.S. Army, formed up on Fifth Avenue, New York City, to allow the people an opportunity to give this symbolic unit a lavish welcome home. They were led on horseback by General Pershing himself, who had always kept that division foremost in his affections. Accompanying the Big Red One was a provisional regiment consisting of representative units from other combat divisions. At 10:00 A.M. promptly, Pershing rode off, starting at 110th Street.

Old cavalryman that he was, Pershing rode his mount at a graceful, calm walk, followed by standard-bearers, staff, and his troops, stopping off once to change mounts and again to call briefly on Cardinal Mercier. At Washington Square, amid teeming hordes of onlookers, Pershing dismounted and climbed in a car for a speedy trip to the Waldorf, where he watched the troops for another hour.[18]

It was Pershing's last duty as commander of the AEF. The saga of Black Jack Pershing and his American Expeditionary Force had come to a close.

EPILOGUE

WHEN THE WEARY DOUGHBOYS of the AEF returned home in late 1918 and all through 1919, they generally assumed, along with the rest of the world, that the Great War had been truly the "war to end all wars." The German defeat had been complete. The former enemy could never again dream of starting another major conflict on the European continent. So it seemed.

It was not to be. In another twenty years Germany, under a dictator far more powerful, destructive, and ruthless than the Kaiser, had destroyed Germany's attempt at democratic government, secretly rearmed her, and launched a second world war even more terrible than the first.

The causes for Germany's military resurgence and reversion to aggression are complex, and many books have been written about them. Suffice it to say that they stemmed largely from the provisions of the Treaty of Versailles, signed on June 28, 1919. That document exacted harsh, humiliating terms that, once the Western nations settled back into peacetime pursuits and underwent the Great Depression, they were not willing to enforce. The treaty deprived Germany of much territory and saddled her with backbreaking financial reparations,[1] but its disarmament provisions did not go far enough to enable the victors to enforce the terms.

On the surface, Germany's military disarmament seemed to be drastic indeed. The left bank of the Rhine River and a strip fifty kilometers wide along the right bank were to be completely demilitarized. The German Army was limited to a strength of 100,000, its Navy to twenty ships and fifteen thousand personnel. All military aviation was prohibited. But the General Staff was not disbanded. "Recreational" aviation, by which future military pilots could be trained, was not prohibited. Thus the seeds of power remained, simply waiting for the day when Adolf Hitler would come along and create a new German war machine in secret. As a result, the two world wars are coming more and more to be viewed as merely two phases of a single conflict.

History would seem to have vindicated General Pershing in his protests against granting Germany an armistice when she requested it in October and November of 1918. Had the Western Allies refused to grant the armistice while Germany was still on French and Belgian soil, had they crushed the German Army completely, occupied all German territory, and deprived her of any means whatsoever to rebuild her armed forces, the Second World War might never have occurred.

That view was shared by most, but not all officers close to Pershing,[2] but their opinions, being outside their military purview, were ignored. Moreover, the views of the American commander were irrelevant to the real world of public opinion and politics. The governments of France, Britain, and Italy, aware of the feelings in their respective countries, would never condone continuing the fighting any longer than necessary. The leaders of those countries, as well as President Woodrow Wilson himself, rejected such views out of hand, even with some irritation. Pershing had advocated the impossible.[3]

With such a small interval between world wars, it is not surprising that the United States Army of 1940 should appear to be a continuum of the AEF of 1918. Pershing's AEF was the first modern Army the United States ever fielded, and the Army of the Second World War was less different from the AEF than the AEF was from the Army that preceded it. Anyone witnessing the mobilization of the draftee Army of 1941 could not help being struck by how much the future GIs of World War II resembled the doughboys of World War I. Soldiers being inducted into service as the result of the draft law of late 1940 were at first issued ill-fitting World War I uniforms, including musty "overseas caps" and even wrap leggings. They were armed with the model 1903 Springfield rifle, which was replaced only when production of the Garand M-1 got under way.[4] Both the heavy machine gun and the light machine gun of the Second World War remained the 1917 Browning models, as did the Browning automatic rifle, which came into the hands of the Americans late in 1918. Bangalore torpedoes, trench mortars, and even rifle grenades changed little between 1918 and 1939.

Perhaps even more important in the development of a modern Army was Pershing's creation of a vast and elaborate supply system that was called Services of Supply in 1917–1918 and Communications Zone (Com-Z) in 1944–1945. This vast organization entailed building and operating large seaports, storage, delivery of all classes of supply to forward supply points utilizing railroads, trucks, and eventually (in the first war) even mules. The Services of Supply, like the Communications Zone of the European Theater in 1944, was organized into three sections (Base, Intermediate, and Advance), with a prescribed level of supply maintained in each. This structure was an innovation of unglamourous but innovative and hardworking staff officers and commanders under Pershing and his headquarters. Nothing so elaborate had existed in the Army before April of 1917.

The staff procedures followed in later years were also developed by Pershing and his staff during the early months of the AEF's existence. Credit for this must be given to Pershing himself, assisted by his chief of staff, James G. Harbord. Their staff organization encompassed the four staff sections—Personnel, Intelligence, Operations, and Supply[5]—in use by the American Army to this day. It is noteworthy that this system was developed by the AEF, not the War Department.

In many important ways, of course, the armies of the First and Second World Wars were different. The division was reorganized from the cumbersome "square division" of four infantry regiments to the "triangular," comprising three infantry regiments. More important, technical advances provided the one thing the generals on both sides had previously been seeking in vain: mobility on the battlefield. The airplane, the tank, the truck, and the efficient two-way radio are generally credited with breaking the stalemate that plagued the earlier conflict. All were in their infancy at the time of Pershing's AEF, but between wars, military aircraft would progress as rapidly as the civilian aircraft industry; the tanks and trucks that broke down more from mechanical difficulties than from enemy guns would grow in reliability, along with the American automobile industry. The walkie-talkie radios would replace carrier pigeons. But the seeds of this progress were planted with the AEF.

AN IMPORTANT LINK between the AEF and the American Army of the Second World War was the military education it gave to many men who served in both. Because of the short interval separating the two world wars—and with a career officer expected to serve about forty years in those days—many of the officers of the AEF returned to serve once more in 1941. Some had remained in uniform during the intervening years; others were recalled as reservists. It was generally assumed, in fact, that service with the AEF in 1918 was almost a prerequisite for responsible positions in the Second World War.[6]

Examples abound of young officers who returned for the second war. Ladislav Janda, that incredibly optimistic twenty-one-year-old who attained command of a battalion at the end of the war, was called up for duty as a reservist in 1942. At the end of that conflict, Lieutenant Colonel Lud Janda had not reached his fiftieth year.

A more noted figure was that of Colonel Theodore Roosevelt, Jr., commanding officer of the 26th Infantry by the last days of the Meuse-Argonne. In November of 1942 Roosevelt went overseas as a brigadier general with the 1st Division and later landed with the 4th Division on Utah Beach on D-Day, 1944.

Another young 1st Division officer, Lieutenant Clarence Huebner, of the 28th Infantry Regiment at Cantigny, came back to the 1st Division as its commander in 1944. He commanded the Big Red One when it landed at Omaha Beach on D-Day.

The most important educational impact of service with the AEF, however, lay in the training of "middle-management" officers, men who were colonels and brigadier generals in 1918. The list includes many—George C. Marshall, Douglas MacArthur, and George S. Patton were only three notables. In the first war these young professionals often performed the difficult day-to-day management of units for their star-bestudded generals. The impact of the war on their mental outlooks varied, of course, depending on their positions and temperaments.

Of the three, Brigadier General Douglas MacArthur, of the 42d Division, certainly enjoyed the most éclat in his spectacular career with the AEF. With flamboyant courage, he participated in one infantry patrol after another, exposing himself far beyond the needs of his office. He was the most decorated American officer in Pershing's force. Yet MacArthur seems to have suffered at least some psychological damage as the result of his experiences in World War I. His miraculous survival while taking extraordinary risks apparently encouraged a mystical feeling of invincibility and destiny, both an asset and a liability. Furthermore, his unhappy relations with Pershing's staff at Chaumont (in which MacArthur was not always to blame) engendered in him an obsession that the "Chaumont Crowd" constituted an organized opposition to him. Even when he was a senior commander in the Second World War, he maintained an obsession that the "Crowd"—now based in Washington—still existed and were still out to get him. He associated George Marshall with that group of imaginary enemies.

Marshall was the one officer whose training in the AEF did the most to fit him for his future responsibilities. As operations officer of First Army during the Meuse-Argonne, Marshall never commanded troops in France, much to his personal disappointment, but it now seems almost providential that he was stationed where he was. A troop commander is concerned with an area only a few miles wide. The future Army chief of staff, however, was at the very center of the operations of the largest fighting force the United States had ever fielded up to that time. Planning, training, and operations, closely tied to logistics, all fell into his purview. There could have been no better spot for Marshall's training for the pivotal role he was to play in the future.

Much of what Marshall saw undoubtedly affected the way he conducted affairs in the Second World War. When the Army began to expand after the draft of 1940, Marshall saw to it, despite his own background as a staff officer, that troop commanders, rather than staff officers, would be given preference in matters of decorations and promotions. He was also determined that troop commanders would be younger men than the commanders of the First War. In the AEF Marshall saw division commanders such as Omar Bundy and Clarence Edwards, men who were older than Pershing himself, turn in less than stellar performances. As a result, the division commanders of 1942 to 1945 were on the average about ten years younger than those of 1918. The Army and the men who served in it benefited.

The last of the three future household names was Lieutenant Colonel George Patton, who commanded the 1st Tank Brigade until wounded on the first day of the Meuse-Argonne. It was there that Patton underwent his conversion to tank warfare. His period between wars, however, was strange. For a while he was able to further the concepts he had been developing in the 1st Tank Brigade. At Fort Meade in 1920, he teamed up with Lieutenant Colonel Dwight Eisenhower, an automotive expert, in developing doctrines for tank warfare. Patton specialized in light tanks, Eisenhower in heavy.

The Patton-Eisenhower partnership was of short duration, but not by their choice. Both ran afoul of the authorities in the War Department for their "heretical" opinions about the employment of tanks, and both were forced to revert to their basic branches. Their views on the massing of tanks were later accepted, but only after the beginning of the European war in 1939. By that time the old traditionalists had been replaced in positions of leadership by more forward-thinking officers such as George Marshall. That, plus the examples set by the German blitzkrieg across France in 1940 and later in Russia, changed Army thinking. Patton returned to the tanks, his tactical views molded on the Aire River in September of 1918.

The senior commanders of the AEF, all of them about Pershing's age, were too old to serve in the Second World War. Pershing himself remained in Europe until after the signing of the Treaty of Versailles and then returned to the United States to serve as Army chief of staff. His name was mentioned in politics, but no groundswell ever developed. Pershing probably realized that, though immensely popular, he lacked political talents. After his retirement he served as the president of the American Battle Monuments Commission in Paris, where he devoted several years to establishing the cemeteries that would be the last resting place of many of his men.

The extent to which Pershing's mystique dominated the psychology of the American Army for many years after the Armistice is remarkable to the modern reader. More than any other American war, the United States effort in the First World War was a single-theater operation. Pershing's position stood alone, essentially unchallenged. Congress rewarded his services by reinstating the mythical rank bestowed on George Washington, General of the Armies, a theoretical six stars. At the same time Congress allowed Pershing's legal superior, General Peyton C. March, to revert to two-star rank, even while still in office.[7] When Pershing was writing his two-volume memoirs of the war in 1930, he felt free to call on his former subordinates—James Harbord, Fox Conner, and many other staff officers—to give him time-consuming assistance. Some of those officers were still on active duty.

To the outsider, however, the last thirty years of Pershing's life—he died in 1948—appear to have been a pathetic anticlimax. Pershing never took on new challenges. Instead, he dedicated his time to justifying his actions for the short period of his life when he commanded the AEF.

There was some need for justification. Pershing's stiffness and self-importance won him few friends; his stubbornness, bordering on recalcitrance, in maintaining that United States forces should be held together practically at all costs has recently come under reexamination. But the basic decision to keep American forces together in a single army, under American command, is generally accepted as necessary, especially since the Americans were basing all organizational plans on prospects for operations in 1919. And it came from President Woodrow Wilson himself, not Pershing.

On the whole, it seems impossible to suggest the name of any other officer who could have performed the duty of commander of the AEF as well as Pershing. Others, while broader thinkers or better tacticians, lacked his grim determination. America was the small dog in World War I; it remained for World War II, when America was the overpowering partner, for it to be magnanimous in dealing with the commanders of other nations.

• • •

ONE QUESTION is still debated: how important was the AEF to the winning of the First World War? It is generally agreed that the threat of the growing power of the AEF, projected into 1919, was critical in convincing the German high command that the war could not be won.[8] It is not agreed as to how much impact American forces had on the fighting itself, especially in the last general offensive that began September 26, 1918.

Americans claim that the AEF was given the most difficult and most important sector on the Western Front, that the Germans sent their best divisions to the Meuse-Argonne, thus making it possible for the Allies, especially the British, to make spectacular gains. While that argument contains some truth, it is difficult to defend unconditionally. There is no question that the American troops fought bravely and were rapidly learning the techniques of conducting modern warfare. They were also taking losses that the French and British could not have afforded. But could the Allies have won without them?

Major General Sir Frederick Maurice, director of military operations of the British General Staff, treated the American contribution generously:

> There are times and occasions in war when the valor of ignorance has its advantages. With greater experience, the American infantry would have learned to overcome the German machine guns with less loss of life, and the services of supply would have worked more smoothly. Had the Americans waited to gain that experience, the war would have been prolonged by at least six months, and the cost in life would have been far greater than it was.[9]

It matters little. Which nation contributed most to the success of the final offensive will never be agreed upon—and need not. But the threat of the growing power of a dynamic AEF could not have failed to exert a critical influence on Germany's decision to ask for peace.

IN SURVEYING the building, training, delivery, supply, and employment of the AEF, the observer must be struck with admiration of what was eventually accomplished once the United States entered the war. A small Army, scattered about the American South and West, the Philippines, and elsewhere, expanded in nineteen months into an army of four million men, half of whom had been delivered overseas and well over a million of whom were fighting on the front lines. One can protest that more could have been done, but I find that argument unpersuasive; the feat was astonishing.

Once deployed, the AEF moved as speedily as it could, and despite the cries of its allies, faster than might be expected. If the United States had not entered the war—or had elected not to send an expeditionary force abroad—there would never have been a Second World War; Germany would have won the first one. On the other hand, in a world with Continental Europe dominated by the Kaiser's Germany, it is difficult to imagine that the United States would have been spared from some future confrontation with that power.

With the declaration of war in 1917 the United States of America became involved in the complexities of the modern world. When it did so, the AEF and John J. Pershing were the emblem and the instrument of that decisive intervention.

MOBILIZATION

As Secretary of War, Newton D. Baker carried responsibilities far beyond the induction, training, and deployment of American soldiers. The mundane matter of construction is a case in point. The draft could never have been implemented had not the Army had established adequate housing for the inductees when they reported. The first of that group were scheduled to report in early September 1917, and Baker had only until then to build cantonments for them. The Regular Army could take care of its new divisions on the posts it already had established. The same applied to the National Guard. But the inductees would have to report to new camps not yet in being.

Baker could be thankful that the bureaus, with all their maddening sense of independence from central authority, had been active in peacetime. Major General Henry G. Sharpe, the Quartermaster General, had preceded the declaration of war by coming up with estimates for facilities to house a million men. Baker soon took the responsibility away from Sharpe—he had too many other responsibilities—and set up a Cantonment Division under Colonel Isaac W. Littel, advised by a New York architect, W. A. Starrett. He then called up the six territorial commanders of the Army to select sites for the new posts. By the end of May 1917, Baker had approved the locations for sixteen National Army cantonments and provisions to equip an equal number of National Guard posts with tents. Strangely, the tents were more expensive than the wooden barracks; canvas, used for haversacks and other equipment, was a scarce item. Through the summer of 1917, then, the Army built thirty-two cities, each to house a population of 40,000 inhabitants.[1]

NEWTON BAKER had another heavy responsibility on his shoulders, to coordinate the mobilization of American industry to support the Army. In some ways this was the more difficult of his tasks, because it was so very new; the United States had never attempted such a thing before. Furthermore, in this field he lacked a core of uniformed professionals to help him.

At the beginning of 1917 American industry was principally and necessarily geared to a civilian economy. The only notable American war industry was that of artillery munitions manufacture. In 1915, early in the European war, American industry had begun producing artillery shells needed by the Allies, and by late 1916 three quarters of all light artillery shells being fired by British guns were manufactured in the United States.[2] On America's entry into the war, however, even that industry needed to expand its production. American needs for ammunition would be great, but they could not be allowed to cut off supply to the British and French. Furthermore, there was no time for retooling plants to fit American guns.

Planning for mobilization of American industry began gradually, starting early in 1916, after the sinking of the *Lusitania*. At that time the Naval Consulting Board was set up for the Navy and the Kernan Board[3] for the Army. These boards made extensive surveys of American industry; the Naval Consulting Board alone surveyed eighteen thousand industrial plants.[4] America's industrial leaders, while cooperative, were determined that the needs of war should not be allowed to shut out civilian consumption. The answer, therefore, was a partnership between government and industry.

Still a sense of urgency was lacking. The Army Appropriation Act of 1916, which set up the Council of National Defense, did so in the form of a rider to another act, not a main provision. Nevertheless the council did come into existence. It consisted of six cabinet officers who were directed to advise with the Commission of Industrialists. The needs of industry were respected, of course, but the nation's needs came first; even the industrialists appointed to the committee were named by the President.[5]

The Council of National Defense wielded almost no power, however, and it was soon succeeded by other, subordinate boards, the most notable of which was the General Munitions Board, set up just before the United States declaration of war. The success of the General Munitions Board was largely due to the efforts of its chairman, Frank A. Scott, pres-

ident of a company manufacturing high-grade machine tools for both the
Army and the Navy. Scott earned Baker's gratitude, and in later years
Baker described him as

> . . . a man of vision and resourcefulness and also a man of tact and sanity.
> Under his leadership, from the beginning, there were understanding, good
> will, and effective cooperation between the officers of the Army, Navy, and
> civilians. . . . Mr. Scott, Mr. [Walter S.] Gifford of the Council of National
> Defense, General Palmer Pierce, and their associates laid the foundation of
> our national mobilization.[6]

These preliminary preparations, though a great step forward,
proved inadequate to prevent confusion among both the government
and industry when war actually came. Much of the problem lay in the old
bugaboo, the independent bureaus, which conducted purchasing independently despite progress made in bringing them under the authority of
the chief of staff. No fewer than five (later nine) separate authorities were
all bidding against one another. In addition to the Navy, other customers
for war-related products included the Shipping Board, the Railroad Administration, and the Red Cross, among many others.

The solution to the problem would have to come from a cooperative
effort, and to administer the sharing, President Wilson looked to a forty-
seven-year-old native of South Carolina, Bernard M. Baruch, much as he
looked to George Creel to mobilize public opinion. Baruch and Wilson
had been friends for some time. Both were progressives, ambitious men,
and Southerners. To Wilson, Baruch combined two ideal qualities: he
was a Democrat who was also a Wall Street financier. Since early summer
of 1916, Baruch had already been participating in an advisory capacity
and by the spring of 1917 he enlisted a group of former business contacts
to administer raw material purchases for the military. Soon he was appointed as Commissioner for Raw Materials in the newly formed War In-
dustries Board.

The coordination of war purchasing may have evolved slowly, but it
was handled with remarkable success. All boards and authorities operated with the power of the President behind them, which included the
power of commandeering. They established a Priorities System, a Price-
Fixing System, and a Conservation System. So effective was the effort
that twelve years later, General Hugh Johnson, the officer so closely associated with it, could rhapsodize in a memo to General Pershing:

> Whole strata of industry were integrated for the first time in our history.
> Competition was adjourned. Industries learned to operate in vast units.
> Patents and trade-secrets were pooled. Hostility was erased and coopera-

tion was instituted. . . . Labor stepped into a new sun. The beneficial effect of doubling the home market for our industry by the simple expedient of higher wages for all employees marked the opening of new vistas of prosperity if not the birth of a vast new economic concept. No coercion was necessary. Men jeopardized their fortunes and industrial futures with the spontaneity of crusaders. Cooperation with Government—so suspiciously regarded in the pre-war era—became commonplace.[7]

Hugh Johnson was an advocate, but he was also an expert. He took great pride in declaring that the American war effort more nearly reached President Wilson's ideal of an "entire nation armed" than did that of any other belligerent nation, Germany included. In the accomplishments he described, however, there was one serious caveat. The full power of America's industrial mobilization was not geared to take effect until the year 1919.

NOTES

PROLOGUE

1. Robert Asprey, *The German High Command*, pp. 292–94.
2. Russia, Italy, and Romania were also on the side of the Allies; Turkey and Bulgaria on the side of the Central Powers. However, none of these nations had troops in the line on the Western Front.
3. Edward House, *The Intimate Papers of Colonel House*, II, p. 436.
4. Ibid., pp. 432–33.
5. Wilson to the Congress, February 3, 1917, cited in ibid., p. 442.
6. Harley Notter, *The Origins of the Foreign Policy of Woodrow Wilson*, pp. 618–19.
7. It is not difficult to explain why. The Kaiser ruled his country in much the way that Carranza would have liked to rule Mexico. Whatever the causes, the privileges Carranza accorded German citizens in Mexico were lavish. He granted permission to the four thousand Germans living in Mexico to establish such fronts as the Union of German Citizens and the Iron Cross Society. He also allowed them to publish a newspaper that distributed German war propaganda. Fifty German military "advisers" were installed in key positions in Carranza's army. One officer, Maximilian Kloss, was appointed Carranza's director of munitions manufacture, with the rank of general in the Mexican Army.
8. John Dos Passos, *Mr. Wilson's War*, p. 195.
9. When Page read the message, he gasped, "This would precipitate a war between any two nations. Heaven knows what effect it will have in Washington."
10. Barbara Tuchman, *The Zimmermann Telegram*, p. 167.
11. Arthur Link, *Woodrow Wilson*, p. 271.
12. Tuchman, *Zimmermann Telegram*, p. 196.
13. *The Public Papers, War and Peace*, I, pp. 6–16, cited in Link, *Woodrow Wilson and the Progressive Era*, 282n.
14. Link, *Woodrow Wilson*, p. 282.

ONE: A VISIT FROM PAPA JOFFRE

1. Cyril Falls, *The Great War*, pp. 263–64, sees jealousy of Joffre's power.
2. Joseph Jacques Joffre, *Memoirs*, II, p. 566.

3. The party included a formidable group of officials, among them Viviani, who represented the civil government; Joffre, who spoke for the French Army; Vice Admiral Chocheprat, for the Navy; and Marquis Jacques Adelbert de Chambrun, a descendent of Lafayette, on behalf of the Chamber of Deputies.
4. Joffre, *Memoirs*, II, p. 567.
5. Ibid., p. 568. The size of the Regular Army, according to Peyton C. March, was only 127,588 officers and men. The National Guard was 66,594 men. March, *The Nation at War*, p. 1.
6. Rod Paschall, *The Defeat of Imperial Germany*, p. 11, puts the Allies at 3.9 million, of which France supplied 2.6 million and the British about half that number.
7. Joffre, *Memoirs*, II, p. 568.
8. Ibid.
9. Elmer Roberts of the Associated Press and Lincoln Eyre of the *New York World*.
10. *New York Times*, April 24, 1917.
11. Later estimated at 187,000 men. Falls, *The Great War*, p. 279.
12. Joffre, *Memoirs*, II, p. 569.
13. Ibid.
14. Ibid.
15. *New York Times*, April 30, 1917. Italics added.
16. See letter, Bridges to Kuhn, April 30, 1917. Bliss papers, Manuscript Room, Library of Congress.
17. British recruits, Bridges pointed out, underwent nine weeks of basic training in England and then only nine days in France. Despite that short indoctrination, however, they gave a "good account of themselves" within those established units, under the supervision of battle-trained officers and NCOs.
18. Bridges to Kuhn.
19. Ibid.
20. Bliss to Baker, 25 May 1917. Cited in Trask, *The AEF and Coalition Warmaking*, p. 4.
21. Bridges to Kuhn.
22. Joffre, *Memoirs*, II, pp. 577–78.

TWO: A NATION AT WAR

1. Dos Passos, *Mr. Wilson's War*, p. 300. Half a century later, Dwight D. Eisenhower, *Waging Peace*, p. 622, expressed the same thought in these terms: "the security of a nation depends upon a balanced strength comprised of morale, economic productivity, and military power."
2. Vardaman insisted that not all the crimes on the high seas had been committed by the Germans. He further stated that "if the people of the United States—I mean the plain, honest people, the masses who are to bear the burden of taxation and fight the nation's battles—were consulted—the United States would not make a declaration of war against Germany today." Congressional Record, Folder 7, Pershing Papers, Manuscript Room, Library of Congress.
3. Creel's most famous book was called *Children in Bondage*, written with Judge Ben B. Lindsey and Edwin Markham, published in 1914.
4. Ironically that tract concentrated on defending the nobility of Wilson's neutrality policy in the war, a position contrary to that which Creel was now to sell the public.
5. Creel was admitted to Wilson's inner circle; like Bernard Baruch, Newton D. Baker, and Colonel Edward House, he was admitted into the President's upstairs quarters in the White House. Dos Passos, *Mr. Wilson's War*, p. 301.
6. Jay Winter and Blaine Baggett, *The Great War*, p. 142.
7. George Creel, *Rebel at Large*, pp. 162–63.

8. "Americans who had marched in pacifist parades only months before enthusiastically participated in loyalty rallies and huge Liberty War Bond Drives. The nation's heroes—soldiers, movie stars, and athletes—led the patriotic movement to support the war. The writers of Tin Pan Alley were called upon to provide a musical expression of the changed attitude toward the war." Thomas Griess, *The Great War*, p. 171. Creel's efforts to take over powers of censorship brought on the wrath of such men as H. L. Mencken. Writing in *The Smart Set* ("Star-Spangled Men"), Mencken castigated him roundly.

9. Frederick Palmer, *Newton D. Baker*, I, p. 115.

10. Josephus Daniels, *The Wilson Era*, p. 451.

11. Russell Weigley, *History of the United States Army*, p. 350. In autumn of 1915, President Wilson found a two-line paragraph in the *Baltimore Sun* that reported the General Staff as preparing a plan in the event of war with Germany. Wilson, described as "trembling and white with passion," ordered an investigation. If the allegation was true, he directed that every officer on the General Staff be relieved and sent out of Washington. Though Wilson later relented, the General Staff was directed to "camouflage" such work in the future. Palmer, *Baker* I, pp. 40–41.

12. Scott's first assignment had been to the 7th Cavalry as a replacement for one of George A. Custer's officers who had been killed at the Little Bighorn in 1876. Scott's heart was still in the West, and he was known to receive visiting Indian delegations in his office, readily communicating with them in their own sign language. Edward Coffman, *The War to End All Wars*, p. 22.

13. Ibid., p. 23.

14. Stimson, who was later to be Secretary of War once more, under Franklin Roosevelt in the Second World War, thought Wood was the finest officer he had ever met until he encountered George C. Marshall. Henry L. Stimson and McGeorge Bundy, *On Active Service*, p. 33.

15. The only war fought largely by regulars was that with Mexico (1846–1848). Even then, half of the regiments were officially "Volunteer," and most of the regulars were signed up after war was declared.

16. Secretary of War Lindley M. Garrison had resigned over the rejection of the Continental Army, which was his pet project.

17. Leonard Ayres, *The War with Germany*, p. 27.

18. When the draft had first been implemented in 1863 the public had protested with bloody riots. Furthermore, the men drafted under that act had always been considered second-class soldiers in the Army.

19. General Peyton C. March, later Army chief of staff, had this to say: "the draft act was the most important piece of legislation enacted by Congress during the progress of the war, and it is a most striking tribute to the common sense of the American people that without apparent opposition and practically overnight they accepted a system which had been hitherto opposed by the nation ever since its organization. Voluntary service gave way to a system which had been stigmatized as Prussian, militaristic, foreign, and opposed to American institutions. The plain fact of the matter is that the voluntary system of raising soldiers for a major war is inherently wrong. In a major war, the ideas of the individual as to what he wants to do must always be subordinated to the common good." *Nation at War*, pp. 237–38.

20. Hugh S. Johnson, memo to Pershing. Pershing papers, Manuscript Room, Library of Congress. When it came to actually writing the original bill, the task fell to Colonel Johnson, a member of the Adjutant General Department. In so doing Johnson attained a reputation that kept him in key public positions for the next twenty years. He became the Administrator of the NRA (National Recovery Administration), a key element of President Franklin Roosevelt's New Deal.

21. Theodore Roosevelt, *The Foes of Our Own Household*, pp. 304–5.

22. At the end of the meeting Roosevelt offered Wilson's aide, Joseph P. Tumulty, a position in his division if it became a reality. Tumulty, *Wilson*, pp. 285–86.
23. Ayres, *The War with Germany*, p. 17. The remaining 1.2 million men who entered service came in as volunteers for the Regular Army or the National Guard. Amusingly, Roosevelt's letter to Pershing requesting command of a brigade was dated the day after the draft act was passed.
24. Palmer, *Baker*, I, pp. 218–19.

THREE: THE SELECTION OF GENERAL PERSHING

1. Joffre, *Memoirs* II, p. 578.
2. When the State, War, Navy Building was completed, shortly after the Civil War, the proud architect is said to have told General William T. Sherman that the edifice was completely indestructible from fire, storm, or earthquake. Sherman is reported to have murmured, "What a pity!"
3. Douglas MacArthur, *Reminiscences*, pp. 46–47. Years later, Baker wrote to Frederick Palmer that MacArthur had mentioned both Pershing and March. MacArthur's version seems more likely, because March was only a lieutenant colonel at the time.
4. This defied the view of the revered General Emory Upton, author of *Military Policy of the United States*, that it required two years to train a soldier.
5. Wood was a Harvard-trained medical doctor, and along with Theodore Roosevelt and Secretary Stimson had access to the Harvard Club in New York and inspired its members to establish the Committee of One Hundred, which consisted of aristocratic young gentlemen who were of a like persuasion regarding readiness for war. The resultant Military Training Camps Association became closely associated with the War Department, which endeavored to give it a role in training reserve officers. The officer training camps that grew out of the Plattsburgh Movement became a major source of junior officers for the Army in the war. Paul Koistinen, *Mobilizing for Modern War*, p. 109.
6. Palmer, *Newton D. Baker*, cited in Frank Vandiver, *Black Jack*, Vol. 7, p. 683.
7. Scott to Pershing, February 24, 1917, Scott papers, Library of Congress, cited in Vandiver, *Black Jack*, II, pp. 672–73.
8. Pershing to Scott, March 3, 1917, Scott papers, Library of Congress, cited in Vandiver, *Black Jack*, II, p. 673.
9. Vandiver, *Black Jack*, II, p. 676.
10. Pershing, *My Experiences in the World War*, I, p. 2.
11. Ibid., pp. 16–17.
12. Ibid., pp. 18, 19.
13. Roosevelt preferred the title of "Colonel" over that of "President."
14. Pershing, *Experiences*, I, p. 23.
15. Ibid., p. 24.
16. Ibid., p. 37.
17. Ibid., pp. 38–40, indicates that Bliss's order came from him, not drawn up by Pershing and Harbord. This version comes from Palmer, *Baker*, I, pp. 170–71. Palmer cites Pershing's lapse of memory simply as evidence of how hectic those early days were.
18. In addition to his official entourage, Pershing had with him on the train members of Lieutenant George S. Patton's family. Patton was going as one of Pershing's aides, and Pershing, in his bereavement on the Mexican border, had become attached to Patton's sister, Nita.
19. George C. Marshall. *Memoirs of My Services in the World War*, p. 3.

FOUR: THE YANKS ARRIVE

1. Actually the story was kept under wraps until after the *Baltic* had arrived at her destination. Pershing, *Experiences*, I, p. 42.
2. Ibid., p. 43.
3. They planned on a daily supply requirement of fifty pounds per man. Sherman had required thirty-seven on his March to the Sea in 1864. American requirements in the Philippines had been about the same. The increase was due to the technologies of modern warfare. James Harbord, *The American Army in France*, p. 74.
4. Pershing, *Experiences*, I, p. 44.
5. *New York Times*, June 9, 1917.
6. Pershing, *Experiences*, I, p. 48.
7. Ibid.
8. Pershing explains Foch's and Pétain's seemingly modest grade, considering his position. The French Army at that time had only two grades of general officer, brigadier and major general. The only rank above major general was that of marshal. In that respect it somewhat represented the general officer structure of the American Army in the Civil War. Pershing, *Experiences*, I, p. 58.
9. *New York Times*, June 15, 1917.
10. Pershing, *Experiences*, I, p. 60.
11. Ibid.
12. Marshall, *Services*, p. 2.
13. Ibid., p. 6.
14. "At 3 A.M., I was standing at the window of the shipping office with the commander of the Port of Embarkation, watching the endless column of infantry pouring slowly through the courtyard. Except for the shuffle of their feet, there was little noise. It was an impressive and forbidding scene. After a long silence, I remarked, 'The men seem very solemn.' In a rather dramatic fashion he replied, 'Of course they are. We are watching the harvest of death.' I hurriedly left the window and hunted up a more cheerful companion from the staff." Marshall, *Services*, p. 6.
15. The 5th Marines left the 1st Division shortly after arrival in France. *The History of the First Division* does not mention it.
16. Marshall, *Services*, p. 12.
17. Ibid., p. 14.
18. *New York Times*, July 5, 1917.
19. James Harbord, *Leaves from a War Diary*, p. 46.
20. Ibid., p. 47.
21. Harbord, *American Army*, p. 85.
22. Harbord, *Leaves*, p. 49.
23. Pershing, *Experiences*, I, p. 63.
24. Harbord, *American Army*, pp. 90–91.
25. Ibid., p. 92.
26. One of the modifications was that predicted by Pershing. Operations and training have indeed been consolidated into one division, G-3. The other major change involved supply and logistics. That was later split out from G-1 to become G-4. The organization from G-1 to G-4 has become fixed, but the term G-5 has carried different meanings in various situations.
27. Pershing, *Experiences*, I, pp. 83–86.
28. Ibid., p. 72.
29. Ibid., p. 81.
30. La Pallice, it will be recalled, was the port originally offered by Marshal Joffre on his trip to the United States.
31. Pershing, *Experiences*, I, pp. 81–82.

FIVE: ORGANIZING THE AEF

1. Harbord, *American Army*, p. 113.
2. As with most large, modern headquarters, Haig's personal command group was separate from the large "Second Echelon."
3. Pershing, *Experiences*, I, p. 114. The British would lose another 500,000 men before the year was out.
4. Ibid.
5. Marshall, *Services*, p. 16.
6. Ibid., p. 18.
7. Memo, French GHQ, Armies of the North and Northeast. Pershing papers, Manuscript Room, Library of Congress.
8. Memo to Chief of Staff, AEF, by Col. H. L. Fiske, AC/S, G-5. Pershing papers, Manuscript Room, Library of Congress.
9. Marshall, *Services*, p. 20.
10. Ibid., pp. 18–19.
11. When Pershing and Harbord visited Haig, Harbord was a lieutenant colonel. His British counterpart was a major general.
12. Marshall, *Services*, p. 31. As evidence of the low opinion the Moroccans had of the regular French infantry, the division's commander sent a small unit across to the east bank of the Meuse to take Camp, a small village on the bank. It was feared that the division attacking northward in parallel with the Moroccans would fail to take that position, thus allowing a German machine gun emplacement to take the Moroccans in flank. As it turned out, that was exactly the case. Marshall, p. 32.
13. Harbord, *Leaves*, pp. 119, 139. Also *American Army*, pp. 131–32.
14. Thomas Sage Wyman, "A Telephone Switchboard Operator with the AEF in France," *Army History*, Fall 1997/Winter 1998.
15. Ibid.
16. "The Hello Girls of the Army Signal Corps," in Lettie Gavin, *American Women in World War I*, p. 77. The article also cites the Report of the Chief Signal Officer to the Secretary of War, 1919.
17. Pershing, *Experiences*, I, p. 175.
18. Ladislav Janda, letter to his mother, September 17, 1917.
19. Paschall, *Defeat of Imperial Germany*, p. 194.
20. Ibid., pp. 195–96.
21. The exact figures are 10,679,814 men registered, of whom 2,666,867 were later taken in. Ayres, *The War with Germany*, p. 17.
22. See chart, ibid., p. 28.
23. The Regular Army divisions were numbered 1 through 20; the National Army divisions were numbered 76 through 93.
24. At least twenty-seven states contributed recognizable units, the largest of which came from Alabama.
25. Ayres, *The War with Germany*, p. 25.
26. Ibid., p. 31.
27. Harbord, *American Army*, pp. 119–120.
28. Harbord, *American Army*, pp. 120–21.
29. Vandiver, *Black Jack*, II, p. 778. He cites USWW 16:52–53, and Harbord, *American Army*, pp. 120–21.
30. Vandiver, *Black Jack*, II, p. 779.
31. Dawes had been friendly with William McKinley and at the age of thirty-one had played a part in McKinley's nomination for President. Later, as a reward, he had been made Comptroller of the Currency. *Dictionary of American Biography*, Supplement 5, p. 159.

32. Dawes would later go on to be ambassador to the Court of St. James and vice president of the United States under Calvin Coolidge.

33. Mitchell had at one time been Chief of the Air Service, AEF, with Major Raynall C. Bolling as Chief of the Air Service in the Line of Communications. He was pleased with his position with the Zone of Advance, because it involved him with actual aerial combat on a day-to-day basis.

34. "We regulars were grateful but nonetheless a little surprised to jump two or three ranks overnight. On the other hand, the civilians [who were made instant colonels and generals] . . . thought that they should have been commissioned a grade or two higher than they were." Benjamin Foulois, *From the Wright Brothers to the Astronauts*, pp. 149–50.

35. William Mitchell, *Memoirs of World War I*, p. 166.

36. Benjamin D. Foulois, with C. V. Glines, *Wright Brothers*, pp. 162–64.

37. American Battle Monuments Commission, *Guide to the American Battlefields in France* (GABF), p. 394.

SIX: THE SUPREME WAR COUNCIL

1. Georg von Rauch, *A History of Soviet Russia*, p. 71.

2. Ibid., p. 72.

3. The Treaty of Brest-Litovsk, signed on March 3, 1918, deprived Russia of the Baltic states, Finland, and Ukraine. Russia lost 26 percent of its population, 27 percent of its cultivated area, 26 percent of its railroads, 73 percent of its iron and steel industry, and 75 percent of its coal mines. Rauch, *Soviet Russia*, p. 76.

4. The Wurtemberg Battalion, a mountain unit, included a company commanded by Lieutenant Erwin Rommel, whose unit spearheaded the German effort.

5. Paschall, *Defeat of Imperial Germany*, p. 93.

6. Ibid., p. 97. They did not all reach there until mid-December, according to the *West Point Atlas*, Map No. 43.

7. Paschall, *Defeat of Imperial Germany*, p. 101.

8. During the period when the crisis in Italy was greatest, the French government sent the chief of staff of the French Army, Ferdinand Foch, to assess the situation on that front. Seeing the Italians holding behind the Piave, Foch quickly concluded that the battle was no longer out of hand. He therefore left the newly arrived French reinforcements in reserve for the moment, refusing to commit them to the front lines. Some troops eventually occupied small sectors on the Italian front, but they were minor.

9. Pershing, *Experiences*, I, pp. 213–14.

10. Ibid., p. 214.

11. Other members were Baker himself, his assistant secretary of war, and five officers from the General Staff. David Trask, *The AEF and Coalition Warmaking*, p. 25.

12. Tasker Bliss to Nellie Bliss, November 8, 1917. Bliss papers, Library of Congress.

13. Tasker Bliss to Nellie Bliss, November 7, 1917. Bliss papers, Library of Congress.

14. Bliss was also a linguist, a respectable geologist, and a highly regarded botanist who specialized in oriental specimens and was consulted by other experts to settle disputes concerning the identification of various types. Proceedings at the presentation of a memorial portrait of Tasker H. Bliss, the Council House, New York City, January 18, 1933. Published by the Council on Foreign Relations.

15. Harbord described House as "the great little man, the man who can be silent in several languages, the close friend of Woodrow Wilson, the man who carried the Texas delegation from Bryan to Wilson at Baltimore, the creator of Governor Hogg, Culbertson, and others. He is one of the few men with practically no chin who were con-

sidered forceful. His eyes are quite good and his expression very pleasant and affable." Harbord, *Leaves*, pp. 196–97.

16. "There were the statesmen, each mindful of retaining power with his people, lest he be unsaddled: Lloyd George, with his supple mind, never at a loss for a word, his bushy hair then only just streaked with white, changing his attitude to suit the moment's demand, never allowing what he said yesterday, if he remembered it, to interfere with what was the thing to do or say today; Clemenceau, with the bright, shrewd eyes of youth, mouth hidden under his mustache, a tried old blade, razor-edged for a concrete phrase which dismissed oratorical poses in discussion, and while his own brand of cynicism and his own brand of fatalism were but the servant of the only love he knew, France, in which he apparently vested his personal hopes of immortality; Orlando, adroit opportunist, adrift between the distinctively French logic of Clemenceau and the winning art of Lloyd George's winged resourcefulness, as he looked right, left, and front for the sustaining hands of Britain, France and America in Italy's distress." Frederick Palmer, *Bliss, Peacemaker*, p. 227.

17. Pershing, *Experiences*, I, pp. 249–50; Harbord, *American Army*, p. 180.

SEVEN: BAPTISM OF FIRE

1. Marshall, *Services*, p. 37.
2. Under the square division of two infantry brigades of two regiments each, unit association within the brigade was close. Thus for an American unit to be in the same brigade with a French unit meant that the two would work closely with each other.
3. Marshall, *Services*, p. 38.
4. Forrest C. Pogue, *Education of a General*, pp. 151–53. The extent of Marshall's technical insubordination is told here in detail.
5. Though this was a quiet sector, it had been the scene of heavy fighting in 1914. General de Castelnau had made his reputation in this sector, protecting Nancy from German attacks from the east.
6. *History of the First Division*, p. 28.
7. Marshall, *Services*, p. 43.
8. *History of the First Division*, p. 28.
9. Ibid., p. 30.
10. Ibid., p. 31. Strangely, the Americans were slow to realize what had happened. In the confusion of the night before, many, including the company commander, thought that the fourteen men had become lost in the relief and would turn up. George Marshall, who was the first officer on the scene to investigate, discovered the white tape that had guided the German patrol into American lines. Marshall, *Services*, p. 47.
11. Ibid., pp. 47–48.
12. *History of the First Division*, p. 31.
13. Marshall, *Services*, pp. 51–52.
14. Vandiver, *Black Jack*, II, pp. 839–40. He cites, among other sources, correspondence "In the Matter of the Investigation of Major General Clarence Edwards," May 1919.
15. Beaumont Buck, of the 1st Division, later commanded the 3d Division; Peter E. Traub later commanded the 35th Division.
16. One of Sibert's assignments was to establish the Chemical Warfare Service, which had previously been a hodgepodge. He had a lucrative civilian career after retiring from the Army with forty years of service.
17. William Manchester, *American Caesar*, p. 84.
18. Ibid., pp. 86–88.
19. *History of the First Division*, p. 48.
20. Ibid., pp. 58–64.

21. Laurence Stallings, *The Doughboys*, p. 55.
22. Pershing, *Experiences*, II, p. 16.
23. Peyton C. March, *Nation at War*, p. 30.
24. Ibid., p. 35. This episode reflects, perhaps, Newton Baker's uncertainty in his position. Placing such heavy responsibility on the sixty-four-year-old acting chief of staff, Tasker Bliss, was unfair to Bliss and to the Army. One can also question the sincerity of March's refusal to declare himself available, though of course that was what he had to claim in writing his memoirs.
25. March, *Nation at War*, p. 36.

EIGHT: THE CALM BEFORE THE STORM

1. Baker to Wilson, March 12, 1918, Reel 6, Baker papers, Manuscript Room, Library of Congress.
2. *New York Times*, March 12, 1918.
3. Even the 41st would soon be virtually deactivated, its personnel transferred to fill out the ranks of other divisions.
4. Ayres, *War with Germany*, p. 53. Maps show nine general storage depots in the St. Nazaire–Nantes area on the Loire; ten in the Bordeaux area, and four around La Rochelle–La Pallice. The Tours area, in the Intermediate Section, shows seven.
5. La Pallice, it will be recalled, was the port originally suggested by Marshal Joffre in his trip to Washington in April 1917. It had since been swallowed up in the greater system because the size of force being supported dwarfed that which Joffre originally had in mind. A fourth port area was that of Marseille, but it was never developed into a major source of supply for the Western Front.
6. Pershing, *Experiences*, I, p. 343.
7. Ibid.
8. *New York Times*, March 17, 1918.
9. Pershing, *Experiences*, I, p. 344.
10. Ibid., p. 345.
11. Ibid., p. 346.
12. *New York Times*, March 20, 1918.
13. The effort to keep the schools at Langres secret was reasonable but probably forlorn. American intelligence knew where each of the German schools were located, the names of their directors, and the curriculum they followed. Alexander Powell, "APO 714," p. 414.
14. *New York Times*, March 21, 1918.
15. Ibid.
16. Harbord, *Leaves*, p. 246.
17. Archibald Roosevelt was luckier than his brother Quentin, who was killed in an air crash on July 14, 1918.
18. Harbord, *Leaves*, p. 253.
19. The 1st, 2d, 26th, and 42d, it will be recalled, had been in France all winter.
20. Liggett, *AEF: Ten Years Ago in France*, pp. 59–60.

NINE: UNIFIED COMMAND AT LAST!

1. Field Marshal Paul von Hindenburg was a member of the Great General Staff. However, his attendance would doubtless have made other commanders question the composition of the meeting. Furthermore, Ludendorff doubtless preferred to operate this way.
2. Barrie Pitt, *1918: The Last Act*, p. 41.

3. Ludendorff, *My War Memories*, II, pp. 220–21. Barrie Pitt offers an additional consideration. Since the British were emerging as a force stronger than the French, it was likely that, if the British were smashed, the French would capitulate. The same might not apply to the British attitude if only the French were destroyed.
4. Pitt, *1918*, p. 42.
5. The Russian emissaries, for example, were being conceded equal right in every respect with the German, with the result that they were making counterproposals of their own.
6. Ludendorff, *Memories*, II, p. 171.
7. The terms were harsh, directed, Ludendorff believed, against the Bolsheviks but also ultimately against Germany's best interests.
8. Hindenburg and Ludendorff had replaced Erich von Falkenhayne on August 28, 1916. No major German offensives had been conducted on the Western Front since then.
9. Asprey, *German High Command*, p. 338. Some writers contend that Hutier was given too much credit for the development of these tactics, that they were the product of many minds. Nevertheless, Hutier used them for the first time and they have become associated with his name.
10. Ludendorff, *Memories*, II, pp. 202–4.
11. Ibid., pp. 204–5.
12. Ibid., p. 205.
13. House, *Intimate Papers*, III, p. 302.
14. Pitt, *1918*, p. 56.
15. Ibid.
16. Ibid., p. 45. See George Allen, *The Great War*, V, pp. 274 and 279.
17. Falls, *The Great War*, p. 331.
18. Pitt, *1918*, p. 75; Vandiver, *Black Jack*, II, p. 871.
19. George H. Allen et al., *The Great War*, V, p. 279.
20. Vandiver, *Black Jack*, II, p. 871.
21. Ibid., p. 869.
22. Pershing, *Experiences*, p. 355.
23. Vandiver, *Black Jack*, II, p 871.
24. Interestingly, Doullens was the planned objective of Ludendorff's drive, though the German troops had not approached dangerously close as yet.
25. In a reverse from his previous views, Sir Douglas now recorded in his diary, "Foch seemed sound and sensible, but Pétain had a terrible look. He had the appearance of a commander who was in a funk." Haig Diary, Robert Blake, ed, *The Private Papers of Douglas Haig, 1914–1918*, p. 298, cited in Falls, *The Great War*, p. 335.
26. Falls, *The Great War*, p. 335.
27. *U.S. Army in World War I* (USAWW), Vol. 2, p. 254.

TEN: "I WILL NOT BE COERCED"

1. Pershing, *Experiences*, I, p. 358.
2. Ibid., p. 359.
3. USAWW, Vol. 2, pp. 254–55.
4. Donald Smythe, *Pershing: General of the Armies*, p. 79.
5. USAWW, Vol. 2, pp. 255–56.
6. Ibid., p. 257.
7. Pershing, *Experiences*, I, pp. 361–62.
8. USAWW, Vol. 2, pp. 261–62.
9. Pershing, *Experiences*, I, p. 364.
10. Pershing, *Experiences*, I, pp. 364–65. Correspondence between Pershing and Pétain

indicates that Pershing made his offer to Pétain before he made it to Foch. That was, of course, the day before the conference at Doullens. Pershing papers, Manuscript Room, Library of Congress.

11. Martin Gilbert, *The First World War*, p. 408. The source cited is Reading's son.
12. Pershing, *Experiences*, I, pp. 373–74.
13. Ibid., pp. 373–77.
14. Ibid., pp. 382–83.
15. Specifically the Six-Division Plan previously mentioned, which called for six American divisions to be brought over in British ships, to serve with the British while undergoing about ten weeks training. Trask, *The AEF*, p. 40.
16. Pershing, *Experiences*, I, p. 384.
17. Pitt, *1918*, p. 141.
18. Haig message, April 10, 1918, cited in Pitt, *1918*, p. 125.
19. Harbord, *American Army*, p. 243, has this to say about Foch: "At Beauvais on April 3 [1918] General Foch was charged with the strategic direction of Allied operations . . . and on April 24th Ferdinand Foch became really Allied Commander-in-Chief. . . . He surrounded himself with a French staff, as was perhaps natural, and to the very end appeared to look to Clemenceau as the authority upon whom his tenure of office depended—notwithstanding the method of his selection. He recognized the fact and bowed to it."
20. Pershing, *Experiences*, II, p. 22.
21. Ibid.
22. Ibid., p. 26.
23. Ibid., p. 29.
24. Ibid., p. 35.

ELEVEN: THE BIG RED ONE AT CANTIGNY

1. A few days later, it will be recalled, the 26th was hit at Seicheprey.
2. The divisional light artillery pulled out with the infantry. The medium (155mm) artillery pieces, too heavy to move easily, were left in place and taken over by the 26th Division artillerymen. The 1st then took over the pieces from the 26th.
3. *History of the First Division*, p. 66.
4. Robert Lee Bullard, *Personalities and Reminiscences of the War*, p. 174.
5. Ibid., p. 175.
6. Bullard, *Personalities*, p. 181.
7. It had not always been so. On January 5, 1918, Bullard had recorded, "Our party had considerable misgivings as to how we would be received by the French general who commands and who was known to be hostile to Americans. Well, with a lot of French talk I slipped up on [Debeney's] blind side and we had little difficulty with him. It was French and Americans in better understanding." Bullard, *Personalities*, p. 120.
8. Ibid., pp. 182–83.
9. Marshall, *Services*, p. 82.
10. Ibid., p. 84.
11. Bullard, *Personalities*, p. 192.
12. USAWW, Vol. 4, p. 266.
13. Bullard, *Personalities*, p. 193.
14. Pershing, *Experiences*, II, p. 53.
15. Vandiver, *Black Jack*, II, p. 886. He does not say where that information came from.
16. Stallings, *Doughboys*, p. 58, describes Ely thus: "If Ely asked his mess attendant for a cup of coffee, the request had the tone of a battalion fire chief ordering a hoseman back into a burning building. When he was silent, which was not too often, he contin-

ually worked a leathery muscle of his jaw, as if banking the fires that smoldered in his rasping vocal chords." Stalling cites no source for this vivid description, however, and it is highly unlikely that he ever set eyes on Ely in person.

17. Colonel Hanson E. Ely, After-action Report, June 2, 1918.
18. Ibid.
19. Ibid.
20. When Kendall's body was found, the authorities gave him credit for having been captured and having resisted interrogation. However, knives were often used on the front lines to avoid attracting the enemy's attention. See Marshall, *Services*, pp. 92–93.
21. Ibid., p. 90.
22. USAWW, Vol. 4, pp. 298–300.
23. Edward Coffman, *The War to End All Wars*, p. 157.
24. RG 120, 1st Division, Box 87, "Operations Against Cantigny, CO 3d Battalion, 28th Infantry, June 2, 1918. Cited in Meirion and Susie Harries, *The Last Days of Innocence*, p. 242.
25. Ely Report.
26. Marshall, *Services*, p. 95. The reason for the vagueness of Marshall's figures lies in the difficulty in differentiating later those killed and wounded in the attack and those lost in the heavy counterattacks later. The prisoner estimate comes from Pershing, *Experiences*, II, p. 60.
27. Bullard, *Personalities*, p. 198.
28. USAWW, Vol. 4., p. 302.
29. Ibid., p. 304.
30. Ibid., p. 305.
31. Ibid., p. 307.
32. Marshall, *Services*, pp. 97–98. He had this to say regarding the effects of artillery fire: "A three-inch shell will temporarily scare or deter a man; a six-inch shell will shock him; but an eight-inch shell, such as those 210 mm ones, rips up the nervous system of everyone within a hundred yards of the explosion."
33. Bullard, *Personalities*, p. 198.
34. Ely Report.
35. Marshall, *Services*, p. 97.
36. Bullard, *Personalities*, p. 199.
37. March, *Nation at War*, p. 39.
38. Ibid., p. 40.
39. March's system was similar to the one Pershing had developed in the AEF. Pershing had designated his staff sections as G-1 (personnel and administration, including supply), G-2 (intelligence), G-3 (operations), and G-4; March called them by their names. 1: Operations, 2: Military Intelligence, 3: Purchase, Storage, and Traffic, and 4: War Plans. Ibid., pp. 40–41. That lack of symmetry must have caused some confusion when the staffs dealt with each other. After the war, when Pershing became chief of staff, he brought with him the system he had used in France. It is still in use today.
40. Ibid., p. 50.

TWELVE: THE 2D DIVISION AT BELLEAU WOOD

1. See Falls, *The Great War*, p. 344.
2. It is easy to forget that the east–west corridor between Metz and Paris was the time-honored invasion route between France and Germany. James Harbord noted, "For fifteen centuries the Marne has been the path of invaders from the east marching on

Paris. Julius Caesar himself marched down it to the pacification or destruction of the Belgae before the Christian era. Clovis in that valley had defeated a Roman General in the last battle for an Empire that had already fallen. In and along this valley had been fought Joffre's great Battle of the Marne, which saved Paris." Harbord, *American Army*, p. 273.

3. Ibid., Pershing, *Experiences*, II, p. 61.
4. Pershing, *Experiences*, II, pp. 62–63.
5. It is interesting to note that two of Pershing's most visible commanders, Bundy and Major General Clarence Edwards, of the 26th Division, were members of the class that, as first-classmen, brought Pershing's class into West Point as plebes. Academically, Edwards ranked number fifty-two in a class of fifty-two members. Bundy ranked only two files above him.
6. Report of Col. LeRoy Eltinge, GS, May 7, 1918, National Archives, cited in Harries and Harries, *Last Days*, p. 247.
7. Ibid., p. 247.
8. Harbord, *American Army*, p. 281.
9. Ibid., p. 280.
10. R. W. Lamont, "Over There," *Marine Corps Gazette*, 1993, cited in Harries and Harries, *Last Days*, p. 248.
11. Harbord, *Leaves*, p. 288.
12. Harbord, *American Army*, p. 278.
13. Oliver L. Spaulding and John W. Wright. *The Second Division, American Expeditionary Force in France, 1917–1918*; quoted in Robert Asprey, *At Belleau Wood*, p. 89. This account of American entry into the lines in June of 1918 has been much simplified to save space. It does not depict the utter confusion that prevailed among the hierarchy of the French command. Preston Brown, for example, reported receiving as many as four conflicting orders from French General Duchêne within the space of only a few hours. Asprey, *Belleau Wood*, 73.
14. Harbord, *American Army*, p. 281.
15. Harries and Harries, *Last Days*, p. 250.
16. See order, Preston Brown to Malone, June 2, 1918, cited in Spaulding and Wright, *Second Division*.
17. Harbord, *American Army*, p. 285.
18. Ibid., p. 289.
19. Harries and Harries, *Last Days*, pp. 256–59.
20. Harbord, *American Army*, p. 291.
21. Cited in Robert B. Asprey, *Belleau Wood*, p. 217.
22. Ladislav Janda to his father, December 18, 1918. Rolfe Hillman Files, Military History Institute.
23. Harbord, *American Army*, p. 291.
24. Ibid.
25. Ludendorff, *Memories*, II, p. 269.
26. Ernst Otto, "The Battles for the Possession of Belleau Woods, June 1918," *U.S. Naval Institute Proceedings*, November 1928.
27. Asprey, *Belleau Wood*, p. 233.
28. Harries and Harries, *Last Days*, p. 264.
29. Ibid.
30. Harbord, *American Army*, p. 293.
31. Brown to Harbord, June 15, 1918, cited in Spaulding and Wright, *Second Division*.
32. Harbord to CO, 7th Inf., ibid.
33. 4BD, June 18, 1918, p. 47, cited in Harries and Harries, *Last Days*, pp. 267–68.
34. Ibid., pp. 52–53, cited in ibid., p. 269.
35. Harries and Harries, *Last Days*, p. 270.

36. Spaulding and Wright place these figures at 319 officers and men killed and 1,450 wounded.
37. Spaulding and Wright, *Second Division*, p. 71.
38. Harbord, *Leaves*, p. 307, calls the operation a "stunt." He was now wearing Marine insignia along with his French helmet.
39. Asprey, *Belleau Wood*, p. 327.
40. Ibid., p. 331.
41. Spaulding and Wright, *Second Division*, p. 72. Conger had been an instructor at the Fort Leavenworth schools and had lived in Europe for several years (thereby becoming fluent in both French and German). He was also extremely thorough.
42. Asprey, *Belleau Wood*, p. 331.
43. Ibid., pp. 331–32.
44. Ibid., pp. 334–35.

THIRTEEN: THE ROCK OF THE MARNE

1. Asprey, *German High Command*, p. 431. The previous operations had been known as Michael, Georgette, Blucher, and Gneisnau. The flu, a virulent disease, hit the German army before it hit the Allied.
2. Association of Graduates, USMA, annual report, 1929, p. 143.
3. Dickman's left was anchored in the town of Château Thierry itself, and the right eight miles to the east at Courthiézy. American Battle Monuments Commission, *Guide to Battlefields*, p. 31. His troop disposition accounts for the availability of the 7th Infantry for Belleau Wood.
4. The detachment of the 7th Infantry to the 2d Division was temporary and brief.
5. Dickman, letter to Spaulding. Italics in original.
6. Ibid. The terrain is reminiscent of Confederate General Robert E. Lee's situation at Fredericksburg in December 1862. Lee contested Union General Ambrose Burnside's crossing of the Rappahannock, but his true main line of resistance was far back, based on Marye's Heights.
7. McAlexander, UG, to Chief, November 3, 1919, Army Historical Section.
8. Jesse Wooldridge, *Giants of the Marne*, p. 29.
9. Ibid., p. 20.
10. 398th Infantry, 6th Grenadiers, and 47th Infantry.
11. Dickman, *Crusade*, p. 83. With the 125th falling back, as expected, the 38th Infantry would eventually be facing four regiments, the 6th, the 5th Grenadiers, the 128th and the 175th.
12. Dickman, *Crusade*, p. 84.
13. ABMC, *Guide*, p. 62.
14. "Their main line of attack and where their bridge was placed was on my front, 'G' Company, and was successful only after every man of my 1st Platoon . . . was killed or put out of action, the lieutenant himself wounded and taken prisoner." Wooldridge, *Giants*, p. 35.
15. Ibid., p. 36.
16. Dickman, *Crusade*, pp. 96–97, Wooldridge, *Giants*, p. 38.
17. Dickman, *Crusade*, p. 97.
18. Col. Conrad H. Lanza, "The 38th Infantry in the Second Battle of the Marne," unpublished and undated manuscript.
19. Dickman, *Crusade*, p. 98.
20. Ibid., p. 99.
21. Lanza report, cited in Harries and Harries, *Last Days*, p. 313. Wooldridge, *Giants*, p. 6, claims that 2,917 of the 38th Infantry strength of 3,400 men "fell." Wooldridge

may have been including those slightly wounded. A reasonable estimate would fall between those two figures.

22. Paschall, *Defeat of Imperial Germany*, p. 160.
23. *Journal of the Royal Artillery*, Vol. 49, 1922–23, p. 339, cited in Dickman, *Crusade*, pp. 111–12.

FOURTEEN: SOISSONS—THE TURNING POINT

1. Hunter Liggett, *Ten Years Ago*, p. 120.
2. Other officers were also becoming corps commanders. I Corps, under Hunter Liggett, had been organized as early as January 1918, and Omar Bundy, of the 2d Division, was being promoted also to corps command. Bundy's promotion carried overtones of being "kicked upstairs." Nobody could risk condemning him outright in view of the lavish publicity the Marine Brigade of the 2d Division had recently attained. However, Bundy's performance had been lackluster at best, and his VI Corps would never see action.
3. Bullard, *Personalities*, pp. 212–13. Since a corps is not a fixed entity, it consists only of a headquarters, to which division, artillery, and engineers are attached.
4. It is a little confusing that both the forest and the town are named Villers-Cotterêts, although the forest is usually referred to by its other name, Forêt de Retz.
5. "It is quite certain that Pershing made the suggestion [of a counterattack] to the Allied Commander in Chief on May 31st. The American Commander had luncheon with him [at Sarcus] that day. He suggested to him a counter-attack against the salient formed by the German attack between Soissons and Reims, which was just that day slowing down at Château Thierry. . . . General Foch said to Pershing that he had such an offensive in mind." Harbord, *American Army*, p. 307.
6. Foch, *Memoirs*, p. 355.
7. Falls, *The Great War*, p. 45.
8. Bullard, *Personalities*, p. 214.
9. A New York lawyer named Paul D. Cravath, Harbord later recorded, topped the scales of flattery. "I would rather be General Harbord tonight," he rhapsodized, "than anyone else in the world; I would rather be General Harbord tonight than to be in Heaven." Colonel Charles Dawes had a less lofty view. When asked about rumors that Harbord had been killed, he said he didn't think so. He had just received a letter from Harbord, and it was not postmarked "Hell." Harbord, *Leaves*, p. 314.
10. Douglas V. Johnson and Rolfe Hillman, *Soissons*, p. 62.
11. Bullard, *Personalities*, p. 215.
12. Harbord, *Leaves*, pp. 314–20.
13. Bullard, *Personalities*, p. 215.
14. Ibid., p. 216.
15. USAWW, Vol. 5, p. 290.
16. "The great strength of XX Corps was the composition of its subordinate units, two-thirds of which were carefully hidden in the great Forêt de Retz. The corps consisted of two huge American divisions and one of the best attack divisions in the entire French Army, the 1st Moroccan. It also had two French divisions in reserve. The three divisions assigned to the attack echelon were numerically equivalent to about five or six normal French divisions. Did it cross Berdoulat's mind that because of the massive structure of the American divisions, four-fifths of his corps' attacking strength came from the AEF, or that none of the soldiers, save the French Foreign Legion's officers and NCO's, were even native Frenchmen?" Johnson and Hillman, *Soissons*, p. 39.
17. Special Orders, French XX Corps, dated July 15, 1918, says, "The liaison between the

Moroccan 1st Division and the American 2d Division must be particularly strong, because the outflanking movement of the 2d Division by the plateau east Verte-Veuille and Le Translon Farms will facilitate . . . the capture of Bois de Quesnoy." USAWW, Vol. 5, p. 291.

18. Bullard, *Personalities*, p. 218.
19. ABMC, *Guide*, p. 37.
20. The Missy-aux-Bois Ravine is "half a mile wide and has heavily vegetated banks sloping at a 60-degree angle. At the bottom was a marshy swamp that measured six hundred yards across." Johnson and Hillman, *Soissons*, p. 46.
21. Berzy-la-Sec had originally been in the sector of the French 153rd Division on the north, which had fallen behind. USAWW, Vol. 5, p. 316.
22. Ibid., pp. 336–38.
23. History, 26th Infantry Regiment, p. 41.
24. Bullard, *Personalities*, p. 221. His source is doubtless the regimental history, which, on p. 41, gives the same figures.
25. Marshall, *Memoirs*, p. 117.
26. ABMC, *Guide*, p. 39.
27. Chester Baker, *Doughboy's Diary*, p. 62.
28. Ibid., p. 73, *passim*.
29. Ibid., pp. 75–77.
30. Pershing, *Experiences*, II, p. 211.
31. Marshall, *Services*, pp. 123–24.
32. Pershing, *Experiences*, II, p. 171.
33. Ibid., pp. 172, 175.
34. Ibid., p. 172.
35. Ibid., p. 175.

FIFTEEN: ST. MIHIEL—DRESS REHEARSAL

1. Baker to Pershing, July 6, 1918, cited in Pershing, *Experiences*, II, pp. 185–86.
2. Harbord, *American Army*, p. 345.
3. Ibid., p. 353. Pershing was able to appoint General Kernan to be senior American representative in a conference to be held in Berne, Switzerland, pointed toward terms for ending the war. It was an ostensible promotion, and Kernan's name went before the Senate for promotion to major general in the Regular Army, along with that of Harbord.
4. Pershing, *Experiences*, II, p. 212.
5. Marshall, *Services*, pp. 117–18.
6. Ibid., p. 121.
7. Ibid., p. 123.
8. Pershing, *Experiences*, II, p. 226, lists thirteen, though he does not specify the date he is referring to. They fall into several categories. He places the 1st and 2d in a class by themselves: "excellent as to training, equipment, and morale." Two other Regular divisions, the 3d and 4th, he classified, along with the 26th and 42d (both National Guard) as "of fine morale and considerable experience." Six of the National Army divisions were in advanced stages of training. They were the 89th, 90th, 33d, 78th, 80th, and 82d. He also lists the 91st, though it had never been in the line and had had less than four weeks training in France.
9. Marshall, *Services*, p. 124. See Paul Braim, *The Test of Battle*, p. 64.
10. Marshall, *Services*, pp. 125–26.
11. Pershing, *Experiences*, II, p. 243. The Aisne River, which flows from east to west at Soissons, flows northward in this area.

12. Ibid., pp. 244–45.
13. Ibid., pp. 244–48.
14. Ibid., p. 251.
15. Ibid., pp. 252–53.
16. On September 1, Pershing sent his chief of staff, Brigadier General James W. McAndrew, to confer at Foch's headquarters with General Maxime Weygand. That meeting doubtless paved the way for the improved atmosphere the next day.
17. Pershing, *Experiences*, II, p. 255.
18. They comprised 701 pursuit planes, 366 observation planes, 323 day bombardment planes, and ninety-one night bombardment planes. USAWW, Vol. 15, p. 230.
19. Writing of Pershing in 1926, Mitchell said, "Pershing did not know, or care to know, much about aviation. . . . I guess he could not swallow the whole hog to begin with. . . . One had to expect that in the organization of a new outfit, and from now on I hoped he would do better." Mitchell, *Memoirs*, p. 238.
20. Ibid., pp. 235–39. Foulois, *Wright Brothers*, p. 178, later wrote, "These were grand-sounding words but actually the missions his units flew were in strict subordination to Pershing's needs on the ground. Mitchell never allowed his planes to operate on more than a 35-mile radius of action."
21. Stallings, *Doughboys*, pp. 207–8.
22. See map, AMBC, *Guide*, p. 107.
23. Pershing, *Experiences*, II, p. 264.
24. Ludendorff, *Memories*, II, p. 361.
25. Ibid.
26. Vicinity of the hill of Les Eparges.
27. ABMC, map p. 164. The town of Regniéville can cause confusion, because some maps carry Thiaucourt as Thiaucourt-Regniéville.
28. Trask, *The AEF and Coalition Warmaking, 1917–1918*, p. 106.
29. The 2d and 3d Machine Gun Battalions each had four machine gun companies. Each regiment also had one. The total was therefore twelve, one company for each of his twelve battalions. See *History of the First Division*, pp. 157, 158.
30. A French critic said that only the Americans could do that. It was because of their big feet. Paul F. Braim, *The Test of Battle*, p. 71.
31. *History of the First Division*, pp. 161–65.
32. Letter, Ladislav Janda to parents, September 17, 1918. Military History Institute.
33. Maury Maverick, *A Maverick American*, pp. 122–24.
34. Vandiver, *Black Jack*, II, p. 950.
35. Paschall, *Defeat of Imperial Germany*, p. 180.

SIXTEEN: THE RACE AGAINST TIME

1. Evaluation reports, whose authors saw the glass as half empty rather than half full, found flaws. Marshall later wrote, "The Allied attachés were busily engaged in seeing everything we had done and, particularly, that which we should not have done as we did do. . . . A veteran of a single battle like the St. Mihiel is prone to draw some erroneous conclusions. Those of the First Division, familiar with the vicissitudes of Cantigny and the terrific fighting at Soissons, felt that they had participated in a maneuver, while the members of a previously inexperienced division considered themselves the victors in a prodigious struggle." Marshall, *Services*, p. 148.
2. Ibid., p. 149.
3. Ibid., pp. 150–51.
4. Coffman, *War to End All Wars*, p. 300.
5. HQ, GHQ, AEF, September 6, 1918. RG 120, Box 338, National Archives (NARA).

6. The ground is so rolling that the author was unable to discern, on inspecting the ground, exactly where each line had been established. The Kriemhilde, for example, could have run along more than one combination of hillocks satisfactorily.

7. The Meuse-Argonne Valley constitutes the "great divide" of France. The Aire River flows west into the Aisne, which joins the Marne, and later the Seine, eventually reaching the Atlantic. The Meuse, on the Americans' right, flows northeastward, eventually reaching the North Sea in Holland, as the Maas.

8. Truesdell Report. Also Pershing, *Experiences*, II, p. 290.

9. Of the nine divisions making the assault, only three had previous combat experience, the 4th, 28th, and the 77th.

10. Kuhn had been commandant of the Army War College in Washington when Joffre had visited eighteen months earlier.

11. Perhaps Pershing's previous interest had been in visiting the 1st Division, and only secondarily personal.

12. Bullard, *Personalities*, p. 258.

13. Ibid., p. 259.

14. Ibid., p. 261.

15. Ibid., p. 262.

16. Ibid.

17. Liggett, *Ten Years Ago*, pp. 167–68.

18. Ibid., p. 168.

19. Baker, *Doughboy's Diary*, p. 90.

20. Varennes, one of the early American objectives, is best known in history as the place where King Louis XVI and Queen Marie Antoinette, attempting to flee Paris during the French Revolution in 1792, were stopped by Revolutionary authorities and returned to Versailles.

21. H. G. Proctor, *The Iron Division*, pp. 247–48.

22. "The position assigned the Pennsylvania regiments was in a forest so dense that to get an area of fire at all, they had to fell the trees before them. But concealment of battery positions in a surprise attack is a vital consideration, and to have cut down hundreds of trees would have been an open advertisement to enemy observation planes of the location of the batteries. To overcome this difficulty, the trees which it was necessary to remove were sawed almost through and wired up to the others in order to keep them standing to the last moment. At dusk on the night of Wednesday, September 25, the artillerymen cut the wires holding the trees and pulled the monarchs of the forest crashing to the ground, leaving the way clear for the artillery fire." Proctor, *Iron Division*, p. 250.

23. Baker, *Doughboy's Diary* p. 94.

SEVENTEEN: MONTFAUCON—OMINOUS VICTORY

1. Field Order No. 20, First U.S. Army, September 20, 1918. RG 120, Box 3381, Folder 112.08, National Archives.

2. The maps show the altitude of Montfaucon as 1,100 feet above sea level. However, the valley surrounding it is generally about eight hundred feet above sea level.

3. Pershing, *Experiences*, II, p. 284, specifies that the only three roads running northward from the line of departure went to Varennes on the west, Avocourt in the center, and Esne on the east. Each was assigned to a corps. The Varennes road was also the best to Romagne, but it was needed by Liggett's I Corps for the assault on Grandpré, Foch's third objective.

4. "The order of battle of the First Army from the Moselle River to the Meuse River for September 25th, from east to west, was as follows: the IV Corps (Dickman) with the

French 69th Division and our 90th (Allen), 78th (McRae), 89th (Wright) and 42d (Menoher) Divisions in line and the 5th (McMahon) in reserve; French II Colonial Corps with the French 29th and 2d Divisions and our 26th Division (Edwards) in line; French XVII Corps with the French 15th, 10th, and 18th Divisions in line and the French 26th Division in reserve." Pershing, *Experiences*, II, p. 290.

5. Trask, *The AEF and Coalition Warmaking, 1917–1918*, p. 123.

6. That was the route which Pershing, in his Field Order No. 20, had specified that Liggett should take to reduce the Argonne. It specified that I Corps "will reduce the FORET D ARGONNE by flanking it from the east." Telling a corps commander how to deploy his divisions may have been a somewhat unusual procedure, but it was probably necessary to insure liaison with V Corps on its right. RG 120, Box 3381, Folder 112.08, National Archives.

7. Ibid.

8. "I had served with [the 33d's] National Guard [units] for long months upon the Rio Grande in 1916, and knew it as reliable. It was, besides, commanded by a regular officer, General George Bell, known to the whole Regular Army as perhaps the most exacting inspector general in it. The division had been serving with the British and I found it in excellent morale, condition, and equipment." Bullard, *Personalities*, p. 268.

9. "The hour after an attack begins is a trying time at Headquarters. There is nothing for a general officer to do but sit with folded hands, and that is not an occupation that suggests itself to a man who has the responsibility of from 15,000 to 1,000,000 lives on those hands. He has done everything he could before H Day, and to try to follow the infantry is folly. . . . The nervous strain is difficult. I have learned to have two packs of cards by me and to lay them out in double solitaire position when an attack is started. That is as good an anodyne as I know." Liggett, *Ten Years Ago*, pp. 174–75.

10. The town square of Varennes is dominated by a huge monument placed there by the state of Pennsylvania to commemorate the actions of the 28th Division in France.

11. At El Paso in 1915 and 1916, Patton's sister Nita had been Pershing's companion in his grief over the loss of his wife and two children in late 1914.

12. Pershing, *Experiences*, II, p. 290; Trask, *The AEF*, p. 123; USAWW, Vol. 9, p. 96.

13. "There were no officers there but me. So I decided to do business. Some of my reserve tanks were stuck by some trenches. So I went back and made some Americans hiding in the trenches dig a passage. I think I killed one man here. He would not work so I hit him over the head with a shovel. It was exciting for they shot at us all the time but I got mad and walked on the parapet. At last we got five tanks across." George Patton, *Patton Papers*, I, p. 616.

14. Patton to his father, 1927, cited in *Patton Papers*, I, p. 613. Patton regarded the death of five men as a vindication of his judgment of the danger of his venture.

15. Ibid., pp. 604–15. This is, it should be remembered, Patton's own version of events.

16. Brett's tank brigade lost forty-three tanks the first day of the Meuse-Argonne battle, and on the third day only eighty-three tanks were still in operation (ibid., p. 619). All this was due to mechanical breakdowns and enemy bullets. According to Harries and Harries, *Last Days*, p. 401, only fourteen tanks were left by November 1.

17. An inspector at Camp Meade had recommended that the division receive more training, but the frantic shipping schedule had resulted in its premature overseas deployment. Colby Eldridge, "The Taking of Montfaucon."

18. Pershing had relieved General William Sibert, another engineer officer, from command of the 1st Division, many thought unfairly. One wonders if Kuhn would have been in command of this attack if the unit in question had been the 1st, not the 79th Division.

19. A source of confusion is that fact that towns and woods, though bearing the same name, could well be some distance from each other. Thus the Bois de Melancourt

was in Sweezey's territory whereas the town of Melancourt was in Oury's. The town of Montfaucon is several hundred yards from the hill known as the Butte de Montfaucon, the division objective.

20. See Eldridge Colby, "Montfaucon," p. 133.

21. Report of Col. C. B. Sweezey to TAG, July 17, 1919. NARA, RG 120, WW I Organizational Records, 79th Division, Box 16.

22. The action of the 4th Division in pushing on ahead to Nantillois without stopping to help the 79th on its left was later the cause for voluminous correspondence and hard feelings. Brigadier General E. E. Booth, commanding the 8th Brigade of the 4th Division, kept up a correspondence defending the action until at least 1924. See NARA, RG 120, AEF Organizational Records, 4th Division, Box 3, Folder "Montfaucon."

23. "You must get by Montfaucon tonight. . . . The 79th Division is holding up the whole army." Colby, "Montfaucon," pp. 135–36.

24. T. M. Johnson, cited in Smythe, *Pershing*, p. 197.

25. In the case of a subordinate officer, relief from command could cause the dreaded consequence of being sent to the reclassification center at Blois, on the Loire River. Kuhn, as a member of the "club," would probably have been spared that humiliation. He would, however, be forever thought of as a failure.

26. Braim, *Test of Battle*, p. 97.

27. All this information was erroneous. The 4th Division was nearly a mile short of Nantillois, even though the corps order assumed that it had been taken. Further, orders were supposed to have been given for the 4th Division to advance as far as Cunel Heights, nearly six miles beyond the line of contact.

28. File, "Brief History in the Case of the Relief of BG Robert H. Noble." NARA, RG 120, 79th Division, Box 18. Noble spent a few days at division headquarters and was then sent to the Officer Classification Depot at Blois, on the Loire River, thence demoted and sent home. Harbord, *American Army*, p. 376, says, "More sad memories cling around Blois than any other city used by the American Expeditionary Forces. . . . For many an American it was the grave of buried ambitions, the temporary home of the hopeless." Noble may have been a victim of poor officer selection. In early June 1918, the commanding general of the 77th wrote: "General Noble has been industrious in going about . . . but the impression is strong that he lacks the background of military knowledge and ability in directing the work of others. . . . I would not be satisfied with General Noble in command of a brigade of this division." "Brief History in the Case of Brigadier General Robert H. Noble."

29. Report, Col. C. B. Sweezey, July 17, 1919, NARA, RG 120, WW I Organizational Records, 79th Division, Box 16.

30. Colby, "Montfaucon," p. 135.

31. Braim, *Test of Battle*, pp. 101, 102.

EIGHTEEN: ARGONNE

1. The performance of the 35th was probably better than could be expected, given their previous lack of experience.

2. Field Order No. 33, October 1, 1918, First U.S. Army. RG 120, Box 3382, NARA.

3. Pershing, *Experiences*, II, p. 290.

4. Field Order No. 39, First U.S. Army, October 5, 1918. RG 120, Box 3382, National Archives.

5. R. T. Ward, "Study of First Army Situation," *U.S. Army in World War I*, Vol. 9, cited in Harries and Harries, *Last Days*, p. 370.

6. Liggett, *Ten Years Ago*, p. 167.

7. Holderman, RG 120, 77th Division, Box 15, "Conversation with Dakota," September 27, 1918, cited in Harries and Harries, *Last Days*, p. 370.

8. Figures vary. Robert Alexander, *Memories of the World War*, pp. 210–11 is the source of the figure of 670. He admits, however, that ninety men were lost in the day's attack, which approximates the figure of 550 in Lowell R. Hollingshead, *History and Rhymes of a Lost Battalion Doughboy*. Companies A, B, and C, from 1st Battalion, Companies E, G, and H. from the 2d Battalion, 308th Infantry, Company K, 307th Infantry, and Companies C and D of the 306th Machine Gun Battalion were cited in the General Orders No. 30, 77th Division, dated April 15, 1919, cited in *History and Rhymes*, p. 44. Company K, 307th Infantry, joined Whittlesey on the morning of the 3d. Alexander, *Memories*, p. 214.

9. Boston Publishing Company, *Above and Beyond: A History of the Medal of Honor*, p. 145.

10. Ibid., p. 146.

11. Each of the four regiments had one machine gun company organic. But the division had three machine gun battalions of four companies each—a total of twelve. Thus the 1st Battalion of each regiment had attached to it the organic regimental machine gun company. Division broke two of the three machine gun battalions into its companies, attaching one to each of the 2d and 3d Battalions of the regiments. Division held the 3d Machine Gun Battalion in reserve, in what seems like an odd procedure.

12. *History of the First Division*, p. 182.

13. Ibid., p. 189.

14. Ibid., p. 194.

15. Maury Maverick, *A Maverick American*, p. 129. He adds, "I have never read in any military history a description of the high explosives that break overhead. There is a great swishing scream, a smash-bang, and it seems to tear everything loose from you. The intensity of it simply enters your heart and brain, and tears every nerve to pieces."

16. Ibid., p. 131.

17. "[Quinn] deserves a book to himself. He is one of the few men I saw who really liked blood-soldiering. Having been a sergeant in the cavalry, he got bored, was busted for drunkness [sic]—deserted, and joined us where death was straight in front of him. Behind the lines he had been the army's best crap-shooter. At the front he was the army's best soldier." Maverick, pp. 132–33.

18. Liggett, *Ten Years Ago*, p. 188.

19. Account of Private Lowell R. Hollingshead, *History and Rhymes of a Lost Battalion Doughboy*, p. 65. Whittlesey denied ever giving the order.

20. Hollingshead, *History and Rhymes*, pp. 65–82.

21. Ibid., p. 63.

22. The relationship was tenuous. Whittlesey's men were relieved on the evening of October 7; York's feat occurred on the 8th. Nevertheless, the crossing of the Aire by York's 328th Infantry is credited with the German collapse on the Argonne front.

23. Liggett, *Ten Years Ago*, p. 194. This claim seems highly unlikely, despite York's prowess. Nobody, of course, was in a position to argue with him later.

24. The main source of this account is Liggett, pp. 192–96. He estimates between twenty and thirty. ABMC, *Guidebook*, p. 230, estimates "over fifteen."

25. Ibid.

NINETEEN: FEELERS FOR PEACE

1. Marc Ferro, *The Great War*, p. 219.
2. Girard Lindsley McEntee, *Military History of the World War*, pp. 528–29.
3. Ferdinand Foch, *Memoirs*, p. 416.

4. This was uttered in the middle of the Cambrai action, which had begun on August 8, 1918. On that date a combined British-French attack on the Somme had, with the aid of tanks and cavalry, advanced about nine miles. But that was not the shocker: for the first time, the German Army had failed to counterattack with zeal. The casualty rate was not spectacular by the standards of the First World War: 22,000 French and British killed and wounded as contrasted to 75,000 German casualties. But of the German casualties, fifty thousand were prisoners, and five hundred guns had been lost. No wonder that Ludendorff called August 8 the "black day of the German army!" Martin Gilbert, *The First World War*, p. 450. See also *Ludendorff's Own Story*, II, p. 332.

5. Asprey, *German High Command*, p. 464.
6. Ibid., p. 467.
7. Ludendorff, *Memories*, II, p. 376.
8. Ibid., pp. 376–77.
9. Asprey, *German High Command*, p. 467.
10. "There is something strangely ironic in the fact that the first democratic Chancellor of Germany should have been a Prussian Major-General, a Prince, and the heir to a Grand Ducal throne. Yet the choice of Prince Max was not altogether an unfortunate one. He had shown distinct democratic tendencies, and his realization of the necessity of peace made him acceptable to the Left. Moreover, his generous work with the Red Cross and prisoners of war had earned him the sympathy and admiration of friend and foe alike." Wheeler-Bennett, *Wooden Titan*, pp. 163–164.
11. Martin Gilbert, *The First World War*, p. 471.
12. Ibid.
13. On September 27, 1918, Wilson had addressed the Liberty Loan Drive at the Metropolitan Opera House in New York. In his speech he attacked the Imperial German rulers but also criticized the Allied imperialists.
14. Pershing, *Experiences*, II, p. 342.
15. Tumulty, *Woodrow Wilson*, p. 307.
16. House, *Intimate Papers*, IV, pp. 73–80.
17. Pershing, *Experiences*, II, pp. 342–43.
18. Ibid., p. 343.
19. Palmer, *Bliss*, p. 338.
20. Ibid., pp. 338–39.
21. Ludendorff, *Memories*, II, pp. 407–8.
22. Pershing, *Experiences*, II, p. 307.
23. Probably referring to the orders Pershing had refused to obey on August 30, 1918.
24. Foch, *Memoirs*, pp. 434–36.
25. Braim, *Test of Battle*, p. 122.
26. Foch, *Memoirs*, pp. 436–38.

TWENTY: FIRST ARMY COMES OF AGE

1. *History of the First Division*, p. 213.
2. The town of Romagne itself nestles down in the valley of the Andon, between the crests of Romagne and Cunel.
3. See folding map, ABMC *Guide*.
4. Liggett, *Ten Years Ago*, p. 189.
5. Bullard, *Personalities*, p. 275.
6. Ibid., p. 278.
7. Ibid., pp. 279–80.
8. Mitchell, *Memoirs*, p. 265.

9. Mitchell, *Memoirs*, pp. 265–66.
10. Ibid., p. 266.
11. Liggett, *Ten Years Ago*, pp. 198–99.
12. Ibid., p. 200.
13. Harries and Harries, *Last Days*, pp. 398–99.
14. Pershing, *Experiences*, II, p. 340. Although Pershing called the Côte Dame Marie "perhaps the most important strong point of the Hindenburg Line on the Western Front," Brigadier General Douglas MacArthur, whose 84th Brigade of the 42d Division was involved at Côte de Châtillon, called that action "the approach to final victory" (*Reminiscences*, p. 67). There may have been some personal jealousy involved in those evaluations, especially on Pershing's part. MacArthur's flamboyant style was not Pershing's. Their relations, outwardly correct, were not friendly.
15. MacArthur, *Reminiscences*, pp. 66–67. The 1st Battalion, 168th, was commanded by Major Lloyd Ross; the battalion from the 167th was commanded by Major Ravee Norris.
16. Stallings, *Doughboys*, pp. 336–38.
17. Liggett, *Ten Years Ago*, p. 207.
18. Morris Schaff, *The Battle of the Wilderness*, cited in Liggett, *Ten Years Ago*, p. 209.
19. Report, Major C. H. Rice, October 22, 1918; report of Col. J. A. Baer, October 15, 1918. Both in NARA, RG 120, AEF Gen Hq, First Army G-3, 120–21, Box 3384.
20. Report on 35th Division by Col. J. A. Baer, date undetermined. NARA RG 120, First Army G-3.
21. NARA (National Archives), RG 120, AEF Gen HQ, G-3, 120–21, Box 3384.
22. NARA, RG 120, 5th Section, G-5, 501–3, Box 3392.
23. To remedy the shortage of front line infantrymen, Pershing reduced the size of the rifle companies from 250 to 175 men and cannibalized two newly arrived divisions to transfer their doughboys to fill the ranks of First Army.

TWENTY-ONE: THE WINDUP

1. Joseph T. Dickman, *The Great Crusade*, p. 193.
2. Marshall, *Services*, p. 188.
3. Pershing, *Experiences*, II, pp. 350–51.
4. Bullard was happy with his chief of staff, Major General Stuart Heintzelman, and especially with his artillery chief, Major General William Lassiter. But aside from himself, Lessiter had no artillery staff.
5. Bullard, *Personalities*, p. 299.
6. Pershing, *Experiences*, II, p. 389.
7. Liggett, *Ten Years Ago*, p. 325.
8. Liggett was glad to have the extra days of preparation (from October 28 to November 1) to recondition his troops. However, he later regretted the delay. One more day of battle would have, in his later opinion, destroyed the German Army completely.
9. The 2d Division, with the 71st Brigade, 36th Division, had been borrowed at the beginning of the Meuse-Argonne offensive by General Gouraud's Fourth French Army for the difficult and all-important attack on Blanc Mont on October 2–10. Liggett had managed to retrieve the infantry elements of this prized division earlier, but it was not until his visit to Gouraud on October 25 that he was able to regain the division's artillery.
10. Liggett, *Commanding an American Army*, p. 113.
11. Brieulles-sur-Meuse has no bridge over the river and no exit roads beyond.
12. French General Paul Maistre, the Army group commander, proposed an alternate plan sent by Foch, which visualized attacking in the woods at the outset. Pershing re-

fused outright on the basis that Foch was exceeding his authority in trying to influence the tactics of the American Army. Maistre's apologetic attitude indicated that Foch realized as much. Pershing ignored the "suggestion." Pershing, *Experiences*, II, p. 355.

13. Oddly, the first crossings were made at Brieulles, where no exit roads existed. On the 5th of November substantial crossings were made at Dun-sur-Meuse.

14. Pershing, *Experiences*, II, p. 381, says, "It was the ambition of the First Army and mine. . . ."

15. Marshall, *Services*, pp. 188–89.

16. Pershing, *Experiences*, II, bears out that Conner had represented him correctly. He claims that French General Maistre "warmly approved" crossing into French territory. He does not mention Sedan by name, however.

17. This is Marshall's version, on pp. 189–90 of his book, *Services*. It is of some amusement to this writer that the two officers who most influenced the career of General Dwight D. Eisenhower, one as a teacher and the other as a patron during World War II, were Conner and Marshall.

18. Memorandum, First U.S. Army, November 5, 1918. Cited in Dickman, *Crusade*, p. 182.

19. Dickman, *Crusade*, pp. 182–84.

20. Dickman, p. 187.

21. Ibid., pp. 187–88.

22. Ibid., p. 188.

23. Liggett, *Ten Years Ago*, p. 229.

24. Dickman, despite his complaints, writes on p. 188 of *Crusade*, "With a fine aggressive spirit the troops of the 1st Division had responded to the demands of their chiefs by exertions in marching, night and day, which had no equal in the American Expeditionary Force."

25. Elton E. Mackin, *Suddenly We Didn't Want to Die*, p. 226.

26. Ibid., p. 259.

27. Ibid., p. 261.

TWENTY-TWO: THE RAILROAD CAR AT COMPIÈGNE

1. Paschall, *Defeat of Imperial Germany*, p. 208.

2. Foch, *Memoirs*, p. 456.

3. Pershing, *Experiences*, II, p. 359.

4. Smythe, *Pershing*, pp. 219–20. Haig later made a lame effort to assuage Pershing's anger over that statement.

5. Pershing, *Experiences*, II, p. 360.

6. Ibid., p. 361.

7. Ibid.

8. Foch, *Memoirs*, p. 460.

9. Pershing, *Experiences*, II, pp. 362–63.

10. Foch, *Memoirs*, p. 461.

11. Asprey, *German High Command*, p. 481.

12. Ludendorff, *Memories*, II, p. 423.

13. Asprey, *German High Command*, p. 483.

14. Ludendorff, *Memories*, II, pp. 424–25.

15. Ibid., p. 426.

16. Pershing, *Experiences*, II, p. 367.

17. Letter from Paul Mantoux (interpreter) to Colonel House, July 6, 1920, cited in House, *Intimate Papers*, IV, p. 91.

18. Ibid., p. 95.
19. The first problem which must be faced was that of the relations between the greater and the smaller Powers of the Allies. At the informal conversation in Pinchot's study, on October 29, the French Foreign Secretary stated that Belgium, like the other Powers, had received from Wilson the correspondence with the Germans; what ought she to do? Ought she not have a representative present in the discussions, especially when it came to the evacuation of Belgium? Japan, also, had suggested that she be consulted.

" 'Would not the other Powers have to be admitted, when we discuss Austria?' asked Balfour.

" 'Yes,' said Lloyd George, 'Serbia and Greece will certainly be in the same category as Belgium.'

" 'If you admit Belgium,' said [Italian Foreign Minister Sidney] Sonnino, 'you cannot possibly exclude the others.' " Ibid., p. 100.
20. *New York Times*, October 27, 1918.
21. Ibid., October 31, 1918.
22. Ibid., November 6, 1918.
23. Ibid.
24. Ibid., November 7, 1918.
25. Ibid., November 8, 1918.
26. Ibid.
27. Foch, *Memoirs*, p. 469.
28. Ibid., p. 470.
29. Ibid., p. 475.
30. Ibid., p. 476.
31. Pershing, *Experiences*, II, p. 382. Hunter Liggett agreed: "Germany still had an army on November 10, but one more day would have reduced it to a mob, in all likelihood. . . . That is when I regretted that we had not opened our final attack on October 28 instead of November 1." Liggett, *Ten Years Ago*, p. 238.
32. Ibid., p. 385.
33. Lloyd C. Grisholm, cited in Smythe, *Pershing*, p. 232. Grisholm's papers are at the Marshall Library.

TWENTY-THREE: THE END OF THE AEF

1. Gregor Dallas, *At the Heart of a Tiger*, p. 553.
2. Thomas M. Johnson, *Without Censor*, pp. 384–85.
3. Paul T. Culbertson, "Your Boy, Paul," pp. 25–26.
4. On October 12 Patton had written his wife, "Peace looks possible but I rather hope not for I would like to have a few more fights." Patton, *Papers*, I, p. 623.
5. Harbord, *Leaves*, p. 391.
6. Baker, *Doughboy's Diary*, p. 114.
7. "Without complaint you have endured incessant toil, privation, and danger. You have seen many of your comrades make the supreme sacrifice that freedom may live. I thank you for the patience and courage with which you have endured. I congratulate you on the splendid fruits of victory which your heroism and the blood of our gallant dead are now presenting to our nation. Your deeds will live forever in the most glorious pages of America's history." Pershing, *Experiences*, II, p. 390.
8. Pershing, *Experiences*, II, p. 397.
9. March, *Nation at War*, p. 254.
10. Ibid., p. 255.
11. Ibid., p. 328.

12. III Corps had 2d, 32d, and 42d Divisions. IV Corps had 1st, 3d, and 4th Divisions, Pershing's best. USAWW, Vol. 10, p. 1.
13. Dickman, *Crusade*, p. 217.
14. March, *Nation at War*, pp. 106, 107.
15. President Theodore Roosevelt's visit to the Panama Canal was not considered a foreign visit.
16. Ayres, *War with Germany*, p. 46.
17. These figures come from the *World Almanac*, 1994, p. 708. Ayres, *War with Germany*, gives slightly lower figures, but that book, published in 1919, can be considered out of date.
18. Vandiver, *Black Jack*, II, p. 1,040.

EPILOGUE

1. Germany was forced to give up Alsace-Lorraine, the entire German overseas colonies, and about 13 percent of its territory in Europe. Most of that ceded territory was located in the East to create the new nation of Poland. Some went to the new Czechoslovakia, and three small counties were given to Belgium.
2. It was not shared by all thinking people, however. Tasker Bliss and Fox Conner, for example, thought that the Versailles treaty should have been more magnanimous. Writing of his service under Conner in 1921, Dwight Eisenhower confirms Conner's views: "One of the most profound beliefs of General Conner was that the world could not long avoid another major war. He did not seek war and he thought that if the United States had been part of the League of Nations, it might have been possible to avoid one. But under conditions as they were he was quite certain that the Treaty of Versailles carried within it the seeds of another, larger conflagration. He urged me to be ready for it." Dwight D. Eisenhower, *At Ease: Stories I Tell to Friends*, p. 195.
3. Some parallel can be drawn between Pershing's recommendations in 1918 and those of Winfield Scott, General-in-Chief of the Union Army at the beginning of the Civil War. Scott rightly believed that the only way to defeat the Confederacy was to occupy the line of the Mississippi and strangle it. Though Scott's strategy was eventually followed, it had no chance of acceptance in 1861.
4. Many people, General Matthew Ridgway among them, always considered the Springfield to be superior. Ridgway carried one personally even during the Battle of the Bulge in late 1944.
5. G-5, at that time designated for Training, has been the staff stepchild, later becoming Military Government in the Second World War.
6. Dwight Eisenhower and Omar N. Bradley, neither of whom were members of the AEF, were notable exceptions. Nevertheless, they both felt at a disadvantage when assuming responsible positions in 1942 through 1945.
7. In 1930 Congress relented and raised March to the retired rank of full general.
8. There is even some argument for a lurking suspicion that the threat of U.S. preponderance in 1919 may have influenced the other Allies to end the war in 1918.
9. Sir Frederick Maurice, *The Last Four Months*, cited in Liggett, *Ten Years Ago*, pp. 203–4.

APPENDIX: MOBILIZATION

1. Coffman, *War to End All Wars*, pp. 29–30.
2. Koistinen, *Mobilizing for Modern War*, p. 124. This circumstance had been brought about early in the European war through the efforts of the New York banking house

of J. P. Morgan, which had financed and coordinated the development, with the help, in the early stages, of the industrialist Edward Stettinius.

3. So named for its chairman, Francis J. Kernan.
4. Memo, General Hugh Johnson to John J. Pershing, September 28, 1930, p. 2.
5. Ibid.
6. Newton D. Baker, "America in the World War," Introduction to Thomas Frothingham, *The American Reinforcement in the World War*, p. xii.
7. Johnson memo, p. 12.

BIBLIOGRAPHY

BOOKS

Alexander, Robert. *Memories of the World War, 1917–1918.* New York: Macmillan, 1931.

Allen, George H., et al. *The Great War.* 5 vols. Philadelphia: George Barrie's Sons, 1915–1921.

American Battle Monuments Commission. *American Armies and Battlefields in Europe.* Washington: Government Printing Office, 1938.

Asprey, Robert B. *At Belleau Wood.* Denton: University of North Texas Press. 1996.

———. *The German High Command at War: Hindenburg and Ludendorff Conduct World War I.* New York: William Morrow, 1991.

Ayres, Leonard P. *The War with Germany: A Statistical Summary.* Washington: Government Printing Office, 1919.

Baker, Chester E. *Doughboy's Diary.* Shippensburg, PA: Burd Street Press, 1998.

Barnett, Correlli. *The Swordbearers: Supreme Command in the First World War.* New York: William Morrow, 1964.

Beach, Edward L. *The United States Navy.* New York: Henry Holt, 1986.

Boston Publishing Company. *Above and Beyond: A History of the Medal of Honor from the Civil War to Vietnam.* In Cooperation with the Congressional Medal of Honor Society of the United States of America. 1985.

Braim, Paul F. *The Test of Battle: The American Expeditionary Force in the Meuse-Argonne Campaign.* Shiffensburg, PA: White Mane Books, 1987.

Brands, H. W. *T.R.: The Last Romantic.* Cambridge, MA: Perseus Books, 1997.

Brook-Shepherd, Gordon. *November 1918.* Boston: Little Brown, 1981.

Broun, Heywood. *Our Army at the Front.* New York: Charles Scribner's Sons, 1918.

Brown, Malcolm. *The Imperial War Museum Book of 1918, Year of Victory.* London: Sidgwick and Jackson, 1998.

Bugnet, Major Charles. *Foch Speaks.* New York: Dial Press, 1929.

Bullard, Robert Lee. *Personalities and Reminiscences of the War.* Garden City: Doubleday, Page, 1925.

Clemenceau, Georges. *Grandeur and Misery of Victory.* New York: Harcourt Brace, 1930.

Coffman, Edward M. *The Hilt of the Sword: The Career of Peyton C. March.* Madison: The University of Wisconsin Press, 1966.

———. *The War to End All Wars: The American Experience in World War I.* Frankfort:

University of Kentucky Press, 1998. Originally published by Oxford University Press, 1968.

Cooper, Sandi E. *Patriotic Pacifism: Waging War on War in Europe*. New York: Oxford University Press, 1991.

Creel, George. *Rebel at Large: Recollections of Fifty Crowded Years*. New York: G. P. Putnam & Sons, 1947.

———. *The War, the World, and Wilson*. New York: Harper and Bros., 1920.

Crozier, Emmet. *American Reporters on the Western Front, 1914–1918*. New York: Oxford University Press, 1959.

Dallas, Gregor. *At the Heart of a Tiger: Clemenceau and His World, 1841–1929*. London: Macmillan, 1993.

Daniels, Jonathan. *The End of Innocence*. Philadelphia: Lippincott, 1954.

Daniels, Josephus. *The Wilson Era, 1910–1917*. Chapel Hill: University of North Carolina Press, 1944.

Dawes, Charles G. *A Journal of the Great War*. 2 vols. Boston and New York: Houghton Mifflin, 1921.

Dewar, George A. B. *Sir Douglas Haig's Command, December 19, 1915–November 11, 1918*. 2 vols. Boston and New York: Houghton Mifflin, 1923.

Dickman, Joseph T. *The Great Crusade*. New York: The Appleton Company, 1927.

Dos Passos, John. *Mr. Wilson's War*. New York: Doubleday, 1962.

Duffy, Francis P. *Father Duffy's Story*. Garden City: Garden City Publishing, 1919.

Eiler, Keith E. *Mobilizing America: Robert P. Patterson and the War Effort, 1940–1945*. Ithaca: Cornell University Press, 1997.

Eisenhower, Dwight D. *At Ease: Stories I Tell to Friends*. New York: Doubleday, 1967.

———. *Waging Peace, 1956–1961: The White House Years*. Garden City: Doubleday, 1965.

Ellis, Captain O. O., and Captain E. B. Garey. *The Plattsburg Manual, A Handbook for Military Training*. New York: Century, 1918.

Esposito, Col. Vincent J. *West Point Atlas of American Wars*. New York: Praeger, 1959.

Falls, Cyril. *The Great War, 1914–1918*. New York: Capricorn, 1959.

Farwell, Byron. *Over There: The United States in the Great War, 1917–1918*. New York: W. W. Norton, 1999.

Ferro, Marc. *The Great War, 1914–1918*. New York: Routledge, 1969.

Foch, Ferdinand, Marshal of France. *The Memoirs of Marshal Foch*. Translated by Col. T. Bentley Mott. New York: Doubleday, Doran, 1931.

Foulois, MG Benjamin D., with Col. C. V. Glines. *From the Wright Brothers to the Astronauts*. New York: McGraw Hill, 1968.

Friedel, Frank. *Over There: The Story of America's Great Overseas Crusade*. Boston: Little, Brown, 1964.

Frothingham, Thomas G. *The American Reinforcement in the World War*. Garden City: Doubleday, Page, 1927.

Ganoe, William Addleman. *The History of the United States Army*. Ashton, MD: Eric Lundberg, 1964.

Garey, E. B., et al. *American Guide Book to France and Its Battlefields*. New York: Macmillan, 1920.

Gavin, Lettie. *American Women in World War I: They Also Served*. Niwot: University of Colorado Press, 1997.

Gerard, James W. *My Four Years in Germany*. New York: Grosset and Dunlap, 1917.

Gilbert, Martin. *Atlas of the First World War*. London: Weidenfeld and Nicolson, 1970.

———. *The First World War: A Complete History*. New York: Henry Holt, 1994.

Griess, Thomas E. *The Great War*. Wayne, NJ: West Point Military History Series, Avery Publishing Group, 1986.

Hagood, Johnson. *The Services of Supply: A Memoir of the Great War*. New York: Houghton Mifflin, 1927.

Hallas, James H., ed. *Doughboy War: The American Expeditionary Force in World War I*. London: Lynn Rienner, 2000.

Hansen, Arlen J. *Gentlemen Volunteers; The Story of American Ambulance Drivers in the Great War, 1914–1918*. New York: Arcade, 1996.

Harbord, MG James G. *The American Army in France, 1917–1919*. Boston: Little Brown, 1936.

———. *The American Expeditionary Force: Its Organization and Accomplishments.* Evanston, IL: Evanston Publishing Company, 1929.

———. *Leaves from a War Diary.* New York: Dodd, Mead, 1925.

Harries, Meirion and Susie Harries. *The Last Days of Innocence: America at War, 1917–1918*. New York: Random House, 1997.

Haythornwaite, Philip J. *The World War One Source Book.* New York: Sterling, 1992.

Hobbs, William Herbert. *Leonard Wood: Administrator, Citizen, Soldier.* New York: G. P. Putnam's Sons, 1920.

Hoffman, Bob. *I Remember the Last War.* York, PA: Strength and Heath, 1940.

Hoover, Herbert Clark. *The Ordeal of Woodrow Wilson.* New York: McGraw Hill, 1958.

Horne, Charles F., and Walter F. Austin, eds. *Source Records of the Great War.* Vol. 6. National Alumni, 1923.

House, Colonel Edward M. *The Intimate Papers of Colonel House.* 4 vols. Charles Seymour, ed. Boston: Houghton Mifflin, 1926 and 1928.

Hunt, Frazier. *The Untold Story of Douglas MacArthur.* New York: Devon-Adair, 1954.

Huston, James A. *The Sinews of War: Army Logistics, 1775–1953.* Office of the Chief of Military History, U.S. Army, 1966.

Hymes, Samuel. *The Soldiers' Tale: Bearing Witness to Modern War.* New York: Penguin, 1997.

Joffre, Marshal Joseph Jacques. *The Memoirs of Marshal Joffre.* 2 vols. London: Geoffrey Bles, 1932.

Johnson, Douglas V. II, and Rolfe Hillman. *Soissons: 1918.* College Station: Texas A&M University Press, 1999.

Johnson, Hubert C. *Breakthrough: Tactics, Technology and the Search for Victory on the Western Front in World War II.* Novato, CA: Presidio Press, 1994.

Johnson, Thomas M. *Without Censor: New Light on Our Greatest World War Battles.* Indianapolis: Bobbs-Merrill, 1928.

Junger, Ernst. *The Storm of Steel.* New York: Howard Fertig, 1996.

Keegan, John. *The First World War.* New York: Alfred A. Knopf, 1999.

Kennedy, David M. *Over Here! The First World War and American Society.* New York: Oxford University Press, 1980.

Koistinen, Paul A. C. *Mobilizing for Modern War: The Political Economy of American Warfare, 1865–1919.* Lawrence: University of Kansas Press, 1997.

Lane, Anne K., and Louise H. Walls, eds. *The Letters of Franklin K. Lane, Personal and Political.* Boston, 1922.

Larson, Cedric. *Words That Won the War: The Story of the Committee on Public Information, 1917–1919.* New York: Russell and Russell, 1939.

Liggett, Hunter. *AEF: Ten Years Ago in France.* New York: Dodd, Mead, 1928.

———. *Commanding an American Army: Recollections of the World War.* Boston and New York: Houghton Mifflin, 1925.

Link, Arthur S. *Woodrow Wilson and the Progressive Era, 1910–1917.* New York: Harper and Row, 1954.

Lloyd George, Earl. *My Father, Lloyd George.* New York: Crown, 1961.

Ludendorff, General Erich von. *My War Memories, 1914–1918.* 2 vols., London: Hutchinson, 1919.

MacArthur, Douglas. *Reminiscences.* New York: McGraw-Hill, 1964.

Mackin, Elton E. *Suddenly We Didn't Want to Die.* Novato, CA, Presidio Press, 1993.

Manchester, William. *American Caesar: Douglas MacArthur, 1880–1964*. Boston: Little, Brown, 1978.

March, Francis A. *History of the World War.* Philadelphia, Chicago, Toronto: United Publishers of the United States and Canada, 1919.

March, Peyton C. *The Nation at War.* Garden City: Doubleday, Doran, 1932.

Marshall, George C. *Memoirs of My Services in the World War, 1917–1918.* Boston: Houghton Mifflin, 1976.

Marshall, S. L. A. *The American Heritage History of World War I.* New York: American Heritage Publishing Company, 1964.

Maverick, Maury. *A Maverick American.* New York: Covici, Friede, 1937.

McCollum, L. C. ("Buck Private"). *History and Rhymes of the Lost Battalion.* 1929.

McEntee, Girard Lindsley. *Military History of the World War.* New York: Scribner's, 1943.

Merrick, Robert G. *World War I: A Diary.* Baltimore: Published by Author, 1982.

Miller, Nathan. *Theodore Roosevelt: A Life.* New York: William Morrow, 1992.

Mitchell, BG William B. *Memoirs of World War I.* New York: Random House, 1960.

Mott, T. Bentley. *Twenty Years as Military Attaché.* New York: Oxford University Press, 1937.

Nelson, Keith L. *Victors Divided: America and the Allies in Germany, 1918–1923.* Berkeley: University of California Press, 1975.

Notter, Harley. *The Origins of the Foreign Policy of Woodrow Wilson.* New York: Russell and Russell, 1965.

Page, Walter H. *The Life and Letters of Walter H. Page.* 2 vols. Burton J. Hendrick, ed. Garden City: Doubleday, Page, 1925.

Palmer, Alan. *The Kaiser, Warlord of the Second Reich.* New York: Charles Scribner's Sons, 1978.

Palmer, Frederick. *Bliss, Peacemaker.* New York: Dodd, Mead, 1934.

———. *Newton D. Baker: America at War.* 2 vols. New York: Dodd, Mead, 1931.

———. *Our Greatest Battle (The Meuse-Argonne)* New York: Dodd, Mead, 1919.

Paschall, Rod. *The Defeat of Imperial Germany, 1917–1918.* Chapel Hill, NC: Algonquin Books of Chapel Hill, 1989.

Patton, George S., Jr. *The Patton Papers.* Martin Blumenson, ed. Vol. 2, 1940–1945. Boston: Houghton Mifflin, 1972.

———. *War as I Knew It.* Boston: Houghton Mifflin, 1947.

Payne, Robert. *The Marshall Story: A Biography.* New York: Prentice Hall, 1951.

Pershing, John J. *My Experiences in the World War.* 2 vols. New York: Frederick A. Stokes, 1931.

Pitt, Barrie. *1918: The Last Act.* New York: W. W. Norton, 1962.

Pogue, Forrest C. *George C. Marshall: The Education of a General, 1880–1939.* New York: Viking Press, 1963.

Price, Alan. *The End of the Age of Innocence: Edith Wharton and the First World War.* New York: St. Martin's, 1996.

Proctor, H. G. *The Iron Division: National Guard of Pennsylvania in the World War.* Philadelphia: John C. Winston, 1919.

Rauch, Georg von. *A History of Soviet Russia.* New York: Praeger, 1972.

Recouly, Raymond. *Foch: My Conversations with the Marshal.* Translated by Joyce Davis. New York: Appleton, 1929.

Roosevelt, Theodore. *The Foes of Our Own Household.* New York: George H. Doran, 1917.

Shrader, Charles R. *United States Army Logistics, 1775–1992.* Washington: U.S. Army, Chief of Military History, 1997.

Simonds, Frank H. *History of the World War,* 5 vols. Garden City: Doubleday, Page, 1920.

Skutch, Alexander F. *Life of the Pigeon.* Ithaca: Cornell University Press, 1991.

Smythe, Donald. *Pershing: General of the Armies*. Bloomington: Indiana University Press, 1986.

Society of the First Division. *History of the First Division During the World War, 1917–1919*. Philadelphia: John C. Winston, 1922.

Spaulding, Oliver L., and John W. Wright. *The Second Division, American Expeditionary Force in France, 1917–1919*. Historical Committee, Second Division Association. New York: Hillman Press, 1938.

Stallings, Laurence. *The Doughboys: The Story of the AEF, 1917–1918*. New York: Harper and Row, 1963.

Stimson, Henry L., and McGeorge Bundy. *On Active Service in Peace and War*. New York: Harper and Brothers, 1947.

Straubing, Harold Elk, ed. *The Last Magnificent War*. New York: Paragon House, 1989.

Terraine, John. *The Great War*. London: Wordsworth Editions, 1965.

Trask, David F. *The AEF and Coalition Warmaking, 1917–1918*. Lawrence: University of Kansas Press, 1993.

———. *Captains and Cabinets: Anglo-American Naval Relations, 1917–1918*. Columbia: University of Missouri Press, 1972.

Tuchman, Barbara W. *The Zimmermann Telegram*. New York: Macmillan, 1958.

Tucker, Spencer C. *The Great War, 1914–1918*. Bloomington: University of Indiana Press, 1998.

Tumulty, Joseph P. *Woodrow Wilson as I Knew Him*. New York: Doubleday, Page, 1921.

Twenty-Sixth Infantry in France, by the Regimental Adjutant. Frankfurt, Germany: Martin Flock, 1919. Military History Institute, Carlisle Barracks, Pennsylvania.

United States Government. *The United States Army in World War I* (USAWW). 17 vols. Washington: United States Army Center of Military History, 1946.

Vandiver, Frank E. *Black Jack: The Life and Times of John J. Pershing*. 2 vols. College Station: Texas A&M University Press, 1977.

Weigley, Russell F. *History of the United States Army*. New York: Macmillan, 1967.

Weintraub, Stanley. *A Stillness Heard Round the World: The End of the Great War, November 1918*. New York: E. P. Dutton, 1985.

Wheeler-Bennett, John W. *Wooden Titan: Hindenburg in Twenty Years of German History, 1914–1934*. New York: William Morrow, 1936.

Winter, Jay, and Blaine Baggett. *The Great War and the Shaping of the 20th Century*. New York: Penguin Studio, 1996.

Wooldridge, Jesse. *Giants of the Marne*. Salt Lake City: Seagull, 1923.

PERIODICALS

Beattie, Taylor V., and Ronald Bowman. "In Search of York: Man, Myth, and Legend." *Army History*, Summer/Fall, 2000.

Brown, Charles H. "Fox Conner: A General's General." *Journal of Mississippi History*, August 1987, Vol. XLIX, No. 3.

Colby, Eldridge. "The Taking of Montfaucon." *Infantry Journal*, March/April 1940, pp. 1–13.

Wyman, Thomas Sage. "A Telephone Switchboard Operator with the AEF in France." *Army History*, Fall 1997/Winter 1998 No. 43.

NATIONAL ARCHIVES

Material on the AEF in the National Archives (NARA) is held in Record Group (RG) 120. Material in RG 120 includes but is not limited to the following:

General Orders and Directives from both Headquarters, AEF, and Headquarters,

First U.S. Army. These include operations orders for the successive phases of the Meuse-Argonne campaign.

Inspector Generals' Reports for the various divisions of First Army.

Table of Organization for the Infantry Regiment, Minimum Strength, dated January 14, 1918.

Report of Colonel (later major general) Hanson E. Ely on the operation against Cantigny, May 28, 1918.

Report from World War Records, First Division, AEF, Regular, Washington, 1928–1930, Vol. 13, Part 2.

Major General Joseph T. Dickman, letter to Colonel O. L. Spaulding, Army Historical Section, February 8, 1920. RG 120, Box 44, 3d Division.

Colonel Conrad H. Lanza, "The 38th Infantry in the Second Battle of the Marne." Unpublished. Undated. RG 120, Box 45, 3d Division.

Brigadier General Ulysses G. McAlexander, letter to Chief, Army Historical Section, November 3, 1919. RG 120, Box 46, 3d Division.

File, "Brief History in the Case of the Relief of BG Robert H. Noble." RG 120, Box 18, 79th Division.

Report, Intelligence Section, 5th Army Corps in St. Mihiel Operations.

Lieutenant Colonel Karl Truesdale, World War I Survey (the Truesdale Report).

MANUSCRIPTS, MILITARY HISTORY INSTITUTE

First Lieutenant Ladislav T. Janda, Report, "M Company, 9th Infantry, Second Division South of Soissons, July 18, 1918." November 19, 1929.

Ladislav T. Janda, Letters home.

MANUSCRIPTS, LIBRARY OF CONGRESS

Newton D. Baker papers.
Tasker H. Bliss papers.
George Creel papers.
Peyton C. March papers.
John J. Pershing papers.

MISCELLANEOUS MANUSCRIPTS

Culbertson, Paul T. "Your Boy, Paul." Letters of Paul T. Culbertson, 1917–1919. Edited by Margaret Culbertson Lott, 1992.

Powell, Alexander E. "APO 714: The University of the AEF." U.S. Military Academy, Patton Papers, Box 7, Folder 18.

ACKNOWLEDGMENTS

The responsibility for any shortcomings in this book is obviously mine alone, but three people, as with previous books, have done so much to make it possible that I must mention them again. They are my wife, Joanne, Mrs. Dorothy Yentz, and Professor Louis Rubin.

Joanne's contribution seems to grow with each book, particularly with this one. She has offered so much conceptual material as to make her in every sense an associate author.

Dorothy W. "Dodie" Yentz, to whom this book is dedicated, continues to be my day-to-day right arm, as she has been over a stretch of four books and twelve years.

Professor Louis D. Rubin, Jr., has again performed an act of true friendship by going over the entire manuscript in detail. Since the subject of the Great War has had more written about it than the subjects of some of my other books, Louis's wide and in-depth reading on the subject has been particularly useful. He was able to challenge me on many points, always to my benefit.

My son, David Eisenhower, took a week out of a busy schedule to jockey me around the Meuse-Argonne region on my second reconnaissance, 1999, for which I am grateful. To do so, he studied the American campaigns in the American Battle Monuments Commission's *Guide to the American Battlefields in France.*

Other friends and professional associates have also been of great help, not only for providing material but also encouragement. Among them are Geoffrey Perret; Dr. Douglas V. Johnson of the U.S. Army War College; Dr. Keith Eiler; Vice Admiral William L. Read; Major General (USAF, Ret.); John Huston, onetime Chief of Air Force History.

Official governmental organizations still hold much untapped material on the subject of the Great War. A major source of primary material is, of course, the National Archives. Within the Archives a researcher is normally assigned to an individual staff member for guidance and assistance. Joanne and I consider ourselves unusually fortunate in having the assistance of Mitchell Yockelson, who assisted us in securing documents, articles, and photographs. In this last category, Mitch was assisted by Kate Flaherty, who went to great length to expedite our searches. Teresa Roy was also helpful. We feel fortunate that Mitch Yockelson became a personal friend as well as professional colleague.

Another organization was especially useful, the Library of Congress. In the Manuscript Reading Room, Mary Wolfskill and Jeffrey M. Flannery have been extraordinary among the many helpful staffers. Bradley Gernand introduced us to that fascinating collection, in which Joanne was able to find material in the papers of Pershing, Bliss, Baker, March, and others.

In the Prints and Photographs Reading Room of the Library of Congress, Ms. Jan

Grenci helped Joanne locate photographs in the usual manner and also instructed her in the use of the online catalogue.

The U.S. Army Military History Institute, at Carlisle Barracks, Pennsylvania, provided much useful material, as it is a repository for unit histories and original documents. It is also an extensive library of published military works. As always at MHI, my closest contact has been with Louise Arnold-Friend, who, with her husband David Friend, has always gone much further than duty requires. Dr. Richard Sommers and David Keogh provided access to files of interviews conducted with veterans of the AEF. Most valuable of these was a complete set of letters written home by Ladislav Janda, a young officer in the 2d Division. We thank Dot Beard, Ellen Milne, and Elizabeth Gonzales, daughters of Major Janda, for making his letters available.

The Imperial War Museum, in London, which Joanne visited in the summer of 1999, gave gracious help in finding many photographs.

The Association of Graduates, U.S. Military Academy, provided us with valuable obituaries of West Point graduates commonly written by a classmate shortly after the death of each individual. Cheryl West, Christine Kays, and Carole Malone were of particular help.

James Knight, in the Office of the Chief of Military History, U.S. Army, Washington, D.C., provided official histories of U.S. participation in World War I.

The George C. Marshall Foundation, at Lexington, Virginia, especially Tom Camden, the Librarian, has been generous in our efforts to understand the role of the then Colonel George C. Marshall in the AEF.

We are also indebted to the Western Front Association, whose American chapter is located in Gainesville, Florida, with Leonard Shurtleff as its head. When Joanne and I made an inspection of the American battlefields in 1998, Mrs. Christina Holstein, the WFA representative, performed great service. She and her husband, Henrik, not only hosted Joanne and me in 1998 but provided maps and arranged for various guides around the battlefields, among them Ingrid Ferrand; Bruno Jurkiewicz; Yves Bufferaut; Bill Graham; and Meredith Sykes. Mrs. Holstein, an expert on the Verdun and Argonne area, provided much information on French commanders not readily available in the United States.

Photographs and maps are tremendous problems for the writer of a book, and our gratitude goes to Chris Robinson, of Maryland Mapping and Graphics, and to Jim Enos, photographer, of Carlisle, Pennsylvania, for their readiness to pitch in. Both did superior work.

I also acknowledge the help of Alan Dickey and Scottie Oliver, of Easton, Maryland, and Deborah Gootee, of Cambridge, Maryland.

INDEX